AEPS™

**Assessment, Evaluation,
and Programming System
for Infants and Children**

SECOND EDITION

**VOLUME
3**

Curriculum for
Birth to Three Years

D1384954

Other volumes in the _AEPS_™ series
edited by Diane Bricker, Ph.D.

AEPS Administration Guide

by Diane Bricker, Ph.D., Kristi Pretti-Frontczak, Ph.D.,
JoAnn (JJ) Johnson, Ph.D., and Elizabeth Straka, Ph.D., CCC-SLP,
with Betty Capt, Ph.D., OTR, Kristine Slentz, Ph.D.,
and Misti Waddell, M.S.

AEPS Test
Birth to Three Years and
Three to Six Years

by Diane Bricker, Ph.D., Betty Capt, Ph.D., OTR,
and Kristie Pretti-Frontczak, Ph.D.,
with JoAnn (JJ) Johnson, Ph.D., Kristine Slentz, Ph.D.,
Elizabeth Straka, Ph.D., CCC-SLP, and Misti Waddell, M.S.

AEPS Curriculum for
Three to Six Years

by Diane Bricker, Ph.D., and Misti Waddell, M.S.,
with Betty Capt, Ph.D., OTR, JoAnn (JJ) Johnson, Ph.D.,
Kristie Pretti-Frontczak, Ph.D., Kristine Slentz, Ph.D.,
and Elizabeth Straka, Ph.D., CCC-SLP

AEPS™
Assessment, Evaluation, and Programming System for Infants and Children
SECOND EDITION

VOLUME 3

Curriculum for
Birth to Three Years

by

Diane Bricker, Ph.D.
University of Oregon, Eugene

and

Misti Waddell, M.S.
University of Oregon, Eugene

with

Betty Capt, Ph.D., OTR, JoAnn (JJ) Johnson, Ph.D.,
Kristie Pretti-Frontczak, Ph.D., Kristine Slentz, Ph.D.,
and Elizabeth Straka, Ph.D., CCC-SLP

PAUL·H·
BROOKES
PUBLISHING CO.®

Baltimore • London • Sydney

Paul H. Brookes Publishing Co.
Post Office Box 10624
Baltimore, Maryland 21285-0624

www.brookespublishing.com

"Paul H. Brookes Publishing Co." is a registered trademark of
Paul H. Brookes Publishing Co., Inc.
"AEPS®" is a registered trademark and *AEPS* is a trademark of Paul H. Brookes Publishing Co., Inc.

Typeset by Barton Matheson Willse & Worthington, Baltimore, Maryland.
Manufactured in the United States of America by
Versa Press in East Peoria, Illinois.

The following AEPS forms can be purchased separately in packs:
Child Observation Data Recording Form I: Birth to Three Years, and II: Three to Six Years
Family Report I: Birth to Three Years, and II: Three to Six Years
Child Progress Record I: Birth to Three Years, and II: Three to Six Years

A CD-ROM of printable masters of the AEPS forms is also available, and also includes a Child
Observation Data Recording Form with Criteria for Birth to Three Years and Three to Six Years not
found in any of the volumes. To order, contact Paul H. Brookes Publishing Co.

Please see page ii for a listing of the other volumes in the AEPS series. All AEPS materials are available
from Paul H. Brookes Publishing Co., Post Office Box 10624, Baltimore, Maryland 21285-0624
(800-638-3775 or 410-337-9580). Find out more about AEPS on www.brookespublishing.com/aeps.

Fourth printing, November 2006.

Library of Congress Cataloging-in-Publication Data

Assessment, evaluation, and programming system for infants and children
    edited by Diane Bricker . . . (et al.)—2nd ed.
      p.   cm.
  Includes bibliographical references and index.
    ISBN-13: 978-1-55766-564-5 — ISBN-10: 1-55766-562-1 (v. 1) — ISBN-10: 1-55766-563-X (v. 2) —
ISBN-10: 1-55766-564-8 (v. 3) — ISBN-10: 1-55766-565-6 (v. 4)
    1. Assessment, Evaluation, and Programming System.   2. Child development—Testing.
3. Child development deviations—Diagnosis.
  RJ51.D48 A87 2002
  618.92'0075—dc21

                2002071124

British Library Cataloguing in Publication data are available from the British Library.

CONTENTS

ABOUT THE AUTHORS

Diane Bricker, Ph.D., Professor, College of Education, and Director, Early Intervention Program, University of Oregon, 5253 University of Oregon, Eugene, Oregon 97403

Diane Bricker is Professor and Associate Dean for Academic Programs, College of Education, at the University of Oregon and a highly respected, well-known authority in the field of early intervention. She has directed a number of national demonstration projects and research efforts focused on examining the efficacy of early intervention; the development of a linked assessment, intervention, and evaluation system; and the study of a comprehensive, parent-focused screening tool. Dr. Bricker directs the Early Intervention Program, Center on Human Development, at the University of Oregon.

Misti Waddell, M.S., Senior Research Assistant/Project Coordinator, Early Intervention Program, University of Oregon, 5253 University of Oregon, Eugene, Oregon 97403

Misti Waddell is a Senior Research Assistant/Project Coordinator at the Early Intervention Program at the University of Oregon. She also has contributed to the development, research, and training of the *Assessment, Evaluation, and Programming System for Infants and Children* (AEPS) since the early 1980s. She has used the AEPS in classroom settings and has coordinated several federally funded, field-initiated research projects and outreach training projects. Ms. Waddell is Project Coordinator for the outreach training project titled "Creating and Sustaining Change Across Diverse Early Intervention Systems (CASCADES)."

Betty Capt, Ph.D., OTR, Research Associate, Early Intervention Program, University of Oregon, 5253 University of Oregon, Eugene, Oregon 97403

JoAnn (JJ) Johnson, Ph.D., Director, Research and Educational Planning Center and Nevada University Center for Excellence in Developmental Disabilities, University of Nevada–Reno, Reno, Nevada 89557

Kristie Pretti-Frontczak, Ph.D., Assistant Professor, Department of Educational Foundations and Special Services, Kent State University, 405 White Hall, Kent, Ohio 44242

Kristine Slentz, Ph.D., Professor and Chair, Special Education Department, Western Washington University, Miller Hall 318b, Mail Stop 9090, Bellingham, Washington 98226

Elizabeth Straka, Ph.D., CCC-SLP, Consultant, New England Early Intervention Consulting, 58 Turtle Cove Lane, Wells, Maine 04090

ACKNOWLEDGMENTS

The second edition of the *AEPS Curriculum for Birth to Three Years* would not be possible without the contributions of the individuals involved in the development of the first edition. Those who provided leadership and contributed to the development of items include Juliann Cripe, Sarah Drinkwater, Tsai-Hsing Hsia, Ruth Kaminski, Angela Losardo, Chris Marvin, Pat Morris, Angela Notari-Syverson, Nancy Reid, Betsy Ryan-Seth, Susan Janko Summers, and Margaret Veltman.

In large part, the changes included in the *AEPS Curriculum for Birth to Three Years, Second Edition,* reflect the input from the many caregivers and interventionists who have been using the curriculum ideas and activities since 1994. In addition to providing valuable feedback for the second edition, their support and commitment has provided inspiration to continue working on the AEPS.

The feedback from AEPS users provided the impetus for two changes reflected in this edition: 1) to streamline the teaching suggestions for the goals and associated objectives so the material presented is more user friendly and 2) to include some specific intervention activities and activity formats that address children's targeted AEPS goals and objectives. The individuals who contributed to this first change by combining the information provided for each of the goals and the associated objectives and eliminating redundancy included Erika Hinds, Meghan Johnson, and Kimberly Murphy. Matty Maxwell is responsible for the formatting change that presents the Activity-Based Teaching Suggestions into typical daily routine categories. Alise Carter, Jantina Clifford, and Natalya McComas were involved in brainstorming ideas for activity formats that are most useful in home and other child care environments. Jantina contributed many of the routine activities targeting multiple goals/objectives garnered from her classroom experiences, and Alise contributed to the Routine Activity Format II contained in Appendix B and the purpose and introductory information for each of the activity formats included in the Appendixes.

A project of this magnitude requires multiple reviews, proof readings, and edits. Contributors to this process include Dave Allen, Karen Lawrence, Erika Hinds, Kate Ray, and Renata Smith. Kate, Renata, and Erika completed the many hours spent word processing. A special thanks to Karen for overseeing all the many pieces of this project and ensuring continuity between the four volumes and to Dave for his willingness to step in and take responsibility for completing a variety of important tasks.

AEPS™

Assessment, Evaluation,
and Programming System
for Infants and Children
SECOND EDITION

VOLUME 3 Curriculum for
Birth to Three Years

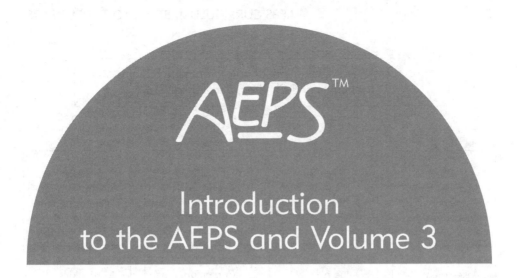

Introduction
to the AEPS and Volume 3

The importance of early experience for young children has long been recognized and has been the foundation for early intervention programs designed for young children who have or who are at risk for disabilities. Early intervention programs have evolved into comprehensive approaches that produce positive change in the lives of participating children and their families. In large measure, the increasingly positive outcomes engendered by early intervention programs have occurred because of the growing sophistication of personnel, curricular materials, and assessment/evaluation tools. Previous approaches that treat program components as isolated and unrelated units are being replaced by approaches that systematically link the major components of assessment, goal development, intervention, and evaluation. The *Assessment, Evaluation, and Programming System for Infants and Children (AEPS®)* is one such linked approach.

This is the third volume of the AEPS series. Figure 1 shows the four volumes and presents an overview of each volume's content. The focus of Volume 3 is the curricular materials designed to accompany the *AEPS Test for Birth to Three Years* contained in Volume 2.

WHAT IS THE AEPS?

The AEPS offers a variety of related materials that enhance the link between assessment outcomes, targeted goals, intervention activities, and evaluation strategies. The AEPS is referred to as a system because its components work together to assist interventionists and caregivers in developing functional and coordinated assessment, goal, intervention, and evaluation activities for young children who have or who are at risk for disabilities. The AEPS is a comprehensive and linked system that includes assessment/evaluation, curricular, and family participation components for the developmental range from birth to 6 years. The AEPS is divided into two developmental levels—Birth to Three Years and Three to Six Years. Also, as shown in Figure 1, each level is composed

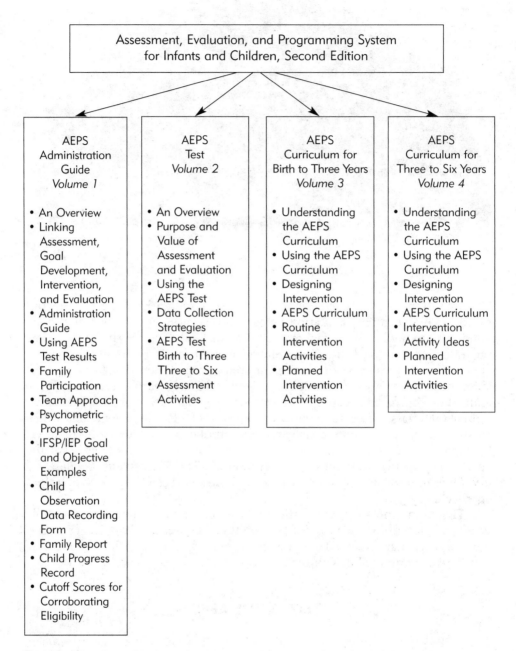

Figure 1.   Four volumes of the *Assessment, Evaluation, and Programming System for Infants and Children, Second Edition.*

of a test contained in Volume 2 and an associated curriculum contained in Volume 3 (Birth to Three Years) or Volume 4 (Three to Six Years).

Volume 1 presents information on the conceptual and organizational structure of the AEPS, how to get started using the system, components of a linked system, interpretation of test outcomes, family involvement strategies in the assessment/evaluation process, and team collaboration suggestions when using the system. Also in Volume 1, a new strategy for using AEPS test results to corroborate standardized, norm-referenced test findings for eligibility determination is described.

Volume 2 contains the test items for the birth to three year level and the three to six year level divided into six developmental areas: Fine Motor, Gross Motor, Adaptive, Cognitive, Social-Communication, and Social. Volume 2 also contains Assessment Activities that are simple scripts to guide the assessment of a range of AEPS test items during specific activities (see Volume 2, Appendix A).

Volumes 3 and 4 contain the curricular material for the developmental range birth to three and three to six years, respectively. In addition, these volumes contain a variety of intervention activities appropriate for a range of children.

OVERVIEW OF VOLUME 3

Volume 3, AEPS Curriculum for Birth to Three Years, is the curricular component of the *AEPS Test for Birth to Three Years* and was developed for two purposes. First, the AEPS Curriculum provides interventionists (e.g., teachers, child development specialists, occupational therapists, physical therapists, psychologists, communication specialists) and caregivers with a range of activities that can be used to facilitate children's acquisition of functional and generalizable skills. Second, the AEPS Curriculum provides a direct link between assessment, goal development, intervention, and evaluation. The AEPS Test and AEPS Curriculum were developed to provide a direct and ongoing correspondence among initial assessment, individualized family service plan (IFSP)/individualized education program (IEP) development, intervention planning, intervention activities, and subsequent evaluation.

Target Population

The AEPS Test and Curriculum for Birth to Three Years is appropriate for children who present a broad range of intervention needs. Some will be infants and young children with identified developmental disabilities such as Down syndrome, spina bifida, or cerebral palsy. Others will exhibit delays attributed to chronic health conditions or unknown causes. The AEPS is appropriate for children who live with high-risk conditions such as poverty and parents with addiction problems. Whatever the cause, the resultant impairments in early skill development require systematic intervention. The content of the *AEPS Test for Birth to Three Years* includes functional skills for children whose development is in the 3 months to 3 year range. This test is appropriate for children who have or are at risk for a wide range of disabilities. Use of the AEPS Test and Curriculum with children whose chronological age exceeds 6 years may require modification of content.

Children with severe disabilities will likely have a team (e.g., occupational therapist, physical therapist, communication specialist, physician, special educator, service coordinator) who will be involved in developing strategies for intervention. The *AEPS Curriculum for Birth to Three Years* lends itself well to a team approach because it permits input from a variety of specialists for embedding individualized objectives, cues, prompts, and correction procedures within activities that are fun and interesting to children.

AEPS Curriculum Content

Volume 3, AEPS Curriculum for Birth to Three Years, is divided into two sections. Section I provides an introductory overview of the AEPS and contains three chapters. Chapter 1 describes activity-based intervention and the linked system approach to assessment, goal development, intervention, and evaluation using the AEPS system. Chapter 2 explains how to use the AEPS Curriculum in conjunction with the AEPS Test. The direct link between the AEPS Curriculum and Test permits efficient movement between the two. Chapter 2 also includes information about working with children with severe disabilities. Chapter 3 describes how to use child initiations, daily routines, environmental arrangements, and planned intervention activities to work on children's goals/objectives. Section II presents specific curricular content and strategies for goals/objectives in the Fine Motor, Gross Motor, Adaptive, Cognitive, Social-Communication, and Social areas of the AEPS Test. Appendixes A, B, and C contain a variety of sample intervention activities using different formats.

The content of the *AEPS Test for Birth to Three Years* is developmentally sequenced beginning with simple skills and moving successively to more advanced skills. This curriculum includes a general and flexible set of considerations, strategies, and activities to address each of the skills. The *AEPS Curriculum for Birth to Three Years* relies on the interventionist to individualize each child's program.

The *AEPS Curriculum for Birth to Three Years* emphasizes an activity-based approach to enhance the behavioral repertoires of young children. Child-initiated activities, daily routines, environmental arrangements, and planned intervention activities are adopted as the contexts for intervention. Focusing on functional skills and on motivating activities is ideal for inclusive program settings that integrate children with developmental delays and disabilities. Because the AEPS Curriculum capitalizes on child-initiated activities, daily routines, environmental arrangements, and planned intervention activities rather than direct instruction of specific skills, it is well suited for use in the home, community-based preschools, or child care settings. The *AEPS Curriculum for Birth to Three Years* has been designed to accommodate a wide range of service delivery locations and models.

SECTION

I

Overview of the AEPS Curriculum

Birth to Three Years

1

Understanding the AEPS Curriculum

The AEPS Curriculum was designed to accommodate an approach to early intervention known as *activity-based intervention (ABI)*. The AEPS Curriculum provides information to the interventionist that encourages integration of goals/objectives into a child's daily activities and life experiences. The format of the AEPS Curriculum emphasizes child-initiated, routine, and planned intervention activities as vehicles for embedding a child's selected goals/objectives.

ACTIVITY-BASED INTERVENTION APPROACH

The ABI approach was designed to take advantage, in an objective and measurable way, of everyday instruction that parents and other caregivers use with their young children:

> Activity-based intervention is a child-directed, transactional approach that embeds children's individual goals and objectives in routine, planned, or child-initiated activities, and uses logically occurring antecedents and consequences to develop functional and generative skills. (Bricker, Pretti-Frontczak, & McComas, 1998, p. 11)

Two features of ABI and the AEPS Curriculum should be emphasized. First, multiple skills (e.g., motor, communication, social, cognitive, adaptive) can be addressed in single activities; for example, a sand box activity can be used to promote communication ("Where is the shovel?"), social skills (playing side by side), adaptive skills (brushing sand off hands), motor skills (reaching and grasping), and cognitive skills (finding a buried toy). For each goal, the AEPS Curriculum has a page titled "Concurrent Goals and Objectives" that helps identify the items that can be targeted during a single activity. Incorporating multiple goals/objectives into one activity is preferable to developing a separate activity for each goal.

A second feature of ABI and the AEPS Curriculum is the inherent reward for children when they participate in fun and interesting activities. When activities are child selected, then they usually provide ample motivation for the child, and artificial contingencies may not be necessary. The AEPS Curriculum provides a description of activities that young children will likely find interesting and engaging.

There are many advantages to using an activity-based format with infants and young children. First, the notion of providing relevant antecedents and consequences within an activity is incorporated into teaching functional skills in the child's usual environment. When the antecedents and consequences are a meaningful part of an activity, motivation and attention tend to increase. Second, ABI addresses the issues of generalization and maintenance. Teaching a particular skill is not limited to just one activity; rather, the skill can be taught by a variety of interventionists and family members across different materials and settings. Third, an activity-based approach helps keep targeted skills functional for the child. If the skills selected for intervention are embedded in daily activities, then they are likely to be useful to the child in coping with environmental demands. A fourth advantage is that, when skill training is embedded in daily activities, other people, such as caregivers and peers, can be used as change agents and teaching resources. Fifth, ABI can be used with heterogeneous groups of young children; for example, an outside riding activity could include children who can pedal, those who need to be pushed, and those who might be pulled in a wagon.

An activity-based approach teaches skills by embedding children's targeted goals/objectives into functional, routine activities of interest to children; for example, rather than establishing special sessions to teach object names, items are named in the context of a relevant activity. Naming body parts might occur naturally during bath time, items of clothing can be named when dressing or during doll play, and labeling foods and eating utensils can be easily worked into snack or mealtimes. The child can practice the target skill of cutting out shapes with curved lines during an art activity.

AEPS Curriculum users who would like more information on how to employ ABI are referred to *An Activity-Based Approach to Early Intervention* (2nd ed., Bricker, Pretti-Frontczak, & McComas, 1998).

LINKING ASSESSMENT, GOAL DEVELOPMENT, INTERVENTION, AND EVALUATION

The AEPS Curriculum provides a direct link between assessment, goal development, intervention, and evaluation. *Assessment* refers to the process of establishing a baseline or entry-level measurement of the child's skills and desired family outcomes. The assessment process should produce the necessary information to select appropriate and relevant intervention goals/objectives and desired family outcomes. Figure 2 illustrates the linked assessment, goal development, intervention, and evaluation approach. The major components are represented by boxes linked by vertical arrows to indicate the sequence in which they should occur. In addition, the diagonal arrows reflect the need for professional collaboration and family participation in each of these components.

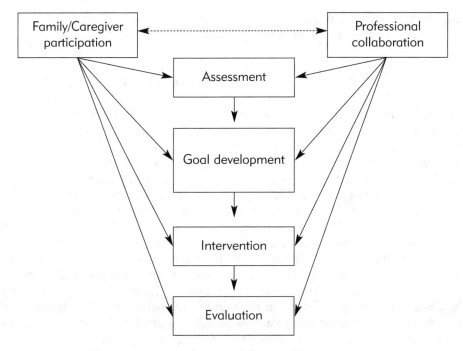

Figure 2. Schematic of a linked assessment, goal development, intervention, and evaluation approach to early intervention with collaborative professional and family participation.

Phase 1: Program Assessment

The link among assessment, goal development, intervention, and evaluation begins when children enter an intervention program. The major purpose of the initial assessment is to formulate useful and appropriate IFSP/IEP goals/ objectives.

In the initial assessment, a curriculum-based measure is administered to determine the content of IFSP/IEP goals/objectives. This content provides the road map for moving children from their beginning skill repertoires to the acquisition of skills specified as annual goals in their IFSP/IEP. For the family, this initial assessment should help determine priority interests to be developed into family outcomes. An accurate assessment of a child's beginning skill level is crucial to the formulation of a useful IFSP/IEP so that an intervention plan can be developed to improve areas in which a child may be lacking. An assessment that measures functional skills and is sensitive to the conditions in which a child is most likely to perform a skill will facilitate the development of appropriate and useful IFSPs/IEPs. For this reason, the *AEPS Test for Birth to Three Years* was developed.

An IFSP allows opportunities to target family outcomes as well as child goals. Family assessment should yield program-relevant information that will aid in developing functional outcome statements, but the process and tools should not be intrusive to family members. Completing the Family Report (Volume 1, Appendix D) is recommended to assist families in developing outcomes they consider relevant and important to their child and family.

Phase 2: Formulation of IFSPs/IEPs

The initial IFSP/IEP will be based primarily on information accumulated during Phase 1. (Results from this initial assessment should be validated at the first quarterly evaluation.) Relevant information is obtained from caregivers' knowledge of their children as well as from professional observation and testing. This initial information is used to develop a plan of action for the interventionists and caregivers to identify specific content areas that the IFSP/IEP will address. The IFSP/IEP should be straightforward so that it can be used as a guide for interventionists and caregivers. It can also be used as a criterion against which success of the intervention is evaluated.

The child's portion of the IFSP/IEP itemizes goals/objectives and a time frame for meeting the selected goals. The family's portion of the IFSP contains a statement of family resources, concerns, and priorities related to enhancing the child's development, based on the family's identification of their interests and needs. Collaborative discussion with appropriate family members establishes priorities. A set of outcome statements evolves from these priorities, and activities, resources, and a timeline for reaching outcomes are all specified. Further information on the development of IFSPs/IEPs can be found in Chapter 4 of Volume 1.

Phase 3: Intervention

Once the IFSP/IEP has been formulated by caregivers and interventionists, the actual intervention activities can be initiated. The child's performance on the program assessment indicates where intervention should begin. Having an assessment tool that directly links to a curriculum, such as the AEPS, assists interventionists in efficiently identifying the activities developed to facilitate acquisition of specific goals/objectives. The AEPS provides a direct correspondence between the assessment items (skills) identified as goals/objectives and the intervention content and strategies specified in the associated curriculum. Chapter 4 of Volume 1 provides an example of how to link assessment outcomes from the AEPS Test to intervention activities in the AEPS Curriculum.

Phase 4: Ongoing Monitoring

A useful IFSP/IEP specifies both the tasks to be conducted and the manner in which success is to be evaluated. A variety of strategies may be used for daily or weekly monitoring of child progress (e.g., trial by trial, brief probes during or after intervention activities). Targeted goals/objectives, program resources, and the need for daily or weekly monitoring to keep intervention efforts on track, will all help determine the strategies selected.

Phase 5: Quarterly and Annual Evaluation

Quarterly evaluations should focus on determining the effect of intervention efforts on goals/objectives specified in the IFSP/IEP. This can be done by using the initial assessment measures (e.g., re-administration of the AEPS Test) in conjunction with the weekly data collection. Quarterly evaluations should be used to compare the child's progress with some standard or expectation for progress. Without assigning expected completion dates for goals/objectives, it is difficult to determine if the child's progress is acceptable.

Annual or semiannual evaluations are used to evaluate the progress of individual children and families as well as the overall effectiveness of the program (i.e., group or subgroup analysis). Without subgroup comparisons, it is difficult to know how to improve intervention strategies for subpopulations of children and families. Methodological design and measurement problems that face the field of early intervention make subgroup evaluations difficult; however, analyses of subgroups may yield important findings on generalization of outcomes for selected groups of children and families.

SUMMARY

The AEPS Curriculum is designed to be used with an ABI approach and emphasizes the use of routine and planned activities to address children's targeted IFSP/IEP goals/objectives. An understanding of ABI serves as an excellent foundation for curriculum users.

The five phases of the linked system emphasize the importance of directly relating the processes of assessment, goal development, intervention, and evaluation. Employing this system allows efficient use of resources, accountability of program impact over time, and individualization through the design of programs specific to the needs of children and their families. Fundamental to such a system is an appropriate assessment/evaluation tool and an associated curriculum, such as the AEPS Test and AEPS Curriculum.

Chapter 2 relates how teams can use the *AEPS Curriculum for Birth to Three Years*, whereas Chapter 3 discusses designing and implementing interventions. Section II contains the curricular suggestions linked to AEPS goals/objectives.

2

Using the AEPS Curriculum

The AEPS Curriculum contains intervention activities and strategies for addressing AEPS Test goals/objectives. The numbering system used in the AEPS Test and Curriculum permits the user to move directly from assessment or evaluation outcomes to appropriate and relevant intervention activities. For AEPS Test goals/objectives, the AEPS Curriculum describes relevant intervention content and a variety of intervention strategies from child centered to adult guided. Prior to using the AEPS Curriculum, it is essential to read the administrative procedures in this chapter that describe the curriculum's format and procedures for its use.

The AEPS Curriculum has important features that make it compatible with the AEPS Test. First, the AEPS Curriculum provides intervention content that is directly tied to the IFSP/IEP goals developed from the AEPS Test results. Program information tied directly to assessment outcomes enhances efficiency of program staff. Second, the curricular content is focused on assisting program staff and caregivers to target functional and useful skills. Finally, information provided in the AEPS Curriculum assists interventionists in implementing an activity-based intervention (ABI) approach, which encourages generalization of learned skills through the integration of targeted goals into daily activities.

AEPS CURRICULUM FORMAT

The AEPS Curriculum is designed to be used in conjunction with the AEPS Test. The content of this test covers the areas of behavior and specific skills considered essential to independent functioning and coping with environmental demands for young children who function in the developmental range of birth to 3 years. Six broad areas of development are used in the AEPS Test and Curriculum: Fine Motor, Gross Motor, Adaptive, Cognitive, Social-Communication, and Social. Each area encompasses a set of skills or behaviors traditionally seen as related developmental phenomena called *strands*.

Strands, which organize related groups of behaviors under a common category, contain a series of items referred to as *goals*. Associated with each goal is an accompanying set of objectives that represent more discrete skills. These objectives enable the examiner to accurately pinpoint a child's developmental level within a specific skill sequence.

The AEPS Curriculum follows the same identification system for strands, goals, and objectives as the AEPS Test, providing a direct correspondence between the assessment and the curriculum. The consistent numbering system ensures that users can move efficiently between the AEPS Test and Curriculum. The identification system associated with the strands (e.g., A, B), goals (e.g., 1, 2), and objectives (e.g., 1.1, 1.2) reflects the sequential arrangement of the test items on the AEPS Test. In addition, the AEPS Curriculum may include programming steps for some goals/objectives. Programming steps offer general guidelines for developing simpler, more basic skills as possible prerequisites to AEPS Test goals/objectives. The programming steps (e.g., PS1.1a, PS1.1b, PS1.2a, PS1.2b) directly correspond with a goal/objective of the AEPS Test.

The cross-referencing system in the AEPS Curriculum utilizes an abbreviated term for the name of the area (e.g., SC for Social-Communication) and then the strand, goal, and objective are listed; for example, Soc A:1.3 refers to the Social Area, Strand A, Objective 1.3; GM B:2 refers to the Gross Motor Area, Strand B, Goal 2. Goals are identified by a single digit, and objectives are identified by the number of the goal, a period, and then the number of the objective. The names of each area are abbreviated as follows:

Fine Motor Area: FM

Gross Motor Area: GM

Adaptive Area: Adap

Cognitive Area: Cog

Social-Communication Area: SC

Social Area: Soc

Section II of this volume contains the curricular activities associated with each AEPS Test item and is divided into the six areas: Fine Motor, Gross Motor, Adaptive, Cognitive, Social-Communication, and Social. The content for each area is organized as follows:

- An outline of the area's strands, goals, and objectives
- Narrative description of the developmental content contained in the area
- Strands listed sequentially (e.g., Strand A, B), the goals associated with each strand also in sequential order (e.g., 1, 2), all associated objectives (e.g., 1.1, 1.2), and programming steps (e.g., PS1.1a, PS1.1b)
- Specific information for each goal and its associated objectives and programming steps:
  - Importance of Skills
    includes Concurrent Goals/Objectives page for each goal

- Teaching Suggestions
  Activity-Based
  Environmental Arrangements
  Instructional Sequences

- Teaching Considerations

Importance of Skills

The Importance of Skills section provides a brief explanation of the importance of the targeted skills to the independent functioning of a child. The hierarchy for the skills and their relationship to other important goals/objectives is also explained. This section also offers information that may help family and team members understand the importance of the goal and its associated objectives.

As shown in Figure 3, each Importance of Skills section contains a page that lists other AEPS Test goals/objectives that can potentially be addressed at the same time as the targeted goal. Identifying other goals/objectives that can be addressed simultaneously with the targeted goal makes it unnecessary to develop separate activities for each priority skill.

```
Narrative Description of Area Content

Outline of area

Strand A

Goal 1

Objective 1.1

Objective 1.2

            Programming Step 1.2a

            Programming Step 1.2b

Importance of Skills

            Concurrent goals/objectives page

Teaching Suggestions

            Activity-Based

            Environmental Arrangements

            Instructional Sequences

Teaching Considerations
```

Figure 3.   Organizational outline for curricular content contained in Section II.

Teaching Suggestions

The Teaching Suggestions section contains appropriate activities for addressing the goal, associated objectives, and, in some cases, programming steps. As shown in Figure 3, this section is divided into three parts: 1) activity-based, 2) environmental arrangements, and 3) instructional sequences. The activity-based part describes how to use routine and planned intervention activities that occur throughout the day (e.g., playtime, travel, bathing, eating, storytime) to work on children's goals/objectives. Addressing target skills during daily activities is likely to be the least intrusive form of intervention and to maximize the use of child-centered teaching techniques. The environmental arrangements part offers ideas for increasing the number of teaching opportunities within settings and activities by taking advantage of the child's physical surroundings. The instructional sequences part offers intervention suggestions that are most intrusive and likely to be adult-directed forms of intervention; however, some children may require carefully structured and directed procedures in order to learn targeted skills.

Teaching Considerations

The Teaching Considerations section lists precautions to be considered while working with children who may need sensory or motor adaptations. The curriculum user should always read this section prior to beginning intervention.

LINKING THE AEPS TEST WITH THE AEPS CURRICULUM

The strength of the AEPS and similar systems that foster a direct link between assessment, intervention, and evaluation activities is the assistance that they provide to caregivers and professionals in moving from assessment results to IFSP/IEP goal development, to intervention planning and implementation, and finally to evaluation. The steps to link child/family outcomes from the AEPS Test to the selection of intervention activities in the AEPS Curriculum are described next.

Step 1:   The professional team completes the AEPS Test for the child by using the Child Observation Data Recording Form while the parent or other caregiver completes the Family Report. Completion of the Family Report is dependent on the family's interest in doing so.

Step 2:   Team members and family members review results from the AEPS Test and Family Report. IFSP/IEP goals are selected and prioritized.

Step 3:   Using the AEPS Curriculum, team members locate the appropriate section for each priority goal/objective. They read the introduction and review the table of concurrent goals/objectives, teaching suggestions, and teaching considerations.

Step 4:   Using the information provided by the AEPS Curriculum, team members develop an intervention plan to address each priority goal/objective.

Step 5:   Team members develop an individual or group activity schedule to guide the embedding of selected goals into routine and planned activities.

Step 6:   Team members develop intervention activities for embedding selected child goals/objectives into specific activities that can be routine, planned, or child initiated.

Step 7:   Team members evaluate the child's progress toward priority goals/objectives using the Child Progress Record and make curricular adjustments as necessary.

An example is provided to illustrate this stepwise progression. Juan is a 2-year-old child with Down syndrome who is eligible for early intervention services in his community. Step 1 requires that, upon entry into the program, the intervention team members observe Juan over a 2-week period using the AEPS Test to guide their observations. During the same period, Juan's parents agree to complete the Family Report.

At the scheduled IFSP meeting, the professional team and Juan's parents share and compare their findings (Step 2). Figure 4 shows a portion of the Adaptive Area from the Child Observation Data Recording Form completed by professionals, and Figure 5 shows a portion of the parent-completed Family Report. An examination of Juan's performance on Strand A: Feeding indicates that his parents and the professionals agree that he met criteria for Goal 1 (Uses tongue and lips to take in and swallow solid foods and liquids) but has not met criteria for Goals 2, 3, 4, and 5.

For Goal 2 (Bites and chews hard and chewy foods), Juan met the criteria for Objective 2.2 (Munches soft and crisp foods), but not for Objective 2.1 (Bites and chews soft and crisp foods). For Goal 3 (Drinks from cup and/or glass), the child met the criteria for Objective 3.2 (Drinks from cup and/or glass held by adult) but did not meet criteria for Objective 3.1 (Drinks from cup and/or glass with some spilling). Juan met the criteria for Objective 4.3 (Accepts food presented on spoon) for Goal 4 but did not meet the criteria for Objective 4.2 and Objective 4.1. He did not meet criteria for any of the objectives associated with Goal 5 (Transfers food and liquid between containers).

As seen in Figure 5, results from the parents' completion of the Family Report are similar to the interventionist's assessment using the AEPS Test. After discussing the results, the early intervention staff and Juan's family select Objectives 2.1, 3.1, and 4.2 as priority targets. The next step is to move directly to the Adaptive Area of the AEPS Curriculum.

Step 3 requires reviewing the AEPS Curriculum section that relates directly to the selected goals/objectives. This section can be viewed on pages 184–197 of this volume. The information provided by the AEPS Curriculum will assist the team in developing an appropriate intervention plan for the selected goals/objectives, an activity schedule (Step 5), and intervention activities (Step 6). Finally, the team will monitor Juan's progress toward the targeted objectives (Step 7).

ADAPTIVE AREA

S = Scoring key	N = Notes
2 = Consistently meets criterion	A = Assistance provided
1 = Inconsistently meets criterion	B = Behavior interfered
0 = Does not meet criterion	D = Direct test
	M = Modification/adaptation
	Q = Quality of performance
	R = Report

Name: Juan

	Test period:	1							
	Test date:	5-02							
	Examiner:	MS							

	IFSP/IEP	S	N	S	N	S	N	S	N
A. Feeding									
1. Uses tongue and lips to take in and swallow solid foods and liquids (p. 71)		2							
1.1 Uses lips to take in liquids from a cup and/or glass		2							
1.2 Uses lips to take food off spoon and/or fork		2							
1.3 Swallows solid and semi-solid foods		2							
1.4 Swallows liquids		2							
2. Bites and chews hard and chewy foods (p. 72)		1							
2.1 Bites and chews soft and crisp foods		1							
2.2 Munches soft and crisp foods		2							
3. Drinks from cup and/or glass (p. 72)		1							
3.1 Drinks from cup and/or glass with some spilling		1							
3.2 Drinks from cup and/or glass held by adult		2							
4. Eats with fork and/or spoon (p. 73)		0							
4.1 Brings food to mouth using utensil		0							
4.2 Eats with fingers		1							
4.3 Accepts food presented on spoon		2							
5. Transfers food and liquid between containers (p. 73)		0							
5.1 Pours liquid between containers		0							
5.2 Transfers food between containers		0							

Figure 4. Portion of a professionally completed AEPS Child Observation Data Recording Form for the Adaptive Area, Strand A for Juan.

Adaptive Area

Adaptive skills are those that involve being able to care for oneself. These skills include eating, drinking, and undressing.

date / 5/02

1. Does your child swallow food and liquids without choking or gagging? (A1)

| Y | | | |

2. Does your child bite off and chew pieces of hard foods such as apples, meat, or hard cookies? (A2)

| S | | | |

3. Does your child drink from a cup by bringing the cup to his or her mouth and putting it down without spilling? (A3)

| S | | | |

4. Does your child eat with a spoon or fork (i.e., spearing, scooping) without much spilling? (A4)

5. Does your child pour liquid and serve food from one container to another without spilling? For example, he or she pours juice into a cup from a pitcher or spoons applesauce from a jar into a bowl. (A5)

Figure 5. Portion of the Family Report, Adaptive Area, completed by Juan's parents.

AEPS CURRICULUM AND CHILDREN WITH SEVERE DISABILITIES

Learning and development can be enhanced in young children with severe disabilities if teams individualize assessment and intervention, accurately target areas of need, and use developmentally and age-appropriate activities. Intervention activities should be tailored to accommodate the individual child's physical or cognitive limitations or both, as well as the environmental demands. Teams should not have a set of intervention activities to be used with all children regardless of their needs or goals but should have a range of intervention activities available. An activity-based approach offers a structure to accommodate a wide variety of intervention activities that can be tailored to meet the needs of individual children.

Teams may find that, for some children with severe disabilities, the objectives in the *AEPS Test for Birth to Three Years* are too complex or advanced, requiring that objectives in this assessment be further refined through task analysis. In general, conducting a task analysis requires three steps: 1) identifying the objective, 2) dividing the objective skill into smaller steps, and 3) sequencing the steps for teaching. The programming steps included in the AEPS Curriculum have divided some goals/objectives into smaller steps. Program staff may find these programming steps useful for developing intervention content for children with severe disabilities. An important consideration when working with children with severe disabilities, regardless of the severity of disability, is to embed targeted goals/objectives in activities appropriate to a child's chronological age. Use of the *AEPS Curriculum for Birth to Three Years* will help in choosing activities appropriate for children functioning in the birth to 3 year developmental range.

Considerations When Working with Children with Severe Disabilities

1. If a special assistant is assigned to a child in a center-based setting, then he or she should only provide assistance as needed and should fade involvement in a child's play whenever possible. One-to-one assistants should consider themselves part of the whole child care or classroom environment and teachers to all children but of special assistance to one particular child when necessary.

2. Children learn how to interact with others in part from adult models, so it is vital to be conscious of the subtle messages that are communicated to children. Interventionists should try to include all children in all activities, at whatever level they are able to participate.

3. Attention should be drawn to children's strengths, and all children should be allowed to take on responsibilities that affect the group (e.g., choosing a book for storytime). Activities should be designed to capitalize on a child's strengths and abilities; for example, during a painting activity, a child with profound hearing and visual impairments may enjoy using the sense of smell or touch to explore materials. Materials can be added or adapted to an activity to provide opportunities for all children to participate to the greatest extent possible.

4. The interventionist should translate a child's behavior whenever necessary. Children with more pronounced disabilities or severe communicative impairments often have difficulties joining play activities with other children. Their peers, who are just beginning to learn to interact, may have difficulty "reading" behaviors and communicative attempts different from those that they know. Adults play a crucial role in translating the child's behavior for peers; for example, during a song at circle time, Denzel, who has cerebral palsy, starts to "sing," but his voice sounds almost like a cry. The children appear alarmed, and the interventionist reassures the children by saying, "I can hear Denzel singing to the music."

5. Adults may need to provide assistance to help children gain access to and participate in different play activities. The child care worker can suggest play ideas (e.g., "How about everyone play in the sand together?") and provide suggestions for how a child with more severe impairments might participate in an activity (e.g., "I bet Tom could dig in the sand, too"). With assistance from teachers, peers can be encouraged to include children with disabilities in activities. Sometimes simple solutions such as altering the location of activities may provide opportunities for children with disabilities to be included.

6. Children may need additional structure and guidance to practice and enhance their social skills. Activities such as rocking a boat, playing seesaw, and playing catch encourage children to play in pairs. Modeling questions such as "Can I play, too?" or "Do you want to play house with me?" or using sign language with nonverbal children are effective strategies.

7. The child should be allowed to be as independent as possible with peers; for example, the interventionist can let peers know that they can approach a child with a visual impairment and say, "Hi, Eric, it's Joey." A child with cerebral palsy who uses a wheelchair might participate in an art project by sitting in a modified chair at a table with other children rather than in the wheelchair.

8. Straightforward, honest answers to questions posed by children will help facilitate understanding of disabling conditions. Specialized equipment may isolate a child if the equipment remains a mystery. The interventionist should be open and honest when answering questions from the child's peers, and allow him or her to explore the adaptive equipment (with the permission of the child) with the understanding that the equipment is a tool and not a toy.

9. The interventionist should assist children without disabilities in learning how to interact and play with peers with disabilities; for example, one can tell the peer that, when he or she colors with a child with a visual impairment, it is helpful to put markers back in the original place; when a peer talks to a child with a hearing impairment, it helps to face the child and speak clearly. Peers should be encouraged to address children with disabilities directly (e.g., "Can I push your wheelchair outside?").

10. It is helpful to enhance the social image of children with disabilities by selecting clothing and toys that are age appropriate and currently popular.

SUMMARY

This introductory material is included to set the stage for efficient and effective use of the AEPS Curriculum in conjunction with the AEPS Test. The user is urged to carefully read this material prior to employing the curriculum. In addition, the authors recommend that the AEPS Curriculum be used in association with the AEPS Test. Without accurate, in-depth knowledge of children's behavioral repertoires, selecting appropriate intervention activities is guesswork, as is monitoring progress. The field of early intervention has become, through legal, professional, and parental interest, a legitimate enterprise that should not tolerate less-than-quality outcomes. Producing outcomes for children and families is dependent on careful and comprehensive assessments that lead to appropriate intervention accompanied by ongoing evaluation. Use of the AEPS Test and AEPS Curriculum may help interventionists attain this quality.

3

Designing and Implementing Intervention

This chapter is designed to assist teams in using the AEPS Curriculum by employing an activity-based approach that emphasizes children's involvement in child-initiated, routine, and planned intervention activities, as well as strategies on how to effectively arrange the learning environment. The primary purpose of this chapter is to address a variety of topics that will assist the user in the understanding and application of the AEPS Curriculum and will help establish a coordinated and cohesive approach to curricular programming.

The content and strategies offered in this curriculum are designed to be used in conjunction with developmentally appropriate practices to encourage child-initiated activities, encourage self-exploration and self-control, promote communication, support problem solving, enhance social interactions and play, and build toward independence. The age and range of disabilities and delays exhibited by the infants and children in a program should be considered when selecting the curricular content, intervention strategies, and environmental arrangements. Promoting effective learning in children who are at risk or who have disabilities requires flexibility in approach, attention to individual needs, and engagement in meaningful activities. Adopting such an approach requires that developmentally appropriate practice is used and opportunities are available that address children's targeted goals/objectives.

Developmentally appropriate practice is predicated on three essential features. First, infants, toddlers, and children are offered a variety of activities, events, and environmental arrangements appropriate to their developmental capacities. Second, these activities, events, and environmental arrangements should be meaningful to young children. A final essential element is that the activities, events, and environmental arrangements provide a balance between children learning to follow the directions of others and learning to initiate activities to meet their own desires and interests.

For young children who have or are at risk for disabilities, it is particularly important that activities be guided into productive endeavors. It is essential to offer children developmentally appropriate activities with multiple opportunities to work on the acquisition and maintenance of targeted goals/objectives. Being developmentally appropriate is not sufficient; activities should offer many opportunities for children to practice behaviors that enhance communication and problem-solving skills and build toward independence. Ongoing observation and evaluation are necessary to ensure that the environment offers adequate opportunity for children to practice their targeted goals. Without careful monitoring of progress, children may engage in fun and meaningful self-initiated activities but fail to improve in targeted areas.

The following sections describe a range of information and strategies that promote developmentally appropriate practice and provide multiple opportunities for targeting children's goals. These strategies include using 1) child initiations, 2) daily routines, 3) environmental arrangements, and 4) planned intervention activities.

CHILD INITIATIONS

When employing an approach such as ABI, the preferred strategy is to follow children's leads and to guide their behavior in desired directions. Following the interests of infants and toddlers is particularly critical because, developmentally, most are poorly equipped to follow an adult's attention or directions. It is important to note that caregivers and interventionists cannot rely exclusively on child initiations to provide the necessary opportunities to practice goals/objectives; therefore, the use of daily routines, environmental arrangements, and planned intervention activities need to be considered, as well as child initiations. However, to the extent possible, caregivers should become careful observers of children's behavior and introduce intervention content into activities that children initiate and choose.

In an ABI approach, the caregiver or interventionist is a facilitator and guide rather than a director of the child's learning. Through observation and interactions with the child, the adult provides the least level of assistance necessary for the child to practice targeted goals or solve problems; for example, Tony's dad noticed that his infant son would babble when put in his infant seat. So, after seating Tony, Dad would wait for his son to babble. Dad would then imitate Tony's babbling and encourage the baby to respond.

Interventionists and caregivers who are sensitive to children's needs in an activity-based program do not stay involved in the children's play longer than necessary. Interventionists and caregivers can use a variety of techniques to facilitate rather than direct learning in children.

Techniques for Encouraging Child Initiations

Follow the Child's Lead

When participating in an activity with an infant or young child, the caregiver or interventionist should follow the child's lead whenever possible and appropriate. Although children can be enticed into activities of the adult's choosing, it is often easier and more effective to subtly change or redirect an activity chosen by the child into a vehicle for practicing a targeted goal/objective; for example, if a toddler is playing in the sandbox, then the child care worker follows the child's lead and joins in the play. If the child picks up a stick and pokes in the sand, then the caregiver imitates the play. To become effective at following a child's lead, it is critical that interventionists and caregivers be good observers of children, watching them to learn about their interests and motivations and their actual capabilities.

Model Desired Behaviors or Draw Attention to Peer Models

Adults and peers with advanced skills can provide excellent models of desired behaviors and targeted goals/objectives throughout child-initiated, routine, and planned intervention activities. This strategy can be used to expand on the child's initiations by taking the activity one step further. In the sandbox activity described previously, the child care worker, knowing that a targeted objective for the child is to grasp objects, might place a few hand-size objects of interest near the child to encourage grasping. A variety of strategies such as modeling, asking for or exchanging toys, or making a simple game out of the activity (e.g., hiding a toy partially under the sand for the child to find, retrieving a toy from the sand) might be used to encourage the child's use of the target grasping response.

Provide the Least Level of Assistance

Prompts provide additional information or support to help a child perform a behavior correctly; however, adults should offer the least assistance necessary for the child to perform the target response. Providing too much support or direction may result in the child becoming overly dependent on the adult for assistance and delay the development of independent skills and problem-solving behavior. Examples of prompts follow, generally from the least intrusive to the most intrusive.

- *Verbal prompts:* Adults make statements that help the child perform the behavior; for example, if the objective is to take off shoes, then a verbal prompt might be, "Take off your shoes."

- *Gestural prompts:* Adults make hand, arm, or other movements that communicate information to the child about what to do; for example, if the objective is to follow a one-step direction such as, "sit down," then a gestural prompt might be patting the chair seat.

- *Model prompts:* Adults or peers demonstrate the desired behavior.

- *Partial physical prompts:* Adults partially physically guide a child's movements.

- *Full physical prompts:* Adults physically guide a child's movements.

Group Children Heterogeneously

Whenever possible, children of varied ages or developmental levels should be grouped together. Heterogeneous groupings provide opportunities for children to learn new skills by observing peer models or enhance their skills by assisting children who are less able.

Plan Time for Children to Complete Tasks

During busy schedules at home and school, adults often find themselves rushing children through activities to stay within a schedule. When possible, adequate time should be allowed for children to complete tasks independently or with as little assistance as possible.

Adjust Speech Complexity

When addressing infants and small children, it is important to adjust the complexity of one's speech to reflect the child's level of understanding (this, of course, does not mean using "baby talk"). It is important to remember that too much adult talk may interfere with the development of the child's communication or with child-to-child communication. Adults should monitor their talk and actions to permit children adequate time to respond or initiate conversations and to communicate with each other.

Use Different Types of Talk

When possible, use a variety of ways to talk to the child, including

- *Self-talk:* Talking aloud to oneself; verbalizing what one sees, hears, does, and feels; describing actions, objects, and events throughout the day for children (e.g., "I'm going to get dinner ready")

- *Parallel talk:* Using talk that focuses on what the child is seeing, hearing, and doing

- *Expansion:* Expanding on what the child says; for example, if the child says "mo" after eating a cracker, then an expansion might be, "More crackers?"

- *Elaboration:* Using the previous example, the interventionist might say, "You want more crackers? You must be hungry."

Provide Choices

Offering choices can prompt a verbal response from children; for example, instead of asking a child, "Do you want more crackers?" offer a choice such as, "Do you want more crackers or more juice?" Choices also provide an excellent strategy to less intrusively direct a child; for example, if a child consistently avoids manipulative activities and needs to practice fine motor goals, then it may be appropriate to offer a limited choice such as, "You can have the puzzle or the blocks."

Use Open versus Closed Questions

Using open questions may require children to use more complex language in response. Open questions cannot be answered in one word and typically begin with "what," "why," "how," or "could" (e.g., "What do you want to do now?" "Why are you sad?"). Closed questions can be answered in one word and often begin with "is," "are," or "do" (e.g., "Do you want to go outside?").

Use the Mand/Model Procedure

In the mand/model procedure, the interventionist may initiate an interaction by making a statement or asking a question (the "mand") that requires a response about the activity in which the child is engaged. If the child does not respond or only partially responds, then the interventionist provides a "model" of the verbal response with an emphasis on a targeted word or phrase; for example, while playing with bubbles, the interventionist holds up the bubble wand and says, "What should I do?" If the child does not respond, then the interventionist might model, "Say, 'Blow bubbles.'"

Try Forgetfulness

The interventionist or caregiver fails to provide the necessary equipment or materials or omits a familiar component of a routine or activity; for example, not having a food immediately available for snack time may provide an opportunity for the children to recognize the missing element (e.g., "Where are the crackers?") and may provide practice in asking questions, searching for materials, and engaging in other problem-solving behavior.

Use Visible but Unreachable

Objects that are desirable or necessary for the completion of activities are placed within sight of children but out of their reach. Children will need to use language and problem-solving skills to retrieve the items; for example, placing a favorite toy on a high shelf may force the child to ask an adult for help.

Violate Expectations

Omitting or changing a familiar step or element in a well-practiced or routine activity violates children's expectations. Children's recognition of change will provide information about their discrimination and memory abilities and provide ideal situations for problem solving; for example, the parent tries to pour juice but has no cups.

Use Interruption

Interruption requires that the interventionist or caregiver stop the child from continuing a chain of behaviors that has become routine; for example, during hand washing, the interventionist or caregiver interrupts the child who is reaching for the soap and asks, "What do you want?" The child must then indicate what is needed to complete the task.

DAILY ROUTINES

Daily routines at home and in community-based preschool and child care programs give children choices about activities, although adults should not give children complete freedom to decide what they will do. Adults create a framework by designing the environment, choosing materials and activities, and taking a facilitative role in the learning process. As children explore their environment and expand on play activities, adults capitalize on child initiations and create additional learning experiences and opportunities.

Daily routines that occur at home or in child care or in school settings can be used to provide multiple opportunities for children to practice targeted goals/objectives across important developmental areas. The use of daily routines (e.g., meals, cleanup, travel, bedtime) should be encouraged for two important reasons. First, daily routines are likely to be important and meaningful to children; therefore, the interventionists or caregivers do not have to create artificial or special activities, nor do they have to find ways to make the activities relevant. Second, daily routines help people get through activities that need to be accomplished on a regular basis (e.g., bathing, eating). Because these activities occur routinely, they can be used effectively and efficiently as teaching times.

An analysis of the home or other child care setting will reveal a variety of activities or events that occur regularly and predictably; for example, upon waking, most families follow bathing, dressing, and eating routines that prepare them for the day. With thought, these routines may be used to assist children in learning and practicing targeted goals/objectives; for example, undressing provides toddlers the opportunity to work on adaptive skills (e.g., taking off pants and socks), social-communication skills (e.g., "Where shoes?"), or cognitive skills (e.g., finding shoes and socks). Breakfast, lunch, and dinner provide numerous opportunities to practice adaptive skills (e.g., chewing, drinking), social-communication skills (e.g., indicating food choices), and motor skills (e.g., sitting, climbing into a chair, transferring or serving food). Without analysis of events and consideration of the child's goals, caregivers may overlook opportunities to use daily routines to target skills. Not all daily routines, of course, will be appropriate teaching times for all families (e.g., families who have tight timelines for getting to work may find it difficult to use breakfast as a teaching time).

A similar analysis of daily routines in a child care setting will yield a variety of routines that can be used to target children's goals; for example, arrival at the center offers opportunities to practice motor skills (e.g., walking up stairs, opening doors), adaptive skills (e.g., removing a jacket, hanging it up), and social skills (e.g., greeting other children). Washing up for a snack gives children the opportunity to practice social skills (e.g., taking turns), adaptive skills (e.g., washing and drying hands), and social-communication skills (e.g., labeling objects, asking for a drink). Through careful observation, interventionists may identify numerous opportunities for children to practice targeted goals/objectives as they engage in daily routines.

To assist caregivers and interventionists in the use of daily routines to target children's goals/objectives, two routine activity planning formats have been developed and are contained in Appendixes A and B of this volume. The first format presents a variety of potential goals/objectives across developmental areas that could be targeted during a specific activity (e.g., mealtime). The second format describes a number of routine activities that could potentially target goals/objectives from a single developmental area (e.g., learning to respond to questions could be targeted during mealtime, playtime, bath time, and bedtime).

Routine activity format I: One activity targeting goals from multiple developmental areas. This routine activity format is designed to assist caregivers and interventionists in using routine activities to target specific goals/objectives across many developmental areas; for example, during routine trips in the car, a caregiver might be able to target cognitive and social-communication goals/objectives such as labeling objects that the child sees, such as cars or trees. An example of this routine activity format is contained in Figure 6. The AEPS goal for each developmental area is listed and, for each goal, specific actions (e.g., what to do) and possible materials necessary for the routine activity are suggested. The "What to Dos" suggested in Figure 6 are illustrative and will likely require modification to be appropriate for individual children. Additional examples of this routine activity format are contained in Appendix A.

Routine activity format II: Multiple activities targeting goals from one developmental area. This routine activity format should assist caregivers and interventionists in using a variety of activities (e.g., mealtime, playtime, bedtime) to target goals from a specific developmental area. As shown in Figure 7, the goals/objectives for a targeted strand from the Fine Motor Area are listed along with possible routine activities that might be used to target those goals/objectives. The goals/objectives, taken from the *AEPS Test Birth to Three Years*, Fine Motor Area, Strand B, are listed to the left in shaded circles. Listed in the columns (i.e., mealtime, bathroom time, outside time, and playtime) are a variety of actions that one might use to embed the targeted goals/objectives that would be appropriate for that particular activity. Activities and actions are illustrative and will likely need modification to meet the needs of individual children and families. Appendix B contains an example of this routine activity format for the entire *AEPS Test Birth to Three Years*, Strand B, Fine Motor Area.

ENVIRONMENTAL ARRANGEMENTS

Children's environments can be arranged in a variety of ways to provide multiple opportunities to practice targeted goals/objectives both in home and out-of-home settings. Such arrangements potentially maximize the impact of intervention activities.

The Home Environment

The manner in which families arrange their home environment is dependent on a number of factors such as family culture and values, economic resources, and available time and energy. The individual nature of children's home environments will dictate what type of physical arrangements caregivers can and will make. Home settings vary from children living in community shelters, motels, and cars, to apartments and single-family dwellings. This enormous range of environments requires intervention teams to think creatively about how to help caregivers make changes in the child's home environment. The suggested environmental arrangements for the home will be dependent both on caregivers' openness to the intervention team's scrutiny of the home and

Routine Activity: Mealtime

FINE MOTOR AREA

Goal/Objective	What to Do	Materials
Turns object over using wrist and arm rotation with each hand. (B:1.1)	Allow and encourage child to feed self with a spoon.	Spoon, food

ADAPTIVE AREA

Goal/Objective	What to Do	Materials
Brings food to mouth using utensil. (A:4.1)	Provide a fork or spoon with food that can be scooped; encourage child to bring filled utensil to mouth.	Fork or spoon, food that can be scooped (e.g., applesauce, yogurt)

SOCIAL-COMMUNICATION AREA

Goal/Objective	What to Do	Materials
Carries out one-step direction with contextual cues. (C:2.3)	Give simple directions for setting the table, passing snacks to peers, and cleaning up afterward.	Napkins, utensils, cups, food items, sponge

GROSS MOTOR AREA

Goal/Objective	What to Do	Materials
Moves up and down stairs. (C:4.2)	Place a step-stool by the sink for washing hands prior to eating.	Step-stool

COGNITIVE AREA

Goal/Objective	What to Do	Materials
Imitates words that are frequently used. (D:2.2)	Label foods and objects while eating.	Food and objects at meal location (e.g., cracker, juice, napkin)

SOCIAL AREA

Goal/Objective	What to Do	Materials
Meets internal physical needs of hunger, thirst, and rest. (B:1.1)	Wait for the child to request food before or during serving.	Food and drink prepared for serving

Figure 6. A sample of a Routine Activity Format I using mealtime to target multiple goals/objectives from the AEPS Test: Birth to Three Years across developmental areas.

AEPS Birth to Three

Fine Motor Area, Strand B: Functional Use of Fine Motor Skills, Goal 1, Objective 1.1

Goal/Objective	Routine Activities			
	Mealtime	Bathroom time	Outside time	Playtime
Goal 1 **Rotates either wrist on horizontal plane**	• Encourage child to remove lids on jars. • Provide jars with the lids already loosened. Gradually make the task more challenging by screwing the lid a quarter turn. • Allow child to make juice by twisting an orange half on a squeezer. • Encourage child to participate in cleaning activities with you, such as washing the table with a sponge or emptying water from cups into the sink.	• Encourage child to flush the toilet. • Close doors to encourage child to turn doorknobs when entering or leaving the room.	• Encourage child to manipulate the handle of a drinking fountain independently. Child may drink from the fountain or simply watch the effect.	• Encourage child to play with toys, such as a Busy Box, that have knobs that can be turned by rotating the wrist. • Play games with cards. Show child how to deal cards and turn them face up. • Provide toys with large, easy-to-manage wind-up mechanisms (e.g., alarm clock, toy train, toy radio). Systematically introduce smaller mechanisms as child begins to develop wrist rotation.

Figure 7. A sample of a Routine Activity Format II using multiple activities to target goals/objectives from one developmental area.

Figure 7. *(continued)*

Goal/Objective	Routine Activities			
	Mealtime	Bathroom time	Outside time	Playtime
Objective 1.1 Turns object over using wrist and arm rotation with each hand	• Allow and encourage child to feed self with a spoon and/or cup. • Allow child to shake or dump the contents of a container into a bowl during baking activities.	• Encourage child to wash and dry own hands, turning the hands back and forth under the water and rubbing soap on the palms and backs of hands.	• Allow child to play with containers in sand, water, dirt, or cornmeal. • Encourage child to dump the contents of one container into another.	• Play at feeding dolls, stuffed animals, and peers "pretend" food or drinks. • During preparation for activities, have child dump crayons, stickers, brushes, blocks or peg people out of storage containers. • Encourage child to turn pages of a book when reading a story with an adult.

caregivers' willingness to make changes. Given these important caveats, the following steps are recommended for environmental arrangements in home settings:

1. Explain to caregivers the reason and purpose for environmental arrangements.

2. Determine the interest and willingness of the caregiver to make changes.

3. Obtain information on the physical features of the home and the family's daily activities.

4. Develop a plan for environmental arrangements.

The first step is to explain to caregivers and families what is meant by environmental arrangements in easy-to-understand language. It is important to explain how environmental arrangements may make the conduct of the families' daily activities easier and more efficient while providing increased opportunities for their child to practice and/or learn new skills. Caregivers who do not understand or appreciate this reasoning should not be pushed to consider changes in their physical environment or daily activities.

The second step is for the professionals on the intervention team to determine, to the extent possible, the caregiver's or families' ability and interest in making changes in the home environment (e.g., a family living in a homeless shelter may have little control over the physical environment or even the flow of daily events). Although some families will not welcome suggestions about changes in the physical arrangement of their home and daily activities, many families will. Using the Family Report, in particular Section I, can be quite useful for families to identify areas that concern them and to indicate their interest to professionals to assist them with changes in environments and routines.

For caregivers/families interested in and willing to consider changes, either a visit to the home or a discussion about the home and family activities is the third step. This visit or discussion allows one to obtain information necessary to design a plan. Some caregivers may be comfortable with only minor changes (e.g., adding toys to the diaper-changing table), whereas others may consider significant shifts (e.g., rearranging furniture).

The final step is to develop a plan tailored to the child and family. Again, depending on the caregiver's interests, the plan could suggest minor adjustments or major changes. Examples of minor adjustments might be changing the type of toys available to the toddler at bath time, tying toys to the infant's car seat, or placing a chair near a window so the toddler can climb up and look out. More extensive adjustments might include rearranging the eating area so that the infant's highchair is closer to mom as she prepares meals, creating a quiet play area in the living room that contains books and table toys, or arranging the child's room to encourage crawling or walking.

Following these or other similar steps may aid caregivers in thinking about and trying environmental arrangements in the home that could benefit the family as well as the child.

The Child Care Environment

A significant number of infants and young children attend child care outside of the home. The caveats discussed about environmental arrangements in the home are also applicable to out-of-home child care settings (i.e., great variability exists across settings and in the willingness and ability of the caregivers to consider environmental arrangements).

The steps suggested for environmental arrangements in the home can also be applied to other child care settings. As with parents, paid child care workers will vary in their interest and ability to make adjustments to the physical environment or the daily activities of the home or center. Section I of the Family Report may assist child care providers in identifying environments or routines that they would like to change.

For those out-of-home caregivers and child care workers who are willing to work with the intervention team, a variety of environmental arrangements may be made that improve the quality of the worker's life as well as enhance opportunities for children to acquire targeted goals/objectives; for example, assisting the child care worker in arranging the environment so that a child with a severe motor disability is more independent should be beneficial for both the child and the child care worker (i.e., the child has greater independence and the child care worker has more time to address other needs). Arranging a child care setting into activity centers (which are described in the next section) may encourage children to remain engaged in activities that enhance their learning without direct intervention by an adult. Helping child care workers think about potential training opportunities for children that can be embedded in daily activities may be another strategy that will prove beneficial to both children and workers.

For individuals or centers that provide child care, working with an intervention team to consider and make changes in the physical environment and daily activities will likely lead to enhanced learning by the child. This leads to greater parent satisfaction with the child's care that, in turn, should increase the child care worker's job satisfaction.

The Preschool Environment

Children's environments can be arranged in a variety of ways to provide multiple opportunities to practice targeted goals/objectives. A useful strategy for young children in center-based programs is to arrange the environment into activity centers, equipping each area with specific materials. Space can be creatively organized to afford multiple opportunities for children to engage in activities that enhance learning. The goal is to design the environment so that multiple skills across areas can be elicited in the activity centers and that multiple opportunities to practice skills are provided.

The use of activity centers is an excellent strategy for encouraging child-initiated activities. When a child initiates an activity—for example, begins to play with a toy, asks a question, or creates a game—the activity is likely to be of considerable interest to the child. Encouraging child initiations capitalizes on children's involvement in activities that they find motivating and fun. Self-selected activities generally do not require artificial reinforcers or other external supports to maintain the child's interest and involvement.

Well-designed activity centers can target a child's interest and effort in multiple skill areas. An activity center with puzzles, blocks, and other manipulatives can be used to promote fine motor and cognitive skills. An obstacle course encourages the use of gross motor and social skills. A book or listening area promotes cognitive and communication skills.

Designing a variety of activity centers allows interventionists to target developing skills across areas. Children can make choices among activity centers, and appropriate assistance from an interventionist facilitates opportunities to learn and practice targeted skills. Activity centers can be a permanent foundation for a center-based program, but a rotation of materials is necessary to capitalize on children's ideas, expand activities, and maintain children's interest throughout the year.

The number and type of activity centers designed will depend on space, daily schedules, the population of children, and available resources (e.g., materials, equipment); for example, programs that have an outdoor play space may not need to develop a gross motor activity center. It is important to provide definition to activity centers and to separate noisy and quiet centers as much as space allows. Shelves or commercial dividers help separate and define spaces.

As children engage in the activities of a center, interventionists should evaluate the usefulness of the activities in moving children toward their IFSP/IEP goals/objectives. Activity centers that do *not* consistently engage children are likely to be ineffective, whereas those that both address target areas and elicit child engagement are likely to be more effective.

The hallmark of effective early intervention is systematic and consistent environmental arrangements that promote learning in children. In center-based programs, thoughtfully designed activity centers provide children with a set of materials and events that are developmentally appropriate and promote opportunities for practice of targeted goals/objectives.

For more information on how to develop and use activity centers see Chapter 3 of Volume 4.

PLANNED INTERVENTION ACTIVITIES

In addition to using child initiations, daily routines, and environmental arrangements, interventionists and caregivers may find it necessary and desirable to offer children a range of planned intervention activities. As with environmental arrangements, specific planned activities may occur much less frequently in home settings than in out-of-home settings; however, in all settings, planning is necessary for successful intervention because it helps ensure that opportunities to practice targeted IFSP/IEP goals/objectives are arranged. This planning is essential at many different levels and should include all team members (e.g., caregivers, specialists) when possible. The information in this section is directed primarily to professional staff who are responsible for planning activities in center-based and child care programs and for helping care-givers select activities appropriate for the home and their family.

The effective use of planned intervention activities requires a framework that assists in targeting important goals/objectives and that permits the efficient use of resources. Components of a useful framework include intervention plans, activity schedules, and intervention activities. Each of these components is described next. These components are also described in-depth in *An Activity-Based Approach to Early Intervention* (2nd ed., Bricker, Pretti-Frontczak, & McComas, 1998).

Intervention Plans

Intervention plans can be used to delineate the intervention content, to outline teaching guidelines, and to determine criteria for monitoring progress on priority goals/objectives. Intervention plans should be developed cooperatively by the intervention staff or team. Input from team members can be shared and then synthesized into a program plan to guide intervention activities and to ensure a cohesive, coordinated approach to addressing the child's/family's goals/objectives.

Intervention plans can specify the goal and its associated objectives for individual children, as shown in Figure 8, or for groups of children. These plans can include intervention strategies, teaching considerations, curricular modifications, procedures for monitoring child progress, and decision rules for change. Intervention plans are much like an architect's blueprint in that they provide the specifications necessary to reach a goal. Intervention plans should be followed and modified as necessary so that interventionists and caregivers always have a specific plan to guide their activities. Volume 1, Chapter 2, provides more detail on how to create intervention plans.

Activity Schedules

Most infants and young children are sensitive to changes in their environment and may become upset if continually unable to anticipate or predict future events. Providing a level of consistency and predictability to home- and center-based environments can greatly enhance a child's independent functioning and increase a sense of security. Families should develop predictable schedules for their daily activities (e.g., meals, bath time, bedtime) to the extent possible, as should child care and preschool programs. The use of weekly and daily activity schedules is one effective way to provide some consistency and predictability. Figure 9 displays a weekly schedule for a child care program. Schedules help staff balance activities and plan opportunities to address children's targeted goals.

Center/Group Activity Schedules

Activity schedules help an interventionist or caregiver determine the best times for children to practice targeted IFSP/IEP goals/objectives. Center-based programs

INTERVENTION PLAN

Child: _Kobe Perkins_____ Team members/Interventionist: _Doug and Regina Perkins_
_(parents), Sandy Tobias (home-based provider), and Elizabeth Burke (occupational therapist)___
Date initiated: _2/02____   Expected date of completion: _5/02_____
Type of setting: ____ Group   ____ Individual   _x__ Home

GROSS MOTOR AREA

Individualized family service plan (IFSP) outcome: Kobe can crawl to get desired objects or people.

Target Goal and Objectives

AEPS Test: Gross Motor Area, Strand A, Goal 3

Creeps forward using alternating arm and leg movements.

AEPS Test: Objective 3.1

Rocks while in a creeping position.

AEPS Test: Objective 3.2

Assumes creeping position.

Intervention Strategies and Teaching Considerations

List of strategies that will be used or what will be done to provide an opportunity for Kobe to practice the targeted skills	List of possible child behaviors: targeted and expected (+) or nontargeted and unexpected (-)	Consequences or what will be done following Kobe's targeted behaviors (+) or nontargeted behaviors (-)
· During floor playtime, place Kobe on rug or other nonslip surface · Place Kobe's favorite toys nearby but out of Kobe's reach · Have caregiver get down on the floor in front of Kobe · Following breakfast, place Kobe on small rug in kitchen	· Creeps forward using alternate arm/leg movements (+) · Assumes creeping position and rocks back and forth (+) · Assumes creeping position (+) · Lies on stomach (-) · Sits (-) · Rolls to back (-)	· Give Kobe desired toy/object (+) · Smile or praise Kobe (+) · If Kobe does not assume creeping position, physically prompt him to do so (-) · Make request again or encourage again (-)

Curricular Modifications

No modifications are needed.

Figure 8. Kobe's intervention plan for Gross Motor Area goal.

Figure 8. *(continued)*

Child Progress Procedures			
Who	Where	When	How
Mother	Kitchen	Once per week, after breakfast	Note if Kobe assumes a creeping position while in the kitchen. Record the information on a chart on the refrigerator.

Decision Rule

If adequate progress does not occur in ___3 weeks___ (specify time frame), then the team will

_x_ modify intervention strategies

___ modify curricular content (i.e., targeted goals, objectives)

___ other (describe): _____

_____

_____

have a variety of daily routines that have potential as excellent training times; for example, arrival can be used to practice adaptive skills (e.g., remove jacket and hat) and foster independence (e.g., select an activity prior to group time). Snack time can be used to practice and improve motor skills (e.g., crawl or walk to a table), social-communication skills (e.g., request food), and adaptive skills (e.g., use a napkin to wipe hands). Clean-up is often an opportune time to promote social interactions and cooperation (e.g., children help pick up toys), improve fine and gross motor skills (e.g., put toys in boxes), and practice social-communication skills (e.g., follow simple directions, ask questions).

Activity schedules can be developed for an individual child or groups of children. The development of activity schedules for young children with disabilities may be vital to receiving adequate opportunities to practice targeted goals/objectives. Figure 10 illustrates an activity schedule developed for three children in a center-based program. The children's names are placed across the top of the matrix and their specific goals/objectives are listed below their names. On the left side of the matrix are the daily classroom activities and times. An "X" is placed in appropriate boxes for each goal/objective to indicate that a training opportunity is likely to occur during that activity. A variation is to insert brief descriptions of possible activities in each box; for example, for

Activity schedule	
Arrival	Greet children; talk to parents
Open play	Children can select area or toy for play
Group story time	Children join one of three groups for teacher to read stories
Outside play	Children play in covered outside area
Snack time	Children sit at tables for snack
Open play	Children can select area or toy for play
Bathroom time	Children use bathroom, or diapers are changed
Lunch time	Children sit at tables for lunch
Nap or quiet time	Children rest on cots; may look at books
Outside play	Children play in covered outside area
Open play	Children can select area or toy for play
Departure	Prepare children; talk with parents

Figure 9. Weekly schedule for child care program.

the 8:30–9:00 activity center, under Robbie's goal "grasps hand-size objects," add a note to introduce a game that requires Robbie to grasp and manipulate a variety of hand-size objects. Activity schedules will differ depending on settings and their restrictions and resources, as well as on the individual needs of children. Figure 11 provides an example of a modified activity schedule that can also be used as a progress monitoring (i.e., data collection) system. As shown in Figure 11, dates are written under each objective, and a child's progress is recorded below the date each time the child independently performs the skill (+), does not perform the skill (–), or performs the skill with assistance or prompting (p). For more detailed information on how to collect daily/weekly child progress data, see Chapter 7 in *An Activity-Based Approach to Early Intervention* (2nd ed., Bricker, Pretti-Frontczak, & McComas, 1998).

Observing each skill daily may be overwhelming; a monitoring system in which observations are staggered (i.e., by child, day, objective, setting) may make the task more manageable; for example, a schedule that staggers the activity being monitored may be helpful (e.g., observations will be made during arrival and departure on Monday, in activity centers on Tuesday, and during

	Child's name: Robbie		Child's name: Lavona		Child's name: Sissy	
	Goal/Obj.	Goal/Obj.	Goal/Obj.	Goal/Obj.	Goal/Obj.	Goal/Obj.
	Grasps hand-size objects	Uses word approxima-tions	Gains attention/ refers to object, person	Indicates need for toilet	Carries out one-step directions	Washes, dries hands
8:20–8:30 Arrival		X	X	X	X	
8:30–9:00 Activity centers	X	X	X	X	X	
9:00–9:20 Circle time		X	X	X	X	
9:20–9:45 Snack	X	X	X	X	X	X
9:45–10:20 Outdoor play		X	X	X	X	
10:20–10:50 Special activities	X	X	X	X	X	
10:50–11:00 Cleanup	X	X	X	X	X	X
11:00–11:30 Circle/story		X	X	X	X	
11:30–12:00 Departure		X	X	X	X	

Figure 10.   Group activity schedule completed for three children.

outdoor play on Wednesday). Another example of a staggered monitoring system that might appeal to staff is to plan observations during planned intervention activities and transition times one week and during free play and routine activities the next week.

Spreading the responsibility for progress monitoring across staff members may be helpful in that team members have reminders to develop opportunities for children to practice targeted skills during daily activities; for example, if a staff person is unable to observe Sissy following one-step directions during arrival because no one-step directions are given, then the staff member can concentrate on providing opportunities for that goal during arrival the next day. The use of planned activity schedules that help ensure opportunities for children to practice identified goals/objectives across each day is essential to effective intervention.

Activity schedule	Child's name: Robbie						Child's name: Lavona						Child's name: Sissy					
	Goal/Objective: Grasps hand-size objects			Goal/Objective: Uses word approximations			Goal/Objective: Gains attention/refers to object, person			Goal/Objective: Indicates need for toilet			Goal/Objective: Carries out one-step directions			Goal/Objective: Washes, dries hands		
	Date 10/12	Date 10/14	Date	Date 10/13	Date	Date	Date 10/13	Date	Date	Date 10/12	Date 10/14	Date	Date 10/13	Date 10/15	Date	Date 10/12	Date 10/14	Date
8:20–8:30 Arrival				+						+	p		–, p	p, p				
8:30–9:00 Activity centers	p, p	–, +		+			p, p											
9:00–9:20 Circle time	+, p			p			p						–, p	+				
9:20–9:45 Snack time																		
9:45–10:20 Outdoor play																		
10:20–10:50 Special activities	p, p	+		+, p			p, +				+							
10:50–11:00 Cleanup	–, p	–														–	–	
11:00–11:30 Circle/story																		
11:30–12:00 Departure													p	+, p				

Figure 11. An activity schedule that includes a progress monitoring system (+ = independently performs skills; – = does not perform skills; p = performs skills with assistance or prompting).

41

Home/Individual Activity Schedules

Activity schedules can also be used effectively in the home. Caregivers are the best source of information to determine which daily routines address certain skills. Each family's schedule, values, and priorities, combined with their knowledge of the child's preferences, interests, and level of involvement in home and community activities, make them, as caregivers, critical to the development of an accurate and useful activity schedule in the home environment. Home/individual activity schedules help us provide structure for families working with children in their routine activities, without creating unnecessary "drill" sessions.

Many possibilities are available to families. Bath time can be a time to expand vocabulary, search for missing objects, or improve adaptive skills. Traveling in the car may be an ideal time to expand the child's communication skills by pointing out people and objects. Figure 12 provides examples of how two IFSP objectives for Michael can be practiced within his family's typical daily routine.

The advantages of using daily routines for teaching are many. First, children are more likely to be motivated to learn a new skill if it is required in the course of a routine; for example, learning to take off the cap in order to put toothpaste on the toothbrush is likely more interesting and certainly more functional than an activity in which the child simply practices wrist rotation by removing jar lids. Second, when a skill is acquired in the course of daily activities, generalization of the skill is more likely. The skill is mastered in the setting where it is used, which eliminates the need to transfer the learned skill from a formal teaching situation. Third, caregivers and interventionists do not have to adopt "training" or "instructional" behaviors because they are already engaging children.

Considerations When Creating Activity Schedules

The development of useful and efficient activity schedules requires consideration of the following factors.

- *Preparation:* Transition time is needed for most children to move from one activity to the next whether at home or in an out-of-home placement. It is helpful to tell children that the activity will end soon and what they can expect next.

- *Time constraints:* It is important to provide adequate time for children, especially those with mobility impairments, to clean up and to move independently to different locations; for example, it may be tempting to quickly put a basket of materials away for a child with a motor delay. However, if the child is provided extra time and encouragement, an excellent opportunity is available for the child to use motor, problem-solving, communication, and social skills to complete the task.

- *Attention:* Whereas some children may require extra time to shift from one activity to another, others may need a quick transition to hold their atten-

HOME/INDIVIDUAL ACTIVITY SCHEDULE

Child: _____Michael_____   Date: ___10/02_____

Routine activity	Routine's time and frequency	Goal/Objective	
		Grasps hand-size objects	Uses consistent word approximations
Dressing	6:30 a.m. (Once per day)	• Offer M. objects (e.g., toothbrush, hairbrush, cup, clothing).	• Model a word to indicate preferred clothing. • Point to family members in the mirror. • Imitate M.'s approximation.
Car travel	8:00 a.m. (Once per day)	• Offer M. books or toys from car pocket.	• Play music from radio/cassettes in car; sing along. • Model a word to indicate familiar location (e.g., store, post office, library).
Bath time	Evening (Once per day)	• Hide objects including soap, shampoo bottle, washcloth, toys, towel, and robe.	• Look at a book, and model words to refer to common objects.

Figure 12.   Home/individual activity schedule for Michael.

tion. Interventionists should anticipate these situations and be prepared to offer additional options to these children; for example, when moving a child from a car seat, provide toys to interest the child until the parent is ready to help the child from the seat.

• *Communication:* It is generally good practice to talk about ending an activity and beginning a new activity. Caregivers can encourage children to do so as well.

Intervention Activities

Planned intervention activities can be used with individuals or with small or large groups of children and should generally meet two important criteria. First, they should be activities or events that children find meaningful, interesting, and engaging; for example, when offered the activity, children should show genuine enthusiasm rather than mere compliance with a request to participate. Second, activities should offer multiple opportunities to learn or practice targeted goals/objectives. Achieving this second criteria will require thought and preplanning. Although planned intervention activities can occur—and often do—apart from daily activities, they can also be meaningfully embedded into daily activities.

Successful intervention requires preplanning and organization. To assist interventionists in preplanning and organizing intervention activities, we recommend using or completing a planned activity form that contains a sequence of nine components:

1. Activity name

2. Materials

3. Environmental arrangements

4. Description of activity

    • Introduction (set up)

    • Sequence of events

    • Closing

5. Opportunities to embed children's goals/objectives

6. Planned variations

7. Vocabulary

8. Peer interaction strategies

9. Parent/caregiver input

A completed planned intervention activity form is contained in Figure 13. Additional examples of planned intervention activities are contained in Appendix C. An intervention activity designed for one group of children can be modified for other children; for example, the Let's Blow Bubbles activity described in Figure 13 can, with modification, be used with most young children. Intervention activities should provide young children experience using a variety of materials throughout the week and should offer children many opportunities and experiences to use and manipulate materials. Intervention activities should also offer children practice in a variety of skills across developmental areas. Many activities can be planned and developed that allow for expansion, change of materials, and differing skill levels. Programs may choose to develop a "bank" of generic intervention activities and modify them as necessary.

Planned intervention activities often require modification because an activity that seems appropriate may not be effective with a group of children or the children may choose to use the materials in ways not anticipated. Following the children's lead within the activity is advisable, as long as IFSP/IEP objectives continue to be addressed.

(1)

Let's Blow Bubbles

(2)

MATERIALS

- Bubble solution
- Bubble wands

(3)

ENVIRONMENTAL ARRANGEMENTS

This activity can happen outside or inside, just make sure there is plenty of space and that the floor surface will not get slippery with bubble solution.

(4)

DESCRIPTION OF ACTIVITY

Introduction

- The interventionist produces a bottle of bubble solution and a handful of wands and begins blowing bubbles where children can see them and/or asks another child to invite some friends to join in blowing bubbles.

Sequence of Events

- Before being given a bubble wand, children are encouraged to ask for one in a way that is appropriate for them.
- Interventionist demonstrates how to blow bubbles.
- Children are each given one turn to immerse their wand in bubble solution and blow bubbles.
- Children are encouraged to request additional turns by asking for them.
- The interventionist helps the children take turns by explaining who is next.
- Children can also be encouraged to try to catch or pop bubbles with their hands or feet, by stomping or jumping.

Closing

- When children are done with the activity or it is time to start another activity, children can return the wands to the interventionist or to another child who has been designated as the interventionist's helper.

(5)

OPPORTUNITIES TO EMBED GOALS/OBJECTIVES

Examples of goals/objectives for Danielle:

Goal/Objective: Uses 50 single words and signs (Soc D:1, modified)
Opportunities:
- Wait for Danielle to request a bubble wand before handing it to her.
- Encourage Danielle to request turns for dipping the bubble wand.

Goal/Objective: Imitates motor action that is not commonly used (Cog D:1)
Opportunities:
- Show Danielle how to dip the wand into the bubble solution and blow bubbles.
- Encourage Danielle to pop bubbles with her hands or feet.

Figure 13. Planned intervention activity: Let's Blow Bubbles. *Note:* Numbers refer to elements of the form.

Figure 13.   *(continued)*

Goal/Objective: Initiates communication with peer (Soc C:2.1)
Opportunity:
- Encourage Danielle to say or sign who will be next ("your turn") and when it is her turn ("my turn").

Whole Group Goals/Objectives

Social-Communication:
- Encourage children to request the bubble wand.
- Encourage children to ask for a turn at dipping the bubble wand into the solution.
- When the activity is finished, children are asked to return wands to the interventionist or helper.

Cognitive:
- Show children how to dip wand into bubble solution and blow bubbles.
- Encourage children to pop bubbles with their hands or feet.

Social:
- Help children wait for their turn by explaining who is next. Encourage children to communicate to others who will be next and when it is their turn.

6 PLANNED VARIATIONS

- Put food coloring into bubble solution and encourage children to blow bubbles onto a large sheet of butcher paper for "bubble art."
- Each child can be given his or her own bottle of bubble solution.
- To encourage group interactions, a large amount of bubble solution may be placed into a tub or into the sensory table. Different types of wands or objects with holes may be offered.

7 VOCABULARY

- Bubble(s), wand(s), bottle
- Big, little, high, low
- Blow, watch, pop, jump, stamp, clap
- Hand, mouth, lips, foot
- Peers' names
- Please, thank you
- More, my turn
- Fun

8 PEER INTERACTION STRATEGIES

- Short-change children on wands and encourage them to share by having one child hold a wand while the other one blows the bubbles. Encourage them to take turns by switching jobs.
- Put bubble solution and wands at the sensory table.
- Have children take turns being in charge of the bottle of bubble solution.

9 PARENT/CAREGIVER INPUT

- Send a bottle of bubble solution or a recipe for bubble solution home with each child and encourage parents to blow bubbles with their child at home.

Considerations When Developing Planned Intervention Activities

The development of useful and effective intervention activities requires consideration of the following factors.

- *Setup and cleanup:* Although many adults consider setup and cleanup their responsibility, these aspects of an activity often provide excellent opportunities to practice targeted IFSP/IEP goals/objectives; for example, a child with the cognitive objective of demonstrating functional use of one-to-one correspondence can hand out one smock and/or one paintbrush to each classmate, a child working on problem solving could find a container to hold water, or two children could work together to wash off the table, promoting social interaction.

- *Introduction and recap: Introduction* refers to a brief preview of an activity before it begins. *Recap* refers to a similar review once the activity has been completed. During the introduction, the interventionist familiarizes children with the sequence of the activity (demonstration with actual objects or pictures may be necessary for some children) and covers basic rules or expectations. The recap provides an excellent opportunity to talk to children about the activity. For children who are preverbal, alternative methods of communication (e.g., pointing, gesturing) can be used.

- *Process versus product:* During an activity, the focus should be on the exploration and learning that occurs during the process rather than on the product; for example, during an art activity, the interventionist may plan to have supplies brought from a counter top or storage area to the work table by the children. Materials may include paper, scissors, glue, and crayons. The interventionist can ask if they can make apples. During the process of the activity, the interventionist focuses on facilitating general skill development across areas and individual children's targeted IFSP/IEP objectives, rather than on children's abilities to create a recognizable product. It is useful at times to be nondirective or nonspecific. The interventionist might present materials by saying, "What can we do with these playthings?" As the activity ends, children can be asked to help return the materials to their storage location.

SUMMARY

The material in this chapter is designed to set the stage for efficient and effective use of the AEPS Curriculum in conjunction with the AEPS Test. In particular, strategies for using child initiations, daily routines, environmental arrangements, and planned intervention activities to embed children's IFSP/IEP goals/objectives are described.

The content of this curriculum can be used by caregivers at home as well as interventionists in center-based programs. The use of routine, child-initiated, and meaningful intervention activities, as well as environmental arrangements, capitalizes on children's interests and motivation and, therefore, should produce effective and efficient learning.

REFERENCES

Bricker, D., Pretti-Frontczak, K., & McComas, N. (1998). *An activity-based approach to early intervention* (2nd ed.). Baltimore: Paul H. Brookes Publishing Co.

SECTION

II

AEPS Curriculum

Birth to Three Years

AEPS™

Fine Motor Area
Birth to Three Years

LIST OF AEPS TEST ITEMS

Fine Motor

The Fine Motor Area addresses a major accomplishment in the infant and toddler years—the use of the hands for precise reaching, grasping, and manipulation. These skills serve the child well throughout life, enabling the child to hold a fork or chopsticks, to insert keys in doors, to turn pages of books, and to sketch drawings or write stories. To manage these sophisticated motor actions, the child begins with the basic fine motor skills contained in this section of the AEPS Curriculum. The Fine Motor Area is divided into two strands: Strand A: Reach, Grasp, and Release; and Strand B: Functional Use of Fine Motor Skills. The first strand delineates the sequence of voluntary development of hand and finger movements. The second strand focuses on the functional use of these new skills to turn, assemble, or activate objects and to copy written shapes.

Much of a child's knowledge of the world is facilitated through the development of fine motor skills; for example, a young child extends a hand to a bright-colored rattle, grasps it, and brings it toward his or her face. In the process, the child shakes the rattle and hears a noise. The child waves the rattle back and forth, watches it, and puts it in his or her mouth and sucks on it. The fine motor skills of reaching and grasping provide this young child opportunities to develop visual, auditory, and oral skills. As fine motor skills develop, opportunities to explore and manipulate the environment increase as well. The child who can intentionally release objects can gain a great deal of attention from caregivers by dropping food, eating utensils, or toys to the floor while smiling and waiting for the caregiver to bend over and pick them up.

The infant has plenty of time for and interest in practicing fine motor skills while lying in the crib, sitting in a swing or stroller, or being carried. Early fine motor practice includes swiping at objects, grasping objects, playing with fingers, and mouthing objects. However, opportunities to practice fine motor skills need to be available. One of the easiest, yet most important, activities is to provide different objects for the infant to watch, touch, taste, smell, and hear. These toys do not need to be expensive; children often prefer common household objects for play. The toys or objects simply must be accessible and safe; it is never too early to check the safety of toys and materials used by an infant. It is also important to consider safety as the child becomes more mobile and capable of manipulating objects.

Reflexes are important in both fine and gross motor development. *Reflexes* are predictable motor responses that follow a specific sensory input; they develop automatically with the maturation of the central nervous system during infancy. Reflexes affect early movements in most positions; for example, when the infant is lying on his or her back and the head is turned to the side, the infant may go into a "fencing posture" in which the arm and leg on the turned side are extended and the other arm and leg are flexed. This reflex, known as the *asymmetrical tonic neck reflex*, can interfere with the infant's ability to bring the hands to the mouth, bring the hands together, or roll over.

Caregivers are often impressed with a newborn's ability to "squeeze" a finger. This ability to tightly grasp a stimulus is a reflex called the *palmar grasp*. It is important for the interventionist to be knowledgeable about reflex development and inhibition in order to explain skills to caregivers and design activities for individual children. Motor abilities develop as a result of the interaction between innate abilities and experience gained in the environment. The AEPS Curriculum is based on this transactional model.

Infants and young children with motor problems form a heterogeneous group. Some children have a disability in which a relatively precise diagnosis can be made, such as cerebral palsy. Other children have disabilities that are described more generally as mild, moderate, or severe. Motor variations may be transient and disappear over time or they may evolve into a more serious disability. It is often difficult for interventionists to make accurate predictions of development; therefore, they should monitor progress carefully. It is also important for caregivers and interventionists to maintain close contact with specialists (e.g., physical and occupational therapists) because their guidance is critical to meeting the needs of children with motor disabilities. The AEPS Curriculum was not written specifically for children with motor disabilities, and adaptations will need to be made when engaging in activities to develop fine motor skills.

Reach, Grasp, and Release

STRAND A

GOAL 1 Simultaneously brings hands to midline

Objective 1.1 Makes directed batting and/or swiping movements with each hand

Objective 1.2 Makes nondirected movements with each arm

IMPORTANCE OF SKILLS

Fine motor skills provide the child with opportunities to explore his or her own body and the external environment. The child begins to actively explore and to visually regard fingers and hands. The child is able, with one hand, to explore objects placed in the other hand. Simultaneously bringing hands to midline aids the development of self-awareness, eye–hand coordination, and the use of the hands to attain desired ends. This is a skill that will be used by the child to hold an object (e.g., bottle) with both hands.

The ability to make directed and nondirected movements indicates the beginning of coordination between motor and visual responses. The child who coordinates looking with hand movements begins to learn the relationship between the position of objects in space and his or her own body movements. The child discovers the relationship between objects as well. The child also develops initial cause and effect relationships and increases his or her attention span as objects are moved and transformed by the child's own activity. The child's random movements with his or her arms will lead to directed movements as the repeated, nondirected movements contact objects. Eventually, the child will learn to purposefully reach and grasp for objects, thus allowing greater independence in exploration and play. Other goals/objectives that can be targeted at the same time as Goal 1 are listed on the following page.

TEACHING SUGGESTIONS

Activity-Based

Playtime

- For the child who holds head erect and bears weight on forearms in prone position (on stomach), present small toys on the floor at midline to encourage manipulation with two hands. (1)

- Encourage the child to play with hands and objects in the sidelying position. Encourage the child to mouth hands and objects if this response is age appropriate. (1, 1.1)

Concurrent Goals/Objectives for Fine Motor Strand A

Cognitive

A:1 Orients to auditory, visual, and tactile events

B:1.1 Visually follows object moving in horizontal, vertical and circular directions

C:1.3 Indicates interest in simple and/or mechanical toy

F:1.4 Uses sensory examination with objects

Social-Communication

A:1.2 Turns and looks toward noise-producing object

A:2.2 Looks toward an object

Social

A:1.2 Responds appropriately to familiar adult's affective tone

Notes:

- During face-to-face play or during feeding or bathing, place an object in the child's hand. Activate toys or objects within the child's visual field (e.g., rattle, squeak-toy, bells). (1, 1.1, 1.2)

- Have siblings or older children play face-to-face with the child and see if the child will bat or swipe at their faces. (1, 1.1, 1.2)

Travel

- Encourage nondirected movements with each arm by using your voice and easily accessible toys. When the child is on his or her back or sitting in an infant carrier or car seat, talk to and engage the child in "conversation," pause and wait for a response; activate crib gym or toy, wait for the child's response by quieting, looking, or moving, and then activate the toy again. (1.2)

- When the child is moving his or her arms and legs, synchronize your voice to the movement. Stop talking when the child stops moving; begin again when the child moves again. (1.2)

Bathing

- Place the child on his or her back on a large sponge in the bathtub. Fill the tub with water so that the child's arm movements will cause splashing, but do not use so much water that the child's ears, mouth, or nose will be submerged. During bathing, hold the child in a secure sitting position. (1.1, 1.2)

- Float an object near the child and encourage batting or swiping. (1.1, 1.2)

Throughout daily routines

- When offering an object to the child, be sure to present the object from the front, to encourage reaching with both hands toward midline. (1)

- Encourage the child to hold the breast or the mother's hand as the child feeds. The child's shoulders should be encircled with the mother's arms while she holds the child close and secure. This will help the hands come to the midline. (1, 1.1)

- Present your face within the child's visual field and talk to the child while changing diapers, bathing, or picking the child up. Activate a variety of simple or mechanical toys such as rattles or squeeze-toys when the child is lying on his or her back or in a supported sitting position (in crib, in infant carrier). (1.2)

Environmental Arrangements

- Position the child to provide increased opportunities for hands to reach toward midline; for example, holding the child with neck and shoulders supported or sitting the child in the corner of the couch both provide easier opportunities for the child than lying flat on the back. (1)

- Arrange soft support for the child's shoulders or elbows when lying or sitting to encourage hands to move toward midline; for example, position a rolled-up towel behind the elbows when the child sits. Gradually remove support as the child begins to bring his or her hands together at midline. (1)

- In order to stimulate the child's interest, present familiar objects in novel ways (use a hand puppet to present a toy, make funny noises and exaggerated facial expressions). Alternate speed and movement pattern to maintain the child's interest. (1.1)

- Present toys or objects within the child's reach. Slowly move the toy or object in a horizontal, vertical, or circular direction, keeping it within the child's visual field. Use objects that are likely to attract the child's attention. Hang or dangle objects or toys (e.g., bells, rattle, crib gym, mobile) within the child's visual field and at the child's midline. Pay special attention to safety with hanging objects. (1.1, 1.2)

- Dangle or wave a pocket mirror near the child's hands so that movement of the arms produces an immediate visual event. Make sure that the child can see the reflective part. Touch the mirror to the child's hand, then remove it slightly. Wait for the child to bat or swipe. (1.1, 1.2)

- Use talking toys or bright-colored objects. Help the child associate movement of the arm with activation. Tie a soft yarn "bracelet" to the child's wrist and to an easily activated toy or mobile. Add noise-producing objects such as jingle bells to produce immediate auditory as well as visual events. Once the child begins to associate movement of the arm with activation, remove the yarn and encourage the child to activate the toy directly. (1.2)

- When the child grasps an adult's finger while feeding, have the adult hold the child's fingers for a moment then release. Repeat as often as the child initiates the behavior. (1.2)

Instructional Sequences

- Place an adult's index fingers in the child's palms and allow the child to grasp the fingers. Slowly move the child's hands to midline while securing the child's grasp on the adult's fingers. (1)

- Pair presentation of a toy or object with auditory or verbal cues by tapping or shaking the object, making exaggerated sounds, or altering the pitch and volume of your voice. (1.1)

- Provide tactile cues by gently touching or tickling the child's arms with the toy, kissing, or making "raspberries" (i.e., putting mouth against skin and blowing) on the child's hands. (1.1, 1.2)

- Physically assist the child in different ways to bring his or her hands to midline and encourage swiping movements by touching the child's arms or shoulders and by stroking and touching the child's arms or hands. (1, 1.1, 1.2)

Combining or pairing different levels of instructions may be helpful when beginning to teach a new and difficult skill. Fade to less intrusive instructions as soon as possible to encourage a more independent performance.

TEACHING CONSIDERATIONS

1. The child should be in a quiet and alert state.

2. Position the child so that his or her head, trunk, and shoulders are stable and symmetrical.

3. Approach the child straight on and to the middle of the body.

4. Free the environment of objects or events that compete with the toy or object presented to the child.

5. Objects should be used that provide cues to which the child with a sensory impairment can respond; for example, use noise-producing toys for a child with a visual impairment.

6. Allow adequate time for the child to respond.

7. Activation of objects should be continued or facilitated to reinforce the child's interest (e.g., help child shake rattle).

8. Consider safety with all objects that the child handles.

GOAL 2   Brings two objects together at or near midline

Objective 2.1   Transfers object from one hand to the other

- PS2.1a The child brings hands together and touches an object with one hand while holding an object in the other hand.

Objective 2.2   Holds an object in each hand

- PS2.2a The child holds an object in one hand.

Objective 2.3   Reaches toward and touches object with each hand

Note: PS = Programming Step

IMPORTANCE OF SKILLS

The ability to bring objects together at the midline, to transfer objects from one hand to the other, and to hold an object in each hand provides new opportunities to combine movements using actions and objects. The transfer of objects from one hand to the other indicates that the child has increased wrist mobility. This facilitates motor activities such as banging objects in an up-and-down vertical pattern and shaking objects from side to side. Holding an object in each hand indicates that the child's grasp is now voluntary. The child begins to perform actions on objects held in each hand.

By directing a reach toward an object and touching it, the child accomplishes a means to an end. The child's actions are purposeful. This skill also fosters eye–hand coordination and visual control as the child uses the eyes to assist directing the hand toward the object. Being able to reach toward and touch an object offers opportunities to explore and learn about objects in the environment.

These skills are important because the hands begin to work independently. The child begins to explore and develop new schemes for acting on objects in the environment, allowing the child to learn more about objects and their relationship to each other and to him- or herself. The child also gains sensory input through visual, auditory, and tactile means. Other goals/objectives that can be targeted at the same time as Goal 2 are listed on the following page.

TEACHING SUGGESTIONS

Activity-Based

Playtime

- Take advantage of opportunities at play to help the child put hands and objects together; for example, play social games such as Pat-a-cake or sing nursery songs such as "Clap, Clap, Clap Your Hands" while the child is holding an object in each hand. Use "rhythm band" instruments that produce exciting auditory and tactile experiences when banged together at midline (e.g., cymbals, sticks, blocks, tambourines). (2, 2.1)

- Encourage the child to transfer objects from one hand to another; for example, during playtime when the child is holding light objects with both hands (e.g., diaper, stuffed animal, foam block), present another object to encourage letting go with one hand to facilitate the transfer of the object to the other hand. (2.1)

Bathing

- During bath time look for ways to help the child bring objects to midline; for example, encourage the child to put the washcloth and soap together or bring bath toys (e.g., toy person and boat) together. (2, 2.1)

- Provide sponges and toys that float for the child to reach for and touch. (2.3)

Throughout daily routines

- Throughout daily routines and activities, provide the child with an object to hold in each hand. Name the objects for the child. Give the child a spoon during feeding or a washcloth during bathing. Increase to two objects to

Concurrent Goals/Objectives for Fine Motor Strand A

Goal 2: Brings two objects together at or near midline

Fine Motor

A:3.2 Grasps cylindrical object with either hand by closing fingers around it

Gross Motor

B:1.6 Holds head in midline when in supported sitting position

Adaptive

A:1.4 Swallows liquids

Cognitive

B:1.1 Visually follows object moving in horizontal, vertical, and circular directions

C:1.2 Acts on mechanical and/or simple toy in some way

F:1.3 Uses simple motor actions on different objects

Social-Communication

A:3.1 Engages in vocal exchanges by cooing

Social

A:2.2 Responds to familiar adult's social behavior

Notes:

encourage an object to be held in each hand. Engage the child in "giving" games in which the adult gives the child objects such as blocks or pop beads to hold in each hand. (2, 2.1, 2.2, 2.3)

- Use opportunities at mealtimes and playtimes to have child hold an object in each hand; for example, present food that the child can hold and feed him- or herself such as crackers or slices of fresh fruit; engage the child in Peeka- boo in which the adult's or child's eyes are covered by hands or cloth. Play finger games such as placing the adult's fingers in the palms of both of the child's hands and letting the child grasp the fingers. When the child grasps one finger of your hand, place another finger in the other hand. (2.1, 2.2)

- During daily routines, encourage the child to reach toward and touch ob- jects with each hand in a variety of ways; for example, when dressing, pre- sent the child with his or her own socks and a shoe. Encourage the child to stroke the fur of a household pet or a stuffed animal. Activate a mobile within the child's reach when the child is lying on his or her back or is in a supported sitting position (e.g., in crib, in infant carrier). (2.2, 2.3)

- At changing time, put a small powder or lotion bottle in one or both of the child's hands. Encourage the child to bring hands together. (2, 2.1)

Environmental Arrangements

- Have the child hold a container at midline and drop small objects inside or remove small objects. (2)

- Introduce objects to the child's hands when arms are positioned close to the body. Vary the size and shape of objects. Objects with different properties of texture, sound, or color will offer interest and variety. (2, 2.1, 2.2, 2.3)

- Provide the child with toys or objects that have surfaces that both hands can touch or hold at the same time (e.g., stacking ring, rattle, diaper, big spoon). Use objects of different textures and firmness for the child to hold, such as a sponge and a plastic rattle. (2, 2.1, 2.2, 2.3)

- Present objects to the left of the child's midline for grasping with the left hand and to the right of the child's midline for grasping with the right hand. Put a container of objects such as small balls or beanbags to one side of the child as he or she is sitting. Give the child objects to put away in the container, offering objects on the child's side that is not next to the con- tainer. (2, 2.1, 2.2)

- Find two objects to hold, one in each hand, similar to the objects already held by the child. Imitate the child's actions with the objects, then intro- duce novel actions; for example, activate the toys by banging them to- gether at midline to gain the child's attention. (2, 2.2)

- Hold an object in each hand and then hold them out to the child. As the child touches the objects, bring them together to activate them. Give the objects to the child. (2.2, 2.3)

- Use objects that produce visual as well as auditory effects when brought to the midline, such as clear rattles with objects inside. Give the child objects that make noise when they are brought together (e.g., blocks, bells). (2.2, 2.3)

- When the child is holding an object in one hand (e.g., spoon during meal-time), present another object (e.g., cracker) at midline for the child to grasp and hold. (2.1, 2.2)

- When the child is holding one object in each hand, clap your hands and say, "Bang, bang, bang!" or "Clap, clap, clap!" Encourage the child to imitate. If grasping and holding onto objects is difficult for the child, then use toys that can be safely attached to the child's hands and allow the child to practice bringing them together. (2.2)

- Use materials such as clay or playdough that the child can initially pull apart and then stick back together. (2.2)

- Initially present objects to the child at chest height at the midline where reaching is easiest. (2.3)

- Blow large bubbles with nontoxic bubble solution, catch the bubble with the bubble wand, and touch it to the child's hand. Pair the activity with the verbal exclamation, "Pop!" (2.3)

Instructional Sequences

- To help the child bring objects to the midline, model the behavior and/or physically assist the child in several ways; for example, model banging two blocks together and say, "Bang, bang, bang!" When the child is holding one object in each hand, face the child and grasp a part of each object without touching the child's hands. Guide the two objects to midline. Pair the action with a verbal statement (e.g., "Bang, bang, bang!" "Boom, boom, boom!"). (2)

- Use verbal, tactile, and physical cues to encourage the transfer of objects from one hand to another such as exaggerated vocal and gestural cues to engage the child's interest. Touch, tickle, or nudge the occupied hand with a second object. Gently guide the occupied hand toward the empty hand. Fade assistance as the child becomes more proficient. (2.1)

- Encourage the child to hold an object in each hand by modeling behavior, using verbal cues, or providing physical assistance if needed; for example, model reaching, or verbally instruct the child to "Get the soft ball." (2.2)

- When the child is holding one object in each hand, tap or support the child's arms behind the elbow; hold the child's shoulders in a stable, slightly forward position and guide the hands to midline from the shoulder. (2.1)

- Initially present objects that the child can most successfully hold (e.g., rattles, squeeze-toys). Slowly introduce slightly more difficult objects. Hold your hand over the child's hand when the child is grasping the object to provide additional sensory input. Gradually fade assistance as the child becomes more proficient. (2.2)

- Use a variety of ways to help the child reach and touch objects with each hand; for example, model reaching toward and touching an object with each hand; use verbal cues to direct the child to reach for and touch an object or make exaggerated sounds, altering voice pitch and volume when presenting a toy or object. (2.3)

- Provide tactile cues by touching or tickling the child with a toy or object; physically assist the child's reaching by holding his or her shoulders or elbow in a stable, slightly forward position and guiding the arm to the object. Gradually fade assistance as the child becomes more proficient. (2.3)

TEACHING CONSIDERATIONS

1. The child should be in a quiet or active alert state.

2. Position the child so that the child's head, trunk, and shoulders are stable and symmetrical.

3. Initially, the grasping behavior will be most successful when the child's hands are positioned with the palms downward.

4. Place objects within reach of the child to prevent frustration.

5. Use objects that can be easily held (e.g., squeeze-toys, rattles) and cannot be swallowed.

6. The environment should be free of objects or events that compete with the toy or object presented to the child.

7. Objects should be used that provide cues to which the child with a sensory impairment can respond; for example, use noise-producing toys for a child with a visual impairment.

8. Allow adequate time for the child to respond.

9. Activation or exploration of objects should be continued or facilitated to reinforce the child's interest.

10. Consider safety with objects that the child handles.

GOAL 3   Grasps hand-size object with either hand using ends of thumb, index, and second fingers

Objective 3.1   Grasps hand-size object with either hand using the palm, with object placed toward the thumb and index finger

Objective 3.2   Grasps cylindrical object with either hand by closing fingers around it

Objective 3.3   Grasps hand-size object with either hand using whole hand

- PS3.3a The child grasps hand-size object with either hand, holding the object on the little finger side of hand and against the palm. The thumb is not holding the object (ulnar palmar grasp).

- PS3.3b The child briefly holds an object placed in either hand.

IMPORTANCE OF SKILLS

Grasping objects allows the hand to explore, manipulate, and control objects of different textures, shapes, sizes, and weights. Using the ends of the thumb and second fingers to grasp demonstrates control and refinement of the grasp skill. Using the palm to grasp with the object held toward the thumb and index finger is a step toward refinement of the grasping response. This refined grasp allows the child greater control for holding onto and manipulating objects. Grasping a hand-size object with the whole hand marks the beginning of the grasp progression in which repetition and modification produce more sophisticated responses. This skill is also the first voluntary grasp and aids in development.

With these skills, the child becomes aware that the object is separate from the self and can be transformed by the child's actions. As the child grasps and manipulates objects, the child learns about properties of objects. The child begins to discriminate between objects and selects different movements to use on various objects. Manual exploration of people and objects stimulates learning and provides the child with greater dexterity for holding and manipulating objects. This is an important skill for later activities such as holding a crayon to color and holding a spoon to eat. These skills also help the child become more discriminating in perception and motor skills and allows the child more interesting exploration and play. Other goals/objectives that can be targeted at the same time as Goal 3 are listed on the following page.

TEACHING SUGGESTIONS

Activity-Based

Playtime

- Allow the child to explore objects that pull apart (e.g., pop beads, Legos, Mr. Potato Head). (3)

- Activate interesting or mechanical toys (e.g., rattle, wind-up toy) in which the child indicates interest. Wait for the child's response. (3, 3.1)

- Set hand-size objects or toys (e.g., blocks, beads, balls) in front of the child whenever the child indicates an interest. Encourage the child to grasp them. (3, 3.1, 3.2, 3.3)

- When passing a toy to the child, offer the part that is easiest to grasp (e.g., leg of teddy bear, wide end of rattle). (3.1, 3.2, 3.3)

Concurrent Goals/Objectives for Fine Motor Strand A

Goal 3: Grasps hand-size object with either hand using ends of thumb, index, and second fingers

Fine Motor

A:5.2 Places and releases object balanced on top of another object with either hand

B:1 Rotates either wrist on horizontal plane

B:2.2 Fits object into defined space

B:3 Uses either index finger to activate objects

Gross Motor

B:1.2 Regains balanced, upright sitting position after reaching across the body to the right and to the left

B:2.2 Maintains a sitting position in chair

C:2.3 Pulls to kneeling position

Adaptive

A:4.2 Eats with fingers

Cognitive

C:1 Correctly activates mechanical toy

D:1.1 Imitates motor action that is commonly used

F:1.2 Uses functionally appropriate actions with objects

Social-Communication

B:2.2 Uses nonspecific consonant vowel combinations and/or jargon

Social

C:1.5 Entertains self by playing appropriately with toys

Notes:

- Encourage the child to take hand-size objects out of a container (e.g., blocks in a basket, cars in a can). (3.1, 3.2, 3.3)

Feeding

- Encourage the child to finger feed self hand-size bits of food (e.g., crackers, cheese sticks). Present cylindrical pieces of finger food at snack times and mealtimes. (3, 3.1, 3.2)
- Encourage the child to hold his or her own bottle or cup. Allow the child to grasp spoon or bottle when he or she is being fed. (3)

Throughout daily routines

- During daily routines, provide the child with cylindrical objects to grasp (e.g., hairbrush with handle when dressing, spoon when feeding, tube of ointment when changing diapers). (3, 3.1)
- Encourage the child to grasp in a variety of ways. Help the child pull up a droopy diaper or pair of pants by grabbing material at waist. When the child is lying on his or her back, encourage him or her to grasp knees or feet. Hold the child's hand briefly when he or she grasps your fingers. (3, 3.1, 3.2, 3.3)

Environmental Arrangements

- Provide the child with toys or objects that activate or produce noise when grasped (e.g., rattle, squeeze-toy). (3)
- Offer the child a hand-size object at chest level toward the center of his or her body. (3)
- Provide objects that pull apart with pieces partially pulled out (e.g., pop beads, Legos). (3.1)
- Put a bead or block on the end of the string of pull-toys (e.g., See-N-Say, Farmer Says) to facilitate pulling. (3, 3.1)
- Use a variety of hand-size objects or toys (e.g., small cars, balls, blocks). Find a preferred grasping object and change gradually to less preferred objects. Pay special attention to safety with small objects. (3, 3.1, 3.2, 3.3)
- Set cylindrical objects or toys in front of the child (e.g., rattle with handle, stick). Encourage child to grasp the toy or object by closing his or her fingers around it. (3.2)
- Hold a toy to the child's mouth and allow oral exploration. Let the object fall to the child's chin and wait for his or her response. (3.3)
- Lower crib gym so that the child can grasp toys while lying on his or her back and bring them to the mouth. (3.3)

Instructional Sequences

- When presenting an object to the child, continue to hold the object until the child approximates grasping the object with the ends of his or her thumb, index, and second fingers. Assist the child's fingers to close around an object by tapping the child's palm. (Be sure that the wrist is in a neutral position, neither extended nor flexed.) (3)

- Model picking up blocks one at a time. Place a block toward the child's thumb and index finger. Have the child grasp the block with the palm. Model holding a cylindrical block with your fingers. (3, 3.1, 3.2, 3.3)

- Place an object in the child's grasp. Allow the child to explore it, then model grasping the object to remove it. Reintroduce the object in a slightly different position. This action should result in the child's involuntary orienting, groping, and, finally, grasping. (3.3)

- Verbally direct the child to pick up objects. Hold an object to the right of the child and say, "Here you go." Touch the child's hand with the object. (3.3)

- Place an object in the child's hand in a position that gives him or her the sensation of the response. Close the child's hand around the object. Prompt the child's fingers to close around an object by tapping or stroking the child's palm or hand with the object or your hand. (3.3)

TEACHING CONSIDERATIONS

1. The environment should be free of objects or events that compete with the toy or object presented to the child.

2. Objects should be used that provide cues to which the child with a sensory impairment can respond; for example, use noise-producing toys for a child with a visual impairment.

3. Use objects that can be easily grasped (e.g., small squeeze-toys, rattles).

4. Allow adequate time for the child to respond.

5. Activation or exploration of objects should be continued or facilitated to reinforce the child's interest.

6. Place objects directly in front of the child so that he or she can grasp objects with either hand.

7. Consider safety with all objects that the child handles.

GOAL 4   Grasps pea-size object with either hand using tip of the index finger and thumb with hand and/or arm not resting on surface for support

Objective 4.1   Grasps pea-size object with either hand using tip of the index finger and thumb with hand and/or arm resting on surface for support

- PS4.1a   The child grasps a pea-size object with either hand using the tip of the index finger and thumb with the hand and/or arm resting on a surface for support. The thumb is to the side of the index finger (inferior pincer grasp).

Objective 4.2   Grasps pea-size object with either hand using side of the index finger and thumb

Objective 4.3   Grasps pea-size object with either hand using fingers in a raking and/or scratching movement

IMPORTANCE OF SKILLS

Grasping objects allows the hand to explore, manipulate, and control objects of various textures, shapes, sizes, and weights. Manual exploration of people and objects stimulates learning in social contexts. The child now attempts to involve the fingers in securing pea-size objects rather than using the whole hand. The use of fingers in a raking or scratching movement develops coordination and strength in the fingers and hands. The adjustment and control of the fingers will evolve from this more primitive response, which is an important precursor to use of the pincer grasp.

The grasping of a small object using the side of the index finger and thumb indicates that the child is beginning to differentiate finger use. The child demonstrates more control of the finger and thumb and is less dependent on the other fingers and the palm of the hand. This grasp facilitates the development of the more refined pincer grasp, which is important to independent eating and play.

As the grasping of pea-size objects becomes more refined, eye–hand coordination and manual dexterity are enhanced. By using the tip of the index finger and thumb, the child becomes more efficient at picking up small objects, which contributes to the child's independence in eating and in play.

Grasping pea-size objects using the tip of the index finger and thumb (pincer grasp) without using the support of a surface for additional stability demonstrates increased dexterity of the fingers. The child is able to use the thumb and index finger separately from the rest of the hand, allowing the child to efficiently pick up tiny objects. This refined pincer grasp increases the child's independence in eating and play. Other goals/objectives that can be targeted at the same time as Goal 4 are listed on the following page.

Goal 4: Grasps pea-size object with either hand using tip of the index finger and thumb with hand and/or arm not resting on surface for support

Fine Motor

B:3 Uses either index finger to activate objects

Gross Motor

B:1.2 Regains balanced, upright sitting position after reaching across the body to the right and to the left

Adaptive

A:4.2 Eats with fingers

Cognitive

C:1 Correctly activates mechanical toy

E:2.1 Uses part of object and/or support to obtain another object

F:1.2 Uses functionally appropriate actions with objects

Social-Communication

B:2.2 Uses nonspecific consonant vowel combinations and/or jargon

C:2.3 Carries out one-step direction with contextual cues

Social

A:3.2 Responds to communication from familiar adult

C:1.5 Entertains self by playing appropriately with toys

Notes:

TEACHING SUGGESTIONS

Activity-Based

Playtime

- Engage the child in play with mechanical toys that have levers that can be grasped with the thumb and index finger (e.g., Busy Box, pop-up toy). (4, 4.1, 4.2, 4.3)
- Give the child pull-toys, extending the toy to the child with the string first. (Remove ring or handle from string so that the child must manipulate the string to activate the pull-toy.) (4, 4.1, 4.2, 4.3)
- Encourage the child to play toy keyboard instruments (e.g., computer keyboard, Linyl keyboard) with his or her index finger. (4, 4.1)
- Present the child with flat objects to grasp. (4.1)

Feeding

- Allow the child to finger feed self small bits of food from a tray or flat surface (e.g., peas, diced cooked carrots, Cheerios). (4, 4.1, 4.2, 4.3)

Storytime

- Provide the child with picture books. Encourage the child to turn the pages of the book. Present thin books and papers on a flat surface where the child can pick them up. (4.2, 4.3)

Throughout daily routines

- Model pointing and poking with the index finger extended (e.g., pop bubbles, poke at holes punched in paper, poke holes in clay, point at pictures in books, dial play telephone). (4, 4.1)
- Allow the child to turn a light switch on and off. (4.3)

Environmental Arrangements

- Begin by presenting larger objects and fade to smaller objects when the child demonstrates competence in obtaining an object using the tip of the index finger and thumb with the hand and/or arm not resting on a surface for support. (4)
- Place a pea-size object near the edge of a surface so that the child is less likely to use the surface for additional support while grasping. (4)
- Offer the child a pea-size object at chest height and toward the middle of the child's body. (4, 4.1)

- Offer the child pea-size objects on a surface that provides high contrast background (e.g., raisins on white table top, oyster crackers on colored plate). (4.1, 4.2, 4.3)

- Offer the child one pea-size object at a time in a way that the child must reach for it; for example, present a pea-size object in your hand for the child to grasp. (4.1, 4.2, 4.3)

- Use pea-size objects that are easily molded to the finger and thumb tips, such as playdough or marshmallows. (4.1, 4.2, 4.3)

- Use a variety of objects (e.g., Cheerios, small pegs, strings). (4.1 4.2, 4.3)

- Put pea-size objects into egg cartons so that the child must reach inside with thumb and forefinger to grasp the object. (4.1, 4.2, 4.3)

Instructional Sequences

- Hold a pea-size object in a pincer grasp until the child grasps the object using the tip of the index finger and thumb with the hands and/or arm not resting on a surface for support. (4)

- Model grasping a Cheerio on the child's highchair tray. (4, 4.1)

- Present a Cheerio on a plate held high enough for the child to reach for and grasp. Gesture and verbally prompt the child to get it. (4.3)

- Provide visual or auditory cues by pointing or tapping a surface on which there is a pea-size object. (4, 4.1, 4.2, 4.3)

- Guide the child's arms to the surface before presenting an object so that the child has adequate support to stabilize arms and grasp successfully. Provide additional support or stability behind the child's elbow. Gradually fade assistance as the child becomes more proficient. (4, 4.1, 4.2, 4.3)

TEACHING CONSIDERATIONS

1. The environment should be free of objects or events that compete with the toy or object presented to the child.

2. Objects should be used that provide cues to which the child with a sensory impairment can respond; for example, use noise-producing toys with a child with a visual impairment.

3. Allow adequate time for the child to respond.

4. Activation or exploration of objects should be continued or facilitated to reinforce the child's interest.

5. Place objects directly in front of the child so that he or she can grasp the objects with either hand.

6. Be sure an adult is nearby to supervise the child's manipulation of pea-size objects. Consider safety with all objects that the child handles.

GOAL 5   Aligns and stacks objects

Objective 5.1   Aligns objects

- PS5.1a The child places an object next to another; for example, the child places a spoon next to a bowl.

Objective 5.2   Places and releases object balanced on top of another object with either hand

- PS5.2a The child places a small object onto a small target (with either the left or right hand), aligning and releasing; the object falls over.

- PS5.2b The child places a small object onto a small object without releasing the object.

Objective 5.3   Releases hand-held object onto and/or into larger target with either hand

- PS5.3a The child releases a hand-held object onto or into a large target with either hand while resting his or her hand on the edge.

Objective 5.4   Releases hand-held object with each hand

- PS5.4a The child releases hand-held object with the left and right hand by pushing or pulling the object against a surface.

IMPORTANCE OF SKILLS

Aligning and stacking objects enables the child to develop eye–hand coordination and manual dexterity as well as discover spatial relationships among objects.

The ability to release hand-held objects indicates increased manual strength, control of wrist (extension), and differentiated use of fingers. The release of a hand-held object onto or into a large target indicates some knowledge of the relationship between two objects in space. The child gains awareness that they are separate from the environment and develops knowledge of cause and effect. Releasing and throwing objects is a sign of emerging differentiated play and provides the child with the opportunity to expand the repertoire of manipulative behaviors.

Placing and releasing one object balanced on top of another indicates that the child is able to combine several movements to produce a desired outcome. Cognitive development is enhanced as the child learns about spatial relationships such as "on top of," "in front of," and "next to."

Fine Motor

These skills provide the child with a new means of independent play and increased opportunities to interact with the environment. Along with developed eye–hand coordination and manual control, the child becomes aware of cognitive concepts such as objects in a series and quantity. The child gains the ability to arrange objects in a specified order (e.g., shortest to tallest), which is a prerequisite to sequencing numbers and letters. Other goals/objectives that can be targeted at the same time as Goal 5 are listed on the following page.

TEACHING SUGGESTIONS

Activity-Based

Playtime

- During playtime, provide the child with toys or objects that stack or align; for example, have the child stack nesting cups, stack or align blocks and sticks to build fences, align toy animals to enter the barn, or align groceries for the cashier. (5, 5.1)

- Encourage the child to release hand-held objects (e.g., blocks, small cars) into a dump truck. Dump the contents from the truck and fill the truck again. (5.2, 5.3)

- Use a variety of activities to help the child release hand-held objects with each hand; for example, allow the child to drop toys into the bathtub before taking a bath. Play ball with the child, rolling the ball back and forth. Play a game by retrieving an object for the child and presenting the object to him or her again. (5.4)

Feeding

- During snack time, provide the child with a variety of finger foods. Give a bowl or cup to the child to practice dropping the spoon and food into it. (5.3)

Dressing

- Encourage the child to hang his or her coat on a hook. (5.2)

Throughout daily routines

- Use a variety of opportunities during the day and at playtime to stack or balance objects on top of another; for example, make a tower with the child by building and stacking blocks. Play a game with the child in which you each take a turn to stack a block. Allow the child to knock over the blocks and stack them again. After mealtimes, encourage the child to help clear dishes from the table by stacking them. (5)

- During daily activities and routines, encourage the child to align at least three objects that are similar. While tidying the house, ask the child to align

Goal 5: Aligns and stacks objects

Fine Motor

A:2 Brings two objects together at or near midline

A:3 Grasps hand-size object with either hand using ends of thumb, index, and second fingers

Gross Motor

B:1.2 Regains balanced, upright sitting position after reaching across the body to the right and to the left

Cognitive

C:2 Reproduces part of interactive game and/or action in order to continue game and/or action

D:1.1 Imitates motor action that is commonly used

E:1 Retains objects when new object is obtained

E:4.1 Uses more than one strategy in attempt to solve common problem

F:1.2 Uses functionally appropriate actions with objects

Social-Communication

B:2.1 Uses consistent consonant–vowel combinations

C:2.3 Carries out one-step direction with contextual cues

Social

A:3.1 Initiates communication with familiar adult

C:1.5 Entertains self by playing appropriately with toys

Notes:

Fine Motor

at least three pairs of shoes, to place books one against the other on the bookshelf, and to place boxes one next to the other in the cupboard. (5.1)

- To help the child release objects, put toys away together, dropping them into boxes or toy chests. Allow the child to play in the garden putting rocks or soil in pots or putting shovels against the wall. (5.3)

- Encourage the child to practice taking objects out and putting them into containers (e.g., take raisins out of a raisin box and put them into a cereal bowl, remove crayons from a box and put them into a cup). (5.3, 5.4)

- Encourage the child to drop paper into a wastebasket. (5.3, 5.4)

- When doing laundry, encourage the child to drop clothes into the basket. (5.3, 5.4)

Environmental Arrangements

- Use magnetic objects to ensure success in balancing one object on another. (5)

- Stabilize the lower object to ensure the child's success in balancing the second object on top. (5)

- Use objects for balancing that are graded in size from larger to smaller (e.g., nesting cups). (5)

- Encourage the child to build or stack objects against a wall. (5)

- Use baskets to store toys on a shelf. (5.1)

- Make a parade or circus train by attaching milk cartons or boxes. Put toy animals or people inside for a ride. (5.1)

- Provide the child with similar objects that can be fitted together in a horizontal direction (e.g., pop beads, magnets) or that are held together by some other means (e.g., beads that the child can string to make a necklace). (5.1)

- Line up plastic eggs in egg cartons. (5.1)

- Have the child align objects by fitting them in defined spaces in a row (e.g., already dug holes to place tulip bulbs) or by placing them within a container (e.g., crayons one next to another in a box). (5.1, 5.3)

- Encourage the child and a peer to take turns aligning objects such as cars, blocks, or books. (5.1)

- Use a variety of hand-held toys or objects to place and release (e.g., different kinds of blocks, spools, empty boxes, jar lids). (5.2)

- Provide the child with containers to drop toys into (e.g., basket, box, bucket). Offer objects to the child in rapid succession so that the child must release one object to get another. Begin with very large targets and small objects.

Fade to objects and targets closer to the same size (e.g., spoon in silverware slot, doll in bed) as the child becomes more proficient. (5.2, 5.3, 5.4)

- Use objects and containers that will produce a loud sound when combined (e.g., blocks and coffee cans, beads and tin containers). (5.3)

- Release objects onto or into targets that produce interesting effects (e.g., sticks off a bridge, rocks into the water) or that have interesting trajectories (e.g., clothing down chutes or slides, a ball or wagon down a curvy incline). (5.3)

- Encourage the child to release objects with each hand in a variety of ways; for example, hold out your hand to the child and encourage the child to release the object into your hand. Roll a ball, truck, or chime ball to position just barely within reach of the child. The child's touch with his or her fingers should propel the object away. (5.4)

Instructional Sequences

- Provide a model for the child; for example, line up objects (e.g., train cars in a row), place and release objects balanced on top of one another, or release a hand-held object onto or into a larger target (e.g., put the blocks away by dropping them into a box). (5, 5.1, 5.2)

- Verbally direct the child in a number of activities; for example, ask the child to stack the nesting cups, put the clothing into the laundry basket, or put the blocks away. (5, 5.1, 5.2)

- Provide the child with visual or auditory cues (e.g., tap surface of object, point to where the child should place the object). (5, 5.1, 5.2)

- For releasing hand-held objects, position the child so that the hands are directly over the target. Encourage the child to hit or tap an object against the inside edge of a container. This will sometimes elicit a release. (5.1, 5.2)

- Provide the child with physical assistance by stabilizing and supporting the child's shoulder or elbow. Assist the child to release an object by gently guiding the child to straighten flexed wrist, by stroking the child's hand, or by gently pulling an object from the child's grasp. Physically guide the child's hand to align objects. Gradually fade assistance as the child becomes more proficient. (5, 5.1, 5.2)

TEACHING CONSIDERATIONS

1. The environment should be free of objects or events that compete with the toy or object presented to the child.

2. Objects should be used that provide cues to which the child with a sensory impairment can respond; for example, use noise-producing toys for a child with visual impairment.

3. If the child has a motor or visual impairment, align lightweight objects that are easy to manage. Use a flannelboard or magnetic board to align objects.

4. If the child has a hearing impairment, use a language approach such as total communication that ensures the child's understanding of your instructions.

5. Use objects that can be easily grasped (e.g., blocks, cups).

6. Allow adequate time for the child to respond.

7. Activation or exploration of objects should be continued or facilitated to reinforce the child's interest.

8. Place objects directly in front of the child so that he or she can grasp objects with either hand.

9. Provide the child with flat, stable surfaces for aligning objects (e.g., table, floor).

10. Focus on spatial concepts and relationships rather than only on fine motor precision. While the child aligns objects, talk about next to, before, behind, beginning, and end.

11. Consider safety with all objects that the child handles.

STRAND B

Functional Use of Fine Motor Skills

GOAL 1   Rotates either wrist on horizontal plane

- PS1a   The child rotates either wrist on a vertical plane

Objective 1.1   Turns object over using wrist and arm rotation with each hand

- PS1.1a The child turns his or her hand and arm from palm-side down (prone) to facing midline while holding an object; for example, child holds two blocks with hands palm-side down and turns them toward each other.

- PS1.1b The child turns his or her wrist and arm over when not holding an object (clasps fingers together and turns wrists and hand; turns one arm and hand while examining fingers).

IMPORTANCE OF SKILLS

A child who rotates either wrist on a horizontal plane demonstrates independent movement of the wrist and the forearm. This skill allows the child the independence to perform many functional skills such as turning on a faucet. When the child turns an object over using both wrist and arm rotation, he or she is preparing to use only one hand to complete some manipulative tasks. These skills offer the child the opportunity to explore objects more completely and to control their movement. It also affords the child the independence to perform more complex manipulation of objects in the environment. Other goals/objectives that can be targeted at the same time as Goal 1 are listed on the following page.

TEACHING SUGGESTIONS

Activity-Based

Playtime

- Encourage the child to play with toys, such as a Busy Box, that have knobs that can be turned by rotating the wrist. (1)

- Allow the child to play with containers in sand, water, dirt, or cornmeal. Encourage the child to dump the contents of one container into another. (1.1)

- Play at giving "pretend" drinks and food to dolls, stuffed animals, and peers. (1.1)

Concurrent Goals/Objectives for Fine Motor Strand B

Goal 1: Rotates either wrist on horizontal plane

Gross Motor

C:4.2 Moves up and down stairs

D:2.1 Pushes riding toy with feet while steering

Adaptive

A:5.1 Pours liquid between containers

B:2.1 Washes hands

Cognitive

C:1 Correctly activates mechanical toy

Social-Communication

D:1.4 Uses 15 object and/or event labels

Social

C:1.3 Plays near one or two peers

Notes:

Feeding

- Encourage the child to manipulate the handle of a drinking fountain independently. The child may drink from the fountain or simply watch the effect. (1)

- Allow and encourage the child to feed him- or herself with a spoon and drink from a cup. (1.1)

Throughout daily routines

- Encourage the child to use horizontal wrist rotation to open doors and remove lids on jars. (1)

- Allow the child to make juice by twisting an orange half on a squeezer. (1)

- Encourage the child to participate in cleaning activities with you, such as washing the table with a sponge after a meal or messy activity or emptying water from cups into the sink. (1)

- Have the child wash and dry his or her own hands, turning the hands back and forth under the water and rubbing soap on the palms and backs of hands. (1.1)

- During preparation for activities, have the child dump crayons, stickers, brushes, blocks, or peg people out of storage containers. (1.1)

Environmental Arrangements

- Play games with cards. Show the child how to deal cards and turn them face up. (1)

- Provide jars with the lids already loosened. Gradually make the task more challenging by screwing the lid a quarter turn. (1)

- Close doors to encourage the child to turn doorknobs when entering or leaving a room. (1)

- Provide toys with large, easy-to-manage wind-up mechanisms (e.g., alarm clock, toy train, toy radio). Systematically introduce smaller mechanisms as the child begins to develop wrist rotation. (1)

- Allow the child to manipulate a bubble gum machine filled with cereal. (1)

- Turn the child's arms and hands over when drying or moisturizing the child after a bath or shower. (1.1)

- When giving the child a requested object, place the object in the child's hand in such a way that pronating hands (palms down) or supinating hands (palms up) will enable him or her to move the object (e.g., pronation to push toy grocery cart, supination to carry large ball). (1.1)

- Provide small objects in containers and show the child how to "dump" the contents. (1.1)

Instructional Sequences

- Model twisting common items. Use exaggerated facial and vocal expressions. (1)

- Remind the child to "twist" the container lid, doorknob, or orange half on the squeezer. (1)

- Create a result from minimal wrist-rotation effort by the child (e.g., complete turn of water fountain handle so water is dispensed, crank toys to the point where minimal effort by the child will result in the toy being activated). Gradually decrease the amount of assistance given. (1)

- Model turning your hand over to receive lotion or a piece of food. (1.1)

- Give verbal directions by saying, "Turn your hand over" when you give the child an object. (1.1)

- Get the child to place palms facing up or down by gently touching the child's hand with the requested object; for instance, if the child requests powder, then pretend to start pouring powder on his or her hand while simultaneously nudging the hand to a palm-up position. (1.1)

- Fully guide the child's hand over to receive an object by turning the wrist and hand simultaneously. (1.1)

- Use minimal physical assistance as necessary. (1, 1.1)

Combining or pairing different levels of instructions may be helpful when beginning to teach a new and difficult skill. Fade to less intrusive instructions as soon as possible to encourage a more independent performance.

TEACHING CONSIDERATIONS

1. Use objects or events to elicit responses that provide cues to which the child with a sensory impairment can respond; for example, use noise-producing toys for a child with a visual impairment.

2. For a child with a motor impairment, initially use objects that can be easily activated (e.g., squeeze-toys, switches).

3. Allow adequate time for the child to respond to toys.

4. Activation or exploration of objects should be continued or facilitated to reinforce the child's engagement in the activity.

5. Consider safety with all objects that the child handles.

> ### GOAL 2 Assembles toy and/or object that require(s) putting pieces together

- PS2a   The child takes apart a toy or object that has pieces.

Objective 2.1   Fits variety of shapes into corresponding spaces

- PS2.1a   The child places round objects into corresponding spaces; for example, the child puts the plug in a drain, a cup in a holder, or peg people in vehicles.

- PS2.1b   The child removes a variety of shapes from corresponding spaces; for example, the child takes out pieces from puzzles or form board, a plug out of the tub, or the cup and toothbrush out of their holders.

Objective 2.2   Fits object into defined space

- PS2.2a   The child puts an object into a defined space in such a way that the object does not fit completely into the space.

- PS2.2b   The child takes an object out of a defined space; for example, he or she removes a block from a dump truck or takes a car out of a toy garage.

IMPORTANCE OF SKILLS

Successful assembly of objects with many different pieces demonstrates the child's ability to translate a visual understanding of a process into motor output. This perceptual motor skill is comprised of finely coordinated bilateral hand activity, the ability to cope with different or changing spatial orientations, greater wrist control, and finger differentiation. The child utilizes problem-solving skills when assembling objects.

Putting shapes into corresponding spaces demonstrates the child's understanding of concepts such as size, form, and position in space. It is indicative of the child's increased ability to express spatial relationships among objects. This skill helps the child coordinate, place, and release objects within a well-defined space. Fitting objects into defined spaces indicates the child's functional coordination of a number of sophisticated fine motor movements of the arms, hands, and fingers. The child is able to combine and manipulate related objects together in different spatial configurations.

These skills aid in the development of perceptual motor and cognitive skills. They provide the child with varied means of play and interaction with objects, they give the ability to combine and manipulate related objects together in different spatial configurations, and they foster creativity as the child designs and build objects. Other goals/objectives that can be targeted at the same time as Goal 2 are listed on the following page.

Goal 2: Assembles toy and/or object that require(s) putting pieces together

Fine Motor

A:5.2 Places and releases object balanced on top of another object with either hand

Adaptive

B:2 Washes and dries hands

B:3 Brushes teeth

C:1 Undresses self

Cognitive

E:4 Solves common problems

G:1.1 Groups functionally related objects

Social-Communication

C:2.3 Carries out one-step direction with contextual cues

Notes:

TEACHING SUGGESTIONS

Activity-Based

Playtime

- Engage the child in games with toys that need to be assembled (e.g., Mr. Potato Head, Cootie, Tinkertoys). (2)

- Provide simple puzzles or form boards with fitting pieces. Pieces do not need to interlock. (2, 2.1)

- Demonstrate for the child how magic marker caps fit on the ends of the markers for storage after using. Have the child help put the markers away. (2, 2.1)

- Encourage the child to play with "sets" of related toys where multiple pieces can be assembled into various combinations during play (e.g., farm, airport, garage, train, Legos). (2.1)

- Give the child coins to put in his or her piggy bank. (2.1)

- Provide numerous containers for the child to play with in functional ways; for example, have separate containers for cars, dolls, balls, or blocks. (2.2)

- Play with dump trucks, buckets, wagons, or toy shopping carts that can be filled with small objects. (2.2)

Feeding

- Serve appealing finger food at snack and mealtime. Encourage the child to put the food into his or her mouth. (2.2)

Throughout daily routines

- Establish a routine for the child to put objects away in containers after play or daily routines; for example, put crayons in a box, peg people in a bus, soap in a soap dish, toothbrush in a holder. (2.1, 2.2)

- Talk about things that fit together or into one another as you cook (e.g., lids on pots, bread in toaster), as you dress the child (e.g., button in hole, shoe on foot), and as you bathe the child (e.g., plug in drain, soap in a soap dish). (2.1, 2.2)

- Encourage the child to fit lids to corresponding containers. Provide two or three different sizes of pots with fitting lids or plastic containers of different shapes and sizes with lids. (2.1)

- Encourage the child to assist with activities that put objects into defined spaces, such as mail in a mailbox, dirt in planter pots, or laundry in a basket. (2.2)

- Encourage the child to put objects away in their correct storage areas (e.g., crayons in a box, books in a bookrack, toys in a toy box or on a shelf, groceries in a cupboard). (2.2)

- When introducing objects to the child, present them so that the object is already in a defined space; the child must remove the object to explore it and then return it to its space. (2.2)

Environmental Arrangements

- Have the child complete the assembly of a toy with the last piece; for example, put the harness on a toy horse and attach the wagon, and then have the child put the toy person in the wagon for a ride. Put all of the children in the bus and have the child put the driver in and drive away. Systematically increase the number of pieces the child contributes. (2)

- Use bristle blocks or Duplos that easily stay together. (2)

- Start with toys that have only two or three pieces and gradually work up to more. (2)

- Use puzzles that have shapes of pieces drawn underneath or trace the shapes yourself. (2)

- Use thick puzzle pieces that are easy to hold and manipulate on a shallow form board. Provide puzzle pieces with handles or attach handles (e.g., thread spools). (2.1)

- Begin with hand-size pieces and gradually choose smaller items; for example, have the child put a cup back in the holder after brushing his or her teeth, then have the child put away the cup and the toothbrush in their places in the holder. (2.1)

- Begin fitting circles into corresponding holes, then progress to shapes that will fit into corresponding holes in more than one way (e.g., square, triangle, cross). (2.1)

- Use color cues to help the child distinguish shape differences (e.g., circles are red, squares are blue). (2.1)

- When introducing shapes and shape sorters or form boards, present them in completed form and let the child remove and replace pieces. (2.1)

- Use objects that can be easily manipulated (e.g., forms with knobs for form boards, plastic eggs for egg cartons). (2.1, 2.2)

- Arrange objects to produce an effect when one object is activated; for example, a bell rings when a ball hits a target or water splashes when an object is dropped into a bucket of water. (2.2)

- Use large receptacles for objects, such as a shoebox for blocks. Decrease the size of the receptacle systematically to a drinking cup size. (2.2)

- Offer the child a second and third object while he or she is still grasping the first object and holding it over an open container. This will encourage the child to drop an object to obtain another. (2.2)

- Begin with two objects that can fit together only one way (e.g., two nesting blocks, baby and cradle, toy car and garage, telephone and receiver). Systematically introduce more and varied combinations as the child begins to fit objects into spaces. (2.2)

Instructional Sequences

- Model assembling a toy such as a Cootie bug. Hand the child the final piece. (2)
- Model the placement of a shape and then let the child try. Give the child a verbal or gestural cue such as say, "That block goes here" while pointing (2, 2.1, 2.2)
- Place pieces near their corresponding space and have the child complete the placement. (2.1, 2.2)
- Give the child materials one at a time. "Here's the baby's bed (child receives the bed) and here's the baby (child receives the doll). Put the baby on the bed so she can take a nap." (2, 2.2)
- Use corresponding spaces that are larger than the pieces and systematically increase the closeness of fit. (2.1, 2.2)
- Place a piece loosely in position and physically guide the child to complete the task. Use minimal physical assistance to guide the child's hand and object. (2, 2.1, 2.2).

TEACHING CONSIDERATIONS

1. Use objects or events to elicit responses that provide cues to which the child with a sensory impairment can respond; for example, use noise-producing toys for a child with a visual impairment.
2. For a child with a motor impairment, use objects (e.g., large puzzle pieces, puzzle pieces with knobs) that can be easily manipulated.
3. Allow adequate time for the child to respond to toys.
4. Activation or exploration of objects should be continued or facilitated to reinforce the child's engagement in the activity.
5. Consider safety with all objects that the child handles.

GOAL 3   Uses either index finger to activate objects

- PS3a   The child isolates his or her index finger by pointing (not necessarily with intent).
- PS3b   The child uses his or her thumb or fingers to poke.

Objective 3.1   Uses either hand to activate objects

IMPORTANCE OF SKILLS

A child using the whole hand or an index finger to activate objects is demonstrating the ability to organize fine motor behavior in a goal-directed manner. Initially, a child will use the whole hand to successfully activate an object. The use of an index finger versus the whole hand indicates that the child's fingers are becoming differentiated and can be used for tasks independent of the whole hand.

With these skills, the child utilizes manual dexterity and a variety of fine motor skills to activate different objects, such as turning knobs. The child learns cause-and-effect relationships and practices problem-solving skills. Other goals/objectives that can be targeted at the same time as Goal 3 are listed on the following page.

TEACHING SUGGESTIONS

Activity-Based

Playtime

- Have the child poke at holes punched in paper, poke holes into clay, point at pictures in books, or push play telephone buttons with the index finger extended. (3)

- Engage in interactive play with blocks, vehicles, balls, and other hand-size objects. (3, 3.1)

- Provide opportunities for the child to explore various toys that provide highly salient feedback when activated. Have a Busy Box, toys with push buttons, musical toys such as a tambourine or jingle bells, or a Happy Apple toy available. Show the child how to activate them. (3, 3.1)

Bathing

- Show the child how to wash his or her belly button and between toes using the index finger during a bath. (3)

- While bathing or playing outside, show the child how to pop bubbles with his or her index finger. (3)

Throughout daily routines

- When the child pats pictures or mirror images, model pointing in return and encourage the child to point as well. (3)

- Give the child the opportunity to activate familiar objects in the environment with an index finger; for example, encourage the child to turn lights on and off, press elevator buttons, push the television or radio buttons, and press doorbells. (3)

Concurrent Goals/Objectives for Fine Motor Strand B

Goal 3: Uses either index finger to activate objects

Gross Motor

B:1 Assumes balanced sitting position

C:1.5 Cruises

Adaptive

A:4.2 Eats with fingers

Cognitive

F:1.2 Uses functionally appropriate actions with objects

Social-Communication

B:1.2 Points to an object, person, and/or event

Social

A:3.2 Responds to communication from familiar adult

B:2.1 Responds to established social routines

Notes:

Assessment, Evaluation, and Programming System for Infants and Children (AEPS®), Second Edition,
edited by Diane Bricker © 2002 Paul H. Brookes Publishing Co., Inc. All rights reserved.

Fine Motor

- Give the child many opportunities to activate familiar objects in the environment. Let the child activate appliances such as the vacuum, toaster, or sink that require use of the entire hand. Encourage the child to push open doors and cupboards and pull open drawers. (3, 3.1)

Environmental Arrangements

- Provide various toys for the child to explore that provide highly salient feedback in response to fine motor movement. Use toy pianos and other musical toys that require touch. (3)

- Give the child pull-toys with string extensions. (Remove the ring or handle from the string so that the child must manipulate the string to activate the object.) (3)

- Provide finger paints and show the child how to "write" with the index finger. Put shiny or interesting toy rings or finger puppets on the child's index fingers and encourage the child to wiggle the fingers to make them move. (3)

- Use pump dispensers for soap and lotion and let the child do the pumping. (3, 3.1)

- Provide materials that lend themselves well to patting, slapping, pushing, and pulling; for example, show the child how to pop bubbles, flatten clay, finger paint, or push floating toys. (3, 3.1)

- Allow the child to push the large buttons on vending machines to receive food or a drink. (3, 3.1)

- Build a tower of blocks and have the child knock it down, pile up bubbles in the bath and have the child pop them, or make a sand tower and have the child flatten it. (3, 3.1)

- Construct special switches (e.g., joysticks, pressure plates) to activate toys for children who have a light touch or who lack coordination. (3, 3.1)

Instructional Sequences

- Model activating the object for the child, then give the child a turn. (3, 3.1)

- Give the child a verbal cue to activate the object, such as, "Push the button" or "Push the car." (3, 3.1)

- Have the child point to an object, then brush the object against the child's finger to activate it. (3, 3.1)

- Use minimal physical assistance to guide the index finger to an object. (3, 3.1)

TEACHING CONSIDERATIONS

1. Use objects or events to elicit responses that provide cues to which the child with a sensory impairment can respond; for example, use noise-producing toys for a child with a visual impairment.

2. Use objects that can be easily activated (e.g., switches, squeeze-toys).

3. Allow adequate time for the child to respond to toys.

4. Activation or exploration of objects should be continued or facilitated to reinforce the child's engagement in the activity.

5. Consider safety with all objects that the child handles.

GOAL 4	Orients picture book correctly and turns pages one by one

Objective 4.1   Turns pages of books

- PS4.1a Child attempts to turn pages.

Objective 4.2   Turns/holds picture book right side up

- PS4.2a Child holds books using both hands.

IMPORTANCE OF SKILLS

Early use of books is an important foundation for emergent literacy and later reading skills. Holding books right side up and turning pages provides opportunities for refinement of eye–hand coordination and grasping and manipulation skills, as well as introducing the child to print and story skills. Other goals/objectives that can be targeted at the same time as Goal 4 are listed on the following page.

TEACHING SUGGESTIONS

Activity-Based

Storytime

- Schedule regular times for shared reading at home or in the classroom (naptime, bedtime, storytime), and look at the same books repeatedly. Once the child is familiar with a book or story, have the child get the book from the shelf, hold it, and turn pages independently. (4)

Concurrent Goals/Objectives for Fine Motor Strand B

Goal 4: Orients picture book correctly and turns pages one by one

Fine Motor

B:1 Rotates either wrist on horizontal plane

Gross Motor

B:2 Sits down in and gets out of chair

Cognitive

D:1 Imitates motor action that is not commonly used

G:3 Recognizes environmental symbols

G:4 Demonstrates functional use of reading materials

G:4.1 Orally fills in or completes familiar text while looking at picture books

Social-Communication

C:2.1 Carries out two-step direction with contextual cues

D:3 Uses three-word utterances

Social

A:3 Initiates and maintains communicative exchange with familiar adult

C:2 Initiates and maintains communicative exchange with peer

Notes:

- Make books from children's drawings. Have each child draw two or more pictures to tell a story. Write a simple narration for each picture as the child dictates, and ask the child to orient the pictures right side up and stack them in order before stapling the pages together. (4)

- While looking at picture books, take turns turning pages. (4, 4.1)

- Purposefully hand a familiar picture book to the child upside down and/or with the back cover facing up. Give reminders to turn the book over only if necessary. (4.2)

- Have the child and a few peers sit in a circle. Give each child a book with directions to find the cover and show it to a neighbor. (4.2)

Playtime

- Play "Simon Says" by giving specific step-by-step directions for locating and looking at a book: "Simon says go get a book," "Simon says find the front cover," "Simon says open the book," "Simon says turn the page." (4, 4.1, 4.2)

- Take pictures of children eating at snack, playing outdoors, or participating in other desirable activities. Have the child orient the pictures right side up and lay them out in sequence (e.g., setting the table, eating, cleaning up; putting on coats, playing outside, lining up to come in). (4.1, 4.2)

Travel

- Take a familiar book on the bus, in the car, or anywhere waiting might be involved. Let the child look at the book while waiting, with reminders to orient it correctly before starting to look at pictures. (4, 4.1, 4.2)

- Go to the library and assist the child to select and look at a few unfamiliar picture books. Point out peers and adults who are reading or looking at books, with special attention to turning pages. (4, 4.1)

Environmental Arrangements

- Assist the child and a few peers to orient books correctly and turn pages in order by having one big book for the teacher and multiple copies of the same book in regular size for children to read along. (4, 4.1, 4.2)

- Provide picture books that are easy to manipulate such as board books, big books, cloth books, or plastic books. (4, 4.1)

- Provide books that have large, high contrast pictures of familiar items (one to a page) to facilitate picture recognition and correct orientation. (4, 4.2)

- Use books and book tapes together, with a sound cue on the tape to cue page turning in concert with the story. (4.2)

- Make picture books from photographs of children taken at home or in the classroom. Put the pictures in plastic photograph pages and have children find one another's photographs by turning the pages. (4.1, 4.2)

Instructional Sequences

- Begin by using big books that have large pictures and pages that are easier to manipulate. Use smaller books with thinner pages as the child becomes more proficient. (4, 4.1, 4.2)

- First, have the child orient single pictures or photographs right side up, then work on finding the front covers of books and turning them upright. (4.2)

- Model turning the book right side up and turning pages, describing what you are doing and having the child imitate. (4, 4.1, 4.2)

- Verbally direct the child to "Turn the book over," "Turn the book right side up," and/or "Turn just one page now." (4, 4.1, 4.2)

- Offer minimal physical assistance to the child; for example, place the child's fingers in a pincer grasp at the corner of a page to be turned. (4.2)

TEACHING CONSIDERATIONS

1. If the child has a visual impairment, increase the intensity and variety of environmental support and cues (e.g., large, bright, high contrast pictures; textured pages). Use books that are easy to manipulate, buy book/tape combinations, or make companion tape recordings for favorite books. Consult a vision specialist for evaluation of the need for large print books, speech output computer programs, and/or braille instruction.

2. If the child has a motor impairment or abnormal muscle tone, consult a physical or occupational therapist about the appropriateness of these skills, related issues, and adaptive devices for holding books and turning pages. Determine a consistent response (e.g., eye point, hand motion) for the child to indicate when a book is correctly oriented or a page should be turned.

3. If the child has a hearing impairment, increase the intensity and variety of cues (e.g., louder verbal cues, exaggerated motions, consistent book reading routines).

4. Provide quiet and comfortable settings with visible covers displayed right side up for some books and accessible storage for others.

5. Integrate books and book making into dramatic play, oral language, art, writing center, and literacy centers of the classroom. Encourage shared reading and family literacy activities in discussion with parents.

GOAL 5   Copies simple written shapes after demonstration

- PS5a   The child traces simple shapes.

Objective 5.1   Draws circles and lines

- PS5.1a   The child draws a circular shape.

- PS5.1b   The child makes a horizontal stroke with a crayon, marker, or pencil.

- PS5.1c   The child makes a vertical stroke with a crayon, marker, or pencil.

Objective 5.2   Scribbles

- PS5.2a   The child makes marks on paper.

IMPORTANCE OF SKILLS

Copying shapes, drawing lines/circles, and scribbling encourages greater control with a writing implement such as a crayon or pencil. These skills aid in the development of perceptual motor skills and eye–hand coordination and foster visual discrimination.

Spontaneous scribbling provides the child with the opportunity to learn the relationship between finger movements that guide the tool and the resulting visual feedback. Circles and lines are the basic elements of numerals and letters, whereas scribbling provides the child with a means of expression and an opportunity to be creative. By reproducing simple shapes, the child practices concepts such as straightness, curves, slants, continuity, enclosure, and intersection. These skills are important precursors to writing and drawing representational pictures. Other goals/objectives that can be targeted at the same time as Goal 5 are listed the following page.

TEACHING SUGGESTIONS

Activity-Based

Art activities

- Take turns drawing pictures with shapes on magic slates, a chalkboard, or paper. Use circles for faces, squares for houses, or triangles for pizza slices. (5, 5.1)

- Use shapes in flannelboard play or art activities, giving the child an opportunity to feel, copy, and match them. (5, 5.1)

Concurrent Goals/Objectives for Fine Motor Strand B

Goal 5: Copies simple written shapes after demonstration

Gross Motor

B:2 Sits down in and gets out of chair

Cognitive

C:1 Correctly activates mechanical toy

F:1.4 Uses sensory examination with objects

Social-Communication

B:1 Gains person's attention and refers to an object, person, and/or event

C:2 Carries out two-step direction without contextual cues

Social

A:2 Initiates and maintains interaction with familiar adult

Notes:

- Encourage the child to make circles, crosses, and triangles with his or her index finger in sand, flour, dirt, mud, or finger paint. (5, 5.1)

- "Paint" with water on the sidewalk, making long lines and big circles. (5, 5.1)

- Provide crayons or markers for drawing. Take turns drawing lines and circles with different colors. (5, 5.1)

- Encourage the child to engage in activities with marking tools, such as painting with paintbrushes or drawing in dirt with sticks. (5, 5.1, 5.2)

- Color together on plain paper or in coloring books without attention to "staying in the lines." (5, 5.1, 5.2)

- Hang large sheets of paper on a wall for the child to color on (e.g., paper grocery sacks cut open work well). (5, 5.1, 5.2)

- Wrap toys in paper and allow the child to "decorate" the packages. (5, 5.1, 5.2)

- Hang the child's work on display to reinforce the activity. (5, 5.1, 5.2)

Bathing

- Use soap crayons in the bath and take turns drawing simple shapes. (5, 5.1)

Throughout daily routines

- Point out shapes in the child's environment (wheels are circles, clocks are circles, windows are rectangles) and trace the shapes in the air with your finger. (5, 5.1)

- While you write letters or pay bills, give the child paper and crayons or markers to use to imitate your activity. (5, 5.1, 5.2)

Environmental Arrangements

- Give the child a template or piece of cutout cardboard that will guide the writing implement around the desired shape. (5, 5.1)

- Give the child pre-cut shapes to paste using glue sticks, or give the child glue bottles to trace the outline of their shape. (5, 5.1)

- Draw dot-to-dots of shapes for the child to trace. (5, 5.1)

- Begin with large exaggerations of desired shapes and gradually diminish the size. (5, 5.1)

- Engage the child's attention to the activity by making dots on the writing surface. The auditory component (tapping) of this action usually captures the child's attention. (5, 5.1, 5.2)

- Make lines and circles in clay or cookie dough and "feel" the configuration. (5, 5.1, 5.2)

- Provide the child with a large piece of paper to write on; gradually decrease the space to the size of writing paper. (5, 5.1, 5.2)

- Move the paper around beneath the child's poised writing implement to create a mark. Call attention to the mark, then wait for the child's response. (5.2)

Instructional Sequences

- Model copying a shape with a pencil, marker, or crayon on paper. (5, 5.1, 5.2)

- Model drawing circles and lines on paper. (5, 5.1)

- Model and verbally encourage the child to scribble on paper. (5, 5.2)

- Use gestures and verbal instructions such as, "Go 'round and 'round," or "One line here, another here." (5, 5.1, 5.2)

- Hold the end part of the child's writing implement as the child makes marks on the writing surface. Gently guide the tool through the desired motion, pairing the action with an auditory cue (e.g., zoom, 'round and 'round, zip). (5, 5.1, 5.2)

- Allow the child to hold an adult's hand or end of a writing implement as the adult makes marks on the writing surface. Guide the tool through the desired motion, pairing the action with an auditory cue (zoom, 'round and 'round, zip). (5, 5.1, 5.2)

- Use minimal physical assistance to guide the child's hand in copying shapes. (5, 5.1, 5.2)

TEACHING CONSIDERATIONS

1. Use objects or events that provide cues to which the child with a sensory impairment can respond; for example, use paper with textured or raised shapes for a child with a visual impairment.

2. Use writing implements that can be easily managed by the child; use necessary adaptive implements for a child with a motor impairment.

3. Allow adequate time for the child to respond to using the writing implement.

4. Consider safety with all objects that the child handles.

Gross Motor Area
Birth to Three Years

LIST OF AEPS TEST ITEMS

Gross Motor

The Gross Motor Area consists of four strands tracing the development of the infant from the earliest movements in the stomach and back positions to sitting and walking and functional use of motor skills in play. The child's efforts in the first year of life are largely concentrated on acquiring new and more complex motor skills. Often, caregiver and infant interactions center on the acquisition of these motor actions, and the actions themselves become important to the child's development in other areas; for example, children use movement to communicate wants and needs when they crawl to the refrigerator and touch the door or reach with extended arms toward a toy that is out of reach. When these movements are combined with vocalizations and interpreted successfully by the caregiver, the basis for communication is being established. Development of motor skills increases interest in and opportunities for exploring. The child is able to make choices through movement and exercise some control over the environment by crawling from one room to another, climbing on and off a riding toy, or sitting on the couch. The child who moves about with increased independence faces new challenges and frustrations.

The first strand in the Gross Motor Area examines the infant's ability to move body parts independently of each other and to position the body on the back and on the stomach to facilitate movement and locomotion. Gross motor development generally follows a predictable sequence, progressing in a cephalocaudal (head to toe) and proximal-distal (from midline to limbs) direction. This means development proceeds from the head down to the feet and from the chest out to the fingers. The infant learns to control the head before the trunk, control arms before fingers, and move the eyes in a controlled manner before stabilizing and turning the head. The infant learns to control his or her body in a horizontal position before a vertical position. Head control is evident while the infant lies on the stomach or back before sitting or standing upright. These body control sequences are predictable but not invariable. Each infant's development may vary widely from others of comparable age but still be typical. It is important to acknowledge normal variations in style and ability when designing developmental activities.

The newborn infant's motor responses are jerky and uncoordinated. Moving or making contact appears to be accidental occurrences of which the infant has little or no control. While the infant is learning to move in new ways, concentration on the action is critical. The child may appear to be moving in slow motion, focusing every ounce of energy on learning a new motor skill. Once the skill is learned, the child will practice it over and over again with obvious enjoyment. Continual use of arms, legs, trunk, head, fingers, and other body parts produces increased control. While on the stomach, the child will use his or her forearms momentarily and will prop higher and for longer periods of time until able to reach for objects with one arm. While in this position, the infant is also exploring with the hands and eyes.

Trunk control is evident when the infant begins to roll and squirm. Movements become skillful and purposeful as the infant becomes adept at exploring the environment through simple locomotion such as pivoting, creeping, rocking, and crawling. The infant may combine many different types of locomotion to gain access to a desired person or object, even relinquishing a new, more sophisticated pattern for a primitive but faster mode.

The second strand in the Gross Motor Area focuses on balance in sitting. Sitting greatly increases the child's freedom of movement and comfort. Sitting requires the infant to balance the head and trunk, initially with support, then independently. When placed in a sitting position, the newborn may lift his or her head and even extend the trunk momentarily before slumping. As body control develops in stomach and back positions and as head righting, equilibrium, and protective responses mature, the infant can not only lift the head and extend the trunk, but also sit without support of the hands. The infant becomes increasingly facile at regaining and maintaining balance in sitting while reaching for and interacting with objects. The infant learns to shift in and out of sitting and into other positions to increase access to the environment. The infant's ability to sit down in and get out of a chair also increases his or her socialization and independence.

A young child who is learning to sit independently may frequently topple over or slump. Back muscles, however, develop strength over time and with use, result in increased stability. It is important with sitting, as with all motor activities, to allow the child's ability to emerge without providing too much adult support. When the child is slow, clumsy, or unsure, the caregiver is easily tempted to provide maximum support that preempts the child's learning of the skill. This curriculum emphasizes the use of the least intrusive support necessary for the child to accomplish the skill independently. Using opportunities throughout the day and arranging the environment to ensure safety is the preferred way for the child to learn skills such as sitting. A few minutes practicing sitting after a diaper change or while propped with towels in a laundry basket helps develop strength for most young children just as well as a 20-minute exercise regimen.

The third strand addresses balance and mobility in standing, walking, and running that are the culmination of muscle development and of practice. This marks a major milestone for caregivers as the child's ability to walk independently eliminates the task of carrying, supporting, or wheeling the child everywhere. Stairs become the ultimate challenge and a frontier that provokes fears in many caregivers.

The development of gross motor skills in the infant and young child is generally carefully watched and proudly acclaimed by the family and caregivers. The gross motor milestones are recorded in baby books and used as comparative measures between generations within the family. Knowing that the father and all of his siblings walked at 9 months places the expectation for early walking upon the child. The combination of this environmental expectation and the possibility of a genetic propensity for early development of gross motor skills may contribute to the development of walking at an early age. High expectations can also lead to discouragement for the child and inhibition in experimenting with motor actions. The child wants to please and is sensitive to the caregiver's impatience and anxiety. A child who has normal movement, tone, and strength, but is still not walking alone when the caregiver thinks he or she should, usually needs more time rather than coaxing or special shoes.

The fourth strand includes play skills. A tricycle and a ball provide opportunities to gain balance and control, as well as to have fun with playmates.

These activities combine motor actions of different levels of complexity, providing the child with practice on new skills while gaining proficiency in old ones. Some activities combine unusual motor expectations such as pushing a riding toy with alternating feet. The sitting position is not a natural way to learn to alternate the feet in motion; therefore, even though sitting is a prerequisite skill for a riding toy, it does not guarantee success. Pushing with legs is very different from walking with legs. Even for the young child with well-developed walking skills, a riding toy poses new challenges.

Infants and young children with motor problems form a heterogeneous group. Children with cerebral palsy have a clearly defined set of motor problems; other children are described simply as delayed or atypical. Motor impairments may be transient and disappear over time or may become more serious. It is often difficult for the interventionist to make accurate predictions about development; he or she must monitor progress carefully. It is also important to maintain close contact with physical and occupational therapists, as their guidance will be critical to meeting the needs of children with motor impairments. The AEPS Curriculum was not written specifically for children with severe motor impairments, and adaptations will need to be made for these children when engaging in activities to develop gross motor skills.

Movement and Locomotion in Supine and Prone Position

GOAL 1   Turns head, moves arms, and kicks legs independently of each other

Objective 1.1   Turns head past 45° to right and left from midline position

• PS1.1a The child turns his or her head 45° to the right and left from midline position.

Objective 1.2   Kicks legs

• PS1.2a The child kicks both legs together.

Objective 1.3   Waves arms

• PS1.3a The child waves both arms together.

IMPORTANCE OF SKILLS

A child's first posture when lying on his or her back (supine) is characterized by the complete flexion experienced in utero. From this position, the child begins to bend and stretch the limbs and turn the head, increasing the range of movement in the legs, arms, and head. This permits the child to practice the antigravity extension movement that will allow an upright posture within the first year of life.

The infant's progression from having arms in full flexion to waving arms freely in all directions builds strength for future reaching and grasping skills. The infant begins to build strength necessary for crawling and walking as his or her leg development progresses from a full flexion posture to stretching out and eventually kicking legs alternately. In the development of head turning, the infant initially looks at objects and follows them with the eyes and head for brief periods. Development progresses to allow the child to turn the head past 45° to a stimulus, demonstrating control of head-turning on a horizontal plane. This controlled movement builds strength necessary for the child to hold the head in an upright position.

The ability to turn one's head, move one's arms, and kick one's legs independently of each other allows the child to visually explore and gain sensory input from the environment. These skills foster the self-awareness necessary for the child to learn that he or she is separate from the environment. Moving body parts independently of one another is basic to all other gross motor skills, such as crawling, sitting, and walking. Other goals/objectives that can be targeted at the same time as Goal 1 are listed on the following page.

Goal 1: Turns head, moves arms, and kicks legs independently of each other

---

Fine Motor

A:1.2 Makes nondirected movements with each arm

Cognitive

A:1 Orients to auditory, visual, and tactile events

B:1 Visually follows object and/or person to point of disappearance

---

Social-Communication

A:1 Turns and looks toward person speaking

Social

A:1.2 Responds appropriately to familiar adult's affective tone

---

Notes:

Assessment, Evaluation, and Programming System for Infants and Children (AEPS®), Second Edition,
edited by Diane Bricker © 2002 Paul H. Brookes Publishing Co., Inc. All rights reserved.

TEACHING SUGGESTIONS

Activity-Based

Dressing

- Dress the child in tights or soft, loose-fitting pants to encourage freedom of movement. Do not overdress the child as movement may be hampered by too much clothing. While putting pants or socks on the child, gently drop the child's legs or feet onto a soft surface, allowing them to "bounce." (1.2)

- Kiss or blow on the child's feet when changing diapers. Wait for the child to respond by kicking. Place your hands close to the child's feet so that when the child kicks, his or her feet will touch your hands. Play a "gonna get you" game. Push gently to offer resistance and increase strength. (1.2)

- When undressing, let the child's arms gently drop out of each sleeve in a coat or shirt. Dress the child in loose-fitting shirts and sweaters to encourage freedom of movement. Do not overdress the child, as movement may be hampered by too many layers of clothing. (1.3)

Bathing

- Encourage the child to use arms and legs to splash and kick water when in the bathtub. (1.2, 1.3)

Feeding

- When feeding the child at the breast, with a bottle, or with a spoon, give the child visual or tactile cues indicating the direction of nourishment. Encourage head-turning response toward food. (1.1)

Playtime

- When the child is engaged with another familiar adult in an interactive game, observe the child for voluntary independent head, arm, and leg movements. (1)

- Give the child opportunities to be held or to lie naked on smooth, soft blankets to encourage pleasurable tactile sensations for body movements. Make sure the child remains warm if lying undressed. (1)

- Encourage head-turning when novel and interesting events occur, such as a pet walking past or a mother, father, or sibling entering the room. (1.1)

- When coming into the child's immediate environment, speak gently to the child from one side and wait for the child to turn toward you. Talk to the child in gentle tones while the child is lying on his or her back in a crib or enclosed space. Pause periodically for the child's response. (1.1)

- Play the child's favorite face-to-face games, encouraging the child's active participation. These early excited movements of the whole body offer many opportunities to wave the arms. (1.3)

- While rocking and singing, gently wave the child's arms or assist the child to clap with the rhythm of the music. (1.3)

Throughout daily routines

- While doing daily chores such as washing dishes and cooking, seat the child in close proximity and talk to and touch him or her occasionally. This encourages the child to attend and respond. Once the child focuses on your face, move slowly from one side to the other while continuing to speak to him or her. Pause periodically and wait for the child's response. (1, 1.1)

Environmental Arrangements

- Safely affix an easily activated mobile to the crib in the child's visual field. Change the location of the mobile to encourage the child to visually explore a larger area. (1)

- If the child has difficulty keeping his or her head from turning to the side or moving out of an asymmetrical tonic neck reflex once in that position, then assist the child's head to midline by shaping a rolled blanket around his or her head, extending it from ear to ear. (1, 1.1)

- When bathing, drying, or putting lotion on the child, stroke one leg, one arm, and one side of the face at a time, encouraging separate responses. (1)

- Hang bold, colorful pictures on both sides of the child's visual field in the crib or next to a chair or infant seat to encourage head turning for visual exploration. (1.1)

- Encourage the child to "track" you either auditorily or visually as you sing or as you play Peekaboo around corners of the crib. (1.1)

- Move a push-toy in front of the child to encourage the child to follow with his or her eyes and head. (1.1)

- Hold the child close to your body or provide him or her with large, soft barriers in the crib (stuffed animals, blankets, towels) so that the child receives tactile sensations for movements of the head or arms. (1.1, 1.3)

- Place tissue paper under the child's feet to produce a crinkly, rattling sound when the child kicks. A squeak-toy or Happy Apple also works well. (1.2)

- Use a soft piece of cloth or yarn to connect the child's ankle to a mobile so that a leg movement will activate the mobile. Gradually make the yarn longer and looser to require stronger kicking. Never leave the child unattended with ties connected to the body. (1.2)

- Provide opportunities to move arms and legs in more supported positions, such as sidelying or supported recline in the bathtub. (1.2, 1.3)

- Safely affix an easily activated mobile or crib gym to the child's crib so that it will move when the child kicks his or her arms or legs. (1.2, 1.3)

- Place your face close to the child and encourage the child to reach and touch. (1.3)

- Long hair, glasses, and jewelry can be interesting to children and provide reason to wave their arms or reach for the object. (1.3)

- Give the child opportunities to move in less demanding positions, such as on stomach supported at chest or in a sidelying posture. Practice independent movements in all positions. (1, 1.1, 1.2, 1.3)

- Sing nursery songs and touch different body parts as a signal for the child to move those limbs or his or her head. Put jingle bells on the child's booties, mittens, or hat so that he or she can control the sounds. (1, 1.1, 1.2, 1.3)

- Place the child gently over your knee and bounce him or her. Watch for leg and arm movements as well as head turning. Do not maintain this position for prolonged periods or if the child expresses displeasure. (1, 1.1, 1.2, 1.3)

- Slightly elevate (with folded blanket or cloth diaper) the child's head and shoulders or hips when the child is lying on his or her back. (1, 1.1, 1.2, 1.3)

- Place a mirror to one side of the child's crib, play area, or changing table. Position the child so that the mirror is sometimes on the left and sometimes on the right. (1, 1.1, 1.2, 1.3)

Instructional Sequences

- Position the child so that his or her head and shoulders are slightly forward and are not held in a stiff, elevated, or retracted fashion. If the child can control his or her own posture, then make the presentation of activities contingent on the child's successful attempt at optimal positioning. (1, 1.1, 1.2, 1.3)

- When the child is lying on his or her back, gently stroke or blow on the bottom of one foot and then the other, on one hand and then the other, and on one ear and then the other, while encouraging single disassociated movements. (1)

- Systematically increase the distance that the child must turn his or her head to see a favorite toy or event (e.g., musical bear, jack-in-the-box). Verbally direct the child to look. (1.1)

- When holding the child in a face-to-face position, hold his or her hand to your mouth and kiss, then gently release. Wait for a response from the child (smile, slight movement, vocalization), then repeat the action. (1.1, 1.3)

- Touch the child's cheek gently with nipple, spoon, or pacifier. This should elicit a rooting response in a very young child who will then turn his or her head to find the food source with the mouth. (1.1)

- Gently guide the child's head in the direction of a favorite toy or activity. (1.1)

Gross Motor

- If the child enjoys raspberries (i.e., putting mouth against skin and blowing), then begin by blowing a raspberry on the child's stomach and then back away. After a signal from the child (smile, slight movement, vocalization), repeat the action, moving slowly toward the child's body. Remain there until the child's hands or feet move toward or touch your head or face. (1, 1.1, 1.2, 1.3)

Combining or pairing different levels of instructional sequences may be helpful when beginning to teach a new and difficult skill. Fade to less intrusive instructional sequences as soon as possible to encourage more independent performance.

TEACHING CONSIDERATIONS

1. If the child has a motor impairment or abnormal muscle tone, consult a physical or occupational therapist about the appropriateness of targeting this skill and about related issues.

2. Provide a quiet and safe space for the child to practice these skills in a comfortable manner.

3. Turning the head to one side may obligate some children to engage in asymmetrical tonic neck reflex.

4. Make sure that the child is turning his or her head voluntarily and not in response to gravity. The child's head should turn, not drop, to each side.

5. Have the child turn his or her head in both directions and not favor one side.

6. For a child with a visual or hearing impairment, stronger or more varied cues may be necessary to elicit responses. Use cues adapted to the impairment to elicit responses; for example, a child with a severe hearing impairment may not respond to kicks of an object that makes a louder noise. This child will more likely respond to tactile stimulation of the feet and legs.

7. If the child with a visual impairment is active in the crib and suddenly becomes still, it may mean that the child is listening carefully to the sounds around him or her. This is a good time to help the child associate sounds with people and objects; for example, direct the child's legs to move the mobile or musical toy.

8. Consider safety with all objects that the child handles.

GOAL 2   Rolls by turning segmentally from stomach to back and from back to stomach

Objective 2.1   Rolls from back to stomach

- PS2.1a The child turns from back to side.

Objective 2.2   Rolls from stomach to back

- PS2.2a   The child turns from side to back.

- PS2.2b   The child positions self on the verge of rolling with one arm extended and the face turned toward the extended arm.

IMPORTANCE OF SKILLS

This goal marks the first time the child independently changes body positions. The ability to move from one location to another fosters curiosity and exploration of the environment. The trunk rotation used in rolling over is important for future movements against gravity, such as assuming sitting, creeping, and standing positions. The child masters a form of movement that allows him or her to move a distance, obtain toys, and escape uncomfortable positions. Other goals/objectives that can be targeted at the same time as Goal 2 are listed on the following page.

TEACHING SUGGESTIONS

Activity-Based

Playtime

- When the child is lying on his or her back or stomach, approach from a position of 2–3 feet away and talk. Present your face to the child in such a way that the child is encouraged to roll 180° to engage in face-to-face interaction. (2, 2.1, 2.2)

- Give the child many opportunities to play with toys or objects on the floor on both the stomach and back. Provide ample space for the child to roll freely without encountering obstacles. (2, 2.1, 2.2)

- Lie on the floor a short distance from the child and engage the child by talking and touching. Encourage the child to move toward you by rolling. (2, 2.1, 2.2)

Dressing

- Dress the child in clothes that will not twist or otherwise constrict rolling. (2, 2.1, 2.2)

Environmental Arrangements

- Place a mirror a slight distance to the side of the child to encourage rolling for a closer look. (2)

- Place the child on a large, partially inflated ball on either his or her stomach or back. Secure the child's body in a slightly upright position by hold-

Goal 2: Rolls by turning segmentally from stomach to back and from back to stomach

Fine Motor

A:2.3 Reaches toward and touches object with each hand

Gross Motor

A:3.5 Bears weight on one hand and/or arm while reaching with opposite hand

Cognitive

A:1 Orients to auditory, visual, and tactile events

B:1.1 Visually follows object moving in horizontal, vertical, and circular directions

F:1.4 Uses sensory examination with objects

Social-Communication

A:1.2 Turns and looks toward noise-producing object

A:2 Follows person's gaze to establish joint attention

Social

A:3.2 Responds to communication from familiar adult

Notes:

ing the child's trunk against the ball with one hand. With the free hand, slowly move the ball either right or left until the child rolls. (2, 2.1, 2.2)

- Place the child on a bed, waterbed, air mattress, or beanbag surface. Rolling is sometimes easier on these surfaces. (2, 2.1, 2.2)

- When presenting the child with a favorite toy, allow the child to focus on it visually, then move it slowly in an arc so that following it will require the child to turn his or her head. Continue moving the toy until it is out of the child's visual range. Encourage a rolling response to see or touch the object. (2, 2.1, 2.2)

- Occasionally place toys out of reach but within child's visual field, instead of giving them directly to the child. Provide ample space for rolling without encountering obstacles. (2, 2.1, 2.2)

- At bath or changing time, use a towel or diaper to gently lift one side of the child to assist in beginning a roll. (2, 2.1, 2.2)

- Place the child on his or her stomach on a slight incline. Gravity will help get the child started. Be sure the movements are not fast or frightening to the child. (2.2)

Instructional Sequences

- Use toys or a peer to encourage the child to roll over. (2, 2.1, 2.2)

- Verbally encourage the child to "Come here" to reach a toy; use a noise-producing toy. (2, 2.1, 2.2)

- Before the child begins to roll, assist by extending the arm on the side on which the child will roll above the child's head so the arm and shoulder do not block the rolling movement. Get the child to extend an arm out and above the head by encouraging the child to reach for an object or toy while lying on his or her stomach or back. (2, 2.1, 2.2)

- If the child initiates rolling but cannot complete it, then assist the child by gently guiding the shoulders and hips in the direction of the roll. Make sure the child's head is leading the movement. (2, 2.1, 2.2)

TEACHING CONSIDERATIONS

1. If the child has a motor impairment or abnormal muscle tone, consult a physical or occupational therapist about the appropriateness of targeting this skill and about related issues. If the child has abnormal muscle tone, do not present toys in a manner that will result in abnormal posture (head and neck extension) by the child.

2. Make sure the child's intended rolling path is clear of obstacles.

3. The rolling surface should be warm, clean, slightly padded, and free of floorboard heating devices or radiators.

Gross Motor

4. For a child with a visual impairment, use cues adapted to the impairment to elicit responses such as bright objects and touch or sound cues; for example, a child with a severe visual impairment will not be attracted to a bright object; however, this child may roll toward a familiar adult in response to touch or sound cues.

5. Use visually appealing objects or touch cues with a child who has a hearing impairment.

6. Consider safety as the child learns to roll and has the potential of rolling off a surface.

7. Some children find the extraneous movement afforded by some surfaces aversive. If the child shows fearful reactions (e.g., increased muscle tone, clinging to parent, gripping surface), introduce these surfaces gradually.

GOAL 3   Creeps forward using alternating arm and leg movements

• PS3a   Child reaches with one arm while maintaining weight on the other hand and both knees.

Objective 3.1   Rocks while in a creeping position

Objective 3.2   Assumes creeping position

Objective 3.3   Crawls forward on stomach

• PS3.3a The child uses arms to propel self backward when lying on stomach.

Objective 3.4   Pivots on stomach

Objective 3.5   Bears weight on one hand and/or arm while reaching with opposite hand

• PS3.5a The child assumes a "swimming" posture with weight primarily on abdomen and with arms and legs stretched out above weight-bearing surface.

Objective 3.6   Lifts head and chest off surface with weight on arms

• PS3.6a The child lifts head and shoulders off a surface.

• PS3.6b The child lifts head off of a surface.

IMPORTANCE OF SKILLS

Lifting head and chest off of a surface, bearing weight on one hand while reaching with the other, and crawling and creeping increases the child's independence and exploration of the environment. As each of these skills develops, the child gains the strength, balance, and coordination essential in future gross motor activities such as sitting, walking, and running.

Initially, the child is able to lift the head and chest off of the supporting surface while bearing weight on the arms, demonstrating advancements in head and shoulder control. From the position of head and chest off of the surface, the child develops upper back extension, a greater awareness of the upper body and arms, and the ability to look at his or her own hands while lying on the stomach. The achievement of weight bearing on one side while reaching with the other in a stomach position represents the development of the "rotary" trunk component and permits the child to reach for and manipulate objects while lying on the stomach.

Pivoting allows the child to shift weight and develop balance, which is necessary for creeping. "Belly" crawling contributes to the child's control of the upper back and shoulders, provides the child with new sensory stimulation and body awareness, and builds stability in the shoulders, back, and pelvis. This provides a more efficient means of moving than rolling because it fosters balance and coordination through shifting weight.

In assuming the creeping position, the child achieves a new position in space that fosters self-awareness and allows the child to view the world from a new orientation. This skill further develops the equilibrium and balance needed for creeping and eventually for upright positions. Rocking while in a creeping position represents experimentation with the hands and knees position and provides a fun and soothing activity within the child's independent control. Creeping is the child's first efficient means of locomotion, allowing the child to cover some distance. Once creeping, the child practices reciprocal movements and maintains balance while shifting weight. These skills are necessary for walking and running.

These gross motor skills lead to increased independence and allow the child a more active means of exploring and gaining access to the environment. Other goals/objectives that can be targeted at the same time as Goal 3 are listed on the following page.

TEACHING SUGGESTIONS

Activity-Based

Playtime

- Slowly move a pull-toy in front of the child to encourage him or her to follow it. (3)

- Creep around the child who is in a creeping position. Chase the child and let the child move after you. (3)

- Allow the child to play in the sand in which creeping will be the most efficient means of locomotion. (3)

- Occasionally place toys out of reach but within the child's visual field instead of giving them directly to the child. When the child has almost

Goal 3: Creeps forward using alternating arm and leg movements

Fine Motor

A:2.3 Reaches toward and touches object with each hand

Cognitive

B:3.1 Looks for object in usual location

C:1.1 Correctly activates simple toy

E:3.1 Moves barrier or goes around barrier to obtain object

F:1.3 Uses simple motor actions on different objects

Social-Communication

A:2 Follows person's gaze to establish joint attention

C:2.3 Carries out one-step direction with contextual cues

Social

A:2.2 Responds to familiar adult's social behavior

Notes:

reached a desired object, move it back a couple of inches. Do not do this more than once or the child may become frustrated and abandon the effort altogether. (3, 3.3)

- Instead of playing with the child's favorite objects or toys on the floor, encourage the child to play on surfaces of varied heights (e.g., low graduated stairs, large foam wedges, large blocks obstructing access to play areas). (3, 3.1, 3.2)

- Play games of imitating family pets by assuming an all-fours position. (3.1)

- Get on the floor with the child, who is in a hands and knees position. Rock back and forth and encourage the child to do the same. (3.1)

- If the child indicates a desire to get down when being held, then place the child in a creeping position facing interesting objects or toys or whatever item engages the child's interest. (3, 3.1)

- Roll balls, toys on wheels, or cylindrical objects between the child's arms while the child is lying on his or her stomach. See if the child will momentarily assume a creeping position to obtain the object. (3.2)

- Place the child on his or her stomach in a very shallow bath or child-size pool and encourage movement toward toys. (3.3)

- Play mirror games in front of the child and encourage crawling for a closer look. (3.3)

- Lie on the floor to the side of the child. Encourage the child with your voice and toys to pivot toward you. (3.4)

- Engage the child in face-to-face interaction. Move your face up and down. Wait for the child's response. (3.4, 3.6)

- Encourage a reaching behavior in all positions by providing toys and objects at arm's length while the child is lying on his or her back or is in a sidelying or supported sitting position. (3.5, 3.6)

Quiet time

- Sing and talk while the child is lying prone against your stomach and chest. Encourage head and shoulder lifting. (3.6)

Nature

- Many small pets are a perfect height for children to rise up and watch. Watching fish in an aquarium on the floor or a low surface is a great way to practice this skill. (3.6)

Dressing

- Provide a mirror at floor level for the child to look at him- or herself. (3.6)

Throughout daily routines

- Vary objects to maintain or engage the child's interest. If the child is more interested in people than objects, then allow the child to reach toward and explore the faces of family members. Family pets, if tolerant of handling by children, are also of great interest. (3.5)

- Give the child opportunities to lift his or her head in other positions, such as when the child is picked up or carried on an adult's shoulder. (3.6)

Environmental Arrangements

- Provide soft rugs and mats for the child's creeping activities. (3)

- Dress the child in clothes that will not ride up or constrict during creeping. (3)

- Place the child over a bolster, making sure that the child's shoulders and hips can move freely and that the child can touch the ground with hands and knees. Present toys to the right or left so that the child will maintain weight on three limbs while reaching with the fourth. (3)

- Set up a "mini" obstacle course with the child creeping through a tunnel or under a table to reach a favorite toy or person. (3, 3.1)

- Give the child the opportunity to move or rock on a scooterboard that supports the trunk. Make sure the device allows the child's shoulders and hips to move freely and that the child can touch the ground with hands and knees. (3, 3.1, 3.3)

- Present toys on elevated surfaces so that the child must get on his or her hands and knees to obtain them. Give the child the opportunity to move on a variety of surfaces to determine which is the most manageable. Begin instruction on the "easiest" surface. (3.1, 3.3)

- Put the child on the floor, arms extended, to play with a favorite pet. Invite the child to come see the pet and to imitate the pet's movements. (3.2)

- Encourage the child to bear weight on limbs by presenting toys on an elevated surface that would otherwise be out of the child's visual field. (3.2)

- Position the child so that the child can push off of a barrier such as a wall or adult's body to propel forward and initiate the crawling movement. (3.3)

- When the child is positioned on his or her stomach, offer an object that is too large to be grasped with one hand and that will roll away when touched (ball, toy vehicle, rolling mirror). If the child becomes frustrated, then hold the object stationary or help the child change position to play with it. Use toys that make noise when the child touches them by reaching from a stomach position (e.g., Happy Apple). (3.3, 3.5)

- Begin by requiring very slight pivotal movements from the child and systematically increase the movements by placing toys at greater distances. Increase distances as the child successfully reaches each one. (3.4)

- Roll or place a soft toy between the child's arms and under one side of the child's chest while the child is lying on his or her stomach. (3.5)

- Hold the child on his or her stomach on a large ball facing a mirror. Make sure the child can see him- or herself in the mirror and then roll the ball to one side until the child can reach for and touch the mirror image with one hand. (3.5)

- Hang toys at shoulder height and within reach to encourage the child to rise up and reach. (Pay special attention to potential dangers with hanging toys.) (3.5, 3.6)

- Support one of the child's shoulders with a rolled-up blanket or towel positioned along one side of the child's body. The roll should be placed behind the child's shoulder and extend part way down the child's trunk. (3.5, 3.6)

- Allow the child to play with a favorite object or toy in a supported upright position and then lower the child to the floor on his or her stomach while the child is still attending. (3.6)

- Introduce a toy on the floor within the visual field of the child lying on his or her stomach. Slowly raise the toy so that the child raises his or her head to follow it visually. (3.6)

Instructional Sequences

- Allow the child to play with a favorite object or toy and then move it to a distance several feet away while the child is watching. When the child rolls to his or her stomach and assumes a creeping position, play with the toy to encourage the child to creep toward it. (3, 3.1, 3.2)

- Model or have a peer model the creeping position. Play games with the child in this position. (3.2)

- Place the child on his or her hands and knees. Hold out a toy and invite the child to "Come on." (3.2)

- Allow the child to play with a favorite object or toy while lying on his or her stomach. Remove the toy to a distance several inches from midline to the left or right while the child is watching. Continue to call attention to the toy by verbally encouraging the child and activating the toy. (3.3, 3.4)

- Allow the child to reach and grasp objects while in a sidelying position, then gently turn the child onto his or her stomach and encourage the child to continue to explore. Move the object to one side within reach of either the left or right hand. Verbally encourage the child to reach. (3.5)

- Position the child on his or her stomach with arms forward. Present a favorite toy so that the child can see it, then move it up out of range. Activate the toy and verbally encourage the child to lift his or her head to view it. (3.6)

Gross Motor

- Allow the child to play with a favorite object or toy while lying on his or her stomach. Move the object to an elevated surface several feet away while the child is watching. After the child assumes a creeping position to look at the object, gently guide the child's hips backward and release. Look repeatedly at the object and move toward it. Gently guide the child's hips and verbally encourage rocking. (3.1)

- Physically assist the child to move forward toward an object by pressing against the soles of his or her feet when the child is in a hands and knees position. (3)

- After the child's bath, place the child on his or her hands and knees on a towel and dry the child in this position. When drying the child's trunk, use strokes that run the length of the trunk (from shoulders to hips), applying enough pressure to rock the child's body back and forth. (3.1)

- If the child is moving toward an object by pulling forward with the arms, then gently stroke the bottom of one foot, then the other, to stimulate movement of the lower limbs. (3.3)

- Physically guide the child's hips and shoulders in a pivoting movement to reach a toy. (3.4)

- When the child is positioned on his or her stomach, offer an object that can be grasped with both hands but is too large to be secured with one. Let the child touch the object with outreached hand(s), then back it away and present it again to one hand. (3.5)

- If the child fails to bear weight on the opposite hand while reaching with the other, then assist maintenance of the position by holding the child's weight-bearing forearm in position before and during reaching. The child should be lying on his or her stomach, bearing weight equally on each arm before an object is presented. (3.5)

- When the child is up on his or her arms, gently rock the child back and forth to help shift weight from one arm to the other. (3.5)

- Place the child on his or her stomach with arms bearing weight. Interact with the child while in this position, causing the child to lift his or her head and chest off the surface. (3.6)

- Position the child on his or her stomach. When the child lifts and turns his or her head to clear airway, interact with the child. (If the child is incapable of clearing his or her airway by lifting or turning his or her head, or if the response is weak, then do not position the child on the stomach.) (3.6)

- Gently grasp and lift the child's shoulders. This will encourage head lifting. (3.6)

TEACHING CONSIDERATIONS

1. If the child has a motor impairment or abnormal muscle tone, consult a physical or occupational therapist about the appropriateness of targeting this skill and about related issues.

2. Some surfaces will afford the child better traction and movement. Begin teaching on surfaces where the child's efforts will result in greater success.

3. The area in which crawling is practiced should be warm, clean, and free of floorboard heating devices or radiators.

4. Some children may find certain textured surfaces aversive. If the child reacts negatively to surface textures (e.g., increased muscle tone, clinging to parent, withdrawing limbs, fussing), use another surface and introduce unfamiliar textures gradually.

5. For a child with a visual or auditory impairment, varied cues may be necessary to elicit responses.

6. Skills that require self-initiated mobility are significantly delayed in a child with a visual impairment. This child is more likely to respond to touch cues to move forward. For a child with a visual impairment, use cues adapted to the impairment to elicit responses; for example:

    *   Place a piece of soft quilt or fabric on the floor. Lie on the floor facing the child. Gently rub the child's lips and mouth with your finger or a pacifier; gradually change the position of the finger or pacifier. This will encourage the child to lift the head and move it from side to side. This is a precursor to the child lifting both head and chest off of a surface.

    *   Place a child with a visual impairment on your lap face down with the child's head over your knees. A soft piece of cloth on your lap may help the child feel secure and comfortable. Stroke the child's neck and spine and softly blow on the child's back. This will encourage the child to lift his or her head while lying on his or her stomach, which is a precursor to pivoting on the stomach.

    *   Present bright-colored or textured toys to prompt the child with a visual impairment to respond by reaching.

    *   A child with a visual impairment may not assume a creeping position in response to a bright-colored toy. This child may, however, respond to touch cues to assume a creeping position.

    *   Use a bolster or large pillow to encourage a child with a visual impairment to sit on his or her heels. This position is a good first step to learning to crawl. Use the bolster to support the child's chest and arms while the legs are folded under the child with the buttocks resting on the heels. Gently roll the bolster forward and backward.

7. Consider safety as the child creeps about the environment and handles various objects.

Gross Motor

STRAND B

Balance in Sitting

GOAL 1   Assumes balanced sitting position

- PS1a   When standing, the child lowers body, bends knees, and shifts weight back to a sitting position.
- PS1b   When on hands and knees, the child rotates the body while extending and pushing with arms and shifts weight to a sitting position.
- PS1c   When in a sidelying position, the child moves to sit by bending at the waist while extending and pushing with arms and bearing weight on the hips to raise the body off the ground.
- PS1d   When on hands and knees, the child shifts weight to lean back and sit on legs; then extends legs out in front to sit on buttocks.

Objective 1.1   Assumes hands and knees position from sitting

- PS1.1a   From a sitting position, the child leans forward, bears weight on hands, and shifts weight from buttocks to knees.

Objective 1.2   Regains balanced, upright sitting position after reaching across the body to the right and to the left

Objective 1.3   Regains balanced, upright sitting position after leaning to the left, to the right, and forward

- PS1.3a   When sitting, the child *leans to the left and right* and then regains a balanced, upright sitting position.
- PS1.3b   When sitting, the child *leans forward* and then regains a balanced, upright sitting position.

Objective 1.4   Sits balanced without support

Objective 1.5   Sits balanced using hands for support

- PS1.5a   When placed in a supported sitting position, the child holds his or her upper back straight.

Objective 1.6   Holds head in midline when in supported sitting position

- PS1.6a   The child lifts his or her head momentarily when in a supported sitting position.

IMPORTANCE OF SKILLS

Sitting skills enhance the child's visual exploration of the environment. The child perceives the world from an upright orientation and is able to view a wider range of events.

The ability to hold the head in midline when in a supported sitting position is the first step in the development of muscular control that proceeds from the head down to the lower back. The child who sits using hands for support has enough head, neck, and back control to maintain this upright position, despite the pull of gravity. The child will practice increased control and equilibrium reactions to maintain balance in this position. This prepares the child for sitting balanced without support, which increases the strength and control of the muscles in the upper and lower back. The firm back that results from the downward extension of muscular control is necessary for balance in standing and walking, as well as for controlled movement in the sitting position.

The ability to regain the sitting position after leaning improves back strength, balance, and trunk control and is important to the increased freedom of the arms and hands for more active exploration. By rotating the trunk, the child's body moves segmentally rather than as a single unit. Instead of moving in line with the body, the arms can move across the body. Across-the-body arm movement enables the child to explore and interact with more of the environment and is critical to one method of getting into and out of the sitting position. Moving out of a sitting to a creeping position represents control over a variety of movements (e.g., rotating trunk, shifting weight, bearing weight on hands and knees). These movements are coordinated into a complex behavior pattern, producing a smooth, balanced, and functional movement.

The ability to assume a sitting position increases balance and motor coordination. The child integrates more complex motor actions into controlled patterns of movement. These skills provide the child with greater mobility, freedom of movement, and independence. They also increase the child's interaction with the environment as the child's hands are free to explore, reach, and play with objects. This increased interaction with the environment facilitates cognitive development. Other goals/objectives that can be targeted at the same time as Goal 1 are listed on the following page.

TEACHING SUGGESTIONS

Activity-Based

Feeding

- To encourage sitting balanced with or without support, sit on the floor facing the child and have a picnic. Present favorite snacks to the child. To encourage the child to assume a sitting position, offer the snack at a height above the child's head. While the child is sitting, offer favorite snacks from a distance so that the child will have to change position to obtain them. (1, 1.1, 1.4, 1.5)

Concurrent Goals/Objectives for Gross Motor Strand B

Goal 1: Assumes balanced sitting position

Fine Motor

A:2 Brings two objects together at or near midline

A:3 Grasps hand-size object with either hand using ends of thumb, index, and second fingers

Adaptive

A:4.2 Eats with fingers

Cognitive

E:4.1 Uses more than one strategy in attempt to solve common problem

F:1.3 Uses simple motor actions on different objects

Social-Communication

C:2.3 Carries out one-step direction with contextual cues

Social

C:1.4 Observes peers

Notes:

- At snack time, sit the child on a table or counter and encourage the child to finger feed. (1.4)

Bathing

- When bathing the child in a shallow tub, offer interesting floating toys while the child is in a semi-reclined position to encourage assuming a balanced sitting position or to encourage the child to reach for the plug, bubbles, or toys presented under the water and out of reach to assume a hands and knees position from sitting. Water will support the transition to hands and knees in the bathtub. (1, 1.1)

Quiet time

- When the child is standing or lying in a crib, encourage the child to use crib rails to help move to a sitting position. (1)
- Sit and hold the child on your lap. Talk to the child, smile, and exaggerate expressions, keeping your face near the child's face. (1.6)

Playtime

- As the child crawls toward you, present toys that must be manipulated with two hands to be activated. (1)
- Engage the child with favorite objects or toys that roll or move away from the child's body when the child plays with them (e.g., balls, balloons, bubbles). Roll a large ball back and forth with the child. (1.1, 1.2, 1.3)
- Activate favorite objects and toys to the child's side while the child is in a sitting position. (1.2)
- Sit facing each other and play Peas, Porridge, Hot or other games that require crossover clapping motions. (1.2)
- Play Peekaboo or "gonna get you" from positions in which the child must reach across to get you. Sit in front of the child and play Peekaboo by placing a cloth over your face. Encourage the child to lean forward to pull the cloth away, then encourage the child to place the cloth over his or her own face and regain an upright position. Repeat the game, sitting on each side of the child so that the child leans to the left or right to pull the cloth from your face. (1.2, 1.3)
- Sing songs or play games with the child that involve swaying motions. Hold the child on your lap or on your knee. Sway the child from side to side as you sing "Row, Row, Row Your Boat," for example. (1.3)

Travel

- Take the child on an outing in a backpack and point out animals, trees, and other objects of interest. (1.6)
- When carrying the child, hold the child away from your body facing outward in a sitting position. Allow the child to lean backward for support of

the head and trunk. Point out people, trucks, and other interesting events or objects for the child to see. (1.6)

Throughout daily routines

- When the child is sitting, stand or squat close by and wait for the child to move out of a sitting position onto hands and knees. Let the child use your body as a support to change position before picking up the child. (1.1)

- During the day, provide opportunities for the child to practice independent sitting on various surfaces (e.g., floor, carpet, couch, crib) to gain stability. (1.4)

- While folding laundry, sit the child in a laundry basket. (1.5)

- While the child is sitting on your lap, position the child to use hands for support. Provide additional support with your own body to prevent falling, if necessary. (1.5)

- Set the child's carrier on a table or work space. Talk to the child while you are working. (1.6)

Environmental Arrangements

- Place pillows under the child as the child practices moving to sitting from standing. (1)

- Hold one end of a blanket while another adult holds the opposite end. Swing the child back and forth inside the blanket. Lift the end of the blanket closest to the child's back until the child assumes a sitting position. (1)

- Place favorite toys and objects near walls or corners of rooms. The walls will function as barriers and assist the child to change position or direction after obtaining the object. (1)

- Play with the child in a sitting position on beds, sofas, or rugs so that unsuccessful attempts to change position will be cushioned. (1.1)

- Allow the child to play with a favorite object or toy (e.g., pull-toy, wind-up toy) while in a sitting position, then move the toy away from the child while the child watches. Activate the toy if the child does not spontaneously assume a hands and knees position. (1.1, 1.2)

- Place favorite objects or toys on stair steps and encourage the child to obtain them. (1.1)

- When drying the child after a bath, with the child in a sidesitting position, put upward pressure on the child's weight-bearing side. Never force the movement; the pressure should be the same as used in normal towel drying. (1.1)

- Play beanbag toss with large targets placed all around the child. (1.2)

- Give the child a set of small objects (e.g., beads, shapes, pegs) and a container. Put the objects on one side of the seated child and the container on the other side. If possible, the container should be unstable or unwieldy so that the child feels the need to stabilize it with the nearest hand. The child must then reach for an object and reach across the body to deposit the object. (1.2, 1.3)

- Sit in front, to the right, and to the left of the child while holding a familiar book. Encourage the child to point to pictures from a distance; this makes the child reach. (1.2, 1.3)

- Present favorite objects and toys on the floor to the right, to the left, and in front of the child just within reach but far enough that the child must lean to reach them. (1.2, 1.3)

- Sit the child in front of a mirror so that the child can reach for his or her image in the mirror. (1.3)

- Give the child opportunities to sit in a car seat, in the corner of a sofa, propped in a chair with pillows, or in an infant carrier in the most upright position possible. (1.4)

- When sitting behind the child, move back so that the child independently maintains balance for brief periods. (1.4)

- Gently stroke the back of the child's neck to help child keep head erect. (1.4)

- Sit the child in a cardboard box or in a swimming ring to provide support. Cover the surrounding area with pillows. (1.5)

- Sit on the floor with the child between your legs facing away from you. Dangle toys or interesting objects in front of the child's face to encourage the child to hold self upright. If the child falls back, your body will block the fall. (1.5)

- Place the child in a sandbox, using sand to support the body. (1.5)

- Use a variety of chairs or seats to encourage the child to hold his or her head in midline (e.g., car seat, infant carrier, front pack, stroller, infant swing, corner of sofa). (1.6)

- Use an object such as foam, cloth ring, towel, or blanket to hold the child's head in midline position when sitting in a car seat, stroller, or infant swing. (1.6)

- Dim lights in a room and use a small flashlight to illuminate objects to gain the child's attention as the child sits supported. (1.6)

- Hold the child at shoulder level and have another person talk to the child over your shoulder. (1.6)

Gross Motor

Instructional Sequences

- Provide a model for the child; for example, sit on the floor from a standing position or model "chase" games and encourage the child to join you. (1, 1.1)

- Sit on the floor and model reaching across your body to get a toy. Then reach across your body with the other hand and move the toy to its original location. Repeat. (1.2)

- Verbally direct the child to sit down beside you on the floor. Verbally encourage the child to "come and get" the adult, a peer, or a toy as the adult, peer, or toy slowly moves away from the sitting child. (1, 1.1)

- While the child is sitting on the floor, hold the child's hand that is nearest a toy; verbally prompt the child to get the toy. (1.2)

- Place the child in a sitting position facing a mirror or an interesting toy on the floor. Verbally encourage the child to lean forward to pat the mirror image by tapping and patting mirror. Activate a toy to encourage the child to reach for it. Begin by placing the child very near the mirror or toy and systematically move the child farther away from it as the child successfully leans and recovers. (1.3)

- Hold the child's hands and gently guide the child to sitting from standing, adding a little bounce on the pillows or mattress. (1)

- Roll a large, partially inflated beach ball to the child while the child is sitting. When the child raises his or her arms to secure the ball, roll the child on top of the ball and allow the child to rock back and forth before resuming a sitting position. (1.1)

- When the child is in a sitting position, give the child an object to hold in one hand and then place another toy (preferably a toy that can be combined with the first toy) in close proximity to the occupied hand. If the child does not have a spontaneous response, then guide the child's free hand from behind the elbow toward the object. (1.2)

- Physically assist the child by gently guiding the child's hip or shoulder. Gradually reduce the amount of assistance. (1, 1.1, 1.2)

- Place the child in a sitting position on your knees, facing you. Hold the child's hands and move one knee slowly up, allowing child to teeter. Then move knee back and allow child to regain balance. Repeat with other knee. Increase the amount that the knees are moved as the child successfully leans and regains an upright sitting position. (1.3)

- Sit the child on the floor between your legs facing away from you. If the child begins to lean backward, then quickly lean forward to bring the child's trunk forward, then lean back beyond the initial point of support. If the child attempts to lean on your legs, then move legs away. Verbally encourage the child to sit up. (1.4)

- Sit the child on the floor and hold him or her by the lower back. Verbally encourage the child to use his or her hands for support. Gradually move your support downward to the child's hips, upper legs, and lower legs while holding lightly. (1.5)

- Support the child between your legs. Gradually move your legs away and place the child's hands on the floor as support. (1.5)

- When carrying the child, hold him or her away from your body, facing outward in a sitting position. Allow the child to lean backward to support the trunk and head. Use your body to guide the child's head and maintain it in midline. (1.6)

TEACHING CONSIDERATIONS

1. If the child has a motor impairment or abnormal muscle tone, consult a physical or occupational therapist about the appropriateness of targeting this skill, the use of equipment to elicit motor responses (e.g., adapted chairs, balls), and related issues.

2. If the child has a hearing impairment, increase the intensity and variety of cues (e.g., auditory cues, toys that produce noise, bright-colored objects). Be aware that the child may be fearful of changing positions. Allow the child to practice this skill on a variety of surfaces (e.g., floor, carpet, grass).

3. For the child with a visual impairment:

    - The child may need to be encouraged to use hands for balance because functional use of hands is often delayed. Gently pull the child up to sitting by pulling on one arm a little more than the other. When pulled by one arm, the child will have to find and maintain his or her balance, as when sitting alone. Provide moderate support for the sitting child by bending at the waist, then place the child's hands on the floor and gently hold them there for support.

    - Encourage the child to reach across the body for a toy by guiding the child's hand. Gently hold the arm and hand nearest the toy on the floor to ensure that the child reaches with the opposite hand. This movement encourages weight shifting.

    - Encourage balanced sitting by varying the child's placement; for example, once the child is sitting steady on the floor, place the child on a low stool or step. The child will have to work harder to regain balance after leaning to the right and left.

    - Encourage confidence in sitting through use of a large body ball. Sit the child on top of the body ball and hold the child securely at the waist in the beginning. As the child becomes more comfortable and begins to find his or her own balance, gradually decrease support by holding the child's legs. Gently move the child back and forth on the ball.

Gross Motor

- Help the child feel secure in a supported sitting position by holding the child just below the chest as the child sits on your lap facing you. As the child becomes more stable sitting and is able to hold his or her head in midline, hold the child less tightly so that the child begins to find his or her balance.

4. Consider safety as the child moves about the environment and handles objects.

GOAL 2   Sits down in and gets out of chair

Objective 2.1   Sits down in chair

Objective 2.2   Maintains a sitting position in chair

- PS2.2a The child maintains a supported sitting position in a chair.

IMPORTANCE OF SKILLS

The ability to maintain an unsupported sitting position in a chair fosters balance and head and trunk control. Sitting in a chair enables the child to move forward at the hips and shoulders in order to bring the arms forward and use the hands for reaching and grasping. The ability to sit down in and get out of a chair requires a smooth movement progression that develops coordination and control over combined movements. This increases the child's independence by allowing the child to get into and out of a chair without assistance and allows more interaction with the environment.

These skills are important for increased independence and will be used throughout life in a variety of settings, such as driving, eating, and reading. Other goals/objectives that can be targeted at the same time as Goal 2 are listed on the following page.

TEACHING SUGGESTIONS

Activity-Based

Feeding

- If the child requests a drink or snack, have the child sit at the table to receive it. (2, 2.1)

- Place the child in a highchair for meals. (2.2)

Dressing

- Encourage the child to sit in a chair for assistance with putting on and taking off shoes and socks or to have pants pulled on up to the knees. Then, have the child get out of the chair to pull pants up to his or her waist. (2, 2.1)

Concurrent Goals/Objectives for Gross Motor Strand B

Goal 2: Sits down in and gets out of chair

Fine Motor

B:2.1 Fits variety of shapes into corresponding spaces

B:5.1 Draws circles and lines

Adaptive

A:3 Drinks from cup and/or glass

A:4 Eats with fork and/or spoon

C:1.3 Takes off pants

Cognitive

E:3.2 Moves around barrier to change location

E:4 Solves common problems

Social-Communication

A:2.1 Follows person's pointing gesture to establish joint attention

C:1.3 Locates common objects, people, and/or events, with contextual cues

C:2.3 Carries out one-step direction with contextual cues

Social

B:2.1 Responds to established social routines

Notes:

Gross Motor

Playtime

- At the playground, encourage the child to get in and out of child-size swings. (2)

- Play "going to the movies"—line up chairs to watch *Sesame Street* or a favorite videotape. (2, 2.1)

- Sit the child in a child-size chair at a low table to play with or manipulate toys or objects. (2.2)

- Have the child sit down in a chair to color. (2.1)

Storytime

- Provide a child-size rocking chair for storytime. (2, 2.1)

Throughout daily routines

- Provide a child-size chair at the snack table and in front of the television and a potty chair in the bathroom. (2, 2.1)

Travel

- Use a safety seat while traveling in a car. Allow the child to climb into the car seat before traveling in the car and to climb out when the car is parked. (2, 2.2)

- When shopping, place the child in a sitting position in the shopping cart. (2.2)

- Take the child for walks in a stroller with the seat adjusted to a sitting position. (2.2)

Environmental Arrangements

- Play musical chairs, or line up chairs in a row and play "choo-choo train." (2)

- Provide a tub of water on a low table for water play. Encourage the child to stand up to get desired toys and sit down to play. (2)

- Before asking the child to sit down or get out of a chair, move the chair out from under a table or turn the seat toward the child. (2, 2.1)

- Use a chair that has arms or sides so that the child has extra support if he or she is feeling insecure. The child can use the arms to lower into or raise out of the chair. (2, 2.1, 2.2)

- Place the chair firmly on the floor to prevent tipping. (2.1)

- Sit in chairs at circle or sharing time, rather than on the floor. (2.1)

- Use a variety of chairs (e.g., chair without sides, rocking chair, cube chair). (2.1, 2.2)

- Hold the child in a sitting position when you carry him or her. The child's back should be toward the adult's body and the child should sit supported by the adult's arms. (2.2)

- Provide a surface on which the child can rest his or her feet. The child's feet should be a few inches apart and rest flatly on the foot support. (2.2)

- Present objects to the child at chest level or on a table surface in front of the child while the child is in a sitting position. Activate toys on the table's surface to maintain the child's attention. (2.2)

- Place the child on a riding toy that has back support; push the child on the riding toy, providing support if necessary. (2.2)

Instructional Sequences

- Model sitting in a chair and getting out several times. (2, 2.1)

- During snack, pat the seat of the chair after asking the child to sit down. Verbally encourage the child to remain seated. Hold arms out toward the child after asking the child to climb out of the chair. (2, 2.1, 2.2)

- Position the child to sit in the chair by pushing the hips against the back of the seat; hold hips until the child extends back to attain a fully upright position. Pull the child's hips forward to the edge of the seat to encourage the child to get out of the chair. Gradually reduce the amount of assistance. (2, 2.1)

- Crouch down close to the chair and allow the child to use your shoulder or arms to pull out of the chair. (2)

- Sit the child down on a straight chair and offer support as the child adjusts position. (2.1)

- Use safety belts to hold the child's hips stable and help the child maintain a sitting position. (2.2)

- Provide support at the child's hips when the child sits in a chair. Gradually reduce the amount of support. (2.2)

TEACHING CONSIDERATIONS

1. If the child has a motor impairment or abnormal muscle tone, consult a physical or occupational therapist about the appropriateness of targeting these skills, the use of equipment to elicit motor responses (e.g., adapted chairs, balls), and related issues.

2. If the child has a visual impairment, increase the intensity and variety of cues (e.g., wider chairs, auditory or verbal cues). Initially, lead the child into and out of the chair and allow tactile exploration of the chair. Be aware that a child may be fearful of moving about freely.

3. Self-initiated mobility is often delayed in the child with a visual impairment; therefore, a child with a visual impairment may need encouragement and support to move in and out of a chair. The child will reach out to grasp a sound cue before he or she will move out in space on hands and knees or feet. The child with a visual impairment may enjoy gaining security in the sitting position by sitting on a body ball with your support. As the child improves his or her balance, decrease the support.

4. If the child has a hearing impairment, increase the intensity and variety of cues (e.g., colorful chairs, louder verbal cues).

5. Be sure that the chair is sturdy and stable; remain nearby as the child sits down in and gets out of the chair.

6. Use adapted chairs for a child with a motor impairment or abnormal muscle tone (e.g., corner chair, bolster, beanbag chair).

7. Consider safety as the child sits and handles objects. Never leave the child unattended in a chair.

STRAND C

Balance and Mobility

GOAL 1   Walks avoiding obstacles

- PS1a   When walking unsupported, the child changes direction without falling.
- PS1b   The child walks unsupported without falling.

Objective 1.1   Walks without support

Objective 1.2   Walks with one-hand support

Objective 1.3   Walks with two-hand support

Objective 1.4   Stands unsupported

- PS 1.4a The child supports him- or herself with one hand while standing.

Objective 1.5   Cruises

- PS1.5a The child stands bearing his or her full weight with support.

IMPORTANCE OF SKILLS

As the child masters each of these skills, he or she is gaining the necessary components to eventually negotiate the environment independently. Cruising is important because it fosters balance, coordination, and strength and allows the child to move in an upright position without the assistance of another person. Standing unsupported increases the strength and control of the muscles in the back and legs and develops balance in an upright position. This new position frees the hands to hold and manipulate objects, allowing greater exploration of the environment. Walking with two-hand support is important because the child begins to take alternating steps (as opposed to side-steps used in cruising), which are necessary for walking without support. Walking with only one hand for support demonstrates increased balance as the child moves in an upright posture and requires less support by caregivers. Eventually, the child can walk around objects, people, and activities independently without falling.

These balance and mobility skills allow the child to move through many settings without assistance and explore with increasing confidence. In addition, the skills provide the child with a new visual experience of the world and are valuable in play because the child is able to follow peers. Other goals/objectives that can be targeted at the same time as Goal 1 are listed on the following page.

Concurrent Goals/Objectives for Gross Motor Strand C

Goal 1: Walks avoiding obstacles

Gross Motor

C:2 Stoops and regains balanced standing position without support

Cognitive

B:3.1 Looks for object in usual location

E:2.1 Uses part of object and/or support to obtain another object

E:3 Navigates large object around barriers

E:4 Solves common problems

F:1.2 Uses functionally appropriate actions with objects

Social-Communication

B:1 Gains person's attention and refers to object, person, and/or event

C:1 Locates objects, people, and/or events without contextual cues

C:2.2 Carries out one-step direction without contextual cues

Social

B:1.1 Meets internal physical needs of hunger, thirst, and rest

B:2.1 Responds to established social routines

Notes:

TEACHING SUGGESTIONS

Activity-Based

Travel

- Encourage the child to walk along garden pathways, down grocery store aisles, through classrooms crowded with activity, and in other environments without disturbing them. (1)

- Encourage the child to maneuver around people or pets in the environment. (1)

- Encourage the child to walk down a hallway and use a wall for one-hand support. (1.2)

- When pushing the child in a stroller, periodically have the child get out and walk along the side of the stroller, holding onto it with one hand. (1.2)

- When traveling or on an outing with the child, walk together and hold the child's hand. Allow the child to practice walking with one- or two-hand support in airports, at the zoo, or on other outings. (1.2, 1.3)

Playtime

- Face the child and move backward slowly, changing directions to avoid objects, people, and activities. Encourage the child to follow or chase you. Walk backward and lead the child with one hand or two hands; give encouragement and reinforcement. (1, 1.2, 1.3)

- Encourage the child verbally or with enticement of toys to change location when standing. (1.1)

- Provide the child with pull-toys with strings that produce novel effects or push-toys such as corn poppers and lawn mowers. (1.1)

- When the child indicates a desire for a toy when being held, stand the child on the floor and take one or both of the child's hands to lead the way to a desired toy. (1.2, 1.3)

- Provide the child with a shopping cart or doll buggy to push. (1.3)

- Encourage the child to push his or her chair to the next activity. (1.3)

- Blow large bubbles for the child to pop as he or she stands holding one hand for support. Offer a bubble to the hand holding onto the support. (1.4)

- Play face-to-face clapping games while the child is standing. (1.4)

- Move together with music, encouraging the child to cruise around you. (1.5)

Dressing

- Place the child in a standing position facing you so that you can remove the child's coat. Hold the coat, but not the child's body. (1.4)

Gross Motor

Throughout daily routines

- Ask the child to transport object(s) to a specified location (e.g., dirty dishes to the sink, trash to the trash can, laundry to the hamper). (1)

- Have parents greet, but not directly approach, the child after an absence. Encourage the child to walk to parents. (1.1)

- Ask the child to do simple errands that require carrying objects, such as bringing a diaper and washcloth to his or her parent or throwing things in the trash. (1.1)

- When the child indicates a desire to be put down when being held, stand the child on the floor nearby without support. (1.4)

- Allow the child to cruise along the rail of a crib or playpen. (1.5)

- When the child is standing at a low, stable support (e.g., table, couch), put the child's bottle or favorite toy out of reach near the edge of the support. (1.5)

Environmental Arrangements

- Create an obstacle course of boxes, baskets, large toys, or pillows. Have the child walk around the obstacles to get to the end of the course. (1)

- Place a favorite toy a short distance in front of the child in an area that has obstacles (e.g., people, furniture, trees). Encourage the child to walk, avoiding obstacles, to obtain the toy. (1)

- Arrange the environment so the child can gain access to both moving and stable objects. (1)

- Play Follow the Leader using peers to walk around objects or people in the room. (1, 1.1)

- Have the child walk without support around obstacles on a variety of surfaces (e.g., carpet, grass, floor). (1, 1.1)

- Place stable objects (e.g., cube seat, low table) in a row across a room, leaving approximately 2 feet between each object. Place interesting toys on the object's surface to lure the child across open spaces from one stable object to another. Provide extra security for the child by encouraging steps between two familiar adults. (1.1)

- Walk a short distance with the child and then rest and play before walking to the next location. (1.1, 1.2)

- Place toys that are typically used together (e.g., doll, bottle, cradle; car, driver, trailer) in different locations but within the child's visual field so the child has to retrieve the toys. (1.1, 1.2, 1.3)

- If the child requests an object or toy that is out of reach, then hold one of the child's hands and let the child reach with the opposite hand. Let the child lead with the free side of his or her body, but control the degree of the child's lean. (1.2)

- Encourage the child to cruise from a low table to one of your outstretched hands. (1.2)

- When walking the child with two-hand support, replace the support of one hand with an object for the child to hold, such as a small ball, block, or the child's bottle. If necessary, help position the object in the child's grasp or against the child's body to secure it. (1.2)

- Use both stationary and moving support for the child to hold onto with one or both hands. (1.2, 1.3)

- After the child indicates a desire to be in a different location, provide a cart, box, walker, or other object that will give the child support when the child pushes or holds onto it with two hands. Control the speed of the object by placing it on a carpet, weighing it down with heavy objects, or by holding onto the front. (1.3)

- Place the child on your feet and walk together, holding onto the child's hands. This is a fun way to "dance" to music. Provide the child with an opportunity to move on his or her own feet also. (1.3)

- Place a peer on a riding toy, and encourage the child to push the toy. (1.3)

- Position a mirror so that the child can see him- or herself standing upright. Talk about different body parts and look for them in the mirror. Decrease your body support as the child becomes interested in the mirror image. (1.4)

- Provide engaging activities that require two-hand manipulation with peers at a low table. (1.4)

- When the child is standing and holding onto support, offer the child a toy or object to hold in one hand. Then offer another toy or object to the other hand. (1.4)

- Hang a Busy Box on the wall and encourage the child to walk along the wall to reach the toy. (1.5)

- Place the child's favorite objects or toys out of reach along the edge of a waist-high, stable support (e.g., table, low shelf, window ledge) while the child stands at the support and reaches. (1.5)

Instructional Sequences

- Model walking around a few "planted" obstacles. Have a peer model walking to an adult for an appealing snack or toy, walking with one- or two-hand support to obtain an appealing snack or toy, or standing unsupported holding a favorite toy. (1, 1.2, 1.3, 1.4)

- Begin by having the child walk or cruise for short distances or stand unsupported for short periods of time. Gradually increase the distance or time as the child becomes more proficient. (1, 1.1, 1.2, 1.3, 1.4, 1.5)

- Verbally encourage the child to cruise, walk around obstacles, or walk to obtain a favorite snack or toy. Crouch facing the child and slowly move backward along a support (e.g., couch), verbally encouraging the child to follow. Follow the child through a cluttered room providing verbal cues as the child approaches obstacles that he or she will have to maneuver around (e.g., "Go around the chair," "Walk around the dog. Shhh, he's sleeping"). (1, 1.1, 1.2, 1.3, 1.4, 1.5)

- Make moving in the environment increasingly challenging, depending on the child's success. Start by introducing a few large obstacles far away from each other and then increase the number and proximity of obstacles while decreasing their size. (1)

- Provide a physical prompt or physically assist the child. Have the child hold onto a rope to form a chain; lead the child around obstacles. Allow the child to grasp a loose portion of your clothing (e.g., coat belt, apron, purse strap) as the child attempts to walk unsupported. Provide support at the hips, shoulders, or hands while the child holds onto another person with one or two hands. Physically assist the child to side-step by providing gentle pressure or guidance to the hips or shoulders. Gradually decrease the amount of assistance. (1, 1.2, 1.3, 1.4, 1.5)

Combining or pairing different levels of instructions may be helpful when beginning to teach a new and difficult skill. Fade to less intrusive instructions as soon as possible to encourage more independent performance.

TEACHING CONSIDERATIONS

1. If the child has a motor impairment or abnormal muscle tone, consult a physical or occupational therapist about the appropriateness of targeting this skill, the use of equipment to elicit motor responses (e.g., adapted chairs, balls), and related issues.

2. If the child has a visual impairment, increase the intensity and variety of environmental support and cues (e.g., environmental sounds). Initially, lead the child through the environment, around obstacles, and along the supported object. Be aware that the child may be fearful of moving about freely. Gently encourage the child with a visual impairment to walk without support, to take one or both of your hands and walk, or to cruise. Have the child learning to cruise practice barefoot to provide additional information about the environment. Pairing of verbal cues and your support is very important to the child's ear–hand coordination and is important to developing the child's confidence in walking alone. Before initiating walking alone, the child may first attempt to reach toward you as you speak.

3. If the child has a hearing impairment, increase the intensity and variety of cues (e.g., exaggerated movements and gestures, louder verbal cues, bright and colorful objects).

4. Avoid slippery surfaces and shoes or socks that do not have adequate traction.

5. Be aware that the child initially may need to be placed in a standing position to practice cruising.

6. Ensure that supports are sturdy and stable.

7. Clear the environment of objects that could hurt the child if the child falls. The area should be padded to cushion falls when first teaching this skill.

8. Consider safety as the child stands or moves about the environment and handles objects.

GOAL 2   Stoops and regains balanced standing position without support

- PS2a   The child uses a support (e.g., furniture, wall, person) to regain a standing position after squatting or stooping.

Objective 2.1   Rises from sitting position to standing position

- PS2.1a The child rises from a sitting to standing position with support.

Objective 2.2   Pulls to standing position

- PS2.2a The child uses support to pull up one foot to a kneeling position with his or her weight resting on one foot and one knee.

Objective 2.3   Pulls to kneeling position

IMPORTANCE OF SKILLS

These skills develop strength, coordination, and balance as the child integrates more complex motor activities into controlled patterns of movement. The ability to independently stoop and then recover indicates that the child can control balance well enough to move in and out of a standing position. This provides a practical advantage for obtaining objects from the floor without having to crawl.

Pulling to a kneeling position or pulling to stand indicates that the child has greater trunk control and can use his or her own power to get into these positions independently. The semi-upright position is a stepping stone to standing. Pulling to a kneeling or standing position is also important because of the increased interaction with the environment as the child changes positions and views the world from a new perspective.

Mastery of these skills increases the child's independence and freedom to explore the environment. In addition, it increases the child's interaction with peers, as the child does not have to rely on support to change positions from sitting to standing. Other goals/objectives that can be targeted at the same time as Goal 2 are listed on the following page.

Goal 2: Stoops and regains balanced standing position without support

Fine Motor

A:3 Grasps hand-size object with either hand using ends of thumb, index, and second fingers

Gross Motor

D:3.3 Throws ball or similar object at target

Cognitive

C:1 Correctly activates mechanical toy

E:1 Retains objects when new object is obtained

E:2.1 Uses part of object and/or support to obtain another object

E:4 Solves common problems

F:1.2 Uses functionally appropriate actions with objects

Social-Communication

B:1 Gains person's attention and refers to an object, person, and/or event

B:2.2 Uses nonspecific consonant–vowel combinations and/or jargon

C:2.3 Carries out one-step direction with contextual cues

Social

A:3.1 Initiates communication with familiar adult

C:2.2 Responds to communication from peer

Notes:

TEACHING SUGGESTIONS

Activity-Based

Playtime

- At home, let the child play with pots and pans in low cupboards. (2, 2.1. 2.2)

- Play games such as Drop the Hanky and encourage the child to participate with assistance. (2)

- Play ball games with the child by rolling the ball on the floor while the child is standing. (2)

- Play games with refrigerator magnets placed at different heights on the refrigerator. (2.2, 2.3)

- Play with or activate a favorite object or toy on a low surface (e.g., couch, shelf, table) while the child watches. The surface should be high enough that the child must pull to a kneeling or standing position to obtain the object. (2.2, 2.3)

Dressing

- Ask the child to retrieve something from a drawer close to the floor. Offer the child many items to hold. If the child drops something, then encourage the child to pick it up. (2)

- Encourage the child to rise from sitting to standing or to stoop and regain a balanced standing position when dressing or undressing. Assist the child to put on pants. Pull the pants up to the knees as the child sits, then have the child stand to complete dressing. Hold a jacket open for the child to put on. Wait for the child to stand to put on the jacket. Encourage the child to pull shoestrings or Velcro straps to unfasten shoes. (2, 2.1)

Nature

- Spend some time outdoors exploring. Pick flowers from the garden. Gather "treasures" on nature walks, squatting and stooping periodically to pick up bugs, leaves, and sticks before walking farther. Encourage the child to bend and straighten while gathering sticks to float in puddles and shallow pools. (2)

Feeding

- When the child is finished at the table, have the child stand to stack dirty dishes or art supplies on a tray or in a bin. (2.1)

- Serve a snack at a low table. (2.3)

Quiet time

- Encourage the child to pull up on the sides of the crib to stand and be picked up. (2.2)

Throughout daily routines

- When the child is sitting, ask if the child wants to be picked up or call his or her attention to a toy or to something outside the window. Wait until the child attempts to stand before you pick him or her up; encourage the child to rise to a standing position to see what is outside. (2.1)

- When the child is near stable objects (e.g., windowsill, wall, shelf), encourage the child to pull to a kneeling or standing position to look out the window, look in the mirror, or reach a shelf. (2.2, 2.3)

- When the child wants to be picked up, hold out your arms above the child's head and encourage the child to pull up on your body to a kneeling or standing position. (2.2, 2.3)

- Encourage the child to engage in face-to-face interaction by pulling to a kneeling position, using your body when you are kneeling or sitting on the floor. (2.3)

Environmental Arrangements

- Occasionally place the child's favorite objects or toys on the floor instead of giving them directly to the child. Keep playthings in containers at ground level. Fill a drawer near the floor with unbreakable toys. Encourage the child to open the special drawer and play. (2)

- Begin by occasionally placing tall objects on the floor for the child to pick up; systematically present smaller objects for the child to grasp. (2)

- Drop an object as you walk across a room in front of the child. Ask the child to pick it up. (2)

- When the child is seated at a table, offer toys or activities that require the child to stand in order to manipulate (e.g., top, playdough factory, pounding toy). Encourage the child to stack objects (e.g., blocks, rings on a post, stacking pegs) so high that the child must stand to finish. Sturdy blocks help provide support for the child. (2.1)

- When the child is sitting, ask if he or she wants to be picked up; extend your arms down toward the child, bending only slightly. Allow the child to use you for support if necessary. (2.1)

- While the child is sitting, hold out a favorite toy above the child's head so that the child must rise to obtain it. (2.1)

- Keep interesting objects or toys on low shelves, walls, stairs, or the couch so that the child must pull to a kneeling or standing position to reach them; for example, tape pictures of the child's family or interesting objects on the wall at a height where the child must stand to look at them. (2.2, 2.3)

- Attach toys or objects to the crib railing so that the child must pull to kneel or stand to manipulate them. For example, hang a Busy Box outside of the crib at kneeling height. (2.2, 2.3)

Instructional Sequences

- Provide a model for the child. Squat to reach a favorite toy while commenting on it and then drop the toy again. Have a peer model rising from sitting to standing or pulling to standing to obtain a favorite snack or toy. Have a peer model pulling to a kneeling position to see something. (2, 2.1, 2.2, 2.3)

- Let the child sit on a stool and bend forward to feel the "squatting" position from a more secure position closer to the ground. (2)

- Provide the child with a verbal direction; for example, "Get the toy on the floor," "You can do it," "Go get your snack," or "There goes an airplane; stand up, and you can see it." (2, 2.1, 2.2, 2.3)

- Hold one side of a large object (e.g., ball, truck, doll) that the child is stooping to obtain. Initially hold the object slightly above the floor so that the child does not have to stoop all the way down. Guide the child back into a standing position with the object. For Objective 2.1, hold one side of a large object (e.g., ball, truck, doll) that the child is playing with while sitting on the floor. Tell the child to put the ball, truck, or doll in a different location or on an elevated surface, then guide the child's movements until the child assumes a standing position. Gradually reduce the amount of assistance. (2, 2.1)

- Provide the child with physical assistance; for example, hold and stabilize the child's hips, helping the child lower into a stoop and rise back to standing or move from sitting to standing. Bend to the child and ask if he or she wants up. If the child does want to get up, then stabilize the child's hips and wait until the child places his or her arms around you. Then, gently lift the child's hips, letting the child assist by pulling with his or her arms. Gradually reduce the amount of assistance. (2, 2.1, 2.2, 2.3)

- Call attention (e.g., tap, point) to a support that the child can use to hoist his or her body. If this does not elicit a response, then hold the child's hands stable when the child pulls to kneel or stand. (2.2, 2.3)

- Place the child's hands on the support that the child will use to hoist his or her body. Stand behind the child and gently lift the child's hips to achieve a kneeling or standing position. (2.2, 2.3)

TEACHING CONSIDERATIONS

1. If the child has a motor impairment or abnormal muscle tone, consult a physical or occupational therapist about the appropriateness of targeting these skills, the use of equipment to elicit motor responses (e.g., adapted chairs, balls), and related issues.

2. If the child has a visual impairment, increase the intensity and variety of environmental support and cues (e.g., tactile cues, toys that activate and make noise, verbal cues). Be aware that the child may be fearful of chang-

ing positions. Provide verbal encouragement to the child with a visual impairment as he or she may not initiate mobility without first reaching out to grasp a sound cue (your arm and your voice). The child may need prompting to achieve ear–hand (your voice–the toy) coordination when trying these skills. Offer your hand as support along with verbal encouragement when the child practices rising from a sitting to a standing position.

3. If the child has a hearing impairment, increase the intensity and variety of cues (e.g., exaggerated movements and gestures, louder verbal cues, bright and colorful objects, toys that activate).

4. Clear the environment of objects that could hurt the child if the child loses balance. Place a cushion under the child to pad the ground for any falls when first teaching this skill.

5. Avoid slippery surfaces and shoes or socks that do not have adequate traction.

6. Ensure that the support is sturdy and stable.

7. Consider safety as the child stands, squats, or kneels and handles objects.

GOAL 3   Runs avoiding obstacles

- PS3a   The child turns a corner when running.

- PS3b   The child stops and starts again when running.

Objective 3.1   Runs

Objective 3.2   Walks fast

IMPORTANCE OF SKILLS

Walking fast, running, and avoiding obstacles help develop balance and coordination as the child remains upright while running around obstacles and changing directions and speeds. These skills are important for developing self-awareness, recreation, and safety. The child experiences freedom of motion and learns about moving through space and about the relationship of his or her body to obstacles in the environment. Besides the pleasure of running, many later recreational activities utilize this skill. Walking fast, running, and avoiding obstacles also provides the child a sense of independence and a quick means of escape in times of danger. Other goals/objectives that can be targeted at the same time as Goal 3 are listed on the following page.

Concurrent Goals/Objectives for Gross Motor Strand C

Goal 3: Runs avoiding obstacles

Gross Motor

D:3.2 Kicks ball or similar object

Cognitive

E:3.2 Moves around barrier to change location

E:4 Solves common problems

Social-Communication

C:2.1 Carries out two-step direction with contextual cues

D:2.3 Uses two-word utterances to express location

Social

A:2 Initiates and maintains interaction with familiar adult

C:1.1 Initiates social behavior toward peer

Notes:

TEACHING SUGGESTIONS

Activity-Based

Playtime

- Play games that require walking fast, running, and running while avoiding obstacles; for example, organize a game of tag in a setting where children must run around obstacles (e.g., trees, large rocks, peers) or play a game of chase with the child ("You can't get me," "I'm going to get you"). Other games to play include soccer; T-ball; Duck, Duck, Goose; Red Rover; Red Light, Green Light; and Follow the Leader. When playing Follow the Leader, begin by having the adult lead the child around obstacles in the environment (e.g., between two trees, around a tricycle, around a bench); then allow the child to be the leader. (3, 3.1, 3.2)

- Play a game and run like different animals (e.g., run fast like a horse, sway like an elephant). (3, 3.1)

Nature

- Take the child on a walk. Stay slightly ahead of the child and encourage the child to catch up by running or walking fast. When walking at the park, encourage the child to run around play equipment, trees, rocks, and shrubs. Alternate walking slowly and walking fast. Say, "Let's go fast now." (3, 3.1, 3.2)

- Encourage the child to run or walk fast when playing outdoors (e.g., in the yard, on a walk, at the playground or park) or when you are in a hurry. (3.1, 3.2)

- Encourage the child to walk fast toward you. (3.2)

Throughout daily routines

- With your arms open, encourage the child to run to you; then pick up and hug the child. (3.1)

- Walk fast to special events and encourage the child to follow. (3.2)

Environmental Arrangements

- Create an obstacle course using boxes, baskets, large toys, pillows, or other obstacles. Require the child to run by and around the obstacles. To assist the child, place tape or a chalk line on the ground for the child to follow. (3)

- When beginning these skills, have the child walk fast or run short distances. Gradually increase the distance as the child becomes more proficient at running. (3, 3.1, 3.2)

- Place a favorite toy a short distance in front of the child and encourage the child to run to it. Do this in an area that has obstacles (e.g., trees, rocks, people) and encourage the child to run around the obstacles to obtain the toy. As the child becomes more proficient at running and avoiding obstacles, increase the distance between the child and the toy. (3, 3.1)

- Throw a ball or other object in front of the child and encourage the child to go after it. (3.1, 3.2)

- Give the child a pull-toy or a push-toy to encourage running or walking fast. (3.1, 3.2)

- To provide some support for fast walking, offer the child a push-toy such as a doll stroller, toy shopping cart, wheelbarrow, or lawn mower. Have the child hold onto the toy and push it fast. (3.2)

Instructional Sequences

- Model walking fast, running, and running around obstacles in the environment. Have a peer model these skills while at a park or playground. (3, 3.1, 3.2)

- Verbally encourage the child to follow you as you run around obstacles, to run to the play equipment at the playground, or to walk fast to "catch" you. (3, 3.1, 3.2)

- Introduce a few large obstacles that are far apart. Gradually increase the number of obstacles, decrease the distance between the obstacles, or reduce the size of the obstacles. (3)

- Begin by requiring the child to walk fast or run avoiding obstacles for short distances. Gradually increase the distance as the child becomes more proficient. (3, 3.1, 3.2)

- Have the child begin these skills using a slower pace and gradually increase how fast he or she walks or runs; for example, begin by having the child walk quickly or run slowly avoiding obstacles. As the child becomes more proficient at avoiding obstacles while running, have the child run faster. (3, 3.1, 3.2)

- Physically prompt the child by holding one hand; by leading the child with a rope, scarf, or other object the child holds; or by gently prodding the child from behind. (3, 3.1, 3.2)

TEACHING CONSIDERATIONS

1. If the child has a motor impairment or abnormal muscle tone, consult a physical or occupational therapist about the appropriateness of targeting this skill and about related issues.

2. If the child has a visual impairment, increase the intensity and variety of environmental support and cues (e.g., verbal cues, tactile cues, bells attached to child). Initially, lead the child through the environment and around obstacles. Be aware that the child may be fearful of moving about freely. If the child has a visual impairment, hold the child's hand as you

walk fast or run. Verbally encourage the child and tell the child of the obstacles that you are avoiding. Pair verbal encouragement with your support, and withdraw support as the child gains steady balance and confidence that he or she will not run into an obstacle. Encourage the child to walk fast or run to you.

3. If the child has a hearing impairment, increase the intensity and variety of cues (e.g., exaggerated movements, arrows on the ground, louder verbal cues).

4. Practice this skill in a wide-open space, preferably outside.

5. Avoid slippery surfaces and shoes or socks that do not have adequate traction.

6. Consider safety as the child walks or runs about the environment.

GOAL 4   Walks up and down stairs

• PS4a   The child walks up stairs holding the rail or wall with one hand.

Objective 4.1   Walks up and down stairs using two-hand support

• PS4.1a   The child walks up stairs using two-hand support.

Objective 4.2   Moves up and down stairs

• PS4.2a   The child moves up stairs.

Objective 4.3   Gets up and down from low structure

• PS4.3a   The child climbs onto a low, stable structure (e.g., low step, raised platform).

IMPORTANCE OF SKILLS

The ability to independently negotiate stairs demonstrates the child's ability to alternately shift weight from one side of the body to the other and maintain balance. This skill is also used when climbing jungle gyms or ladders, running, and riding a tricycle. By using one hand for support, if needed, the free hand is available to carry objects and to protect self when falling.

The child begins by getting up and down from a low structure and moving up and down stairs using any movement pattern (e.g., creep, crawl) to practice the skills necessary to climb stairs. When getting up and down from a low structure, the child enhances strength and balance and demonstrates body awareness and the ability to coordinate movement patterns to achieve a desired event. Moving up and down stairs increases the child's independence and interaction with the environment as the child moves to change locations and reverse directions. Other goals/objectives that can be targeted at the same time as Goal 4 are listed on the following page.

Concurrent Goals/Objectives for Gross Motor Strand C

Goal 4: Walks up and down stairs

Gross Motor

D:4 Climbs up and down play equipment

Cognitive

B:3.1 Looks for object in usual location

Social-Communication

B:2 Uses consistent word approximations

C:2.2 Carries out one-step direction without contextual cues

Social

A:3.1 Initiates communication with familiar adult

C:2.2 Responds to communication from peer

Notes:

TEACHING SUGGESTIONS

Activity-Based

Travel

- Have the child go up and down stairs leading to and from the house, church, and child care. Encourage the child to walk up and down stairs independently or with support. Let the child find the wall or rail for support; then stand near enough for the child to grasp your hand for assistance when beginning to walk up and down the stairs. If the child, who is not yet walking up and down stairs, indicates a desire to be put down while you are walking up or down stairs, then place the child on a step and supervise closely. (4, 4.1, 4.2)

- Step up and down street curbs when on a walk with the child. (4.1)

- Rather than carry the child up and down short flights of stairs, put the child down and have an adult on each side of the child take a hand. Allow the child to initiate the stepping action. (4.1)

Playtime

- Play with a Slinky on the stairs. (4, 4.1, 4.2)

- Activate toys out of the child's reach but within the visual field on a stairway, rather than giving them directly to the child. (4, 4.1, 4.2)

- Play Follow the Leader using stairs. Guide the child to lead going up and follow going down. (4, 4.1, 4.2)

- Pull a pull-toy up and down the stairs as the child reaches for it. (4.2)

- Provide the child with cushions, large pillows, or large stuffed animals on the floor during play. Build a barrier around the child on the floor with the objects, requiring the child to get up and over the barrier to reach you. (4.3)

- Allow the child to play with large cardboard blocks. (4.3)

- Play tumbling games on thick mats. Guide the child to get up and down. (4.3)

Throughout daily routines

- Place a step stool by the bathroom sink, near a drinking fountain, near a coat rack, or other locations that the child frequents. (4.3)

- Encourage the child to climb up and down a low bed or futon. (4.3)

Environmental Arrangements

- Replace a ladder on a slide with a three- or four-step staircase for the child to climb. (4, 4.2)

- Lead the child to the banister or handrail of stairs leading to and from the house, church, or child care. (4, 4.1)

- Arrange obstacle courses or treasure hunts that involve stairs. (4, 4.1, 4.2)

- Make "mini" stairs by placing a thick catalog or book in front of a step stool. Place along the wall for support. (4)

- Place the child's favorite objects or toys on a stair landing. Encourage the child to obtain the toy. (4, 4.1)

- Use carpeted stairs to reduce slipping and increase confidence. (4, 4.2)

- Carry the child halfway up or down a short flight of stairs with railings and then put the child down on the stairs. Proceed, and encourage the child to follow, remaining close enough to prevent falls. (4, 4.2)

- Guide the child to step up on and then off of a solid box while you hold both hands. (4.1)

- Begin stair climbing by using slides or ramps for descending. (4.1)

- Set the child on the lowest step or on a stool to put on shoes and socks. Encourage the child to get up and down independently. (4.3)

- Play a "follow the toy" or "come and get me" game by pulling a pull-toy over a cushion, pillow, or stuffed toy as the child reaches for it. (4.3)

- Put a favorite toy or bottle up on a low platform and encourage the child to get it. (4.3)

- Place a mirror up on a low platform and draw the child's attention to his or her reflection. (4.3)

Instructional Sequences

- Begin by having the child walk up and down a few stairs. Increase the number as the child successfully negotiates stairs. (4, 4.1, 4.2)

- Use gestures and verbal cues to encourage the child to move up and down stairs or get up and down from a low structure. (4, 4.1, 4.2, 4.3)

- Model walking up stairs independently to obtain a toy. Comment on the toy and set it down again. Have a peer model getting on and off a low surface or crawling or climbing up stairs. (4, 4.1, 4.2, 4.3)

- Provide the child with physical assistance in one or more of the following ways: (4, 4.1, 4.2, 4.3)

  - Walk up and down stairs with the child, initially giving two-hand support. Release support with one hand and allow child to continue to walk up and down the stairs with one-hand support.

  - Walk up and down stairs behind the child, stabilizing the child's hips as needed.

Gross Motor

- Walk up and down stairs behind or to the side of the child. Support the child's arm just below the shoulder joint.

- Walk down the stairs backward, facing the child. The child's hands should be on your shoulders, and your hands should stabilize the child's hips.

- Gradually decrease the amount of assistance as the child becomes more proficient.

- Begin a climbing activity with a low structure that is only slightly higher than the floor. Increase the height of the structure as the child becomes more proficient. (4.3)

TEACHING CONSIDERATIONS

1. If the child has a motor impairment or abnormal muscle tone, consult a physical or occupational therapist about the appropriateness of targeting this skill and related issues.

2. If the child has a visual impairment, increase the intensity and variety of cues (e.g., verbal cues, tactile cues, toys that activate and make noise, bells attached to child). Be aware that the child may be fearful of moving about. Initially, lead the child up and down the stairs or low surface. If the child has a severe visual impairment, pair verbal encouragement with a helping hand (or two hands if needed) when the child walks up and down the stairs. Pair verbal encouragement with gentle physical prompting as the child moves up and down a low structure. The child may need this ear–hand coordination prompting (your voice–physical touch) before the child feels confident to move out into space independently. Stairs may be frightening until the child builds confidence and ear–hand coordination.

3. If the child has a hearing impairment, increase the intensity and variety of cues (e.g., exaggerated movements and gestures, louder verbal cues).

4. Be sure that the low structure is sturdy and stable.

5. Remain near as the child moves up and down stairs and low structures.

6. Avoid slippery surfaces and shoes or socks that do not have adequate traction. Remain near as the child walks up and down stairs.

7. Consider safety as the child moves about the environment and handles objects. Never leave the child unattended on the stairs.

STRAND D
Play Skills

GOAL 1   Jumps forward

- PS1a   The child jumps forward with one foot landing at a time.

Objective 1.1   Jumps up

- PS1.1a The child bends at the knees, raises up on his or her feet or toes, and jumps up with one foot at a time.

- PS1.1b The child bends at the knees and raises up on his or her toes while feet remain on the ground (i.e., child "jumps up" without his or her feet leaving the ground).

Objective 1.2   Jumps from low structure

- PS1.2a The child step-jumps or hops (leads with one foot) from a low, stable structure to a supporting surface.

IMPORTANCE OF SKILLS

These jumping skills are important for play, developing balancing skills (shifting weight and landing upright), strengthening leg muscles (protecting the body against gravity), and body awareness. Jumping up becomes a problem-solving strategy for obtaining objects out of reach. The child continues to develop self-awareness as he or she learns a new way to move his or her body through space and control motions to accomplish this skill. Active physical play allows the child to release energy and is an enjoyable way to interact with peers. Jumping is a skill used throughout life in many games and sports. Other goals/objectives that can be targeted at the same time as Goal 1 are listed on the following page.

TEACHING SUGGESTIONS

Activity-Based

Playtime

- Sing songs or nursery rhymes and encourage the child to jump to the songs (e.g., "Jack Be Nimble," "Bunny Hop"). (1, 1.1)

- Play a game of jumping in patterns or to directions; for example, jump two times fast and two times slow. Demonstrate for the child if necessary. (1, 1.1)

Concurrent Goals/Objectives for Gross Motor Strand D

Goal 1: Jumps forward

Cognitive

D:1.1 Imitates motor action that is commonly used

Social-Communication

C:2.1 Carries out two-step direction with contextual cues

D:2.3 Uses two-word utterances to express location

Social

C:1.1 Initiates social behavior toward peer

Notes:

- Play motor games such as Mother May I and Simon Says; include jumping forward, jumping up, and jumping from a low structure. (1, 1.1, 1.2)

- Play a game with the child and pretend to be an animal. Create a story or scene that has an animal jumping; act it out; for example, pretend to be a frog jumping into a pond or a cat leaping from a tree. (1, 1.2)

- At the playground or park, encourage the child to jump into the hopscotch squares. Jump over the cracks in the sidewalk, jump from low, stable structures such as rocks, railroad ties, or a low platform. (1, 1.2)

- Blow bubbles high into the air. Encourage the child to jump up to reach them. (1.1)

- Stand in front of a full-length mirror and encourage the child to jump. (1.1)

- Encourage the child to jump into sand from the sturdy edge of a sandbox. (1.2)

Environmental Arrangements

- Place an object on the floor or ground for the child to jump over; for example, draw a line with chalk or put a stick or jump rope on the ground. (1)

- Make a shape (e.g., square, circle) with chalk or put a string on the floor or ground; have the child jump into the shape or step into the shape and jump up. (1, 1.1)

- Play music on a radio or record player and encourage the child to "dance," jumping up and forward. Vary the tempo of the music. (1, 1.1)

- Create an obstacle course of boxes, baskets, and ropes. Within the obstacle course, set up a few objects for the child to jump over (e.g., a small box, a rope) or have the child jump from a low structure such as a low sturdy box or crate. Allow peers to participate with the child in the obstacle course. Have the child and peers take turns being the leader through the obstacle course. (1, 1.2)

- Do exercises or actions to music. (Some videotapes and television programs model parent–child aerobic exercises.) (1, 1.1, 1.2)

- Provide a trampoline, mattress, or mat for jumping games. (1, 1.1, 1.2)

- Hang objects (e.g., balloons, streamers) above the child's head so that the child must jump up to touch the objects. Use caution with balloons and hanging objects. (1.1)

- Attach a noise-producing object (e.g., bells on a string) to the child's ankle so that a noise is produced when the child jumps. (1.1)

- Place objects on the floor or ground beside a low, stable structure so that the child jumps onto the objects (e.g., pillows, mat). (1.2)

Gross Motor

Instructional Sequences

- Model the jumping skill, or have a peer demonstrate. Jump forward, jump up, or jump from a low structure. (1, 1.1, 1.2)

- If the child does not readily jump, then verbally prompt the child to jump (e.g., "You can do it"). Provide specific instructions to the child (e.g., "Bend your knees," "Lift up from your toes"). (1, 1.1, 1.2)

- Extend an object for the child to grasp (e.g., hula hoop, stick, rod). (1.1)

- Physically prompt the child by holding the child's hands. Reduce assistance as the child gains skill. (1, 1.1, 1.2)

Combining or pairing different levels of instructions may be helpful when beginning to teach a new and difficult skill. Fade to less intrusive instructions as soon as possible to encourage more independent performance.

TEACHING CONSIDERATIONS

1. If the child has a motor impairment or abnormal muscle tone, consult a physical or occupational therapist about the appropriateness of targeting this skill and about related issues.

2. If the child has a visual impairment, increase the intensity and variety of environmental support and cues (e.g., verbal cues and tactile cues, bells attached to the child); for example, allow tactile exploration of the low structure. Be aware that the child may be fearful of moving about freely. If the child has a severe visual impairment, offer gentle verbal and physical encouragement to the child to jump. The child may need to reach out to where a sound came from (you) before moving out independently to jump.

3. If the child has a hearing impairment, increase the intensity and variety of cues (e.g., louder verbal cues, exaggerated facial expressions and gestures). Make the low structures visually appealing (e.g., bright colors).

4. Ensure that the low structures are sturdy and stable; remain near the child.

5. Avoid slippery surfaces and shoes or socks that do not have adequate traction.

6. Consider safety as the child jumps.

GOAL 2   Pedals and steers tricycle

- PS2a   When sitting on a tricycle with feet on the pedals, the child pedals the tricycle forward.

- PS2b   When sitting on a tricycle with feet on the pedals, the child pedals the tricycle backward.

Objective 2.1   Pushes riding toy with feet while steering

- PS2.1a   When sitting on a riding toy with his or her feet on a surface, the child pushes forward with feet.

- PS2.1b   When sitting on a riding toy with his or her feet on a surface, the child pushes backward with feet.

Objective 2.2   Sits on riding toy or in wagon while adult pushes

IMPORTANCE OF SKILLS

These skills are important for the development of balance and coordination and for play and recreation. Sitting upright without support while on a tricycle, push-toy, or wagon develops balance. Coordination is enhanced through the reciprocal motion of pedaling, steering (eye–hand coordination), and simultaneous actions of pedaling and steering. Pedaling and steering a tricycle provide amusement, active play, and transportation, as well as some skills necessary for riding a bicycle. Other goals/objectives that can be targeted at the same time as Goal 2 are listed on the following page.

TEACHING SUGGESTIONS

Activity-Based

Nature

- Go to a playground or park. Bring along a tricycle, riding toy, or wagon. Push the child on a riding toy at the playground or park or encourage the child to sit on a riding toy and push with his or her feet while steering. Offer the tricycle for the child to ride and steer while at the park. (2, 2.1, 2.2)

- Pull the child in a wagon or bring a tricycle or riding toy for the child to ride while going for a walk around the neighborhood or when playing outdoors. Ask the child to indicate (verbally or by pointing) which direction to go. (2, 2.1, 2.2)

Travel

- Encourage the child to ride the tricycle or riding toy up and down a path, driveway, or sidewalk. (2, 2.1)

- Use the tricycle, riding toy, or wagon as transportation when traveling reasonable distances. (2, 2.1, 2.2)

Goal 2: Pedals and steers tricycle

Cognitive

D:1 Imitates motor action that is not commonly used

E:3 Navigates large object around barriers

E:4 Solves common problems

F:1.2 Uses functionally appropriate actions with objects

Social-Communication

D:3.3 Uses three-word action–object–location utterances

Social

C:2.1 Initiates communication with peer

Notes:

Playtime

- Play a game with the child and a few peers and pretend that the tricycles or riding toys are cars. Create a gas pump (i.e., use a box and garden hose) where the "cars" can fill up with gas. (2, 2.1)

- Encourage the child in imaginary play with the riding toy or tricycle (e.g., play race car driver, cowgirl, police). (2, 2.1)

- Encourage the child to play "Follow the Leader" or "Copycat" with a few peers while riding tricycles or riding toys. Allow the child and peers to take turns being the leader. (2, 2.1)

- Take an imaginary trip (e.g., pretend the riding toy is a train or car and go visit Grandma). (2, 2.1)

Environmental Arrangements

- When teaching tricycle riding, begin on a very slight incline so that pedaling is assisted by gravity and the child can concentrate on steering. (2)

- Decorate the tricycle with streamers, crepe paper, and balloons. Attach a bell or horn to the tricycle. Encourage the child to pedal and steer the decorated tricycle with peers in a parade through the neighborhood, playground, or park. (2)

- Give the child a favorite doll or stuffed animal to take for a ride. (2, 2.1, 2.2)

- Place a few obstacles in a configuration and encourage the child to pedal and steer the tricycle or steer the riding toy in and out and around the obstacles. Use cones, large blocks, or boxes to make a circle, triangle, or square. (2, 2.1)

- Begin by having the child ride short distances on a tricycle or riding toy. Gradually increase the distance as the child becomes more proficient. (2, 2.1)

- Make a road with tape or blocks on the ground for the tricycle or riding toy to follow. (2.1, 2.2)

- Place a peer in the wagon with the child. (2.2)

- Pull the child from room to room in the laundry basket. (2.2)

- Use a variety of riding toys (e.g., tyke bike, tricycle, Big Wheel, wagon). (2, 2.1, 2.2)

- Have the child ride in a grocery cart when grocery shopping. (2.2)

Instructional Sequences

- Have a peer model riding a tricycle, pushing a riding toy with his or her feet while steering or sitting on a riding toy or in a wagon. (2, 2.1, 2.2)

- Provide verbal instructions (e.g., "Push the pedals with your feet," "Turn the handle bar," "Come sit on your bike"). (2, 2.1, 2.2)
- To initially get the child moving on the tricycle, push the pedal for the child. (2)
- Push the tricycle or pull it with a rope while the child has his or her feet on the pedals and hands on the handlebars. (2.1, 2.2)
- Physically assist the child on the riding toy by pushing while the child steers. (2.1)
- Provide physical assistance by holding the child on a riding toy or wagon (i.e., place a hand on the child's back and guide the child's hands to the handle bar). (2.2)

TEACHING CONSIDERATIONS

1. If the child has a motor impairment or abnormal muscle tone, consult a physical or occupational therapist about the appropriateness of targeting these skills and about related issues.

2. If the child has a visual impairment, increase the intensity and variety of environmental support and cues (e.g., horn on riding toy or tricycle, larger seat, verbal cues, colorful tape on handlebars). Allow tactile exploration of the tricycle, riding toys, or wagon. If the child has a visual impairment, place the child on the tricycle as you hold the child's hands on the handlebars and gently pull the tricycle forward. Then, hold the child's waist and encourage the child to pedal. Continue verbal and physical prompting until the child develops steady balance and a sense of direction on the tricycle. When on a riding toy, hold the child's hands on the handlebars and encourage the child to push the toy with his or her feet. Physically help the child establish balance and direction on the toy as you verbally encourage the child.

3. If the child has a hearing impairment, increase the intensity and variety of cues (e.g., louder verbal cues, colorful attachments to tricycle and riding toy, exaggerated facial expressions and gestures).

4. Use a seat belt or padding (e.g., towels, blanket) to support the child in a wagon.

5. A tricycle that is low to the ground is easier to pedal. Attach blocks to the pedals for a child who cannot reach the pedals. Strap the child's feet to the pedals to assist the child.

6. Use an adaptive tricycle (e.g., pedal with hands or arms) with a child who has limited use of his or her legs.

7. Teach these skills in a wide open space.

8. Consider safety as the child moves about the environment. Never leave the child unattended on the riding toy.

GOAL 3 Catches, kicks, throws, and rolls ball or similar object

Objective 3.1 Catches ball or similar object

- PS3.1a When a large object is tossed to the child, he or she stretches out two arms in front.

Objective 3.2 Kicks ball or similar object

- PS3.2a Kicks a ball or similar object while holding onto support (e.g., adult's leg, wall, railing).
- PS3.2b When an object is in front of the child's feet, the child walks into the object and moves object forward.

Objective 3.3 Throws ball or similar object at target

- PS3.3a The child throws an object forward with one or two hands.
- PS3.3b The child flings an object with one hand.

Objective 3.4 Rolls ball at target

- PS3.4a Child rolls a ball.
- PS3.4b The child moves a ball forward (e.g., bats it, kicks it).

IMPORTANCE OF SKILLS

These ball-playing skills are important for enhancing strength, coordination, and balance; for creating chances for social interactions with peers; and for providing recreational opportunities (e.g., baseball, bowling, basketball, soccer). Catching, kicking, throwing, and rolling a ball helps strengthen leg and arm muscles and develop eye–hand coordination and cause-and-effect relationships. Other goals/objectives that can be targeted at the same time as Goal 3 are listed on the following page.

Goal 3: Catches, kicks, throws, and rolls ball or similar object

Gross Motor

C:3 Runs avoiding obstacles

Cognitive

C:2 Reproduces part of interactive game and/or action in order to continue game and/or action

D:1 Imitates motor action that is not commonly used

E:3.1 Moves barrier or goes around barrier to obtain object

F:1.2 Uses functionally appropriate actions with objects

Social-Communication

C:2.1 Carries out two-step direction with contextual cues

D:3 Uses three-word utterances

Social

A:2 Initiates and maintains interaction with familiar adult

A:3 Initiates and maintains communicative exchange with familiar adult

C:1 Initiates and maintains interaction with peer

C:2 Initiates and maintains communicative exchange with peer

Notes:

TEACHING SUGGESTIONS

Activity-Based

Playtime

- When playing with a ball inside or outside, roll or throw the ball back and forth between the child and yourself. Encourage the child to catch the ball in midair as well as when rolled. Place the ball on the floor or ground and encourage the child to kick it. (3, 3.1, 3.2, 3.3, 3.4)

- Play games such as kickball, soccer, and catch. Kickball and soccer require kicking, whereas a game of catch allows the child and adult to take turns throwing and catching. (3.1, 3.2, 3.3)

- When playing outside, encourage the child to throw a ball against a wall (e.g., side of a house or garage) and catch the ball as it bounces back. (3.1, 3.3)

- Toss and catch balloons. Helium-filled balloons with weights attached (e.g., pieces of candy) move slowly and are colorful and fun for children. (Remember to use caution when playing with balloons.) (3.1, 3.3)

- Use an incline (e.g., hill, driveway) for ball play. Encourage the child to roll or kick the ball up and down the incline. (3.2, 3.4)

- Take a ball to the playground or park and roll the ball up and down the slide. Kick or roll the ball back and forth to each other on the grass or cement. (3.2, 3.4)

- Choose a target such as a tree in the environment. Take turns throwing the ball at the target; keep a record of how many times each person hits the target. (3.3)

- Play "Hot potato," throwing a "hot" stuffed sock or soft ball to the child and a peer. (3.3)

- Have the child and peers sit in a large circle. Spread the children's feet and make a star by placing their feet together (adjacent feet touch). Encourage the child to roll the ball back and forth to peers, keeping the ball within the star. (3.4)

Throughout daily routines

- When folding laundry, roll up socks for the child to throw in the laundry basket. (3.3)

Environmental Arrangements

- Use a variety of balls or similar objects that can be rolled, thrown, kicked, or caught (e.g., balls of yarn, gym balls, beach balls, rolled-up socks, soft balls, beanbags, small stuffed animals, soft blocks, soccer balls). (3, 3.1, 3.2, 3.3, 3.4)

- Assist the child and a few peers to stand in a circle. Encourage the child to throw and catch the ball with peers. (3.1, 3.3)

- Have the child sit on the couch and catch pillows as you toss them. (3.1)

- With catching, allow the child to sit in a stable position before throwing the ball. Begin by using a ball that can easily be caught (e.g., a larger and lighter ball). Use a smaller and heavier ball as the child becomes more proficient. (3.1)

- Make a goal using two cones, large blocks, pillows, or boxes placed a short distance apart. Encourage the child and a few peers to kick the ball between the two objects. (3.2)

- Kick heavy balloons and watch the result. (3.2)

- Line up several chairs, one in front of another, so that the child rolls or kicks the ball through the legs of the chair. (3.2, 3.4)

- Present a household object (e.g., laundry basket, box turned on its side) that can be placed on the ground and encourage the child to roll, throw, or kick a ball or similar object into it. (3.2, 3.3, 3.4).

- Line or stack up objects that can be knocked down when the ball is rolled, thrown, or kicked; for example, place cans along a low wall or stack blocks on the ground. (3.2, 3.3, 3.4)

- Attach a hoop (e.g., coat hanger, Nerf basketball hoop) to the wall so that it is slightly lower than the child's height. Encourage the child to throw the ball through the hoop. (3.3)

- Place a large target such as a circle or square on the wall or ground (use chalk or masking tape). Encourage the child to hit the target with the ball. (3.3)

- Set up bowling pins (e.g., milk cartons, soda cans). Encourage the child to roll the ball to knock down the pins. (3.4)

- Build roads and tunnels with blocks so that the child rolls the ball on the road and through the tunnels. (3.4)

Instructional Sequences

- Model rolling and throwing a ball or similar object at a target, kicking and catching a ball; have peers demonstrate. (3, 3.1, 3.2, 3.3, 3.4)

- Begin by using a ball that can be easily rolled, thrown, or kicked by the child (e.g., large and light ball). Use a smaller and heavier ball as the child becomes more proficient. (3.2, 3.3, 3.4)

- Initially, have the child use these ball skills from a short distance; for example, have the child initially roll or throw a ball or similar object only a short distance from the target, kick the ball only a short distance, or catch a ball while standing a short distance from the person throwing the ball. Gradually increase the distance as the child becomes proficient. (3, 3.1, 3.2, 3.3, 3.4)

- Verbally direct the child to roll or throw the ball at a target, kick the ball to you, or catch the ball as you throw. When the child is catching, tell him or her to "hold arms out." (3, 3.1, 3.2, 3.3, 3.4)

- Offer minimal physical assistance to the child; for example, hold the child's hands and roll or throw the ball together. Allow the child to use some support when kicking such as holding onto your arm, a railing, the wall, or some other stable object with one hand. Physically prompt the child to catch by standing behind the child and guiding the child's hands or arms. (3, 3.1, 3.2, 3.3, 3.4)

TEACHING CONSIDERATIONS

1. If the child has a motor impairment or abnormal muscle tone, consult a physical or occupational therapist about the appropriateness of targeting this skill and about related issues.

2. If the child has a visual impairment, increase the intensity and variety of environmental support and cues (e.g., large or bright-colored ball, ball with bells inside, textured objects, contrasting target). Use balls or objects that can be easily grasped (e.g., soft ball, soft blocks). Allow tactile exploration of the ball or object. For kicking, assist the child to feel where the ball or object is located on the ground. Pair verbal encouragement with physical assistance. For rolling and throwing, use a target that makes a sound when the ball or object hits; for example, throw a ping-pong ball in a basket of many ping-pong balls. Throw a rock in a pond or river. Use another person as the target and have the person give an audible response as the ball hits the target. With catching use large, soft balls or soft objects with bells and help the child learn to be "ready" to catch the large object. Gradually withdraw physical assistance as the child becomes oriented to the ball's placement or the target.

3. If the child has a hearing impairment, increase the intensity and variety of cues (e.g., bright-colored or textured ball, louder verbal cues, contrasting target, exaggerated motions).

4. Practice this skill in a wide open space.

5. Supervise ball play carefully.

6. With kicking, avoid slippery surfaces and shoes or socks that do not have adequate traction. Make sure the ball stays still on the floor or ground. It is easier for the child to kick the ball when it is not moving.

7. Consider safety with all objects that the child handles.

Gross Motor

GOAL 4   Climbs up and down play equipment

- PS4a   The child climbs up ladders.

- PS4b   The child climbs down from adult-size furniture (e.g., chair, couch, bed).

- PS4c   The child climbs onto adult-size furniture (e.g., chair, couch, bed).

Objective 4.1   Moves up and down inclines

- PS4.1a The child moves down inclines.

- PS4.1b The child moves up inclines.

Objective 4.2   Moves under, over, and through obstacles

- PS4.2a The child moves over obstacles.

- PS4.2b The child moves through obstacles.

- PS4.2c The child moves under obstacles.

IMPORTANCE OF SKILLS

Climbing up and down play equipment or inclines and moving under, over, and through obstacles are both functional for the child and provide valuable play skills. The skills are fun and provide a good way for the child to release energy. The child develops self-awareness of how to move and control the body through space while interacting with objects and exploring the environment. Strength, balance, and coordination are developed as the child uses reciprocal motor actions in new ways to climb up and down play equipment. These skills afford the child more mobility and independence in play. Other goals/objectives that can be targeted at the same time as Goal 4 are listed on the following page.

TEACHING SUGGESTIONS

Activity-Based

Playtime

- Play a game and pretend to be firefighters. Climb up and down a ladder to put out the "fire" in a house. Wear fire hats and use a hose and buckets as props. (4)

- Take a trip to the playground or park. Encourage the child to move up and down the slide and climb up and down the play equipment (e.g., jungle gym, slide ladder, climbing bars). Use the playground equipment for the

Concurrent Goals/Objectives for Gross Motor Strand D

Goal 4: Climbs up and down play equipment

Gross Motor

D:1.2 Jumps from low structure

Cognitive

E:3.2 Moves around barrier to change location

E:4 Solves common problems

Social-Communication

D:1.2 Uses five action words

D:2.1 Uses two-word utterances to express agent–action, action–object, and agent–object

Social

C:1 Initiates and maintains interaction with peer

Notes:

Gross Motor

child to move under, over, and through obstacles; for example, have the child climb under and over jungle gym bars, crawl through and over a barrel, or move over a low platform. (4, 4.1, 4.2)

- Engage in dramatic play (e.g., mountain climbing, hiking) and use ramps and slides. (4.1)

- When playing in a sandbox, encourage the child to crawl in and out of the sandbox. (4.2)

Throughout daily routines

- When encountering ladders (e.g., stepladder, bunk-bed ladder, slide ladder) or inclines (e.g., ramps, slides) in the environment, encourage the child to climb or move up and down. (4, 4.1)

- Allow the child to move under dining and coffee tables and between and through chairs. (4.2)

Environmental Arrangements

- Use a variety of play equipment (e.g., jungle gym, ladders, climbing structures) of varying difficulty. To provide a cushion in case of falls, place the climbing structure or slide in a sandbox. Begin with play equipment that is low to the ground. As the child becomes more proficient at climbing, use play equipment that requires the child to climb higher. (4)

- Create an obstacle course in which there are a few obstacles for the child to climb up and down (e.g., stepladder, slide) and into and over (e.g., sturdy box). Add a line of chairs or a box with open ends for the child to crawl through. Allow peers to participate with the child in the obstacle course; have the children take turns as the leader. (4, 4.2)

- Make a ramp with a board or turn stairways into ramps by placing pillows on the steps. Encourage the child to move up and down the ramp or have the child slide down the pillows. (4.1)

- Make a "train" on the slide by assisting the child and one or two peers to line up one after another. Have the children move together down the slide. (4.1)

- Place a favorite toy at the top or bottom of an incline or on the other side of an obstacle. Encourage the child to move up or down the incline to obtain the toy or to obtain the toy by moving over, under, or through the obstacle. (4.1, 4.2)

- Start with a low grade when encouraging the child to go up and down inclines. As the child becomes more proficient, use steeper inclines. (4.1)

- Hold up a rope or large stick and encourage the child to move under it. (4.2)

- Place a sheet over a card table to make a tent. Encourage the child to go in, move under, and move through. (4.2)

Instructional Sequences

- Model or have peers model climbing up and down play equipment, moving up and down an incline, and moving under, over, and through obstacles. (4, 4.1, 4.2)

- If the child does not readily climb up and down play equipment, then move up and down an incline or move under, over, and through obstacles, verbally prompting the child (e.g., "You do it"). Provide specific instructions (e.g., "Put your hand on this bar," "Step up with this foot," "Get on your hands and knees," "Duck your head"). (4, 4.1, 4.2)

- Physically assist the child by providing light support at the hips or by holding his or her hand. (4, 4.1, 4.2)

TEACHING CONSIDERATIONS

1. If the child has a motor impairment or abnormal muscle tone, consult a physical or occupational therapist about the appropriateness of targeting this skill and about related issues.

2. If the child has a visual impairment, increase the intensity and variety of environmental support and cues (e.g., bright colors, large objects, contrasting objects, noise-producing objects, tactile cues, verbal cues). Initially, lead the child up and down the play equipment; up and down inclines; and over, under, and through obstacles, allowing tactile exploration of play equipment and obstacles. Be aware that the child may be fearful of moving about freely. Pair verbal encouragement with physical support as the child climbs up and down play equipment, moves up and down inclines, and moves around obstacles. Gradually withdraw physical support as the child gains confidence and becomes oriented to the equipment and obstacles. Use your voice to help the child establish direction on inclines. Physically catch the child or provide a verbal reward when the child reaches a destination.

3. If the child has a hearing impairment, increase the intensity and variety of cues (e.g., exaggerated movements, loud verbal cues, tactile cues).

4. Ensure that the play equipment, inclines, and obstacles are sturdy and stable. Stay near and supervise carefully as the child climbs on play equipment and moves under, over, and through obstacles.

5. Avoid slippery surfaces and shoes or socks that do not have adequate traction.

6. Consider safety whenever the child climbs. Never leave the child unattended when climbing.

Gross Motor

AEPS™

Adaptive Area
Birth to Three Years

LIST OF AEPS TEST ITEMS

Adaptive

173

The Adaptive Area includes goals/objectives in the areas of feeding, personal hygiene, and undressing. The skills mastered in these areas exemplify the child's growing independence, perhaps more than in any other area. The ability to meet personal needs allows the child to feel good about what he or she can do independently, fostering self-esteem.

As the child acquires abilities in eating, drinking, toileting, hand washing, teethbrushing, and undressing, the support provided by adults in caregiving activities is gradually reduced. For most adaptive activities, the caregiver initially performs the entire skill for the child. Adults hold the bottle, hold a baby to nurse, hold the cup for drinking, or manipulate the spoon for semi-solid foods. Likewise, toileting, bathing, dressing, and brushing teeth are completed with only minimal assistance from the child at first.

As each adaptive routine becomes familiar, the infant or young child learns to cooperate; for example, the child opens his or her mouth for food or pulls an arm out of a sleeve. Caregivers build on these cooperative behaviors to teach new skills and promote independence.

The balance between facilitating development of a new skill and providing ongoing assistance can be difficult to strike, especially for the child who acquires adaptive skills slowly. Both the adult and child can become accustomed to an efficient, adult-completed routine and experience difficulty affording the child time to learn the skill independently. With each developing skill, however, the caregiver should gradually decrease the amount of assistance provided, yet still provide enough support for the child to successfully complete the task.

Soon after birth, reflexive feeding behaviors develop into the basic skills required to close lips around a nipple, suck, and swallow liquids. Infants are sustained by liquid nourishment for many months, and this demands a number of coordinated skills (e.g., sucking, swallowing).

The introduction of solid foods is an important new experience, and a child may be initially negative about both the spoon and the texture of the food. The infant initially continues to use the sucking motion that efficiently takes liquid from a nipple, only to push puréed food back out of the mouth. The infant may then overreact and develop a tendency to bite down on the spoon. With practice, most young children learn to efficiently use their lips to remove semi-solid foods from the spoon and swallow.

The child who grasps at the spoon or puts hands on the bottle or breast may be indicating a readiness for finger foods. Initial attempts may be awkward because the child uses the whole hand to pick up food, and the food falls from the fist before it reaches the mouth. With practice, the child learns to coordinate picking up the food and putting it in the mouth. Sucking finger food to make it soft is eventually replaced by munching and then biting and chewing.

The infant may tend to suck or munch on the cup when it is first introduced, having successfully sucked from nipples and munched on finger foods. The child may initially pull back from the cup or inhale liquid, surprised at how easily it enters the mouth. Coughing, sputtering, and spilling are common at first, and more liquid may spill than enters the mouth. In time, sputtering and spilling decrease as the child learns to close his or her lips around the rim of the cup to prevent spilling, to regulate the amount of liquid taken in, and to swallow without dribbling. Spilling returns when the child begins to hold the cup, bring it to the mouth, and tip it to drink independently. Eventually, the child coordinates picking up and setting down the cup without spilling.

Most children master spoon feeding before learning to use a fork because the spoon is familiar, and scooping requires a less precise movement than stabbing with a fork. The child's first attempts to bring the loaded spoon to the mouth may result in most of the food falling off the spoon, but with experience the child learns to coordinate scooping and bringing the food to the mouth.

It is typical for the child who is learning to use utensils to continue to use the fingers. Similarly, when introduced to the fork, the child attempts to use it like a spoon. As more refined skills develop, the child realizes the increased advantages of using the correct utensils.

The oral-motor abilities of the infant with a neuromuscular impairment require careful evaluation by a specialist prior to the development of mealtime intervention plans. Certain reflexive patterns and high, low, or fluctuating muscle tone may interfere with the development of typical sucking, chewing, and swallowing skills. In addition, individualized prosthetic utensils and positioning aids may be necessary to support the development of self-feeding. It is critical that the child with a neuromuscular impairment receive support in learning new adaptive skills so that the experience is positive and promotes maximum independence.

Mealtime is a valuable learning time for the child and a typical social setting for families and peers. It is important for the young child to happily anticipate mealtimes and be a social participant at the table. Many of the specific suggestions in the feeding strand are aimed at creating a relaxing and positive atmosphere when teaching new feeding and eating skills. Most children will experiment with new foods and make a mess in the process. Allowing an acceptable amount of food play helps the child learn about qualities of the new foods. The nonproductive playing with food should decrease as the foods and the skills become more familiar to the child.

Toilet training requires a number of complex skills, and success relates to the child's physical and social maturity. Muscle control is necessary to regulate elimination; as the child matures, the time between eliminations increases to a couple of hours. The child gradually develops the control to stay dry or unsoiled between adult-initiated trips to the toilet.

Subtle internal signals indicating the need to go to the toilet must be recognized if the child is to "hold it" between trips. Occasional accidents are common. Eventually, the child indicates the need to eliminate and relies less on adult-initiated trips. Finally, the child independently initiates toileting and remains dry and unsoiled between trips. Remaining dry through the night is usually the last skill to develop.

Toilet training is a sensitive area for teaching and learning new skills, and sometimes it creates a struggle between the adult and the child. It is important not to pressure children about toilet training and to avoid a punishing situation for the child. Follow the child's interest and plan variations in the training schedule if the child becomes resistant.

Even after a child is toilet trained, relapses and accidents often occur. Stress, fatigue, exciting play, or new surroundings can all disrupt the toileting routine or the child's ability to read internal cues. A supportive and neutral adult attitude throughout toilet training has a positive impact on the child's success.

Hand washing is usually the child's first attempt to keep clean independently. It is helpful to teach the child the importance of clean hands for hygiene and social acceptability. A regular hand washing routine prior to meals and after toileting is critical, and adult and peer models are powerful teaching tools. When hand washing is first attempted, playing with soap and water are more common than getting the hands clean. Adult assistance should be encouraging and ensure cleanliness. The child will gradually develop the component skills and motivation to perform hand washing and drying routines independently.

Brushing teeth develops in the same manner as other adaptive skills because the child initially holds the mouth open for the adult. Care of the baby teeth can affect the permanent teeth, and a regular brushing routine helps establish a lifelong pattern of dental hygiene. Even after a child has mastered the basics of teethbrushing, an adult should assist to make sure all teeth are clean. The fine motor control required to brush all teeth thoroughly is beyond most 3-year-old children, and dentists recommend adult assistance until at least age 4.

The child learns undressing skills by first having the caregiver remove clothing. As the child becomes aware of the routine, he or she cooperates by raising and pulling arms and legs for clothing to be removed. The child also experiments with independently removing a hat, socks, and shoes. Eventually, the skills to manipulate shirts, pants, coats, and jackets enable the child to undress. Caregivers may be responsible for undoing fasteners, however, long after the child learns to remove clothing.

Undressing is included in this curriculum because the skills required to pull clothes off are less complicated than those required to put them on. Adults can foster undressing skills by approaching the task as a partnership, allowing the young child to do as much as possible and decreasing assistance to match emerging skills.

As with feeding, the consultation of a specialist is critical to the successful mastery of hygiene and undressing skills by the child with a neuromuscular impairment. Specially designed toothbrushes, soap dispensers, sinks, and clothing can promote more efficient acquisition of adaptive skills for this child and prevent unnecessary frustration for teachers, family, and the child.

Teaching skills in the Adaptive Area is fun. Many functional and motivating opportunities for the child to eat, wash, toilet, and undress occur throughout the day. Mastery of adaptive skills provides an early start to independence in home, school, and community and increases the degree to which the young child socializes and learns with peers.

Adaptive

STRAND
A

Feeding

GOAL 1   Uses tongue and lips to take in and swallow solid foods and liquids

Objective 1.1   Uses lips to take liquids from a cup and/or glass

Objective 1.2   Uses lips to take food off spoon and/or fork

Objective 1.3   Swallows solid and semi-solid foods

- PS1.3a   The child swallows solid foods.

- PS1.3b   The child swallows semi-solid foods.

Objective 1.4   Swallows liquids

IMPORTANCE OF SKILLS

Use of the tongue and lips allows the child to eat/drink a variety of foods and liquids and promotes oral motor development, which is important for the production of speech.

The child's ability to voluntarily swallow is both life sustaining and an important step toward independent eating. The suck–swallow reflex present at birth is usually inhibited at about 2 months of age and replaced by a voluntary swallowing pattern. Swallowing solid and semi-solid foods enables a child to feel a wider variety of different textures in the mouth.

Controlled lip movement is important for functional eating skills and is a step toward independent eating and drinking. Using the lips helps the child obtain and maintain liquid in the mouth and actively remove foods from eating utensils. The ability to take food from utensils and drink from cups and glasses allows the child to participate more fully in social eating activities at home and in the community. In addition, utensils can be used to eat many foods that are difficult to manage with fingers, hands, or a bottle. Coordination and control of lip movement is also vital to speech production.

The ability to take in solid foods and liquids is central to participation in social interactions with family and friends at mealtime. These skills provide the opportunity for many communicative, social, adaptive, cognitive, and fine motor skills to be practiced in a frequent and highly motivating routine. Other goals/objectives that can be targeted at the same time as Goal 1 are listed on the following page.

Concurrent Goals/Objectives for Adaptive Strand A

Goal 1: Uses tongue and lips to take in and swallow solid foods and liquids

Fine Motor

A:3.3 Grasps hand-size object with either hand using whole hand

Adaptive

A:3.2 Drinks from cup and/or glass held by adult

A:4.3 Accepts food presented on spoon

Cognitive

D:1.1 Imitates motor action that is commonly used

Social

B:1.1 Meets internal physical needs of hunger, thirst, and rest

Notes:

Adaptive

TEACHING SUGGESTIONS

Activity-Based

Feeding

- Present liquids in a cup or glass during snack and mealtimes. Put the child's favorite drink in a cup rather than a bottle. (1.1)

- Provide liquids at regular intervals during the meal, alternating between food and drinks. Take care to offer liquids more often when the child is eating salty or sticky foods. (1.1)

- Give the child opportunities to play with empty plastic cups and glasses and engage in imaginary drinking. Practice smacking lips on cup when "drinking" liquids. (1.1)

- Gain the child's attention before putting the filled spoon into the mouth. Help the child anticipate the utensil by playing lip-smacking games while bringing the food to the mouth. Encourage the child to imitate. (1.2)

- Have tea parties using toy dishes and small amounts of snacks or drinks. (1.1, 1.3)

- Offer the child opportunities to play with spoons and forks during mealtimes. Use child-size utensils and wait to introduce them until the child's initial hunger is satisfied. (1.2)

- Fill the spoon or fork and place it at the center of the child's mouth. Wait to see if the child will use lips to remove the food, rather than pull the utensil directly out of the child's mouth. (1.2)

- Give the child fruit popsicles to practice lip and tongue movements. Use foods and liquids with attractive colors to motivate the child. Present foods of appropriate size so that the child can manage easily. (1.2)

- Wait for the child to attempt to use lips and tongue to remove food that accumulates around the mouth during feeding, rather than wipe the child's face after each bite. The presence of food on the mouth may encourage the child to close lips around the food. (1.2)

- Introduce solid and semi-solid foods to the child during regular snack and mealtimes. When solids are first given, the child may use a sucking movement, similar to sucking from a bottle or breast. (1.3)

- Present solid and semi-solid foods on child-size utensils, using small bites to decrease gagging and choking. Most children initially prefer warm, but not hot, food. (1.3)

- Whenever possible, purée or grind for the child the same foods that are served to others at the meal. Introduce only one new food at any given meal. (1.3)

- Be sure the child is provided frequent opportunities to drink in addition to regular snack and mealtimes. Infants and young children should be offered liquids routinely throughout the day, even if they are not giving clear signals that they wish to eat or drink. (1.1, 1.4)

- Respond consistently to the child's cues for hunger/thirst. Present the bottle or breast on demand or according to the child's schedule of feedings. A relaxed, consistent feeding routine may facilitate swallowing in a smooth suck-swallow-breath sequence. (1.4)

- Present a variety of liquids appropriate to the child's developmental age, such as milk, juice, or water. Use the liquids that the child likes most to encourage swallowing. Smile and talk softly to the child while feeding to establish feeding as an enjoyable part of the daily routine. (1.4)

- Follow diet recommendations from family and physician to ensure that developmentally appropriate foods are used. (1, 1.1, 1.2, 1.3, 1.4)

Environmental Arrangements

- Try different types of chairs (car seat, highchair, adaptive chair) to find the upright position most comfortable for eating and drinking. (1, 1.1, 1.2)

- Present the liquid in "fun" glasses that motivate the child. Try to find glasses of favorite sizes, colors, or characters. Use a cup with a built-in straw to encourage sucking and swallowing at the same time. (1.1, 1.4)

- Try several kinds of cups such as a small, short cup that fits comfortably next to the child's lips or soft plastic that can be bent by the adult to help the child control liquid intake. Use cups that have been cut out on one side to allow the cup to be drained without the child tipping back the head. These cups also give the adult a clearer view of the child's lip movements. (1.1, 1.4)

- Start with a small amount of liquid in the cup so that the child does not have to control too much liquid too quickly. Gradually increase the amount as the child learns to drink. (1.1, 1.4)

- Establish the child's attention to the cup in anticipation of drinking. Wait for the child to open lips before bringing the cup or glass to the mouth. (1.1)

- Use thickened liquids for easier control. Provide milkshakes, nectars, yogurt thinned with juice or milk, milk thickened with pudding or cereal, or juice blended with fruit or cereal. Gradually thin drinks to normal consistency. (1.1)

- If the child is initially resistant to both the feeding utensil and new textures, then consider use of a bottle with a juice nipple to present thickened liquids. (1.1)

- Put a dab of peanut butter on child's lips and encourage the child to close his or her lips and taste it. Once the child has begun to use lips, put the dab on your finger, and wait for the child to remove it with his or her lips. Systematically move from presenting food on your finger to presenting it on a spoon and then a fork. (1.2)

- Present on forks and spoons highly reinforcing foods that are difficult to eat efficiently with hands, fingers, or a bottle. Try applesauce, mashed bananas, pudding, yogurt, mashed potatoes, and ice cream to find the child's preferences. As the child begins to use lips to take these foods, gradually introduce more lumpy foods. (1.2)

- Gradually increase the thickness of liquid foods by adding cereal or fruit. Smooth semi-solid foods such as yogurt and applesauce can be easily thickened. (1.3)

- Combining new foods with old favorites may be useful initially in getting the child to try new tastes and textures. At first, combine a small amount of the new food with a bite of familiar foods. Gradually reduce the amount of familiar food until the child is eating the new food alone. (1.3)

- Alternate solid and liquid foods during feeding. Initially, present small amounts of more solid foods toward the middle of a feeding, when the child is slightly, but not terribly, hungry. Gradually increase the amount of solid nourishment offered at each feeding. (1.3)

- Foods can be ground, chopped, or blended to allow easier swallowing. Juice, milk, or gravy can be used instead of water to thin foods without diluting taste. (1.3)

- Positioning is important to facilitate swallowing. Be careful not to recline the child too far, or choking may occur. Put the child in his or her favorite position to facilitate swallowing. (1.3, 1.4)

- For infants, try a variety of nipple sizes, materials, and shapes (e.g., orthodontic, preemie, rubber, latex) or breast shields for retracted or difficult-to-grasp nipples. (1.4)

- Bottle nipples with regular-size holes, in combination with thickened liquids, are helpful to control the amount of liquid taken with each suck. (1.4)

- Begin practicing these skills with only favorite foods. Choose a snack or mealtime with few distractions, ample time allotted, and multiple opportunities in a familiar and comfortable environment. Soft lights or music may be helpful. (1.1, 1.2, 1.3, 1.4)

- Consult a qualified speech-language, occupational, or physical therapist for advice about lip control, adaptive sucking/swallowing procedures for children with cleft lips or palate, or adaptive devices for utensils. (1.1, 1.2, 1.3, 1.4)

Instructional Sequences

- Demonstrate drinking from the cup, then give the cup to the child. The cup or glass should initially be relatively full so that the child can drink easily without tipping the head back. Gradually decrease the amount of liquid offered and assist the child in taking in more liquid at each oppor-tunity. (1.1, 1.4)

- Model the lip movements. Sitting with the child in front of a mirror may be helpful. (1.1, 1.2)

- Model swallowing food and comment about it, as in "Mmm, good." (1.3)

- If the child does not close lips when food is placed in the mouth, then ver-bally encourage the child to do so. (1.3, 1.4)

- Verbally encourage the child to drink from a cup or glass, giving specific di-rections such as, "Swallow," "Take a small sip," "Tip your head back to get to the bottom of the glass," or "Keep your lips together when you swal-low." (1.1, 1.4)

- Once food is placed in the child's mouth, touch the lips gently as a re-minder to the child. Avoid scraping the food off the utensil with the child's gum ridge, teeth, or upper lip. (1.2)

- Watch for the child to move the upper lip slightly toward the spoon or fork, then move the utensil gradually to the child's mouth. Require more lip movement before bringing each successive spoonful to the child's mouth. (1.2)

- Place the food in the child's mouth, pressing down firmly on the middle of the tongue with the utensil. Wait for the child to use the upper lip to help remove food. (1.2)

- Place food toward the back of the child's mouth to induce the child to swallow. Systematically move the food forward as the child becomes more proficient. (1.3)

- Touch the child's lips and gently stroke the child's lower jaw and neck to facilitate swallowing. (1.1, 1.4)

- Physically assist the child to place the cup between the lips, tip a small amount of liquid into the mouth, and withdraw the cup. (1.1, 1.4)

Combining or pairing different levels of instructions may be helpful when beginning to teach a new and difficult skill. Fade to less intrusive instructions as soon as possible to encourage more independent performance.

TEACHING CONSIDERATIONS

1. Seat the child in an upright position to avoid choking. Avoid hot liquids.

2. The child may prefer hardened plastic or plastic-coated utensils that do not conduct the temperature of the food and are less harsh to the sensitive areas of the lips and tongue. Use plastic-coated utensils for a child who tends to bite during feeding.

3. The child may initially refuse milk from a cup/glass or food from utensils if accustomed to drinking from the bottle or breast.

4. For the child with an oral-motor problem, consult a qualified specialist for teaching ideas.

5. Drooling is often associated with poor swallowing ability.

6. The child who is fed by gastrostomy or nasogastric tubes may also benefit from oral stimulation. Have a qualified specialist assess the child and introduce appropriate oral activities.

7. Consider safety with straws and other utensils.

8. Swallowing as addressed in this skill should be an automatic process. For this reason, any instructions used to develop the skill should be eliminated as quickly as possible.

GOAL 2   Bites and chews hard and chewy foods

- PS2a   The child chews hard and chewy foods.
- PS2b   The child bites hard and chewy foods.

Objective 2.1   Bites and chews soft and crisp foods

- PS2.1a The child chews soft and crisp foods.
- PS2.1b The child bites soft and crisp foods.

Objective 2.2   Munches soft and crisp foods

- PS2.2a The child munches crisp foods.
- PS2.2b The child munches soft foods.

IMPORTANCE OF SKILLS

Biting and chewing are necessary to make the transition from puréed foods to solid foods and may affect the ability of the growing child to receive adequate nutrition.

Before teeth emerge, a munching pattern appears, which is a precursor to chewing behavior. Munching enables the child to eat nonpuréed foods and obtain nutrition from a variety of sources, making meals and snacks more tasty and interesting. As the child develops teeth, the munching pattern is replaced by the more powerful and effective rotary jaw movements of chewing. Controlled rotary chewing also reduces the risk of choking because food is moved between the teeth and around the mouth in one mass.

The ability to bite and chew foods expands the variety of tasteful meals and snacks to include fruits, meats, and vegetables. Other goals/objectives that can be targeted at the same time as Goal 2 are listed on the following page.

TEACHING SUGGESTIONS

Activity-Based

Feeding

- Allow the child to handle hard and chewy or soft and crisp foods freely at meal and snack times, without always requiring that the food be eaten. The child may be less hesitant to bite and chew new foods if he or she becomes familiar with the texture of the foods by handling them. (2, 2.1, 2.2)

- Feed each other bites of a cracker or cookie during snack times. (2.1, 2.2)

- Make eating a relaxed and pleasant experience for the child. Use the child's preferences for foods and favorite mealtimes to introduce hard and chewy foods. (2)

- Provide regular opportunities for the child to eat hard and chewy foods, such as carrot slices, bread sticks, raw vegetables, fruit rolls, and meats during snack and mealtimes while adults and peers are eating the same foods. (2)

Environmental Arrangements

- There are many kinds of chewy foods that vary in the degree of difficulty to bite and chew. Hot dogs, ham, hard-boiled eggs, chicken, ground beef, whole grain bread, and fish are chewy. More chewy are steak, pork chops, roast beef, and bread sticks. Begin with easier foods and systematically introduce chewier and harder foods as the child begins to bite and chew. (2)

- Provide foods that are appropriate for finger feeding. The child may be more interested in trying a new and harder to eat food if finger feeding than if fed by an adult. (2, 2.1, 2.2)

- Initially introduce only a small amount of one soft and crisp or hard and chewy food at each meal. Alternate soft and crisp or hard and chewy foods with other foods and liquids that the child manages easily. Gradually introduce more soft and crisp or hard and chewy foods as the child learns to bite and chew them. (2, 2.1, 2.2)

- Begin by using foods that the child prefers to eat. Cook a small amount of a fruit, vegetable, or meat to make it soft. Gradually cook the same food less and less (with the exception of meat) to encourage the child to bite through the same food in a harder form. Apples, carrots, broccoli, celery,

Goal 2: Bites and chews hard and chewy foods

Fine Motor

A:3.1 Grasps hand-size object with either hand using the palm, with object placed toward the thumb and index finger

Adaptive

A:4.2 Eats with fingers

Cognitive

B:1 Visually follows object and/or person to point of disappearance

B:2.3 Reacts when object and/or person hides from view

D:1.1 Imitates motor action that is commonly used

E:1.2 Retains object

Social-Communication

A:2 Follows person's gaze to establish joint attention

Social

A:2.2 Responds to familiar adult's social behavior

A:3.1 Initiates communication with familiar adult

B:2.1 Responds to established social routine

Notes:

and zucchini are examples of foods that can be eaten fully cooked, partially cooked, or raw. (2, 2.1, 2.2)

- Gradually begin to toast bread to introduce a crisp texture, toasting longer and longer until the child can eat a piece of crisp toast. (2.1, 2.2)

- Once a child has begun to manage some soft and crisp foods, snacks such as peeled and pitted peaches, melons, and berries; peanut butter crackers; and occasional pie, cake, and cookies are tasty choices for encouraging the child to practice biting and chewing. After the child takes a bite, encourage him or her to move food from side to side in the mouth with the tongue. (2.1, 2.2)

- There are many kinds of crisp foods that vary in the degree of difficulty to bite and chew. Saltine crackers, rice cakes, celery sticks, apples, and Cheerios are crisp. More crisp are melba toast, potato chips, raw carrots, and corn chips. Begin with easier foods and systematically introduce crispier foods as the child begins to bite and chew. (2.1)

- Provide foods that melt, crumble, or disintegrate easily, such as teething cookies, zwieback, or graham crackers, to give the child the feel of soft and crisp foods without having to take a large mass into the mouth at once. (2.2)

- The transition to soft and crisp foods that require munching can begin with the addition of "lumps" to puréed foods. Fruit pieces in yogurt, cooked macaroni in mashed vegetables, or commercial "junior" baby foods are easy to introduce at regular mealtimes. (2.2)

Instructional Sequences

- Gain the child's attention before putting the food into the child's mouth. Help the child anticipate the food by playing lip-smacking games while bringing the food to mouth. (2, 2.1, 2.2)

- Model munching or biting and chewing. Munch soft and crisp foods, bite through hard and chewy foods moving the jaw up, down, and in a rotary motion. Encourage the child to imitate, using a mirror if necessary. (2, 2.1, 2.2)

- Verbally encourage the child to imitate munching motion ("Keep munching," "Up and down with your teeth") or verbally encourage the child to bite through hard and chewy or soft and crisp foods and chew each bite ("Bite hard," "One bite at a time," "Keep chewing"). (2, 2.1, 2.2)

- Physically assist the child to bite by placing food between child's side teeth or front teeth and applying gentle pressure on the chin. Gently stroke the child's lips and chin to facilitate munching. (2, 2.1, 2.2)

Adaptive

TEACHING CONSIDERATIONS

1.   Seat the child in an upright position to avoid choking.

2.   When the child is biting hard and chewy food, make sure the child chews thoroughly and swallows before taking another bite.

3.   The child may initially refuse to eat hard and chewy foods if accustomed to drinking/eating only liquid, soft, or crisp foods.

4.   Use plastic-coated utensils for children who tend to bite during feeding. Insert spoon only partially into the mouth to avoid gagging.

5.   The child may prefer plastic utensils that do not conduct the temperature of the food and are less harsh than metal to the sensitive areas of the lips and tongue.

6.   The child may initially refuse food with texture (lumps) if accustomed to eating only puréed, strained, or liquid foods.

7.   For the child with an oral-motor problem, consult a qualified specialist for teaching ideas.

8.   The child who is fed by gastrostomy or nasogastric tubes may also benefit from oral stimulation. Have a qualified specialist assess the child and introduce appropriate oral activities.

9.   Have the child with a visual impairment touch the hard and chewy foods as you describe them.

GOAL 3   Drinks from cup and/or glass

- PS3a   The child drinks from a cup or glass by bringing it up to the mouth without spilling. The child may release the cup before returning it to the surface.

Objective 3.1   Drinks from cup and/or glass with some spilling

Objective 3.2   Drinks from cup and/or glass held by adult

- PS3.2a The child sucks and swallows from bottle or breast.

IMPORTANCE OF SKILLS

The ability to drink from a cup allows the child greater independence in managing physical needs. The child learns to manage the amount of liquid intake by coordinating lip movements with tipping the cup while holding it. Eye–hand coordination is also developed as the child picks up the cup, brings it to the mouth, and returns the cup to the surface without spilling. Drinking from a cup without spilling is a desirable skill for eating meals and snacks in social situations (e.g., restaurants, school, friends' and relatives' homes). Other goals/objectives that can be targeted at the same time as Goal 3 are listed on the following page.

TEACHING SUGGESTIONS

Activity-Based

Feeding

- Offer drinks from a favorite cup when the child indicates thirst or at times when the child usually nurses. Provide repeated opportunities to drink from a cup or glass at snack and mealtimes. Expect some spilling at first. (3, 3.1, 3.2)

- Put the child's favorite liquid in a cup or glass. Provide drinks in cups at regular intervals when children are playing outside, especially during physical activities like tumbling, running, swimming, and riding tricycles. (3, 3.1, 3.2)

- Make a game of copying each other and taking turns as you sip juice, milk, or water. Model cup drinking, and let the child practice where spilling is okay. (3.1)

- Provide the child opportunities to observe other people drinking from cups and glasses. As the child becomes interested, offer a sip from your drink. Make a game of taking sips from an adult's cup or glass using milk, juice, or water. (3.2)

Playtime

- Have a tea party for the child and peers, dolls, and stuffed animals to encourage drinking from cups and glasses. A picnic is also a fun activity that can feature special drinks and foods. (3, 3.1, 3.2)

Environmental Arrangements

- Positioning is important to allow the child to grasp, tip, and return the cup to the table without spilling. Use table and chairs or highchair with tray to provide comfortable support in an upright position while the child's forearms rest on the table or tray. (3, 3.1)

- Select cups or glasses that are an appropriate size and weight for the child. Present liquid in "fun" cups of interesting designs and colors or familiar characters. (3, 3.1)

- Cups with handles are easier for the child to grasp. Weighted cups (tippee cups) are easier to release without spilling. Begin by using weighted cups with handles and move to regular glasses as the child becomes more proficient. Avoid plastic glasses that tip easily. (3, 3.1)

- Transparent cups help the child anticipate the changing level of liquid while drinking. (3, 3.1)

Adaptive

Goal 3: Drinks from cup and/or glass

Fine Motor

A:3.2 Grasps cylindrical object with either hand by closing fingers around it

A:5.3 Releases hand-held object onto and/or into a larger target with either hand

Adaptive

A:5.1 Pours liquid between containers

Social-Communication

B:1 Gains person's attention and refers to an object, person, and/or event

Social

A:3 Initiates and maintains communicative exchange with familiar adult

Notes:

- Use cups that have been cut out on one side to allow the cup to be drained without the child tipping head back. These cups also give the adult a clearer view of the child's lip movements. (3, 3.1, 3.2)

- Experiment with the optimal amount of liquid for each child. Try filling the cup only one third full to give the child less liquid to control and less weight to manage. (3, 3.1, 3.2)

- Try a cup that is relatively full so that the child can drink easily without tipping head back. Gradually decrease the amount of liquid so that the child learns to drink all of the liquid from the glass without spilling. (3, 3.1)

- Begin by using preferred liquids or "special" drinks such as a milkshake from a restaurant. Gradually introduce a variety of liquids in the glass or cup. (3.2)

- Establish the child's attention to the cup before bringing it to the child's mouth. Use encouraging facial expressions and vocalizations to prepare the child to drink from the cup as you hold it. Raise your eyebrows, purse or smack your lips, and say, "Mmm" or "Yummy." (3.2)

- Alternate drink with food to make the child more thirsty. Stop offering the cup if the child resists or loses interest. (3.2)

- Consult a qualified speech-language, occupational, or physical therapist for advice about adaptive devices and procedures for drinking. (3, 3.1, 3.2)

Instructional Sequences

- Model drinking from a cup or have peers and siblings demonstrate cup drinking at snack and mealtimes. (3, 3.1)

- Verbally encourage the child to drink the liquid from the cup as you tip it upward or have the child bring the cup up to the mouth, drink, and put the cup back on the table; for example, place the rim of the cup on the child's lower lip. Verbally encourage the child to drink the liquid from the cup as you tip it upward, being careful not to cause the child to lean backward. (3, 3.1, 3.2)

- Stroke the child's throat gently to facilitate swallowing after the child takes in liquid from a cup held to the lips. (3.2)

- Stand behind the child. Let the child see the liquid in the cup first. Physically guide the child's hand to lift the cup toward the mouth, drink from the cup, and put it down on the table. (3, 3.1, 3.2)

TEACHING CONSIDERATIONS

1. Seat the child in an upright position to avoid choking.

2. The child may initially refuse to drink liquids from a cup or glass if accustomed to drinking only from the breast or bottle.

3. Be prepared for frequent spills. Use bibs or towels, and have a mop handy!

4. For the child with an oral-motor problem, consult a qualified specialist for teaching ideas.

5. A child who is fed by gastrostomy or nasogastric tubes may also benefit from oral stimulation. Have a qualified specialist assess the child and introduce appropriate oral activities.

6. Have the child with a visual impairment feel the cup or glass as you assist in drinking.

GOAL 4   Eats with fork and/or spoon

- PS4a   The child eats by stabbing food with a fork.

- PS4b   The child eats by scooping with a spoon and/or fork.

Objective 4.1   Brings food to mouth using utensil

Objective 4.2   Eats with fingers

Objective 4.3   Accepts food presented on spoon

IMPORTANCE OF SKILLS

The ability to independently bring food to the mouth and eat using utensils allows the child to feel grown up and competent and allows independence from caregivers. The child begins by accepting food presented on a spoon, which increases the variety of foods that the child can eat. This skill promotes attention to and interaction with the person who is presenting the spoon, which provides a positive and regular setting for building social skills. Eating with fingers is an independent eating skill that is used for a lifetime. It facilitates the development of the pincer grasp and chewing skills. The child gains further independence in eating by using a fork or spoon to eat foods that are difficult to eat with fingers. By bringing the utensil to the mouth, the child develops eye–hand coordination and fine motor control. This skill involves combining and coordinating many complex motor behaviors.

Using these skills, the child can be involved formally in mealtimes at home and in the community, and these provide excellent opportunities to learn table manners and socialize. Other goals/objectives that can be targeted at the same time as Goal 4 are listed on the following page.

Goal 4: Eats with fork and/or spoon

Fine Motor

B:1.1 Turns object over using wrist and arm rotation with each hand

Cognitive

F:1.2 Uses functionally appropriate actions with objects

Social-Communication

C:2.3 Carries out one-step direction with contextual cues

D:1.1 Uses five descriptive words

Social

B:2.1 Responds to established social routine

C:1.4 Observes peers

Notes:

Assessment, Evaluation, and Programming System for Infants and Children (AEPS®), Second Edition,
edited by Diane Bricker © 2002 Paul H. Brookes Publishing Co., Inc. All rights reserved.

Adaptive

TEACHING SUGGESTIONS

Activity-Based

Feeding

- Give the child a spoon to hold while you feed the child. Allow the child to play with and manipulate the spoon; encourage a few independent bites. Be prepared for some mess! (4.1)

- Provide a fork or spoon with food that can be scooped during snack and mealtimes. It may be necessary to scoop the food for the child. Encourage the child to bring a filled spoon to the mouth and eat. Use favorite foods to motivate the behavior. (4.1)

- Provide various finger foods during snack and mealtimes. Encourage the child to grasp food and eat. Use easy-to-grasp foods such as breadsticks, crackers, or string beans. (4.2)

- Introduce finger feeding by letting the child lick fingers and hands after dipping them in favorite foods. Take turns feeding the child finger food and having the child feed you. Include giving bites to dolls or stuffed animals. (4.2)

- Gain the child's attention before putting the filled spoon into the mouth. Help the child anticipate the utensil by playing lip-smacking games while bringing the food to mouth. (4.3)

- Provide the child many opportunities to observe others eating semi-solid foods (e.g., applesauce, pudding, yogurt) from spoons. If the child opens and closes mouth, smacks lips, or sucks lips/tongue while watching someone else eat with a spoon, then offer a very small bite. (4.3)

- Before presenting a utensil, allow the child to dip fingers into semi-solid foods such as cereal, applesauce, and yogurt and suck the food off. (4.3)

- Present food in a small amount on a spoon during regular snack and mealtimes. Most children will open their mouth as the spoon approaches and use a suck-swallow pattern to remove the food from the spoon. Formula or breast milk thickened with cereal or fruit are often the earliest foods to be spoon fed. (4.3)

- Once the use of utensils has been introduced, practice using spoons with applesauce, yogurt, pudding, and ice cream, which are reinforcing snacks. Chunks of meat, fruit, or vegetables are best for stabbing. (4, 4.1, 4.2, 4.3)

- Include the child in family meals and snacks. Have the child observe others using utensils. Specific eating skills should be included as part of an enjoyable mealtime experience. Making meals a regular time of information sharing and social interaction facilitates development of socially appropriate eating behaviors. (4, 4.1, 4.2, 4.3)

Playtime

- Provide opportunities for the child to use eating utensils during play. Have the child pretend to cook, serve, and eat food when playing with play-dough, water, cornmeal, and sand. Set the child's place with utensils, plate, and bowl, and encourage the child to use them. (4)

- Allow the child to explore spoons of all sizes as toys before using them as tools. Mouthing is a predominant form of early exploration. Dip the spoon in food and let the child suck on the spoon in the course of manipulation and exploration. (4.1)

Environmental Arrangements

- To practice eating with utensils, use sticky foods such as oatmeal, peanut butter, and mashed potatoes that stay on the spoon or fork allowing the child to maintain a grasp until the food gets to the mouth. Expect some spilling. Gradually introduce more difficult foods to scoop and spear, to provide practice and variety for the child. (4, 4.1)

- Give the child small portions to help reduce spills. Have the child ask for more and practice using larger utensils to transfer food from serving bowls to eating bowls. (4)

- Stabbing chunks of food may be easier for some children than scooping with a spoon. (4)

- Plates with special features, such as suction cup bases and high rims, may facilitate scooping. Bowls may be easier than plates to manipulate. (4)

- Alternate use of utensils with finger feeding or being fed by an adult. Introduce utensils toward the middle of a meal when the child is still hungry but less likely to be frustrated by the slowness of using a spoon. (4.1)

- The size of food should facilitate grasping and require less chewing. Foods such as raw vegetables should be presented after crackers, bread pieces, cereal, cheese, and bananas have been mastered. (4.2)

- Play hide-and-seek games with small cookies, crackers, or cereal. Place them under cups or napkins, and have the child find and eat them before you hide other pieces. (4.2)

- Try different types of chairs (e.g., car seat, highchair, adaptive chair) to find the upright position most comfortable for introducing utensils. (4.3)

- Begin introducing the spoon with only favorite foods. Choose a snack or mealtime with few distractions, ample time allotted, and multiple opportunities in a familiar and comfortable environment. Soft lights or music may be helpful. (4.3)

- Lighting and position should permit the child to see the food on the spoon as it approaches the mouth. Establish the child's attention to the spoon before touching it to the mouth. (4.3)

Adaptive

- Foods should be at the appropriate temperature: not too hot or too cold. Try spoons of various sizes and shapes. Offer semi-solid foods first and move to solid foods. (4.3)

- Put a dab of peanut butter on the child's lips and encourage the child to close lips and taste it. Once the child has begun to use lips, put the dab on fingers and wait for the child to remove it with lips. (4.3)

- Systematically move from presenting food on the child's fingers to your finger, then to a spoon. (4.3)

- Try utensils of various materials, sizes, and designs (built-up or bent handles) to find those that work best for the child. (4, 4.1, 4.2, 4.3)

- Consult a qualified speech-language, occupational, or physical therapist for advice about adaptive utensils. (4, 4.1, 4.2, 4.3)

Instructional Sequences

- Model eating with a spoon or fork. Exaggerate opening your mouth to accept the spoon and closing your mouth to remove food. Have siblings and peers model eating from a spoon or fork. (4, 4.1, 4.2, 4.3)

- Present the food and verbally instruct the child to pick it up, scoop or stab it, and bring it to the mouth to eat. (4, 4.1, 4.2)

- Use verbal and facial cues to help the child anticipate the spoon and open the mouth to take in food. Say "Aaahh" while opening mouth wide and "Mmmm" as you place the spoon in the mouth. (4.3)

- Stand behind the child and put the child's hand on the handle of utensil. Scoop the food, and guide it to the child's mouth. (4, 4.1)

- Place finger food in the child's hand and guide it toward the mouth as you encourage the child. (4.2)

- Once the child is attending to the spoon, gently stroke or tap the child's lips to encourage the child to open his or her mouth. Place the spoon on the tongue and slowly remove it, pulling straight out, to leave food in the mouth. (4.3)

TEACHING CONSIDERATIONS

1. Seat the child in an upright position to avoid choking.

2. Provide postural support to allow the child to concentrate on eating skills. Make sure that the child's feet, back, and hips are well supported so that balance is stable and arms are free for eating.

3. The child may initially refuse to use utensils if accustomed to eating/drinking only from the breast, bottle, or with fingers.

4. The child may prefer plastic or plastic-coated utensils that do not conduct the temperature of the food and are less harsh to the sensitive areas of the lips and tongue. Use plastic-coated utensils for the child who tends to bite during feeding.

5. For the child with an oral-motor problem, consult a qualified specialist for teaching ideas.

6. A child who is fed by gastrostomy or nasogastric tubes may also benefit from oral stimulation. Have a qualified specialist assess the child and introduce appropriate oral activities.

7. Have the child with a visual impairment feel the utensils before using them with food. Describe what the child is touching.

GOAL 5   Transfers food and liquid between containers

Objective 5.1   Pours liquid between containers

- PS5.1a Child empties container of liquid or solids by dumping contents (child holds container and rotates wrists to empty it).

Objective 5.2   Transfers food between containers

- PS5.2a The child uses a utensil to remove food from a bowl or plate.

IMPORTANCE OF SKILLS

The skill of transferring food and liquid is an important step toward independent eating. It allows the child more opportunities to participate in group activities and interact with others.

The ability to transfer food and pour liquid is the basis for many leisure and daily living skills used throughout life. Transferring food using a utensil is a useful skill for cooking and gardening. Pouring liquid from one container into another involves the coordination of fine motor control, an understanding of spatial relations, and the anticipation of the movement of the liquid. Pouring water is a form of play enjoyed by most children, providing recreational opportunities in addition to increased independence in meeting physical needs.

These skills enable the child to function more independently during mealtime activities, increasing opportunities to interact with other people in socially appropriate ways. Other goals/objectives that can be targeted at the same time as Goal 5 are listed on the following page.

Adaptive

Goal 5: Transfers food and liquid between containers

Fine Motor

A:5.2 Places and releases object balanced on top of another object with either hand

Adaptive

B:3 Brushes teeth

Social-Communication

B:1 Gains person's attention and refers to an object, person, and/or event

B:2 Uses consistent word approximations

C:2.1 Carries out two-step direction with contextual cues

Social

A:3 Initiates and maintains communicative exchange with familiar adult

B:2.1 Responds to established social routine

C:2 Initiates and maintains communicative exchange with peer

Notes:

TEACHING SUGGESTIONS

Activity-Based

Feeding

- Provide regular opportunities for the child to practice pouring. Offer drinks during outside play, picnics, and regular snack and mealtimes, and have the child pour from a pitcher into individual glasses. (5, 5.1)

Playtime

- Include toy pitchers, cups, and tall containers of various sizes in the sink, bathtub, wading pool, or water table. Let the child practice filling and dumping from one container to another. (5, 5.1)

- Have a tea party for the child and peers, dolls, or stuffed animals. Have the child take turns pouring pretend drinks and serving pretend food with utensils for guests, to practice the transferring motion without having to control actual foods and liquids. (5, 5.1, 5.2)

Nature

- Include the child in gardening activities; have the child dig scoops of dirt and transfer them to a bucket. (5.2)

Throughout daily routines

- Include the child in simple cooking chores. The child can pour water and the box of Jell-O into a bowl for Jell-O, pour soup into a pan to heat, and pour milk and spoon flour and sugar into cake batter. Doing the dishes afterward provides more pouring opportunities to transfer liquids. (5, 5.1, 5.2)

Environmental Arrangements

- Use pourable solids to introduce the pouring motion. Children can pour sand, cornmeal, macaroni, beans, rice, and cereal from one container to the other, using the same tipping motion with the wrist that is required to pour liquids. Start with larger items (cereal, beans) and systematically introduce smaller particles (rice, cornmeal, sand). (5, 5.1)

- Squeeze-bottles are easy to control when first practicing pouring because they are lightweight and retain liquid when tipped. (5.1)

- Begin pouring activities by using thick liquids (smoothies, milkshakes, ketchup) that pour slowly. As the child gains control over tipping the container to start and stop the flow of liquid, gradually introduce thinner liquids. (5.1)

- Use a small container and fill it half full of liquid. A measuring cup with a handle and spout may be easiest for a child to first learn to pour. (5.1)

Adaptive

- Use a heavy container with a sturdy base as a receptacle so the child will not tip it over when pouring. (5.1)

- Include toy bowls, plates, and utensils of all types in the sandbox and garden and on the cornmeal table. Let the child practice transferring dirt, sand, and cornmeal from one container to another. (5.2)

- Begin by letting the child transfer finger foods such as toast and fruit chunks. Introduce a spoon or fork after the child has established transferring food by hand. (5.2)

- Use bigger serving utensils that may be easier for the child to manipulate. (5.2)

- Use foods such as mashed potatoes, pudding, casseroles, applesauce, and yogurt that stick to the serving utensil. As the child becomes more proficient at transferring food, introduce drier and less sticky foods. (5.2)

- Arrange special snacks that allow opportunities to transfer food. Cut bananas in chunks rather than offer them whole; cut strawberry or peach slices to spoon onto a dish one or two at a time. (5.2)

Instructional Sequences

- Model pouring liquid into a container. Have peers and siblings demonstrate pouring in a group activity like filling a large pot with water. (5.1)

- Model or have peers and siblings model transferring food with utensils. (5.2)

- Verbally instruct the child to pour liquid from a small container to a cup by offering details ("Tip the cup down," "Pour slowly," "Tip it back up now"). (5.1)

- Verbally instruct the child to use a spoon or fork to transfer food from a bowl to a plate by offering details ("Slide the spoon under the food," "Pick it up," "Put it on the other plate"). (5.2)

- Help the child pick up the container and offer minimal physical assistance to guide the pouring movement. Try to prompt only the initial tipping of the container to pour or to stop pouring. (5, 5.1)

- Use minimal physical assistance to hold the child's hand around the utensil, then scoop and transfer the food. You may need to stabilize the bowl or plate that receives the food. (5.2)

TEACHING CONSIDERATIONS

1. The child should be seated or standing in a supported, balanced position so that concentration is on the fine motor activity of pouring.

2. Avoid heavy or breakable containers and hot liquids.

3. Provide smock, bib, and floor covering; be prepared to mop up spills when the child is first learning this skill.

4. For the child with a motor impairment, consult a qualified specialist for teaching ideas.

5. Have the child with a visual impairment feel the pitcher and receptacle with hands before actually pouring solids or liquids. Describe the object that the child is touching.

Personal Hygiene

GOAL 1   Initiates toileting

- PS1a   The child initiates toileting in unfamiliar and seldom-visited community settings (e.g., store, park, restaurant, doctor's office).

- PS1b   The child initiates toileting in familiar, frequently visited out-of-home settings (e.g., car, grandparent's or neighbor's house, classroom).

- PS1c   The child initiates toileting in most familiar and frequent settings with regular caregivers (e.g., home with caregiver, child care, classroom, extended family member's home).

Objective 1.1   Demonstrates bowel and bladder control

- PS1.1a   The child sits on a potty chair or toilet regularly and accomplishes bowel and bladder functions some of the time.

- PS1.1b   The child sits on a potty chair or toilet regularly, without necessarily accomplishing bowel or bladder function.

Objective 1.2   Indicates awareness of soiled and wet pants and/or diapers

IMPORTANCE OF SKILLS

Independence in toileting is viewed by parents and professionals as an important adaptive skill. Awareness of wet or soiled pants and the ability to control the bowel and bladder is essential for a child to independently take care of toileting needs. These are motivating factors for the child to become toilet trained. The child gains independence from the caregiver, allowing the caregiver freedom from a frequent and messy chore. Along with allowing the child to function more independently, being toilet trained decreases the behaviors that set the developmentally young child apart from other children and thus increases social acceptability. Other goals/objectives that can be targeted at the same time as Goal 1 are listed on the following page.

Concurrent Goals/Objectives for Adaptive Strand B

Fine Motor

B:4 Orients picture book correctly and turns pages one by one

Gross Motor

B:2.2 Maintains a sitting position in chair

Adaptive

C:1.3 Takes off pants

Social-Communication

B:2 Uses consistent word approximations

C:2 Carries out two-step direction without contextual cues

C:2.2 Carries out one-step direction without contextual cues

D:1.1 Uses five descriptive words

Social

A:3.1 Initiates communication with familiar adult

B:2.1 Responds to established social routines

Notes:

Adaptive

TEACHING SUGGESTIONS

Activity-Based

Toileting

- Take the child to the bathroom during established, toileting routines. Prior to taking the child to the toilet, ask if the child needs to use the toilet. (1, 1.1)

- Encourage the child to indicate whenever he or she needs to use the toilet. When you take the child to a new place, indicate the location of the bathroom and tell the child to let you or another adult know if he or she needs to use the toilet. (1, 1.1)

- Whenever reasonable, make use of natural consequences for being wet or soiled; for example, require a change to dry clothes before allowing the child to sit on your lap, eat lunch, ride in the car, or play with peers. (1, 1.1)

- Allow the child to follow an adult or peer into the bathroom; let the child sit on the potty chair at the same time someone else is using the bathroom. (1.1)

- If the child informs you verbally or by gesturing that his or her pants are wet or soiled, then reinforce the child by changing his or her pants quickly. (1.2)

- When you notice that the child has wet or soiled pants, ask what happened and then pause and wait for an indication that pants are wet or soiled. Provide gestures and facial expressions to indicate that being wet or soiled is unpleasant. Change the child's pants as soon as possible to prevent the child from becoming comfortable in soiled pants. Wash the child's hands, as you wash yours, after changing. (1.2)

- As you change the child's diaper, clearly label it as "wet" or "soiled." Have the child repeat the label with an appropriate sign, gesture, or word. After changing, label the diaper or pants as clean and dry. Use unpleasant and pleasant facial expressions and voice tone to emphasize wet or soiled and dry or clean, respectively. (1.2)

- Use the labels "clean," "dry," and "soiled" to describe objects and events throughout the day; for example, label muddy shoes as "soiled," washed and dried hands as "clean and dry," and a bath sponge as "wet." Exposure to more examples of clean, dry, and soiled may assist the child in developing terms to describe diapers or pants. (1.2)

Throughout daily routines

- At various times throughout the day, pair using the toilet with a regularly occurring activity; for example, before taking a nap, going for a ride in the car, going outside to play, or after waking from a nap or night's sleep, ask the child about using the bathroom. (1, 1.1)

Environmental Arrangements

- Provide child-size potty chairs or toilet seats so that the child is secure and comfortable when going to the bathroom. (1, 1.1)

- Dress the child in training pants during waking hours. Training pants are easier for the child to remove independently and are less absorbent than diapers. This may motivate the child to initiate toileting to avoid drippy, soaked clothes. (1, 1.1, 1.2)

- At routine toileting times during the school day, have children line up to go to the bathroom. (1, 1.1)

- Obtain a schedule of the child's regular elimination times. Record each time elimination occurs during the day. If the schedule shows a pattern of toilet times, then sit the child on the toilet just prior to these times. (1, 1.1, 1.2)

- Dress the child in easy-to-remove outer pants to avoid struggles with clothing and to allow easier undressing for the child who goes independently to the toilet. (1)

- Provide opportunities for the child to observe other children initiating and going to the toilet. Sit the child on a potty chair next to a peer who is using the toilet, allowing the child to observe what the peer is doing. While the child is sitting on the potty chair, run water from the faucet. The sound of running water may trigger the child to urinate. (1, 1.1, 1.2)

- Provide washable books or lap toys near the potty chair or toilet to occupy the child while sitting. Initially, require a brief period of sitting and gradually increase the time as the child becomes accustomed to the activity. (1, 1.1)

- Increase the amount of liquids and fiber in the child's diet to increase the number of times the child will need to use the toilet. (1, 1.1)

- Some children may find more discomfort in a soiled diaper than a wet diaper. Begin by verbally making the child aware of soiled diapers and then wet diapers. (1.2)

- To help the child gain awareness, describe other indicators of wet or soiled diapers. Ask if the child smells something. Ask if the child sees wet pants in the mirror, hears the squish of a wet diaper when sitting, or hears the rattle of a wet plastic diaper. Combine multiple cues to help the child identify wet or soiled pants. (1.2)

- Cloth diapers make it easier for the child to feel wetness and become aware of urinating. Whenever possible use cloth diapers to work on this skill. (1.2)

If this goal is particularly difficult for a child, then it may be necessary, within activities, to use an instructional sequence.

Adaptive

Instructional Sequences

- Have an adult or peer model using the toilet. Ask the child at the same time if he or she needs to go the toilet. (1, 1.1)

- For the child who demonstrates bowel and bladder control, physically direct the child to the toilet on a regular schedule. If the child squirms or crosses legs at other times, then ask, "Do you need to go to the bathroom?" and take the child to the toilet. (1)

- Provide verbal direction for the child to use the toilet such as a word, sign, or gesture as a cue that the diaper is wet or soiled. Model the cue and have the child imitate before changing pants. (1, 1.1, 1.2)

- Acknowledge the child's wet or soiled diaper by labeling. (1.2)

- To encourage awareness of soiled or wet pants, place the child on the toilet for 5 minutes on a regular schedule (at least once every hour). Give the child a drink of water 10–20 minutes before this time. (1, 1.1)

- Physically direct the child to look at or touch the diaper and label it as wet or soiled. (A soiled diaper is usually also wet, so have the child touch the wet part only.) Wash the child's hands immediately after changing. (1.2)

   Combining or pairing different levels of instruction may be helpful when beginning to teach a new and difficult skill. Fade to less intrusive instructions as soon as possible to encourage more independent performance.

TEACHING CONSIDERATIONS

1. Toilet training requires family involvement. Be sure toilet training is a priority at home before requiring the skill at school.

2. Consult with the family to determine how they refer to toileting needs (e.g., potty, toilet, bathroom). Use the same words when the child is practicing toileting.

3. Generally, a child gains bladder control before bowel control and becomes daytime trained before nighttime.

4. In order for the child to become toilet trained, he or she must have sphincter control. Consult with medical personnel if there are concerns about sphincter muscles or urological disorders.

5. Some children do not become aware of wet or soiled pants until after gaining bowel and bladder control. For these children, it is advisable to work on Objective 1.2 and Objective 1.1 simultaneously.

6. When training a male child, teach him to sit rather than stand to urinate. He can learn to urinate standing after he learns to distinguish between the need to urinate and to have a bowel movement.

7. Teach the child who is nonverbal a manual sign, signal, or gesture to use to initiate or request toileting.

8. Consult an occupational or physical therapist for adaptations and positions for the child with a motor impairment. Adaptive toileting equipment may be needed.

9. Be prepared to change pants and sometimes socks as the child learns to toilet independently.

10. For the child who has no feeling in the genital area, teach awareness of a wet or soiled diaper by smell or vision.

11. After toileting (or diaper change) is a good time to practice the adaptive skill of washing hands.

GOAL 2   Washes and dries hands

- PS2a   The child washes and rinses and dries hands effectively with a towel.

- PS2b   The child washes hands with soap, rinses with water, and rubs hands on towel without necessarily drying them.

Objective 2.1   Washes hands

- PS2.1a   The child makes attempts to rinse hands after washing with soap.

- PS2.1b   The child grasps soap and rubs it on his or her hands.

- PS2.1c   The child places his or her hands under running water or in a sink full of water.

IMPORTANCE OF SKILLS

As the child learns to wash and dry his or her own hands, the child begins to develop independence in grooming. This is important, as the child no longer depends on the caregiver to always be available to wash and dry hands. It is also important that the child develops good personal hygiene habits because washing hands helps stop the spread of germs. A clean appearance is socially acceptable and will help the child be more readily accepted by peers and adults. Washing hands also helps the child develop motor control and is a functional activity for practicing many fine motor skills. Other goals/objectives that can be targeted at the same time as Goal 2 are listed on the following page.

Goal 2: Washes and dries hands

Fine Motor

A:5.3 Releases hand-held object onto and/or into a larger target with either hand

B:1 Rotates either wrist on horizontal plane

Cognitive

E:4 Solves common problems

Social-Communication

C:2.1 Carries out two-step direction with contextual cues

C:2.3 Carries out one-step direction with contextual cues

Social

B:1 Meets observable physical needs in socially appropriate ways

B:2.1 Responds to established social routines

Notes:

TEACHING SUGGESTIONS

Activity-Based

Playtime

- Encourage activities that will get the child's hands messy and require them to be washed after the activity. Some fun messy activities are finger painting, playing in the dirt, spreading shaving cream over a table surface, making playdough, and cooking. (2, 2.1)

- Play imaginary games and sing songs such as "This is the way we wash our hands . . ." (2, 2.1)

Throughout daily routines

- As the child goes through the daily routine and encounters situations that require clean hands, pause and wait for the child to independently wash and dry hands. Ask, "What do we do to clean up?" This may be accompanied by the adult washing and drying hands, too. (2, 2.1)

- Provide opportunities for the child to wash and dry dishes, dolls, and toys. The child can practice washing and drying objects and his or her own hands. (2, 2.1)

- Establish hand washing as a part of regular daily activities, as in before and after eating, after toileting, before bedtime, while taking a bath, and after engaging in a messy activity. (2, 2.1)

Environmental Arrangements

- Water activities (e.g., washing dishes, floating boats) can be used to give the child opportunities to dry his or her own hands during and after the activity. (2, 2.1)

- Towels that are attached to a rack or holder may be easier for the child to manipulate. (2, 2.1)

- Colorful towels or towels with favorite characters can be used to encourage hand drying. (2, 2.1)

- Some environmental adaptations can make the skill easier. Faucet knobs that turn are easier for a child to operate than those that pull. (2, 2.1)

- Practice hand "rubbing" by allowing the child to apply hand lotion or baby powder after hands are clean. This gives a visual cue to "get all the spots" and is usually a pleasant treat. (2, 2.1)

- If the sink or towel is too high for the child to reach, then have a sturdy stool available for the child to stand on. (2, 2.1)

- Soap in a pump dispenser may be easier to use than a large bar of soap or powdered soap in a push-up dispenser. Also, small bars of soap (hotel size) are easier to handle than large ones. (2, 2.1)

Instructional Sequences

- Have an adult or peer model washing and drying hands, and have the child imitate the steps (e.g., turn on water, wash with soap, rinse, dry, throw away paper towel). (2, 2.1)

- Give the child verbal cues for the hand-washing routine (e.g., "Turn on the water," "Use the soap," "Rinse off the soap," "Dry your hands," "Put the towel away"). (2, 2.1)

- It may be necessary to break this skill down into its critical components. Complete the entire skill, even if you are teaching just one component of it, such as using soap. (2)

  - The child turns on the water, washes and rinses his or her own hands, and turns off the water.

  - The child obtains a towel.

  - The child rubs the towel on all sides of his or her hands until they are dry.

  - The child returns a cloth towel to the towel rack or throws a paper towel away in the trash can.

- Prompt the child by pointing to the next step in the routine; for example, if the child does not dry his or her hands, then point to the towel. (2, 2.1)

- Physically assist the child as needed to help completely wash and dry hands. (2, 2.1)

TEACHING CONSIDERATIONS

1. Ask the parent what type of faucet knobs the child uses most often at home. Begin teaching this skill with that type of knob, if possible.

2. Some children may not be able to regulate the water temperature when learning to wash hands. Check the water or teach the child to use just cold water. Use safety precautions.

3. The child may find it easier to dry hands on a soft hand towel rather than on paper towels. If using hand towels at school, then each child will need his or her own to prevent the spread of germs.

4. Be sure adequate support is given to the child with a motor impairment to allow the child to perform the skills.

5. Teach the child who is nonverbal a manual sign, signal, or gesture to indicate a desire to wash his or her hands.

GOAL 3   Brushes teeth

- PS3a   The child makes a persistent attempt to brush in one spot.
- PS3b   The child moves the toothbrush around in his or her mouth, briefly contacting the teeth.
- PS3c   The child puts the toothbrush in his or her mouth and chews on the bristles.

Objective 3.1   Cooperates with teeth brushing

- PS3.1a   The child tolerates an adult lightly brushing his or her teeth and gums.
- PS3.1b   The child tolerates the rubber tip of a toothbrush or an adult's finger covered with terry cloth moving along his or her gums and teeth.
- PS3.1c   The child tolerates an adult's finger moving along his or her gums and teeth.
- PS3.1d   The child opens his or her mouth on request.

IMPORTANCE OF SKILLS

Good oral hygiene is essential to maintaining good health. It helps prevent cavities, gum disease, bad breath, and germs. A child with poor oral hygiene may develop tooth decay and swollen gums, and an unattractive appearance may separate the child from peers. Allowing an adult to brush the teeth establishes the habit and routine before the child is able to brush his or her own teeth. As the child learns to brush teeth, the child becomes more independent in taking care of grooming needs. Other goals/objectives that can be targeted at the same time as Goal 3 are listed on the following page.

TEACHING SUGGESTIONS

Activity-Based

Brushing teeth

- Establish regular times during the day for the child to brush teeth. Incorporate brushing teeth into morning, evening, and going-out routines. Tell the child why brushing teeth is important and how to do it. (3)
- Have the child brush teeth when other children or adults are doing the same. (3)

Concurrent Goals/Objectives for Adaptive Strand B

Goal 3: Brushes teeth

Fine Motor

A:3.2 Grasps cylindrical object with either hand by closing fingers around it

B:1.1 Turns object over using wrist and arm rotation with each hand

B:2.2 Fits object into defined space

Adaptive

A:3 Drinks from cup and/or glass

A:4.1 Brings food to mouth using utensil

Cognitive

B:3.1 Looks for object in usual location

D:1 Imitates motor action that is not commonly used

F:1.2 Uses functionally appropriate actions with objects

Social-Communication

C:2.3 Carries out one-step direction with contextual cues

Social

A:3.1 Initiates communication with familiar adult

B:1.1 Meets internal physical needs of hunger, thirst, and rest

B:2.1 Responds to established social routines

Notes:

- Assist the child in putting toothpaste on the brush, if necessary. While the child is learning this skill, you may need to complete brushing for the child. (3)

- Plan regular visits to the dentist for children starting at age 3. Use the type of brush recommended by the hygienist. (3)

- When the child's teeth first begin to come in, clean them after the child eats and before bedtime by rubbing them with a washcloth. (3.1)

- As the child gets more teeth, brush them after every meal and at bedtime. Initially, do not put toothpaste on the brush; as the child begins to tolerate brushing, add a small amount of toothpaste. (3.1)

Throughout daily routines

- Take advantage of opportunities in the community to expose a young child to dental information. Go to health fairs, have a dental hygienist speak at the preschool, or provide books about teeth and teeth brushing. (3)

Environmental Arrangements

- Stand behind the child with your arms around him or her, enabling the child to watch in the mirror. This is a good position to begin encouraging the child's participation through physical assistance. (3, 3.1)

- Specially flavored toothpaste encourages its use; however, toothpaste is not necessary for cleaning teeth and may be eliminated if the child does not tolerate it. Toothpaste may be rinsed out by putting water on the toothbrush and rubbing it over the teeth. (3, 3.1)

- Let the child put the toothbrush in his or her mouth and suck off the water and a minimal amount of toothpaste. The child may also chew on the toothbrush. (3, 3.1)

- Give the child a carrot stick to suck on to practice grasping and putting something into his or her mouth. Encourage the child to rub the carrot over his or her teeth. (3, 3.1)

- Practice "spitting" drinking water in the sink. (3, 3.1)

- An electric toothbrush may be used if the child is not afraid of the noise; this brush does not have to be moved up and down. (3, 3.1)

- For the child who resists the toothbrush in his or her mouth, begin by introducing your finger with a dab of yogurt or applesauce into the mouth. Systematically introduce a washcloth on your finger and then a toothbrush. (3.1)

- Try using one of the child's stuffed animals for brushing teeth. "Is George going to help brush your teeth?" (3.1)

Adaptive

- For the child who has a bite reflex or hypersensitive mouth, have a speech-language, physical, or occupational therapist evaluate and suggest ways to desensitize or adapt for dental hygiene. (3, 3.1)

Instructional Sequences

- Have an adult or peer model brushing teeth. (3, 3.1)

- Verbally direct the child to brush teeth. If necessary, give verbal directions for each step of the skill (e.g., "Brush the front teeth"). (3)

- Verbally prompt the child to keep his or her mouth open while the teeth are being brushed. (3.1)

- Have the child brush teeth in front of a mirror. (3, 3.1)

- For the child who does not have voluntary control of opening the mouth (or who resists opening), it may be necessary to physically assist in opening the mouth so that the teeth can be brushed. Place your thumb under the chin, your index finger along the side of the jaw, and your remaining fingers just below the bottom lip. Gently press down on the chin. (3.1)

- For the tactilely defensive child, use other soft materials to clean the teeth before introducing a toothbrush. (3.1)

- Give minimal physical assistance to start the child moving the toothbrush over the teeth. (3, 3.1)

TEACHING CONSIDERATIONS

1. Use a child-size toothbrush with soft bristles.

2. When using toothpaste, use a very small amount.

3. Keep each child's toothbrush covered and separate from others to prevent spread of airborne germs.

4. An adult should complete the brushing to ensure the teeth are clean for a child who is not able to properly clean teeth.

5. The child may be resistant to an adult brushing his or her teeth and may want to do it alone.

6. Certain medications may cause side effects that alter dental hygiene needs. Check with the child's doctor or dentist to coordinate care of teeth, gums, and mouth.

7. Be sure that the child is positioned and supported so that the child does not fall and injure him- or herself with the toothbrush.

8. For the child with motor or oral-motor impairment, consult a qualified specialist for teaching ideas.

9. Teach the child who is nonverbal a manual sign, signal, or gesture to indicate a desire to brush teeth.

10. For the child who has oral-tactile defensiveness, brushing teeth is a good way to help the child become more tolerant of food and objects that will be placed in the mouth.

Adaptive

Undressing

GOAL 1   Undresses self

Objective 1.1   Takes off pullover shirt/sweater

- PS1.1a The child removes the shirt/sweater part way; for example, the child removes a shirt from one arm by pulling it over his or her head.

- PS1.1b The child persists in pushing and pulling at arms, neck, and front of the shirt in an attempt to remove it.

- PS1.1c The child tugs at the shirt, vocalizes, points, or otherwise indicates to an adult a desire to remove the shirt.

Objective 1.2   Takes off front-fastened coat, jacket, or shirt

- PS1.2a The child removes his or her coat, jacket, or shirt part way; for example, the child removes a sleeve from one arm, removes the coat from one shoulder, or pulls off the coat that has been removed from one side.

- PS1.2b The child persists in pulling at sleeves, lapels, or collar in attempt to remove the coat, jacket, or shirt.

- PS1.2c The child tugs briefly at a coat or jacket, points, or otherwise indicates to an adult a desire to have the coat removed.

Objective 1.3   Takes off pants

- PS1.3a The child removes pants part way; for example, the child takes off pants that have been pulled down to the knees, or the child pulls down pants to the knees.

- PS1.3b The child persists in pulling and pushing at legs, waist, or cuffs of pants in an attempt to remove them.

- PS1.3c The child tugs at pants, vocalizes, points, or otherwise indicates to an adult a desire to remove pants.

Objective 1.4   Takes off socks

- PS1.4a The child removes socks part way; for example, the child removes a sock that has been pulled over the heel or pulls down a sock to the ankle.

- PS1.4b The child persists in pushing and pulling at heel, toe, or foot of socks in an attempt to remove them.

- PS1.4c The child tugs briefly at socks, vocalizes, points, or otherwise indicates to an adult a desire to remove socks.

Objective 1.5   Takes off shoes

- PS1.5a The child removes shoes part way; for example, the child pulls shoe from off the heel or removes a shoe that has been pulled off of the heel.

- PS1.5b The child persists in pushing and pulling at shoes in an attempt to remove them.

- PS1.5c The child tugs briefly at shoes, vocalizes, points, or otherwise indicates to an adult a desire to remove shoes.

Objective 1.6   Takes off hat

- PS1.6a The child removes a hat part way; for example, the child pulls off a hat that has been removed from one side of his or her head.

- PS1.6b The child persists in pushing and pulling at the hat in an attempt to remove it.

- PS1.6c The child tugs briefly at the hat, vocalizes, points, or otherwise indicates to an adult a desire to remove the hat.

IMPORTANCE OF SKILLS

Children gain independence by taking care of their own basic needs. Undressing represents one of the initial areas that allows a child independence from his or her caregiver. Undressing activities provide many opportunities for practicing fine and gross motor skills, learning concepts, and engaging in social interactions in a functional context. Learning adaptive skills also decreases the difference between developmentally young children and their peers. A child's self-concept may be influenced by his or her level of independent functioning in the Adaptive Area. The skills involved in undressing allow the child to become less dependent on other people for daily adaptive needs, and uses a variety of gross and fine motor skills in a functional and frequent activity. Other goals/objectives that can be targeted at the same time as Goal 1 are listed on the following page.

TEACHING SUGGESTIONS

Activity-Based

Dressing

- Taking off a pullover or front-fastening coat or jacket is best taught as a natural consequence to coming in from outside. A child might become confused or irritated if you try to teach this skill by putting on a coat and removing it without going outside. (1.1, 1.2)

- When undressing the child, play a game of Peekaboo by pulling the child's T-shirt to just above the nose, and let the child pull it the rest of the way. Gradually let the child take more of it off before you say "Peekaboo." (1.1, 1.2)

Concurrent Goals/Objectives for Adaptive Strand C

Goal 1: Undresses self

Fine Motor

A:3 Grasps hand-size object with either hand using ends of thumb, index, and second fingers

B:1 Rotates either wrist on horizontal plane

Gross Motor

B:1.2 Regains balanced, upright sitting position after reaching across the body to the right and to the left

B:2 Sits down in and gets out of chair

Adaptive

B:1 Initiates toileting

Cognitive

B:3.1 Looks for object in usual location

D:1 Imitates motor action that is not commonly used

E:4.1 Uses more than one strategy in attempt to solve common problem

G:1.1 Groups functionally related objects

Social-Communication

B:1 Gains person's attention and refers to an object, person, and/or event

B:2 Uses consistent word approximations

Social

A:3.1 Initiates communication with familiar adult

B:1 Meets observable physical needs in socially appropriate ways

B:2.1 Responds to established social routines

Notes:

- A favorite time to remove pants or shirts is when they are replaced by a garment that symbolizes "fun," such as removing pajamas to get dressed for going outside, removing clothes for a bath, or removing clothes to put on a swimsuit. (1.2, 1.3)

- When changing the child's diaper or when helping the child use the toilet, encourage the child to assist in pulling down his or her own pants. (1.3)

- Encourage the child to remove pants, shirt, socks or shoes during daily caregiving routines such as undressing at bath time, bedtime, or when changing into clean clothes. If the child does not initiate taking off pants, shirt, or socks, then offer a reminder (e.g., "Don't forget your pants"). (1.3, 1.4, 1.5)

Travel

- When a child arrives at a new destination (e.g., school, home, coming in from outside) wearing a coat or a jacket, encourage the child to remove it. If the child does not initiate removing the coat, then offer a reminder (e.g., "Don't forget to take off your coat now that you're indoors"). (1.1, 1.2)

Playtime

- When playing with paint, water, playdough, or other messy substances, put a large shirt on the child to keep clothes clean. After the activity, ask the child to remove the shirt. (1.1, 1.2)

- Engage the child in dramatic play activities. Provide various coats, shoes, hats, pants, and so forth for the child to use in dress-up play; for example, put together a dress-up box of clothes that are loose, fun, and representative of favorite characters such as Superman or Mickey Mouse as well as including pretend characters in dramatic play activities (e.g., doctor, cowboy/cowgirl, firefighter). Play foot doctor or shoe store to practice taking off shoes, or chefs and firefighters wearing hats that can be taken off. (1.1, 1.2, 1.3, 1.4, 1.5, 1.6)

- When the child is wearing shoes or socks, play a game of Peekaboo with the child's toes. Place the shoe or sock just over the tips of the child's toes and say, "Where are (Jenny's) toes?" After the child pulls off the shoe or sock, say, "Peekaboo," and tickle the child's feet. This game can also be played with "This little piggy went to market." Peekaboo is also a fun game for practicing taking off hats. (1.4, 1.5, 1.6)

- Allow the child to try on adult hats found in the home, school, or in stores. Let the child look in the mirror to see how hats appear and practice taking them off. (1.6)

Throughout daily routines

- Whenever appropriate, have peers or siblings remove jacket, pants, shirt, socks, shoes, or hat; for example, when undressing for swimming, bedtime, or after dress-up, let children undress together. Only children who know

Adaptive

each other well (e.g., siblings, regular playmates) should undress together to promote learning about privacy. (1.1, 1.2, 1.3, 1.4, 1.5, 1.6)

- Encourage the child to remove wet or muddy shoes after coming in from outdoors. (1.5)

Environmental Arrangements

- When teaching the child to remove front-opening garments, begin teaching with vests and short-sleeve shirts and systematically introduce long-sleeve shirts as the child demonstrates the intent and behaviors to remove shirts. (1.1, 1.2)

- When teaching the child to remove pullover shirts, let the child practice using sleeveless undershirts and large T-shirts. Gradually introduce shirts of an appropriate size and with longer sleeves. (1.1, 1.2)

- Taking off a coat or jacket can be taught by using a cape. As the child demonstrates the intent and behavior of removing an outer garment, introduce loose-fitting coats and jackets. As the child learns to remove the loose jacket, teach the child to remove a jacket or coat that is the appropriate size for the child. (1.1, 1.2)

- Lightweight jackets are often easier to remove than heavy coats or sweaters. Coats with cuffs are slightly more difficult. Begin teaching with the easiest clothing available and systematically introduce more difficult coats and jackets. (1.1, 1.2)

- Play a hiding game by putting a special sticker or name tag on the back of the child's coat where it cannot be seen until the coat is taken off. (1.1, 1.2)

- Have a mirror by the door where the child takes off his or her coat or sweater to allow the child to watch him- or herself remove the article of clothing. (1.1, 1.2)

- Use "fun" and "wild" underwear or diapers beneath pants to motivate the child to remove outer pants. Have the child look for the characters on undergarments by taking off outer pants. A bandage on the knee is also a good hidden object to uncover. (1.3)

- Short pants are easier to remove than long pants. Begin teaching the removal of pants by using underpants and shorts. Introduce long pants once the child demonstrates the ability to remove short pants. (1.3)

- Use loose or large pants at first. Drawstring sweatpants and elastic-waist pants are easy to remove. Begin teaching with these pants and introduce pants with zippers and buttons as the child becomes proficient at removing pants. (1.3)

- The child who needs support when taking off pants may be assisted by leaning against a wall or holding onto a chair or handrail. Some children find it easiest to pull pants down to the knees while standing and then sit to pull the legs out of the pants. (1.3)

- Put adult-size socks on the child and let the child remove the socks after playing "Mommy" or "Daddy." Let the child pull off an adult's socks or a peer's socks. Once the child demonstrates the behavior and intent of taking off socks, introduce socks of the appropriate size. (1.4)

- Put nail polish or tiny stickers on the child's toes to encourage the child to remove socks and find the "surprise." (1.4)

- Plan activities for which removing shoes is appropriate; for example, trace the outline of the child's foot or make finger-paint footprints. (1.5)

- As the child begins to learn to remove shoes, flip-flops and slip-on house slippers may be used prior to introducing shoes and boots. (1.5)

- Adapt materials by using a scarf or diaper as a hat that the child can remove. Once the child demonstrates the intent and behavior of removing the "hat," introduce loose-fitting caps and hats, as they are easier for the child to remove. When the child has learned to remove loose-fitting hats, use hats that are the appropriate size for the child. (1.6)

- Have the child take hats and scarves off of dolls or stuffed animals when playing dress-up with toys. Use a variety of styles of hats to ensure generalization (e.g., baseball caps, knitted hats, bonnets). Some of these may need to be unfastened. (1.6)

Instructional Sequences

- Model taking off your garment (e.g., coat, pants, shirt, socks, shoes, hat) or have a peer demonstrate removing the garment; then have the child imitate the behavior. (1.1, 1.2, 1.3, 1.4, 1.5, 1.6)

- Give the child a general verbal or nonverbal cue to remove garment (e.g., coat, pants, shirt, socks, shoes, hat). Pause and wait for the child to begin taking off his or her garment. (1.1, 1.2, 1.3, 1.4, 1.5, 1.6)

- Give the child specific verbal cues to remove the garment (e.g., "Grab the sleeve with your other hand," "Pull your arm out"). (1.1, 1.2, 1.3, 1.4, 1.5, 1.6)

- Give the child visual or tactile cues. Pull on or point to the sleeve of the garment to prompt the child to remove an arm. (1.1, 1.2)

- Help the child remove a pullover garment such as a shirt with minimal assistance as needed; for example, the child takes off a shirt that has been pulled up to the chest or when one arm is in and the other arm removed to just below the elbow or when the other arm is completely removed. Assistance can be provided at several steps such as when the shirt has been removed to around the neck or above the nose or the crown of the head. (1.1)

- Help the child remove the front-opening garment with minimal physical assistance as needed; for example, the child takes off a coat or shirt that has been moved just off the shoulders or has been moved just below the elbows. (1.2)

- Help the child take off a coat or shirt when the dominant arm is already out of the sleeve or when the garment is partially off the nondominant arm or totally off the dominant arm. (1.1, 1.2)

- Help the child remove pants with minimal physical assistance as needed. While in a standing position, the child takes off pants that have been pulled down to the middle of the hips or pulled down to the middle of the thighs. While sitting, the child will take off pants that have been pulled down to the ankles or will pull pants off that are just around one ankle. (1.3)

- Help the child remove both socks with minimal physical assistance as needed; for example, the child removes socks after being assisted to grasp the back of the cuff of the sock with the thumb and fingertips; the child removes the sock when the heel has been removed and the sock is positioned around the ankle or on the lower half of foot; the child removes a sock that is positioned just over the tip of the toes. (1.4)

- Help the child remove shoes with minimal physical assistance as needed; for example, the child takes off a shoe when the heel is slipped halfway off his or her heel or all the way off; the child takes off a shoe when the shoe is just covering lower half of foot. (1.5)

Combining or pairing different levels of instructions may be helpful when beginning to teach a new and difficult skill. Fade to less intrusive instructions as soon as possible to encourage more independent performance.

TEACHING CONSIDERATIONS

1. The child can learn different methods of taking off a garment; for example, when taking off a coat or shirt, the child can remove one sleeve at a time, extend arms back and remove arms from sleeves from behind, or swing the coat or shirt over his or her head and pull off the sleeves from the front. Choose the method that is most appropriate for the child.

2. Supervise the child while removing a pullover shirt so that the child does not become "stuck" and frightened.

3. The child may find it easier to remove socks or shoes when sitting in a chair rather than on the floor.

4. The adult may unfasten shoes before the child removes them.

5. Consult a qualified specialist for adaptations and positions for a child with a motor impairment. Adaptive clothing (e.g., snaps, Velcro) may be necessary.

6. The child must be in a balanced or supported position that allows free use of arms.

7. The child with a visual impairment may need more manipulative, tactile, and auditory cues to replace models, gestures, and pointing.

Adaptive

AEPS™

Cognitive Area
Birth to Three Years

LIST OF AEPS TEST ITEMS

Cognitive

Cognitive

The Cognitive Area is the largest area in the AEPS Curriculum, which indicates the scope and complexity of early cognitive development. Prior to the mid-1970s, the cognitive abilities of infants were rarely addressed in early intervention programs. The area of pre-academic skills (e.g., shapes, colors, categories) was regarded as the earliest cognitive content relevant to students in special education. The application of Piagetian theory of sensorimotor development to early intervention curricula has provided a valuable framework for understanding the cognitive skills of infants and young children. The Cognitive Area in the AEPS Curriculum is organized to reflect Piaget's theoretical framework, which incorporates sensory stimuli, object permanence, causality, imitation, problem solving, interaction with objects, and early concepts.

Newborn infants, with few exceptions, are perceptually equipped to respond to environmental stimuli. Sight, touch, and sound are important sources of sensation and information for the developing child. Initial responses may involve only a change in activity level, but the infant quickly learns to orient to the source of stimulation. Thus, a baby will snuggle into a parent's arms, look toward a mobile, and later reach toward a musical toy. The process of selecting certain stimuli out of the infinite variety of sights, sounds, and touches available provides the foundation for more sophisticated interactions with the environment.

Every interaction between caregivers and young children provides sensory stimulation. The human face holds special visual interest, and the human voice is a salient auditory stimulus for most infants. Many of the activities suggested in the AEPS Curriculum involve face-to-face interaction between adult and child. Saying an infant's name, making eye contact, and smiling when picking up a baby provide auditory, visual, and tactile stimulation in the space of seconds in a familiar and meaningful context.

Object permanence refers to the child's ability to form a mental representation of objects outside of the immediate perceptual field. Initially, the child learns to control his or her own perceptual field by following objects visually and locating objects after seeing them hidden or covered. These skills culminate in the child's ability to look for missing or lost items.

The child who masters object permanence makes a significant cognitive leap from concrete and immediate experience to abstract experience. Object permanence also promotes many related learning opportunities. The child who has a firm concept of objects is likely to realize that the toy he or she plays with today is the same toy that a particular action activated yesterday. The child can immediately try that action again and move on to explore more sophisticated alternatives.

Cognitive

The notion of familiar adults is a specific case of object permanence, sometimes called *people permanence.* The infant develops a mental representation of a caregiver and associates the caregiver with comfort. Once an infant develops a mental image of his or her mother, for example, crying becomes a means to an end, rather than just an expression of discomfort.

Causality refers to the child's ability to infer cause-and-effect relationships from action on objects or from interactions with people. A prerequisite to understanding cause and effect is the use of one means to achieve a specific end; for example, the infant uses vocalization as a means of soliciting adult attention or pushes a musical toy to produce a tinkling sound. The use of actions to accomplish a particular objective shows the child's intentional control over the immediate environment.

The repetitive use of specific actions with people and objects allows the child to develop means for achieving predictable ends. Young children can happily play Peekaboo or manipulate a Busy Box many times, making sure that the same actions will produce similar results each time. These concrete experiences eventually culminate in the child's ability to mentally predict an outcome or infer the cause of a particular effect.

The development of cause-and-effect hypotheses is another example of the child's ability to move from concrete to abstract representations and from immediate to delayed associations. The child who purposely knocks a toy into the bathtub to create a splash has come a long way, cognitively, from the younger child who does not associate the toy falling with the water splashing.

Imitation is a valuable learning strategy available to infants and young children. Children observe and listen to adults and peers, learn from what they see and hear, and imitate. Children who can imitate are able to associate their own actions with those of others and then produce new behaviors. The efficiency of this strategy over trial-and-error learning is obvious.

Children begin to imitate by seeing their own actions performed by another person. Adults often mimic infant actions and vocalizations, and the infant responds by continuing the movement or sound. This game of mutual imitation is enjoyable and important for building imitative skills. Soon the child will follow an adult's lead and imitate actions or sounds that are familiar and easy to produce. Eventually, the child makes use of imitation strategies to learn new and difficult skills.

Actions that children can see are generally easier to imitate than ones they cannot see. Patting the top of the head is more difficult than clapping hands because the child can see the hands and match the action to a model of the action. Similarly, vocal and/or verbal imitations are more difficult than other actions because the movements required to make sounds are often not visible, even with a mirror.

Imitation is an important component of successful problem solving. Faced with a problem at home, school, or in the community, a child's best strategy is often to see what peers or adults are doing in a similar situation; for example, the child who has too many blocks to carry may observe a peer using a wagon and find a wagon for the blocks. Parents and teachers typically show a young child how to do something, rather than do it for the child or explain a sequence of actions.

Problem solving requires the child to combine and use objects and people in novel ways to achieve certain ends. Skills developed in the areas of object permanence, causality, and imitation all come into play when the child successfully approaches and solves problems. The ability to solve common problems at play, in caring for self, and during interactions with adults and peers give the young child a measure of independence and increase confidence in negotiating social and physical environments.

The young child initially approaches problems by persevering in one familiar strategy or solution; for example, the child who has used a low stool to reach the bathroom sink may try to use the same stool to reach the kitchen sink. As the ability to see the relationships between objects increases, the child will attempt alternative solutions. The child attempting to reach the counter may try to climb on an adult-size chair or may open a drawer and stand on it. Gradually, the child develops the skills to evaluate the situation, compare it with others from previous experiences, and determine a workable solution.

The development of play in young children has social, motor, and cognitive components. It is included in the Cognitive Area in the AEPS Curriculum because the sequence of play skills progresses from concrete to abstract, from simple to complex, and from unintentional to intentional. These simple-to-complex sequences are central to sensorimotor development and mark the way that the child applies many of the skills delineated throughout the area.

The earliest object play involves the infant holding and exploring objects. At first, all objects are explored with the same limited set of actions—sucking, banging, and throwing. The child soon determines that certain actions are better suited for certain objects. At the same time, the schemes include increasingly complex actions. Dolls and stuffed animals are for hugging, cars and balls are for rolling, fingers and rubber toys are for sucking, and paper and fabric are for crumpling.

Once a child begins using objects in functionally appropriate ways, the stage is set for more abstract and symbolic play. The child who knows to talk into a toy telephone, rock a doll, comb hair with a brush, and sweep with a broom has a mental representation of each object and its function. When the correct object is not available, the child substitutes another object to perform the same function. A small box, for example, can serve as a shoe or as a bed for a doll. A block can be a telephone. The child's mental picture of the object and knowledge of its function allows one object to represent another.

Finally, the child can play without the benefit of object props. The child's imagination creates the object or event, and play becomes an abstract endeavor. The freedom and creativity available to children who can pretend is evident in imaginary play. No longer limited to available objects and events, or hindered by the immediate time frame of reality, children revel in imaginary scenes, perform feats of strength and daring, create new friends, and travel to the ends of the earth. Whether playing with superheroes, assuming exciting identities, creating new worlds, or simply doing something one cannot really do (e.g., pretending to drive a car), imaginary play is a wonderful resource for entertainment and learning.

Cognitive

Early concepts in this curriculum include categorization, one-to-one correspondence, and early literacy skills. These skills are prerequisite to learning to use basic concept labels, perform precise manipulations of objects, and develop computational math and reading skills.

The ability to categorize objects based on similar properties is an initial step in concept development. Matching similar objects or pictures and objects shows the child's ability to perceive similarities and differences between items. This skill is necessary for the identification of specific qualities such as size, shape, and color.

A child can sort objects into groups based on specific qualities long before the child can name the size, shape, or color of the objects; for example, a child might sort blocks into piles by shape or sort cars into containers by color. The same child, however, may not be able to label or even recognize circles, triangles, or squares, or red, blue, or yellow.

Grouping functionally related objects requires the child to evaluate the use of each item and associate it with those of a similar function; for example, a child may put a fork and plate together because both are used for eating. A blanket and doll will go together because both are put into the crib for sleeping.

Ultimately, the young child develops conceptual classes such as vehicles, furniture, people, animals, and buildings. At this point, the child can start with the conceptual category and select items that represent it; for example, a child might take all of the animals from a farm scene and put them in a different box than the buildings. Categorization and the development of concepts allow the child to organize people, objects, and events into a meaningful and interrelated mental framework. More sophisticated understanding of superordinate and subordinate concepts, and the relationships between levels, is dependent on early categorization skills.

The child also learns in the early concepts strand to match one, and only one, item to another. This skill has many functional and practical applications in daily living; for example, each foot gets one sock, each plate one fork, and each child one cracker. One-to-one correspondence is perhaps the earliest math skill. It is a necessary prerequisite to understanding the concepts of more than, less than, and equal to. Rational counting has as its basis the assignment of one numeral to each object, an obvious extension of the one-to-one concept.

Finally, early literacy skills are addressed. The child begins to associate symbols with a particular meaning and learn that pictures can represent the people, objects, or events in their lives. Children enjoy looking at picture books and filling in text from familiar books as adults read to them. As the child begins to experiment with rhyming words and repeat simple nursery rhymes, he or she is developing early reading skills.

Cognitive skills for birth to 3-year-olds span the continuum from response to external stimulation to creation of imaginary play scenarios. The interventionist is constantly challenged not to underestimate the abilities of young children in the area of cognition. Our job is to detect the discrepancy between what children can already do and what skills they need to master next. We must design environments that encourage and interest children in problem solving while making certain that the problem is indeed solvable. Most important, we must try to see the world through the eyes of each child and find the excitement, challenges, and rewards that will motivate and maintain cognitive gains.

As you design learning environments, you must also consider the significance of cognitive development for all children, despite their levels of impairment. The challenge is to facilitate cognitive development so that the child's disability does not impede progress. At times, this will require consulting a qualified specialist for techniques for the child with a visual, auditory, or motor impairment.

Cognitive

STRAND A

Sensory Stimuli

GOAL 1 Orients to auditory, visual, and tactile events

Objective 1.1 Orients to auditory events

Objective 1.2 Orients to visual events

- PS1.2a The child uses reflexive pupillary and blinking responses. Present bright lights to elicit constriction of the pupils of the eyes, or slowly approach the child's face with an object to elicit blinking.

Objective 1.3 Orients to tactile stimulation

- PS1.3a The child displays reflexive responses, such as the rooting response, to tactile events. During feeding, stimulate the sides and upper and lower portions of the mouth to facilitate oral searching or head rotation prior to placing the nipple directly in the infant's mouth.

Objective 1.4 Responds to auditory, visual, and tactile events

- PS1.4a Research to date has not shown a consistent developmental sequence among different sensory modalities. Soon after birth, infants are capable of detecting correspondences between different senses (internodal perception). Begin teaching with the sensory modality to which the child is most likely to respond and progress to those modalities that initially elicit the least interest.

- PS1.4b Use multiple sensory cues and fade to each individual type of cue (auditory, visual, tactile).

IMPORTANCE OF SKILLS

Children actively construct knowledge through exploration of the environment. Infants react to visual stimuli by scanning visual patterns, to auditory awareness by localizing sounds, and to tactile stimuli with reflexive and voluntary responses. Observation of the infant's reactions will provide the observer with information about the infant's differential responses and preferential modes to specific sensory modalities.

The child actively processes information in the environment, using auditory, visual, tactile, and olfactory modalities. Orientation to auditory and visual stimuli are essential for the acquisition of practical communication skills and the development of both information processing and social interaction. Tactile sensitivity is necessary to assist children in their awareness of extreme temperatures and pain to maintain good health and in avoiding physical danger. Locating, orienting, and responding to auditory, visual, and tactile events in the environment allow the child to exercise basic sensorimotor schemes on a variety of social and nonsocial objects. Other goals/objectives that can be targeted at the same time as Goal 1 are listed on the following page.

TEACHING SUGGESTIONS

Activity-Based

Playtime

- Play with noise-producing objects (e.g., bells, rattle, crinkly paper, music box, squeeze toy). (1, 1.1)

- Make funny sounds (e.g., tongue clicks, animal imitations) while interacting with the child. (1, 1.1)

- Call to the child from behind or the side; whisper in the child's ear. (1, 1.1)

- Vary facial expressions and engage in face-to-face interaction games such as Peekaboo. (1, 1.2)

- During playtime use a variety of objects, from social to nonsocial, with simple and complex patterns and with colors of varying brightness. (1, 1.2)

- Present visual stimuli that do not produce a sound (e.g., colored ball, face of a doll, person smiling) within the child's visual field and encourage the child to turn, look, reach, or move toward the visual event. (1, 1.2)

- Play nursery games that involve tactile, auditory, or visual stimuli, such as "This little piggy," "Up we go," or Pat-a-cake. (1, 1.1, 1.2, 1.3, 1.4)

Quiet time

- When the child is lying on his or her back in the crib, activate a mobile. (1, 1.2, 1.4)

- When the child cries, rock, touch, stroke, or sing to elicit a quieting response. (1, 1.4)

- Look for blinking responses when turning on a soft light in a dark room or when opening curtains. (1, 1.4)

Bathing

- While bathing, gently splash the child or pour water over the child's back or side and observe whether the child turns his or her head toward the source of stimulation. (1, 1.3)

Cognitive

Concurrent Goals/Objectives for Cognitive Strand A

Goal 1: Orients to auditory, visual, and tactile events

Fine Motor

A:1.2 Makes nondirected movements with each arm

Gross Motor

A:1 Turns head, moves arms, and kicks legs independently of each other

---

Adaptive

A:1.4 Swallows liquids

Cognitive

B:1.2 Focuses on object and/or person

Social-Communication

A:1.1 Turns and looks toward object and person speaking

A:2.2 Looks toward an object

Social

A:1.2 Responds appropriately to familiar adult's affective tone

---

Notes:

Feeding

- During feeding, move the nipple gently in and around the mouth to stimulate response to tactile stimulation. (1, 1.4)

Throughout daily routines

- Expose the child to noises in the daily environment, such as vacuum cleaners, doorbell, garbage disposal, mixer, train, voices, and animals. Encourage the child to orient to sounds that occur near him or her by turning, looking, reaching, or moving in the direction of the sound. (1, 1.1)

- Talk to the child frequently during daily caregiving routines (bathing, dressing, feeding, and play) and vary pitch, intonation, and intensity. (1, 1.1)

- Use a variety of sounds by varying the pitch of your voice, sounding bells or maracas, or playing soft and loud music, to determine the cues to which the child most readily responds. Begin with auditory cues to which the child most readily responds and gradually present other cues until the skill is generalized across a variety of auditory cues. (1, 1.1)

- Provide sights in the daily environment, such as the child's own image in a mirror, colorful posters on the wall, and sunlight coming in a window. (1, 1.2)

- Encourage the child to turn, look, reach, or move toward tactile events as they occur in the daily caregiving routine (e.g., gentle touch, stuffed animals, water, bottle or breast, adult or child's face, lotion). (1, 1.3)

- Touch the child with warm or cold objects, such as a warm bottle, warm clothing just out of the dryer, or cold hands. (1, 1.3)

- Watch for gaze direction or fixation when the infant is approached by a familiar person. When a familiar person talks to the infant or when a noise occurs in the environment (e.g., door slams, radio is turned on), watch for cessation or increase of motor activity. (1, 1.4)

- Throughout the daily routine (e.g., dressing, changing, bathing, feeding), present toys and/or objects within the child's visual field and noise-producing toys and/or objects (e.g., rattle, squeak-toy). (1, 1.4)

Environmental Arrangements

- Help the child differentiate between sounds and silence. Speak and then pause or turn on the radio and then shut it off and wait for the child to respond. (1.1)

- Give the child a noise-producing object to manipulate (e.g., rattle, crinkly paper). (1.1)

- Cease activity and listen to sounds in the environment such as dogs barking, children shouting, appliances, and airplanes. Take the child to locate the noises. (1.1, 1.4)

Cognitive

- Alternate low tones (use wooden objects) and high tones (use plastic objects) and loud sounds (sing) and soft sounds (whisper). (1.1, 1.4)

- Hide yourself or a toy and continue to speak or make a noise with the toy. (1.1, 1.4)

- Attach noise-producing objects to child's arms or legs (e.g., jingle bells on socks or wrist). (1.1, 1.2, 1.3, 1.4)

- When the child focuses visually on an object, slowly move the object to elicit tracking, head turning, or reaching and to maintain visual contact. (1.2)

- Use a variety of colors and patterns over time to determine the cues to which the child most readily responds and then orients toward. Begin with those cues and gradually present others until the skill is generalized across a variety of visual cues. (1.2, 1.4)

- Hold objects directly in the child's visual field at a distance where accommodation is best (approximately 12 inches). (1.2, 1.4)

- Use large, bright-colored objects or objects that move (e.g., hand puppet, small balloon, mobile). Present objects or figures with patterned surfaces, curved lines, and bright colors. After playing with an object, maintain the child's interest by introducing new but visually similar objects. (1.2, 1.3, 1.4)

- Rub lotion or blow gently on different parts of the child's body. (1.3)

- Provide materials that stick to the child's fingers, such as cereal, finger paint, or playdough. Wipe off the materials with a cloth. (1.3)

- Carefully pass balloons across the child's visual field and observe if the child recognizes and then orients to the balloons. (Pay special attention to the potential dangers of balloons.) Use bright, shiny Mylar balloons and banners of different colors and shapes to attract and hold the child's attention. (1.2, 1.4)

- Vary the texture of tactile cues over time to determine the cues to which the child most readily responds and orients. Begin with those cues and gradually present others until the skill is generalized across a variety of tactile cues. (1.3, 1.4)

Instructional Sequences

- Increase intensity of auditory, visual, and tactile cues. Use louder, more distinct sounds (e.g., drum, shout, larger bells) in place of speech and music; use contoured, bright-colored, large, or quickly moving visual stimuli; and rough towels (gently), sand, soft feathers, or Jell-O for increased tactile cues. (1, 1.1, 1.2, 1.3, 1.4)

- Pair auditory events with visual or tactile cues; for example, talk to the child while moving your face within the child's visual field. Touch the child's leg with a bright-colored toy or a noise-producing object; talk and touch the child within the child's field of vision. (1, 1.1, 1.2, 1.3, 1.4)

- Gently assist the child to move, turn, or reach toward noise-producing, visual, or tactile objects (1.1, 1.2, 1.3)

Combining or pairing different levels of instructions may be helpful when beginning to teach a new and difficult skill. Fade to less intrusive instructions as soon as possible to encourage more independent performance.

TEACHING CONSIDERATIONS

1. Be cautious about eliciting a startled response from some children with loud or sudden noises.

2. The child should be in a quiet and alert state.

3. The environment should be free of auditory, visual, or tactile events that compete with the visual stimuli presented.

4. When presenting paired cues to elicit a response to an auditory or visual event, select those cues to which the child is most responsive (auditory, visual, or tactile).

5. The child with a visual or hearing impairment may require cues that are more intense (e.g., louder, increased size or brightness paired with tactile or visual cues). Consult a qualified specialist for techniques for a child with a hearing or motor impairment.

6. Be cautious about balloons and consider safety with all objects that the child handles.

Cognitive

Object Permanence

GOAL 1 Visually follows object and/or person to point of disappearance

Objective 1.1 Visually follows object moving in horizontal, vertical, and circular directions

- PS1.1a The child visually follows an object moving in a circular direction.
- PS1.1b The child visually follows an object moving in a vertical direction.
- PS1.1c The child visually follows an object moving in a horizontal direction.

Objective 1.2 Focuses on object and/or person

IMPORTANCE OF SKILLS

The child who is able to actively accommodate his or her own actions (e.g., looking, turning head) to maintain visual contact with moving objects demonstrates knowledge that objects have a certain permanence. Visual tracking plays an important role in cognitive development. It is an intermediate step between the mere perception of an object and the active search for an object that has disappeared from the visual field. Visual tracking constantly provides the foundation for learning from objects and interactions in a moving environment. Focusing on an object or person represents the first step toward the active search for objects that have disappeared from sight. The ability to visually accommodate a stable object is basic to the subsequent skill of tracking a moving object. In addition, the ability to maintain a visual focus allows the child to explore the properties of objects in the immediate environment. With these skills, the child begins to understand that objects are permanent and constant entities, even when moving through space. Other goals/objectives that can be targeted at the same time as Goal 1 are listed on the following page.

TEACHING SUGGESTIONS

Activity-Based

Feeding

- During feedings, hold the bottle within the child's visual field momentarily before bringing it to the child's mouth. (1.1, 1.2)

Goal 1: Visually follows object and/or person to point of disappearance

Fine Motor

A:1.1 Makes directed batting and/or swiping movements with each hand

Gross Motor

A:1.1 Turns head past 45° to the right and left from midline position

Adaptive

A:4.3 Accepts food presented on spoon

Cognitive

C:1.2 Acts on mechanical and/or simple toy in some way

F:1.4 Uses sensory examination with objects

Social-Communication

A:1.2 Turns and looks toward noise-producing object

Social

A:1.3 Smiles in response to familiar adult

Notes:

Cognitive

- At snack time, pass food from one person to another in front of the child, bring food down from shelves, and move plates and cups from the counter to the table. Move the child's cup or spoon under the table or around and behind him or her, encouraging the child to follow the movement visually. (1, 1.1, 1.2)

- When feeding the child, present the spoon and move it in circular, horizontal, or vertical directions before bringing it to the child's mouth. Make airplane noises or similar sounds. (1.1, 1.2)

Quiet time

- When the child is lying on his or her back in the crib, activate a mobile. (1.1, 1.2)

Travel

- Point out people crossing streets, people going into buildings, and cars going down the street as you drive. (1, 1.2)

Playtime

- Play face-to-face interaction games, such as gazing intently at the child before smiling. Vary your facial and vocal expressions. (1.2)

- While playing with the child, change location frequently by moving around the child or behind a barrier, such as a doorway. Watch for the child to follow as you slowly disappear from view. Re-appear and play again. (1, 1.1)

Throughout daily routines

- Encourage the child to visually follow objects and people moving in horizontal, vertical, and circular directions within the child's visual field. Play with objects that can be rolled horizontally (e.g., balls, cars). Talk to a pet cat or dog that is within the child's visual field. Turn toy dials and wheels in clockwise and counterclockwise directions. "Fly" toy birds or airplanes. Toss a balloon in the air several times. Push floating bath toys while in the tub. (1, 1.1, 1.2)

- Move objects out of the child's visual field by having toys drop to the floor from your lap or a table, or have food such as crackers drop from a highchair. (1, 1.1)

- Throughout daily routines (e.g., bathing, rocking, feeding, changing the child), move your face within 6 inches of the child's face. Look at and talk to the child. (1, 1.2)

- Encourage visual exploration of an object that the child is manipulating. Move the object in different directions. (1, 1.1, 1.2)

Environmental Arrangements

- Present objects that are interesting or novel to the child. Cause a toy that the child is playing with to drop to the floor, or slowly move the toy to another location. Make objects more interesting by attaching appealing stickers. (1, 1.1)

- Over time, present objects with a variety of colors and patterns to determine the type of cues and objects to which the child most readily responds. (1, 1.1)

- Dangle objects in front of the child (e.g., crib gym, toys tied to a rope) so that when the child bats at the object, it will move in horizontal, vertical, or circular directions. (1, 1.1)

- Vary the distance at which you present an object to determine the optimal distance for the child to focus. Hold the object until the child focuses on it before you move it. (1, 1.1)

- Place objects on a high shelf, or roll a ball under a bed. Repeat several times. (1, 1.1)

- Vary the direction in which objects move (left to right, right to left) in order to generalize the skill. (1, 1.1, 1.2)

- When the child's eyes are on the dog, ask the dog to come. Continue to speak to the dog so that the child's eyes will follow the dog. (1, 1.1, 1.2)

- Pair visual with auditory cues. Speak to the child while moving out of sight. Use noisy, wind-up toys, and let them drop off the table. Call the child's name if the child stops tracking before the person or the object disappears. (1, 1.1, 1.2)

- Use objects that move easily such as wind chimes, mechanical toys, a rocking clown, or a toy that rights itself when tipped over. (1, 1.2)

- Present objects within the child's visual field at a distance where accommodation appears to be best (usually about 10–12 inches from the child). Move the object briefly to gain the child's attention. (1.2)

- Keep the objects stationary for more than 4 seconds to allow the child to sustain focus. (1, 1.2)

- When playing face-to-face with the child, introduce variations to maintain the child's focus. Sing, talk, and vary facial and vocal expressions. (1, 1.2)

- Use lights and shiny surfaces to increase visual appeal. (1, 1.2)

- Hold a mirror in front of the child's face. (1, 1.2)

- Place bold, colorful designs within the child's visual field when the child is in a crib, chair, or car seat. (1.2)

- Allow the child to scan without distractions or interruptions. (1, 1.2)

Cognitive

Instructional Sequences

- Begin by having the child follow an object or person with his or her eyes only. Then, have the child turn his or her head to maintain visual contact. Finally, have the child turn his or her body to keep the object or person in sight until the point of disappearance. Physically direct the child if necessary. (1, 1.1, 1.2)

- Pair visual cues with auditory cues. Use noise-producing objects (e.g., clear ball with bells inside, noisy wind-up toys). Make airplane noises while pretending to make a plane fly. When the child begins to lose attention, increase auditory cues by shaking a bell or changing the tone of the airplane noise. Slowly fade the use of auditory cues in combination with visual cues. (1, 1.1)

- Verbally direct the child to look at an object or follow an object to the point of disappearance (i.e., "Look at the dog. Where is she going?"). (1, 1.1, 1.2)

- Pair visual cues with tactile cues. Use gentle physical assistance to make the child move an object held in the hand. If the child loses sight of the object, then bring the object back into the child's visual field. Once the child focuses on the object again, continue to move it. (1, 1.1)

- Make social, verbal, and tactile reinforcers contingent upon visual contact with a face or object; for example, wait until the child attends to your face before you talk or smile, or activate a mechanical toy after the child visually focuses upon it. Gradually increase the length of time (from immediate to 4 seconds) between the presentation of the object and the reinforcement. (1, 1.1)

Combining or pairing different levels of instructions may be helpful when beginning to teach a new and difficult skill. Fade to less intrusive instructions as soon as possible to encourage more independent performance.

TEACHING CONSIDERATIONS

1. The child should be in a quiet, alert state.

2. The environment should be free of auditory, visual, or tactile events that compete with the stimuli presented.

3. If the child has a visual impairment, then increase the intensity and variety of cues (increased size or brightness); for example, use noise-producing objects with the child who has a visual impairment; observe the child's ability to track the sound and/or object to the point of disappearance. Encourage sustained tactile exploration of the object.

4. If the child has a hearing impairment, gain the child's interest in the object and/or person through visual or tactile means (e.g., use bright-colored objects, touch the child with the object).

5. If the child has a motor impairment, be aware of limitations and position the child to facilitate visual tracking/focusing.

6. Consult a qualified specialist for techniques for the child with a visual, auditory, or motor impairment.

7. Consider safety with all objects that the child handles.

GOAL 2   Locates object in latter of two successive hiding places

- PS2a   After the child sees an object hidden first in one place, then another, the child searches for the object in the first hiding place, then in the next hiding place.

- PS2b   After the child sees an object hidden first in one place, then another, the child searches for the object in the first hiding place.

Objective 2.1   Locates object and/or person hidden while child is watching

- PS2.1a   The child searches for the object by continuing to follow the object's path after it disappears; for example, the child looks for a toy train at the end of the tunnel through which the train has disappeared.

- PS2.1b   The child looks for a hidden object at the point where the object was last seen before it disappeared; for example, the adult takes a doll from the child's lap and covers it with a blanket. The child searches for the doll in his or her lap or in the adult's hand.

Objective 2.2   Locates object and/or person who is partially hidden while child is watching

Objective 2.3   Reacts when object and/or person hides from view

IMPORTANCE OF SKILLS

These skills represent the child's ability to generalize the notion of permanence of objects to situations in the daily environment. The child becomes aware that objects have an existence that is permanent and independent from the child's actions. That is, the child learns that objects continue to exist even if they are not seen or manipulated directly. The child begins to understand that objects that disappear can be found again. These skills are critical to the child's sense of control of the environment and sense of trust and afford the child more play opportunities. Other goals/objectives that can be targeted at the same time as Goal 2 are listed on the following page.

Cognitive

Goal 2: Locates object in latter of two successive hiding places

Cognitive

E:3.1 Moves barrier or goes around barrier to obtain object

E:4 Solves common problems

Social-Communication

C:1 Locates objects, people, and/or events without contextual cues

C:2.2 Carries out one-step direction without contextual cues

D:3.2 Asks questions

Social

B:2.1 Responds to established social routines

Notes:

TEACHING SUGGESTIONS

Activity-Based

Playtime

- Hide objects in clothes with two or more pockets or in bags with two or more compartments. (2, 2.1)

- Play guessing games by hiding objects in your hands or under boxes, cups, or sheets of paper. Objects serving as covers should be similar. Encourage the child to look in the second hiding place to find the objects. (2, 2.1)

- Make toys disappear under sand or bubble bath. During water and sand play activities, partially hide objects under soap bubbles or in the sand. Cover floating toys with a washcloth. Hide small objects in your hand during interactive games. (2.1, 2.2, 2.3)

- Play hiding games, such as Peekaboo, with the child. Cover face or parts of face with hands, a pillow, or a cloth. Hide behind furniture or in a doorway. Encourage the child to find the people underneath. Encourage the child to take turns hiding and act excited when you "find" the child. (2.1, 2.2)

- When the child is playing with a toy, hide the toy (e.g., behind an adult's back, under a blanket, in a container) and encourage the child to find it. Intentionally make toys, cars, or balls roll out of sight. (2.1. 2.2)

- Present the child with toys that have parts that disappear and appear again, such as pop-up toys or jack-in-the-boxes. Activate the toy and encourage the child to find the part that disappeared (e.g., lift lid on jack-in-the-box). (2.1, 2.3)

Throughout daily routines

- Move toys, clothes, or household objects from their usual places to other hiding places. Encourage the child to look in the successive hiding places. (2)

- Place objects (e.g., toys, clothes, food) out of sight in dressers or cabinets that have similar drawers or doors. Place objects and food in boxes and paper bags and wait for the child to find them. (2, 2.1, 2.2)

- During daily routines, pick up and place the child's favorite foods and toys in the refrigerator and cupboards while the child is still interested in them. Encourage the child to search for them. (2.1)

- Ask the child to find objects that are partially covered by blankets in the crib or by napkins at the table, objects that are partially hidden under furniture, or objects that are stacked on one another in the toy box. Name objects and point to them if necessary; for example, say, "Where's your teddy bear?" when only the bear's legs are visible under a cover. If the child does not locate the bear, then point to it and encourage the child to pull it out from under the cover. (2.2)

- When giving an object to the child, hold the object in such a way that part of it is covered with your fingers, a cloth, or a paper bag. (2.2, 2.3)

- Make objects that the child is playing with disappear from the child's visual field by dropping them on the floor, placing them on a high shelf, or covering them with a larger object. (2.2)

- Observe the child's reactions when a person leaves the room or when a desired toy or food is placed behind a cupboard door or in a drawer. Draw the child's attention to the object or person who disappears from sight. (2.2, 2.3)

Environmental Arrangements

- Use objects that are clearly interesting to the child to ensure the child's attention. Hide objects the child is about to reach for or with which the child is playing; for example, cover an object held in the child's hand or lying in the child's lap, then slowly displace the object and hide it close to the child within easy reach (e.g., under clothing, under a blanket the child is sitting on). Use covers of different color, size, or shape. (2, 2.1, 2.2)

- Provide visual cues. Begin by using transparent covers, such as drinking glasses, clear plastic, or cupboards with glass doors. Use soft covers that make the contour of the hidden object visible. Covers should be easy for the child to remove (e.g., a lightweight lid, cloth, pillow, your hand). Avoid tight lids and heavy objects. (2, 2.1)

- Use familiar opaque objects as covers and avoid bright, shiny covers so that the object remains more interesting than the cover. (2)

- Hide and reveal objects repeatedly; for example, open and shut your hand while holding a small toy, or cover and uncover a cracker with a napkin. (2.1)

- Pair visual cues with auditory cues by partially hiding noise-producing objects or by talking to the child if playing Peekaboo. Hide a musical toy under a cloth while the toy is still playing music. (2.1, 2.2)

- Pair visual cues with tactile cues by covering or partially covering an object that the child is manipulating or by gently touching the child with an object that is partially covered. (2.1, 2.2)

- Use toys and/or objects that have strings attached (e.g., pull-toy, car with yarn attached) so that the child pulls the string to obtain the partially hidden toy. (2.2)

- Hide toys or objects that the child is playing with under a blanket, towel, or box. (2.1, 2.2, 2.3)

- While the child is sitting on the adult's lap or in a highchair, hand the child a large, interesting toy that is likely to drop from the child's hands and visual field because of its size. (2.1, 2.2, 2.3)

- Play with balls and other objects likely to roll out of view. (2.2, 2.3)

- Use objects such as wind-up toys that will continue to make noise while out of sight. Continue to talk to the child while moving behind the doorway, behind a large piece of furniture, or under a blanket. (2.2, 2.3)

Instructional Sequences

- Model opening two successive cupboard doors to find the child's favorite toy. (2, 2.1, 2.2, 2.3)

- Verbally direct the child to look in two successive places for a favorite toy. (2, 2.1, 2.2)

- Hide an object while the child is watching, and then model finding it. (2.2)

- After placing the object in one hiding place, slowly move the object to another place where it is only partially hidden. (2, 2.1, 2,2)

- Physically assist the child to open cupboards to find a toy. (2.1, 2.2)

TEACHING CONSIDERATIONS

1. If a cover (e.g., cup, blanket, paper, box, lid) is used to hide an object, then it is important to differentiate the child's search for the object from pulling at the cover to play with the cover itself. In general, if the child removes the cover and immediately reaches for the object, then it can be assumed that the child is looking for the hidden object.

2. If the child does not have the motor skills to reach for or grasp the object, then the child may indicate awareness of its location by looking or pointing.

3. If the child has a visual impairment, increase the variety and intensity of cues (e.g., objects of increased size or brightness, noise-producing objects).

4. Consult a qualified specialist for further techniques for the child with a visual, hearing, or motor impairment.

5. Consider safety with all objects that the child handles.

Cognitive

GOAL 3   Maintains search for object that is not in its usual location

- PS3a   The child asks the adult for an object when the object is not found in its usual location.

- PS3b   The child maintains a search for an object in its usual location; for example, the child searches a second time in a toy box for a favorite toy.

Objective 3.1   Looks for object in usual location

- PS3.1a The child looks for an object in the proximity of its usual location; for example, the child goes into the kitchen and requests a cracker or goes to the corner where the toys are kept to look for a ball.

IMPORTANCE OF SKILLS

These skills represent the beginning of an understanding of the permanence of objects. In addition, these skills require the child to practice long-term memory skills and associate familiar objects with stable locations that are familiar reference points in the child's environment. These skills enhance the child's exploration of the environment and increase opportunity for play. Other goals/ objectives that can be targeted at the same time as Goal 3 are listed on the following page.

TEACHING SUGGESTIONS

Activity-Based

Playtime

- Play a "You're getting warmer or colder" game and give the child clues as he or she searches for the missing object or peer. (3, 3.1)

- Ask the child to look for the dog inside when you know that the dog is outside or in a closed room. (3, 3.1)

- During play activities, avoid providing all necessary materials so the child has an opportunity to search for objects; for example, give the child only one of two functionally related objects, such as a formboard without shapes, crayons without paper, people and animals without the barn, or strings without beads. (3, 3.1)

- Play games such as Hide-and-Seek with objects. (3, 3.1)

Feeding

- Ask the child to get bread out of the cupboard when it is really in the refrigerator or in a grocery bag. (3, 3.1)

- Give the child only one of two functionally related objects, such as a bowl of applesauce without a spoon, or a cup without a pitcher of juice. Wait for the child to notice something is missing; encourage the child to look for it. (3, 3.1)

Goal 3: Maintains search for object that is not in its usual location

Cognitive

E:3.1 Moves barrier or goes around barrier to obtain object

E:4 Solves common problems

Social-Communication

C:1 Locates objects, people, and/or events without contextual cues

D:3.2 Asks questions

Social

B:2.1 Responds to established social routines

Notes:

Cognitive

Throughout daily routines

- Set up daily activities so that the child can independently search for familiar objects in their usual locations; for example, when it is time to go outside, ask the child to find his or her coat. When it is time for a change of clothes or diapers, ask the child to go get them. Announce bath time, and wait for the child to proceed to the bathroom. (3.1)

Environmental Arrangements

- Arrange the environment so that objects are not in their usual location; for example, tell the child to look in the cupboard for a particular color or shape of glass that is in the sink and not yet washed. Place the object in another location similar to its usual location; for example, place the child's teddy bear, which usually rests on the child's bed, on the parent's bed. (3, 3.1)

- Arrange objects so that they are visible to the child when the child is searching for the object in its usual location; for example, place fish food on a nearby stool when the child goes to get the fish food in its usual location on a shelf. (3, 3.1)

- Encourage the child to look for an object just after the child has placed it in its usual location; for example, the child places a box of crackers in the cupboard, the peer requests a cracker, and the child returns to the cupboard to get a cracker. (3, 3.1)

- Give the child one item of a pair, such as one shoe or sock, and ask the child to find the mate. (3, 3.1)

- Encourage the child to look for an object in its usual location when the object is within the child's visual field; for example, ask the child to get a book from an open bookshelf. (3, 3.1)

- Have the child look for the dog in its doghouse or bed. (3.1)

Instructional Sequences

- Model searching for an object that is not in its usual location. Comment as you find it. (3, 3.1)

- Verbally encourage the child to continue looking for an object that is not in its usual location (e.g., "Where else could your teddy bear be?"). (3, 3.1)

- Suggest places for the child to search; for example, as the child looks for the pet dog in the backyard suggest that the child look on the front porch. (3, 3.1)

- Accompany the child in the search and physically assist the child to look in several places. (3, 3.1)

TEACHING CONSIDERATIONS

1. Be sure that the object and its usual location are familiar to the child.

2. The mastery of this skill does not require the child to find the object. If, however, the child appears to become upset about not finding the object after searching in more than one place, then give the child the object or direct the child to it.

3. If a cover (e.g., cup, blanket, paper, box, lid) is used to hide an object, then it is important to differentiate the child's search for the object from pulling at the cover to play with the cover itself. In general, if the child removes the cover and immediately reaches for the object, then it can be assumed that the child is looking for the hidden object.

4. If the child has a visual or motor impairment, the child may indicate awareness of the location by some other means (e.g., vocalizing, blinking, pointing).

5. Consult a qualified specialist for techniques for the child with a visual, hearing, or motor impairment.

6. The environment should be free of auditory, visual, or tactile events that compete with the object presented. Arrange objects systematically in the same locations within the child's reach.

7. Consider safety with all objects that the child handles.

Cognitive

Causality

GOAL 1   Correctly activates mechanical toy

- PS1a   The child touches or attempts to manipulate a button, key, or switch to activate a mechanical toy.

- PS1b   The child touches the part of the mechanical toy that produces a movement or a sound (e.g., the child touches the tail of a toy animal that wags when wound up).

Objective 1.1   Correctly activates simple toy

Objective 1.2   Acts on mechanical and/or simple toy in some way

Objective 1.3   Indicates interest in simple and/or mechanical toy

IMPORTANCE OF SKILLS

These skills represent the child's ability to produce actions that take into account the specific properties of the object. The child differentiates responses that activate specific objects from those that merely produce interesting results. Initially, the child learns to associate specific actions with certain items (e.g., balls roll and bounce, rattles shake and make noise) not apparently connected to the child's action. Eventually, the child begins to perceive his or her actions as the causes of interesting results. This is an important early step in the child's exploration of the environment and affords the child more interesting play opportunities. Other goals/objectives that can be targeted at the same time as Goal 1 are listed on the following page.

TEACHING SUGGESTIONS

Activity-Based

Playtime

- Present the child with a variety of mechanical toys and objects that must be manipulated (e.g., push-button, knob, handle) to be activated. Use many different examples of toys that are manipulated in a variety of ways; for example, a dump truck activated by pushing a button or pulling a lever, a musical toy activated by pulling on a string, a wind-up toy activated by turning a key, or a toy piano played by hitting a key. Demonstrate the toy's correct action, if necessary. (1)

- Select and offer toys that produce effects that are interesting to the child. (1, 1.1)

Concurrent Goals/Objectives for Cognitive Strand C

Goal 1: Correctly activates mechanical toy

Fine Motor

B:1 Rotates either wrist on horizontal plane

B:3 Uses either index finger to activate objects

Cognitive

D:1.1 Imitates motor action that is commonly used

E:2.1 Uses part of object and/or support to obtain another object

E:4.1 Uses more than one strategy in attempt to solve common problem

F:1.2 Uses functionally appropriate actions with objects

Social-Communication

C:2.3 Carries out one-step direction with contextual cues

Social

A:3.2 Responds to communication from familiar adult

C:1.5 Entertains self by playing appropriately with toys

Notes:

Cognitive

- Offer toys that are activated by different actions; for example, rattles and bells are activated by shaking; larger objects, such as a roly-poly toy, are activated by a push with the arm and hand; and squeeze-toys are activated by squeezing. (1.1, 1.2)

- Make sure that the child has time to thoroughly explore and exercise a number of actions (e.g., mouthing, shaking, banging) on an object before you expect correct activation. (1.2, 1.3)

- Introduce objects within an interactive, turn-taking game, and demonstrate the toys' correct use. (1.1, 1.2, 1.3)

- Provide the child with a variety of mechanical and simple toys that produce an interesting effect as a result of the child's action on them (e.g., squeeze-toy, mobile, roly-poly toy, chime ball). Encourage the child to exercise simple actions on objects (e.g., swiping, banging, mouthing, shaking). (1.2, 1.3)

- Make your own pull-toy by threading yogurt cartons or spools on yarn. (1.2, 1.3)

- Wind a musical toy for the child. When it winds down, ask if the child would like to hear it again. (1.2, 1.3)

- Activate a variety of interesting simple or mechanical toys, such as a rattle, bell, squeeze-toy, wind-up radio, or jack-in-the-box. (1.3)

Quiet time

- Routinely activate a mobile above the child's crib when you put the child down or get the child up from a nap. (1.3)

Throughout daily routines

- To stimulate the child's interest, use familiar objects in novel ways (e.g., bang a spoon on a metal or plastic bowl to produce a noise; use a hand puppet to shake a rattle; make funny noises and exaggerated facial expressions). (1.3)

Environmental Arrangements

- Start by using toys that are easily activated by pushing a button or lever, as opposed to turning a key or dial. Increase the complexity as the child's skills increase. (1)

- Select toys that produce interesting effects that are tangible to the child (e.g., a water pistol that squirts water on the child, a flashlight or slide projector in a dark room). Demonstrate the toy or object's correct use, if necessary. Begin with simple, highly interesting items, such as a doorbell or light switch. (1)

- Try demonstrating the use of a mechanical toy that the child is already using in some way. Increase the complexity of the child's play by using similar toys with mechanical features; for example, for a child who enjoys doll play, introduce a doll that walks or talks when a button is pushed or a string is pulled. (1, 1.2)

- Many mechanical toys require considerable effort to produce an effect (e.g., a long pull-string on a See-N-Say, a wind-up television or radio, many cranks of a jack-in-the-box handle). Assist the child by doing the initial pull or crank; let the child complete the task to produce the effect. Systematically reduce your input and require more participation by the child. (1, 1.2)

- Use toys that continue a movement after an initial activation (e.g., rocking horse, wobbly toy, wind chimes, toy with pendulum). Use toys that produce a sound (e.g., bell, drum) or a visual effect (e.g., a transparent rattle full of beads). (1, 1.1, 1.2, 1.3)

- Join in the child's play with the toy. Demonstrate the correct use of a toy the child is already using or manipulating. Encourage the child to incorporate new movements into play if he or she is holding a rattle with moving parts (demonstrate how to make other parts move). (1.1, 1.2)

- Hang a rattle or chime toy on the side of the crib or hang a swing toy within swiping range when the child is lying on his or her back. Always be cautious of the danger of hanging objects in the crib. (1.2)

- Place toys in close proximity to the child's hands or feet so that the child might accidentally activate them. Encourage the child to repeat the movement. (1.2, 1.3)

- Create noises for toys that do not typically make noise (e.g., cry for the baby doll when you hold it, make a "vroom" sound when you push a toy truck). (1.3)

- Use objects that are likely to attract the child's attention, such as large, bright, or noise-producing toys (e.g., attach measuring spoons or jingle bells to the car seat). Alternate activation of the toy with abrupt interruptions to maintain the child's interest. (1.2, 1.3)

- Model interest in the toy by exclaiming surprise when the toy activates. (1.3)

- Introduce toys during face-to-face interactions when the child is showing interest in your behavior. (1.3)

Instructional Sequences

- Model or have a peer model activating a toy, and then hand it to the child. If necessary, give specific instructions (e.g., say, "Shake the bells," "Push the button"). (1, 1.1, 1.2, 1.3)

Cognitive

- When the child purposely or accidentally activates a toy (e.g., sets a spinner in motion on a crib mobile), verbally acknowledge the movement by saying, "That's the way. Do it again." (1.1, 1.2)

- If the child does not use a simple toy correctly, then provide verbal directions to encourage the child and to focus the child's attention (e.g., say, "Look at this," "Something funny is going to happen"). Verbally encourage the child to activate the toy (e.g., "Make it move") and provide instructions (e.g., "Push the button"). (1.1, 1.2, 1.3)

- Pair presentation of the toy with visual or verbal cues by presenting the object in the child's visual field or by telling the child to look. (1.3)

- Place toys in the child's hands, on the child's lap, or by the child's feet. Assist the child to act on the toy by touching, kicking, moving, or swiping. (1.2)

- Physically assist the child to activate simple toys. (1.2, 1.3)

Combining or pairing different levels of instructions may be helpful when beginning to teach a new and difficult skill. Fade to less intrusive instructions as soon as possible to encourage more independent performance.

TEACHING CONSIDERATIONS

1. The child should be in a quiet, alert state.

2. The environment should be free of objects or events that compete with the toy presented to the child.

3. Choose a toy that is appropriate for the child's motor/sensory skills. Toys should provide cues to which the child with a sensory impairment can respond (e.g., noise-producing toys for the child with a visual impairment, moving toys for the child with a hearing or motor impairment).

4. A child with a motor impairment may indicate awareness that a toy can be acted on in ways other than manual exploration; for example, active visual exploration of an object may replace manipulation.

5. If the child has a visual impairment, allow tactile exploration before expecting the child to activate the toy. Provide verbal and tactile cues rather than a visual demonstration of the toy.

6. When the child indicates interest, continue activating the toy to reinforce the interest.

7. Consult a qualified specialist for techniques for the child with a visual, hearing, or motor impairment.

8. Consider safety with all objects that the child handles.

GOAL 2   Reproduces part of interactive game and/or action in order to continue game and/or action

- PS2a   The child indicates a desire for the adult to continue a game and/or action by touching a part of the adult's body used to produce the game and/or action; for example, the child touches the adult's hand or eyes to indicate the desire to continue playing Peekaboo.

Objective 2.1   Indicates desire to continue familiar game and/or action

- PS2.1a   The child reproduces an action (e.g., waves arms, vocalizes, smiles) after an adult is attentive to the child's initial behavior.

IMPORTANCE OF SKILLS

The child learns how to reproduce an action or part of a game to cause others to repeat actions that they have initiated. The child no longer uses random actions to make interesting events continue but reproduces a precise action related to a specific type of interaction. The child also uses a variety of actions to cause a particular effect, indicating that the child is becoming aware of the effect of personal actions on people, objects, and events. The child learns to perceive the causal relationship between personal actions and their consequences. These behaviors also represent the first signals used intentionally by the child to communicate, which is an important first step in the communication process. Other goals/objectives that can be targeted at the same time as Goal 2 are listed on the following page.

TEACHING SUGGESTIONS

Activity-Based

Playtime

- Sing interactive songs or songs with motor actions such as "Row, Row, Row Your Boat," "Eency Weency Spider," and "Twinkle, Twinkle Little Star." (2)

- Play "This Little Piggy" on the child's bare foot; stop after the second toe. (2)

- Engage the child in interactive games or actions with or without objects. Observe the child's reactions (e.g., looking, smiling, moving body, waving arms). Once the child's interest is gained, cease the activity and wait for

Cognitive

Concurrent Goals/Objectives for Cognitive Strand C

Fine Motor

B:3.1 Uses either hand to activate objects

Adaptive

A:4.3 Accepts food presented on spoon

Cognitive

B:2.1 Locates object and/or person hidden while child is watching

D:1.1 Imitates motor action that is commonly used

D:2.2 Imitates words that are frequently used

Social-Communication

A:3 Engages in vocal exchanges by babbling

Social

A:3.2 Responds to communication from familiar adult

Notes:

the child to indicate a desire to continue the game or action, or reproduce part of the game or action to continue it; for example, play Pat-a-cake or Peekaboo. Then, pause and wait until the child claps hands, covers eyes, or vocalizes, waves arms, shakes head, arches, or rocks as a signal for you to continue. (2, 2.1)

Throughout daily routines

- Engage in simple motor activities that entertain the child and that the child can reproduce (e.g., bang or push objects, open and close hands, make funny noises, gesture good-bye, splash water). (2)

- During diapering, place a diaper or cloth over the child's face or your face to play Peekaboo. Play airplane while feeding the child with a spoon. While dressing the child, tickle his or her feet, tummy, or neck. (2.1)

- Repeat the child's sounds or actions, pausing to allow the child to respond. (2.1)

- During feedings, stop offering the bottle or spoon and wait for the child to indicate desire for more. (2.1)

Environmental Arrangements

- Engage in actions, using visual, auditory, and tactile stimuli. Play with shiny, noisy, or tactilely interesting objects (e.g., flashlight, aluminum foil, noise-producing toys, feathers, or soft stuffed animals). (2)

- Pair actions with additional cues (e.g., vocalize, exaggerate facial expressions) to make the game or action interesting to the child. (2)

- Engage in actions that have a direct effect on the child's body (e.g., gently tickle the child's tummy, kiss and blow on the child's arm). (2.1)

- Play with objects that produce auditory, visual, and tactile stimuli (e.g., noisy mechanical toys, a radio set at increased volume, a flashlight, soft and furry toys, feathers, water). (2.1)

- Imitate a behavior initiated by the child and integrate it into a social game (e.g., if the child bangs an object, then imitate the action). Ascertain the child's interest by observing the child's reaction. Cease imitating to allow the child an opportunity to indicate a desire to continue the action. (2.1)

Instructional Sequences

- Integrate an action initiated by the child in an interactive game; for example, if the child bounces up and down while sitting on your lap, then ask, "Do you want to play horsie?" Bounce the child up and down, making clicking noises with your tongue. Cease the activity and wait for the child to bounce again or make clicking noises. (2, 2.1)

Cognitive

- Model interactive actions such as clapping your hands and pausing for the child to do the same. (2, 2.1)

- Give the child verbal instructions ("It's your turn" or "More!"). Ask the child, "More?" or "Again?" (2, 2.1)

- Physically clap the child's hands together and then exclaim, "Good job! You're clapping." (2.1)

TEACHING CONSIDERATIONS

1. Be sure that the actions are developmentally appropriate for the child to reproduce.

2. Make sure that the interaction is familiar and interesting to the child. Try a variety of behaviors until the child manifests interest with a smile, look, or kick.

3. If the child has a sensory impairment, make sure that the child is capable of reproducing the stimuli presented and the responses required.

4. Games and actions should provide cues to which the child with a sensory impairment can respond (e.g., noise-producing toys for a child with a visual impairment, moving toys for a child with a hearing or motor impairment).

5. Speak loudly and use gestures for the child with a hearing impairment. Play touching or tickling games with the child with a visual impairment.

6. Consult a qualified specialist for techniques for the child with a visual, hearing, or motor impairment.

7. Consider safety with all objects that the child handles.

STRAND D

Imitation

GOAL 1   Imitates motor action that is not commonly used

- PS1a   The child imitates an unfamiliar motor action demonstrated by the adult with an object that the child is playing with or with parts of the body the child has just used; for example, the child claps his or her hands, the adult opens and closes his or her fingers, and the child imitates, or the child places some beans in a container, the adult puts some beans in a row, and the child imitates.

- PS1b   The child responds to a model of an unfamiliar motor action by performing a similar but different action involving the same body part(s); for example, the adult turns around, and the child jumps up and down.

Objective 1.1   Imitates motor action that is commonly used

- PS1.1a   The child reproduces a motor action similar to, but different from, the adult's model; for example, the adult opens and closes his or her fingers and the child waves his or her hand.

- PS1.1b   The child imitates a simple motor action that is commonly used after the adult imitates an action initiated by the child; for example, the child sticks out his or her tongue, the adult imitates, and the child repeats the action within a turn-taking interaction.

IMPORTANCE OF SKILLS

The child's ability to reproduce an action that he or she is not yet using is important for the acquisition of new behaviors and skills. The child learns to modify familiar actions with respect to new models. Imitation of novel gestures requires the child to engage in problem-solving behaviors as the child tries different actions (means) to reproduce the modeled action (goal). At first, the child imitates only actions that he or she can already do. Imitation is important to the development of representation and language because the child uses gestures to indicate formerly perceived objects and events. Reciprocal imitation also represents a form of early communicative exchange. Imitation enables the child to learn about people, objects, and events by reproducing new behaviors and actions performed by models. Other goals/objectives that can be targeted at the same time as Goal 1 are listed on the following page.

Concurrent Goals/Objectives for Cognitive Strand D

Goal 1: Imitates motor action that is not commonly used

Fine Motor

A:5.1 Aligns objects

B:2 Assembles toy and/or object that require(s) putting pieces together

B:5 Copies simple written shapes after demonstration

Gross Motor

D:1 Jumps forward

D:3.2 Kicks ball or similar object

Adaptive

A:5 Transfers food and liquid between containers

B:2 Washes and dries hands

B:3 Brushes teeth

Cognitive

C:2 Reproduces part of interactive game and/or action in order to continue game and/or action

E:4 Solves common problems

F:1.2 Uses functionally appropriate actions with objects

Social-Communication

C:2.3 Carries out one-step direction with contextual cues

Social

A:2.2 Responds to familiar adult's social behavior

C:1.2 Responds appropriately to peer's social behavior

Notes:

TEACHING SUGGESTIONS

Activity-Based

Playtime

- Engage the child in interactive activities (e.g., playing musical instruments, acting out and telling stories, playing with dolls and animals) and introduce a turn-taking interaction (e.g., the child imitates the adult hitting a bell with a drumstick; the adult tells a story about a bird and flaps his or her arms in the motion of wings, and the child imitates the motion). (1)

- Play games such as Simon Says, introducing uncommon actions (e.g., rub feet, place hand under arm, touch forehead with one finger). (1)

- Sing novel songs with motor actions (e.g., "Wheels on the Bus," "Open/Shut Them"). Encourage the child to join by imitating the novel motor actions. (1)

- Engage the child in turn-taking activities, such as building a tower, in which each person takes a turn placing a block. Play games taking turns clapping each other's blocks, as in Peas, Porridge, Hot. (1.1)

Throughout daily routines

- As the child demonstrates interest during daily activities, seize the opportunity to demonstrate actions and the use of objects with which the child is not yet familiar. Show the child the functional use of objects (e.g., comb hair, brush teeth, scribble with a pencil), communicative gestures (e.g., shake someone's hand, blow a kiss, stroke a pet), or movement (e.g., step over an obstacle, kick a ball). Encourage the child to imitate the action. (1)

- During daily routines and when the child is in a position that allows eye contact, smile, stick out your tongue, move your head from side to side or up and down, or produce any visible motor action and observe whether the child reproduces the same action. Bring a hand within the child's visual field, then move your fingers, wave bye-bye, open and close one hand, or move both hands together and apart. Encourage the child to imitate. (1.1)

- When the child demonstrates interest in an object, act on the object, using actions that the child can perform; for example, shake a rattle, bang a spoon on the table, push a ball, or splash water. (1.1)

- Encourage children to learn signs for a few basic words. (1.1)

Environmental Arrangements

- Encourage the child to imitate less familiar actions within the child's visual range (e.g., swing a leg, put on a bracelet). (1)

Cognitive

- Stand with the child in front of a mirror so that the child can see him- or herself. Demonstrate different actions (e.g., place an object on your head, try to touch the tip of your nose with your tongue). Encourage the child to imitate the action while observing him- or herself in the mirror. (1)

- Exaggerate actions and pair them with auditory or tactile cues (e.g., make noises while kissing or blowing the child's ear or leg, hit your stomach and groan, wrinkle your nose or sniff at a strong-smelling substance and make an exclamation, pat your mouth while making sounds). (1)

- Play imitative games beginning with imitation of commonly used, visible gestures. Gradually introduce gestures not commonly used. (1, 1.1)

- Sing motor imitation songs such as "Head, Shoulder, Knees, and Toes" or "The Hokey Pokey." Have another child demonstrate the action as a model. (1, 1.1)

- Encourage the child to imitate movements performed with parts of the body that the child can see on him- or herself. Use hands, arms, legs, or feet rather than parts of the face; shake hands rather than open and close eyes; or touch your knee rather than your nose. (1, 1.1)

- Perform actions that produce intense stimuli or interesting results for the child; for example, bang on a loud drum, bring a bottle to your mouth, splash water, or shake a flashlight. (1.1)

- Pair visual, auditory, and tactile cues. Put sticky tape on the tips of your fingers and vocalize while gently drumming fingers on the child's arm or leg. Encourage the child to move his or her own fingers. (1.1)

- Make a desired event contingent on the child's imitation; for example, during meals, open and close your mouth and encourage the child to imitate before placing food in the child's mouth. (1.1)

- Engage other children as models in interactive games of imitation. (1.1)

- Encourage the child to imitate a model in action. While shaking a rattle, hand the child a similar rattle to shake. (1, 1.1)

Instructional Sequences

- Model common motor actions (i.e., kicking a ball). (1, 1.1)

- Encourage the child to imitate the model in action; for example, during a magic show, continue to move your hand in a circular motion over a blanket and say, "Abracadabra" until the child imitates. (1, 1.1)

- Give verbal directions (e.g., "You do it," "Your turn"). (1, 1.1)

- Physically assist the child by gently touching the part of the body to be engaged in the action. (1.1)

Combining or pairing different levels of instructions may be helpful when beginning to teach a new and difficult skill. Fade to less intrusive instructions as soon as possible to encourage more independent performance.

TEACHING CONSIDERATIONS

1. Initially, select actions that the child has been observed to perform.

2. When selecting actions that the child has not yet performed make sure they are functional and useful.

3. Motor actions should be only slightly beyond the child's current abilities.

4. Do not provide the child with extra cues, such as verbal directions, unless intentionally used for assistance. The child needs to focus on the motor act, not the verbal direction.

5. The focus is on the ability to reproduce a previously performed action and not on the motor complexity of the action.

6. If the child has a motor impairment, select motor actions not commonly used that are within the child's ability (e.g., pat knee, rub eyebrow).

7. The child with a visual impairment may need special adaptations such as verbal direction (e.g., say, "Jump up and down like me"). This goal may not be appropriate for a child with a severe visual impairment.

8. A child with a hearing impairment may require directions using sign language or total communication.

9. Consider safety with all objects that the child handles.

Cognitive

GOAL 2   Imitates words that are not frequently used

- PS2a   The child imitates a word that he or she does not frequently use and that is a modification of a child-initiated sound or word (e.g., the child says, "Ball." The adult says, "It looks like a ball, but this is a balloon." The child imitates and says, "Balloon").

Objective 2.1   Imitates speech sounds that are not frequently used

- PS2.1a   The child imitates an adult's modification of a child-initiated speech sound or word approximation (e.g., the child says, "Baba"; the adult responds "Bobbie"; and the child imitates, "Bobbie").

Objective 2.2   Imitates words that are frequently used

- PS2.2a   The child imitates simple, familiar consonant–vowel words when the model is an imitation of a word that the child has just used (e.g., the child says, "Go"; the adult says, "Go"; and the child imitates).

- PS2.2b The child imitates the adult's expansion of a child-initiated word approximation (e.g., the child says, "Wa"; the adult says, "Water"; and the child imitates, "Wa wa").

- PS2.2c The child imitates vocal sounds that are frequently used (e.g., the adult vocalizes, "Baba, ah-goo"; and the child imitates, "Baba, ah-goo").

- PS2.2d The child responds to the adult's vocalization with a similar but different vocalization (e.g., the adult coos, "Gege"; and the child responds, "Ee").

- PS2.2e The child responds vocally to the voice of others (e.g., the child coos when mother talks).

IMPORTANCE OF SKILLS

Through imitation of words that are not frequently used, the young child's basic vocabulary can be broadened to include words referring to both more general and more specific categories. The child learns to reproduce new vocalizations to match the novel model by modifying vocal behaviors already in his or her repertoire. These new vocalizations become meaningful speech sounds that the child can use to refer to objects or events. The child's increased flexibility in adapting behaviors with respect to an external model represents experimentation with different strategies to solve a problem. The imitation of speech sounds and words plays an important role in the acquisition of language. By imitating familiar words, the child can learn to generalize newly acquired words over settings and to other objects. In addition, imitation is a form of turn-taking communication between the child and caregiver. Other goals/objectives that can be targeted at the same time as Goal 2 are listed on the following page.

TEACHING SUGGESTIONS

Activity-Based

Playtime

- Point to and label novel body parts (e.g., knee, elbow, cheek). Encourage the child to imitate. (2, 2.1, 2.2)

- Engage the child in play with toys and other materials or social games in which sound patterns can be easily integrated in the game; for example, play with toy animals and produce animal sounds. Say, "Moo" when playing with a cow and "Meow" when playing with a cat. (2.1)

- Engage in pretend play or play with hand puppets; for example, pretend to be a magician and use magic words such as "poof." (2, 2.1)

- Engage in turn-taking interactive games by making "funny" sounds. Encourage the child to imitate unfamiliar speech sounds. (2.1)

Concurrent Goals/Objectives for Cognitive Strand D

Goal 2: Imitates words that are not frequently used

Cognitive

E:4 Solves common problems

Social-Communication

B:1.1 Responds with a vocalization and gesture to simple questions

C:1.2 Locates common objects, people, and/or events in familiar pictures

C:2.3 Carries out one-step direction with contextual cues

D:1 Uses 50 single words

Social

A:3.2 Responds to communication from familiar adult

C:2.2 Responds to communication from peer

Notes:

Cognitive

Storytime

- Look at books with the child, and label the pictures. Encourage the child to imitate the frequently used and novel words. (2, 2.1, 2.2)

Throughout daily routines

- If the child displays an interest during daily activities, then use the opportunity to refer to people, objects, or events with words that the child does not yet use; for example, say the proper name of a relative (e.g., "Grandma Helen" if the child uses only "Grandma") and encourage the child to imitate the name. (2, 2.2)

- Respond to the child's questions of "What's that?" by labeling unfamiliar objects, people, or events; give the child a chance to imitate. (2, 2.1)

- During daily routines, label objects in the immediate environments that are of interest to the child; for example, label foods while eating meals. (2, 2.2)

- During daily interactions, talk to the child. Speak in short sentences about people, objects, and events that are in the immediate environment. Use words that the child frequently uses and observe whether the child imitates them. (2, 2.2)

- While feeding, dressing, and playing with the child, comment on objects that are being used (e.g., the adult says, "Here's your shoe," the child imitates, "Shoe"); people who are present (e.g., the adult says, "Look at Daddy," the child imitates, "Daddy"); and actions that are performed (e.g., the mother says, "Mommy drinks juice," the child imitates, "Drink"). (2, 2.2)

Environmental Arrangements

- Name either a more general or more specific category of an object or event for which the child uses a single term; for example, if the child labels all four-legged animals "doggie," then tell the child, "That's a cow." If the child asks for an apple, then tell the child that an apple is a fruit. If the child identifies a girl skipping as "jumping," then tell the child the girl is skipping. Encourage the child to imitate the new word. (2, 2.2)

- Introduce objects similar to, but slightly different from, those that the child likes. If the child likes books, for example, then show the child a glossy, colorful magazine. Name the new object and encourage the child to imitate the new word. (2, 2.1)

- Place novel objects similar to highly desired objects out of reach but within the child's visual field. Make obtaining the object contingent upon the child's imitation; for example, the child sees yogurt in the refrigerator and asks for ice cream. Tell the child that it is yogurt; wait for the child to imitate before offering the yogurt. Make the novel object or event interesting to the child—tell the child that yogurt is very good. (2, 2.2)

- Play interactive verbal imitation games, and begin by having the child imitate frequently used words; for example, play guessing games. Hide an object under a cover and tell the child that you will uncover the object only if the child imitates the correct word. Alternate familiar and unfamiliar words. (2, 2.2)

- Have other children demonstrate verbalization of words unfamiliar to the child. Engage other children in conversation and have them provide a model for imitation. (2, 2.1, 2.2)

- Associate sounds with objects and events that are of particular interest to the child. Imitate the child's pet dog by saying, "Woof," or make the car noise, "vroom," if the child wants to go for a ride. (2.1)

- Use picture books or sounds to stimulate imitation of animals, vehicles, and environmental sounds. (2.1)

- Associate a speech sound with a motor action (e.g., say, "Sh, sh," while gesturing for quiet). Encourage the child to imitate both the action and the sound. (2.1)

- Pair a speech sound to a child-initiated action (e.g., if the child pulls a string attached to a bell, then say, "Ding dong"), and encourage the child to imitate the sound. (2.1)

- Associate sounds to tactile–kinesthetic stimulation, such as tickling and bouncing. Hold the child in the air and say, "Boom," while rapidly bringing the child down. Repeat actions without vocalizing and observe whether the child repeats, "Boom." Engage other children as imitative models in verbal games. (2.1)

- Repeat the sound or word often, speak slowly, and emphasize each syllable. (2.1, 2.2)

- Comment on novel, changing objects or events (e.g., the adult says, "Mama's home," "The doggie runs fast"); encourage the child to imitate part of the sentence (e.g., "Mama," "Doggie"). (2, 2.2)

- Simplify sentences by using only one- or two-word utterances (e.g., if the child gestures to be picked up, then ask the child, "Up?"; if the child wants to activate a mechanical toy, then tell the child, "Push there"). Pair utterances with visual or tactile–kinesthetic cues; for example, bounce the child up and down while saying, "Up and down"; hide an object behind a screen and label the object while you slowly make it reappear; wave and say, "Bye-bye." (2, 2.2)

Instructional Sequences

- Repeat the word or sound several times, pausing to allow the child to imitate; for example, while playing with a doll, say, "Baby, baby sleep." If necessary, repeat until the child imitates. (2, 2.1, 2.2)

Cognitive

- Give verbal directions (e.g., say, "You say milk"). (2, 2.1, 2.2)
- Physically assist the child by gently touching the child's mouth. (2.1, 2.2)

TEACHING CONSIDERATIONS

1. Sounds should be developmentally appropriate for the child's developmental level but not frequently used by the child. The focus is not on the complexity of the speech sound but on the degree to which the sound differs from sounds already within the child's repertoire.

2. Integrate imitations within a game (e.g., Peekaboo, Simon Says) and make them meaningful (e.g., animal sounds, onomatopoeic sounds associated with objects and motor actions). Introduce turn-taking activities.

3. For Objective 2.2, select words that are related to objects and events in the child's immediate environment and/or words used frequently by the child. Refer to objects and events that are meaningful to the child, such as an object the child is playing with.

4. If the child has a hearing impairment, the use of total communication may be appropriate. Encourage the child to watch lip movements. Speak clearly and combine words with signs. Consult a communications specialist for further ideas for the child with a hearing impairment.

5. If the child has a motor impairment, proper positioning may facilitate sound production.

6. If the child has a visual impairment, provide descriptions of what the new words and labels represent; for example, "A teddy bear is furry and soft. It has four legs." Provide descriptions of the new sounds and words (e.g., say, "When I blow the candle out, it goes 'poof' "). Allow the child to feel your mouth while you speak new words.

Problem Solving

GOAL 1   Retains objects when new object is obtained

- PS1a   The child retains two objects and acts upon a third; for example, the child holds a cracker and a spoon and bangs the highchair tray.

- PS1b   The child retains two objects while regarding a third object.

Objective 1.1   Retains one object when second object is obtained

- PS1.1a   The child retains an object with one hand while acting on a second object; for example, the child holds a block while banging another block with the other hand.

- PS1.1b   The child retains one object while regarding a second object.

Objective 1.2   Retains object

- PS1.2a   The child momentarily grasps an object that is placed in his or her hand.

IMPORTANCE OF SKILLS

When the child has two hands occupied, the presentation of a second or third object leads the child to search for a different strategy to retain all of the desired objects. The child learns to plan, sequence, and coordinate different actions to attain a desired goal. This skill allows the child to engage in more interesting play activities by holding more than one toy or object. The ability to voluntarily grasp an object is a first step toward the development of the use of a tool. The child learns that the hand and other body parts can be used as tools for obtaining and retaining objects. This behavior demands the use of means (e.g., body parts) to attain desired ends (e.g., objects). Other goals/objectives that can be targeted at the same time as Goal 1 are listed on the following page.

TEACHING SUGGESTIONS

Activity-Based

Playtime

- While the child is manipulating or playing with two or more objects, present the child with an additional object. Make sure that the new object is of interest to the child and related to the activity in which the child is engaged; for example, if the child is holding two toy cows, then give the child

Concurrent Goals/Objectives for Cognitive Strand E

Fine Motor

A:2.1 Transfers object from one hand to the other

B:2 Assembles toy and/or object that require(s) putting pieces together

Gross Motor

A:3 Creeps forward using alternating arm and leg movements

Cognitive

E:4 Solves common problems

F:1.2 Uses functionally appropriate actions with objects

Social-Communication

C:1.3 Locates common objects, people, and/or events with contextual cues

Social

A:3.2 Responds to communication from familiar adult

Notes:

a toy horse. The child may place the toy animals in his or her lap, freeing the hands to obtain the additional animal. If the child is shaking a bell in each hand, then hand the child a maraca; the child may transfer the bells to one hand and then obtain the maraca with the free hand. (1)

- Place a variety of objects and toys of different sizes, colors, weights, and textures within the child's reach. Encourage the child to take two objects, or hand the child two objects, one at a time. Observe the child's ability to retain toys in one hand, under one arm, in his or her mouth, or by any other means. If the child initially demonstrates interest in only one object, then let the child manipulate or play with that object for a while before presenting a second object. (1.1, 1.2)

- Provide objects and toys that are similar or are functionally related so that the child can use two objects in a meaningful manner; for example, encourage the child to bang two blocks together, fit two pop beads together, place an apple in a paper bag, or drop blocks in a bucket. (1, 1.1, 1.2)

Feeding

- Have the child hold one cracker in each hand. Offer a third cracker so that the child must place one cracker in his or her mouth or other hand to obtain the third. (1, 1.1)

Throughout daily routines

- During clean-up time, have the child carry several items to his or her bedroom; for example, give the child two shoes and a toy to be carried to his or her bedroom. (1, 1.1)

- During daily routines, give the child an object that the child looks toward. While the child is holding the toy or object, talk about it. Model using a similar toy or object to motivate the child to retain the object. (1.2)

- While the child is holding a doll or similar large object, invite the child to follow you into another room and bring the doll along. (1.2)

- Present the child with familiar objects that the child can manipulate. (1.2)

Environmental Arrangements

- Give the child objects that can be easily retained: clothing or small blankets that the child can drape over an arm; sheets of paper that the child can easily hold in one hand; small objects (e.g., raisins, crackers, small foam sponges, miniature toys) of which several fit in one hand; or stickers that the child can stick on his or her body or on another object. (1, 1.1)

- Prior to presenting a third object, give the child two objects, one of which assists in retaining the other; for example, a blanket can be draped over a doll, a sticker can be stuck on a sheet of paper, a spoon can be placed in a cup, and pop beads can be fitted together.

- When the child is manipulating an object, present a second object that is functionally related to the first and will lead to an interesting result for the child; for example, hand the child a toy hammer or screwdriver when child is manipulating the nuts and bolts on a toy workbench. (1.1)

- Place one object inside another, such as a sock inside a shoe, and give it to the child. Encourage the child to remove one object while holding the other. (1.1)

- Give the child toys and objects that are easily retained because of their shape or texture (e.g., soft furry balls or animals, small blankets or clothing, rattles, spoons). (1.2)

- Offer objects that are especially interesting to the child, such as noise-producing toys, bright-colored paper crumpled in a ball, or favorite foods. (1.2)

- Use materials that stick easily, such as soft playdough, sticky tape, or thick finger paint, to help the child retain them. (1.2)

- Tie an object to a piece of yarn. Place the object in the child's hand, and use the yarn to keep it in place. (1.2)

Instructional Sequences

- Model retaining several objects; for example, place objects in your lap, hold several crayons in one hand, or place crackers in a cup. Encourage the child to imitate. (1, 1.1, 1.2)

- Give the child verbal suggestions, such as, "Put one of the crackers in your mouth," "Put the monkey under your arm," or "Put the spoon in the cup." (1, 1.1, 1.2)

- Remind the child verbally to hold on to the first object while securing the second. Say, "Hold your doll, and take his bottle to feed him." (1.1, 1.2)

- Present a third object and physically assist the child to retain it; for example, when the child's hands are full with a bar of soap and bottle of shampoo, touch the child's arm with a washcloth. Assist the child to extend his or her arm to obtain the cloth. Or, when the child's hands are full, touch the child's lips with a cookie, and see if the child opens his or her mouth to obtain it. (1, 1.1)

- Place part of an object in the child's hand, under the child's arm, or in the child's mouth, and continue to hold onto the object. Use objects of appropriate shapes and sizes, such as cloths, plastic rings, or rattles with long handles. (1.1, 1.2)

- Encourage the child to use more than one means simultaneously to retain an object; for example, while feeding, place the bottle in the child's mouth, and encourage the child to grasp it. (1.2)

Combining or pairing different levels of instructions may be helpful when beginning to teach a new and difficult skill. Fade to less intrusive instructions as soon as possible to encourage more independent performance.

TEACHING CONSIDERATIONS

1. Make sure that the child visually fixates on the object before you offer it to the child.

2. Objects should be interesting to the child so that the child will want to retain them all.

3. Make sure that the child is in a posture that allows free use of body parts to retain objects; for example, hold the child upright rather than lying down.

4. If the child has a visual impairment, allow sufficient time for tactile exploration (e.g., while the adult holds the object) so that the child can identify the object before you expect him or her to retain it.

5. Observe the child's ability to attend simultaneously to all objects (e.g., the child visually explores one object after the other and then returns to explore the first object again).

6. Consider safety with all objects that the child handles.

Cognitive

GOAL 2   Uses an object to obtain another object

- PS2a   The child uses a person to obtain an object; for example, the child asks for the object, looks at the person, and points toward the object; the child looks at the object, looks at the person, and returns the gaze to the object.

- PS2b   The child uses an object to act upon another object; for example, the child hits a drum with a stick or draws a line with a stick in wet sand.

Objective 2.1   Uses part of object and/or support to obtain another object

- PS2.1a   The child acts on part of an object or support to produce a visible or auditory effect; for example, the child pulls a place mat, and the dish rattles, or the child pulls a string, and the toy moves.

- PS2.1b   The child moves his or her own body parts to produce an effect on an object; for example, the child kicks a mobile.

IMPORTANCE OF SKILLS

The child combines a succession of different actions to find a strategy to solve a problem. First, the child has to search for and then use an object as a tool to obtain another object. In addition, the child has to spatially coordinate the two objects so that a contact occurs, enabling the child to obtain the desired object. This skill allows the child more independence in getting the things that he or she wants and needs. The child learns that strings, handles, and supports, as well as direct actions, can serve to act upon other objects, and that spatial contact between objects are necessary for this to happen. This skill aids the development of cause-and-effect relationships. Other goals/objectives that can be targeted at the same time as Goal 2 are listed on the following page.

TEACHING SUGGESTIONS

Activity-Based

Playtime

- As the child colors at the table, have crayons just out of reach. Make available a ruler or rubber scraper for the child to use to obtain crayons. (2, 2.1)

- When playing outdoors, have the child use a toy rake to obtain a ball that has rolled away. (2, 2.1)

Throughout daily routines

- During daily routines and play activities, place objects and toys that the child typically uses just out of reach; for example, place food on the far end of a table, favorite toys in a crib, or clothes on high shelves. Make available objects that the child can use as tools to obtain the desired object; for example, have a wooden spoon or rubber scraper for the child to obtain a cracker, a broom or plastic bat for the child to reach into the crib or behind a couch to obtain a toy, or a chair or stool for the child to climb on to get mittens before going outside. (2, 2.1)

- Encourage the child to obtain objects that are functionally related to the objects used as tools by using a fork, for example, to pick up a piece of meat or a paintbrush to transfer paint. (2, 2.1)

- Give the child toys or objects that have parts that the child could use to obtain the objects (e.g., pull-toy, toy with handle, toy telephone with cord). (2, 2.1)

- If the child shows an interest in having a toy or other object during play or daily caregiving activities, then place the object out of immediate reach on various supports (e.g., pillow, blanket, towel, diaper). Verbally encourage the child to pull the support to obtain the object. Provide a demonstration. (2, 2.1)

Concurrent Goals/Objectives for Cognitive Strand E

Goal 2: Uses an object to obtain another object

Fine Motor

A:3.2 Grasps cylindrical object with either hand by closing fingers around it

Gross Motor

C:4.3 Gets up and down from low structure

Adaptive

A:4.1 Brings food to mouth using utensil

Cognitive

B:3 Maintains search for object that is not in its usual location

E:4 Solves common problems

F:1.2 Uses functionally appropriate actions with objects

Social-Communication

B:1 Gains person's attention and refers to an object, person, and/or event

Notes:

Cognitive

- Place dolls almost out of reach, and observe whether the child pulls on the hair, ribbon, or dress to get the doll. (2, 2.1)

Environmental Arrangements

- Provide tools that serve as an extension of the hand, such as a toy rake, broom, or long spoon. Encourage the child to reach for objects that are easily obtained; for example, use a toy rake to obtain a soft furry animal toy, a broom to obtain a ball or toy car that rolls easily, or a long spoon to obtain an apple or a box of raisins. (2, 2.1)

- Provide the child with a duster on a stick (not a feather duster, as this could be hazardous) to obtain a toy that has been pushed too far back on a shelf. (2, 2.1)

- Place cooked macaroni on a fork and allow the child to eat it from the fork. Gradually require the child to spear macaroni pieces. (2, 2.1)

- Initially, have both the object and the tool close to the child and within the child's visual field. Gradually require the child to look around for the tool. (2, 2.1)

- Identify a number of objects in the child's environment that can be obtained by using part of the object (e.g., shoelace to get shoe, handle to pull wagon, string to pull toy) or by using a convenient support (e.g., place mat under a dish, book under a toy, pillow under a doll). Provide the child with these objects. (2.1)

- Create a game by hiding or partially hiding an object with a string attached (e.g., under a blanket or low table, behind a chair). Present the string to the child. (2, 2.1)

- Tie strings on toys that produce auditory, visual, and other feedback when moved. (2, 2.1)

- Initially, shorten strings and place supports in close vicinity to the child so that accidental touching or pulling will produce an effect on the objects. (2.1)

Instructional Sequences

- Model using an object to obtain another object; for example, poke the end of a paintbrush into a ball of playdough to obtain the playdough. (2, 2.1)

- As the child tries to get a toy out of reach on a shelf, gesture toward a nearby stool. (2, 2.1)

- Give the child verbal instructions (e.g., say, "Climb on the chair," "Reach with the spoon"). If the child is trying to obtain an object with another object but is not making contact, then provide physical assistance by pushing the desired object toward the tool. (2, 2.1)

- Have the child begin to use a fork and spoon at mealtimes. Verbally direct the child to "Use your spoon to get some cereal," or "Use your fork to get a piece of meat." (2, 2.1)

- Use minimal physical assistance to help the child to pull a string or support to obtain an object. Reduce the assistance to give the child an opportunity to continue independently. (2, 2.1)

- Provide a direct connection between the child and an interesting toy by tying a soft string, ribbon, or yarn to the child's wrist so that moving the arm produces a visible or auditory effect on the toy. Start with shorter lengths of string and gradually lengthen. When the child has learned to move each arm to activate a toy, present the toy still attached to the string, but no longer tied to the child's wrist. (2, 2.1)

- Physically assist the child by guiding the use of the tool. (2.1)

TEACHING CONSIDERATIONS

1. Objects should be interesting to the child (e.g., bright-colored and noisy toys for the child with a visual impairment).

2. Place the object where the child cannot obtain it without use of a tool. Be sure, however, that the object can be reached with the tool.

3. Be sure that the actions required to obtain the object are developmentally appropriate for the child's level of functioning and are in the child's repertoire.

4. If the child has a visual impairment, give both objects to the child to explore tactilely before placing one out of reach. Allow him or her to tactilely explore the toy and the string or support. Put the toy at a distance and place the string or part of the support in the child's hand. Talk about the toy.

5. If the child has a motor impairment, use tools that require a minimum of fine motor skills (e.g., attach a magnet to the end of a stick, use T-shaped tools), add a handle (e.g., a wooden bead to a string), use easily grasped supports, and assist the child in pulling.

6. In order to demonstrate that the child has used the support or part of the object to obtain it, the child should manipulate the object in some way once it's obtained.

7. Consider safety with all objects that the child handles.

GOAL 3 Navigates large object around barriers

- PS3a   The child moves a large object from one location to another without barriers in the pathway; for example, at mealtime the child pushes a chair from the corner of the room to the table nearby.

Objective 3.1   Moves barrier or goes around barrier to obtain object

- PS3.1a   The child moves a barrier to obtain an object.
- PS3.1b   The child goes around a barrier to obtain an object.

Objective 3.2   Moves around barrier to change location

IMPORTANCE OF SKILLS

The child learns to coordinate his or her own movements and the movements of an object with respect to another object. The child has to simultaneously solve the problems of navigating an object and of moving around a barrier. The child learns to situate not only him- or herself in relation to a point in space, but also to situate objects in spatial relationship to each other. In order to obtain an object, the child modifies the position of the barrier in relation to the object, or the child re-adjusts his or her own movements as a function of the position of the barrier or the desired object. These skills allow the child more independence of movement and more freedom in play. Other goals/objectives that can be targeted at the same time as Goal 3 are listed on the following page.

TEACHING SUGGESTIONS

Activity-Based

Playtime

- Play with dolls that the child can place in a carriage; play grocery store so that the child can place groceries in a cart. Arrange the environment so that the child can move from one part of the room to another, moving around barriers; for example, pretend to visit a friend's house in another corner of the room, or place the cash register at the far end of the room for grocery store play. (3, 3.1)

- Set up and move through an obstacle course. Play Follow the Leader on tricycles or while pulling wagons or carrying dolls. (3, 3.1, 3.2)

- While playing with the child, place objects that the child will want behind other objects; for example, place a small toy behind a larger toy and observe whether the child moves the larger toy to obtain the smaller toy. (3.1)

Concurrent Goals/Objectives for Cognitive Strand E

Gross Motor

C:1 Walks avoiding obstacles

D:2.1 Pushes riding toy with feet while steering

Social-Communication

C:2.3 Carries out one-step direction with contextual cues

Social

A:3.2 Responds to communication from familiar adult

C:1.3 Plays near one or two peers

Notes:

Cognitive

Assessment, Evaluation, and Programming System for Infants and Children (AEPS®), Second Edition, edited by Diane Bricker © 2002 Paul H. Brookes Publishing Co., Inc. All rights reserved.

- Have the child play with objects that roll away easily under barriers and behind pieces of furniture; for example, play ball near a sofa or bed so that the child can retrieve a ball that rolls away by moving around to the other side. (3.1)

Feeding

- Place a snack for the child on the far side of a table so that the child must walk around the table to get it. (3.2)

Throughout daily routines

- Provide the child with large objects that can be easily moved (e.g., toy wagon or truck, doll carriage, tricycle, small chair, stuffed animals). Encourage the child to move around pieces of furniture, toys on the floor, flower beds, or people while carrying, pushing, or pulling the object. (3, 3.2)

- During daily activities, place objects that the child frequently uses behind barriers or slightly out of reach. Encourage the child to obtain objects normally used in daily routines that have been left in another room. At bedtime, let the child get a favorite toy left in the living room; at snack time, tell the child to find a favorite snack on a shelf behind the table. Observe whether the child moves around pieces of furniture to obtain the object. (3.1)

- During daily inside and outside activities, have the child move around pieces of furniture, large toys, a fence, and flower beds in order to reach a designated location. At mealtime, observe the child's ability to move around a doll carriage to get to the table or to walk around a chair to join an adult or peer. Have the child help clean up after snack and move around furniture to take objects to the sink. (3.1, 3.2)

- During clean-up time, ask the child to get a stuffed animal that has fallen on the other side of the bed. (3.2)

- Ask the child to take objects to a person who is at the far end of a room or behind a piece of furniture. (3.2)

Environmental Arrangements

- Begin with stationary barriers, and then use moveable barriers that the child can move themselves (e.g., push- or pull-toys) as the child becomes more proficient. (3)

- Arrange the situation so that there is no alternate path to the child's desired destination. (3, 3.1)

- As the child carries, pushes, or pulls objects, obstruct the child's path by standing so that the child must move around you. (3, 3.1)

- Place a barrier between the child and an object or toy that the child is playing with; observe whether the child moves or goes around the barrier to continue play; for example, when the child pushes a toy car across the table, make the car drop over the opposite side of the table and encourage the child to go around to retrieve it. Push a toy car or roll a ball slowly around a piece of furniture so that the child can visually follow the object, and then follow the same path to retrieve the object. (3, 3.1)

- Call the child from the opposite end of the room or from behind a barrier such as a door or couch. Remain visible to the child while the child moves around the barrier. (3, 3.2)

- Have the child follow a peer as they both hold an object and navigate around barriers. (3, 3.2)

- Use barriers that allow the object to remain at least partially visible to the child; for example, place a tricycle between the child and a large ball that the child is rolling. Encourage the child to move the tricycle. Place a toy in a transparent plastic container or under a clear heavy plastic sheet so that the child will dump the container, remove a loose-fitting lid, or pull off the plastic sheet. (3.1, 3.2)

- Use lightweight barriers such as empty milk cartons that the child can easily move while reaching for an object; for example, partially hide the child's bottle behind an empty milk carton. (3.1)

- When on the opposite side of a room or a barrier, call the child to participate in an activity. Place yourself close to the barrier so that you are visible to the child; for example, situate yourself on the opposite side of a table from the child and ask the child to come around to join you for a snack or activity. When the child is on the other side of the sofa, sit down and call the child to come and look at a book. If the child hesitates or stops moving, then call the child again. (3.2)

- Have a peer call the child from the other side of a barrier and encourage the child to join the peer. (3.2)

- Walk and hold the child's hand or have the child follow a rope. (3.2)

- Devise a situation that provides no alternate way of reaching the desired location except to move around a barrier. (3.2)

Instructional Sequences

- Provide a model for the child; for example, model maneuvering a wagon around the flower bed or other barriers. (3, 3.1, 3.2)

- Give the child verbal directions to move around the barrier while continuing to push or pull an object. Direct the child which way to move the object. (3, 3.1, 3.2)

- Give the child a small object to navigate and systematically increase the size of the object. (3.1, 3.2)

- Navigate a large object around a barrier, and then physically assist the child in navigating the same object. (3.1)

- Physically assist the child to remove the barrier, or physically guide the child around the barrier to obtain the object. (3.1, 3.2)

TEACHING CONSIDERATIONS

1. Make sure that the solution to the problem is meaningful for the child.

2. Physically assist the child who has a motor impairment to move the object while allowing the child to indicate the direction to move. Use barriers that the child can move with minimal physical effort, or ask the child to gesture or tell how to obtain the object. Ask the child to gesture or tell how to change location. Allow enough space for the child who uses a walker to maneuver around barriers.

3. If the child has a visual impairment, use noise-producing toys to help the child locate the object. Allow the child to tactilely explore the barrier; talk to the child to help identify the location. Motivate the child to change location by calling the child. Keep talking to help the child identify your location.

4. If the child has a hearing impairment, use gestures and signs as well as words.

5. Ensure the child's safety by using barriers that are free from sharp corners and rough edges.

6. Consider safety with all objects that the child handles.

GOAL 4   Solves common problems

- PS4a   The child uses an adult to assist with solving a common problem; for example, the child hands a container to an adult to help open it.

Objective 4.1   Uses more than one strategy in attempt to solve common problem

- PS4.1a   The child repeats the same strategy to solve a common problem; for example, the child pulls on his or her mother's pants to get attention, the mother ignores the child, and the child pulls again.

IMPORTANCE OF SKILLS

Finding a solution to common problems by trial and error represents the child's ability to modify actions as a function of their outcomes. After the first unsuccessful attempt, the child not only tries another strategy but also adjusts successive strategies in response to outcomes of preceding strategies. In this way, the child attains the solution to the problem through gradual approximations and trial-and-error procedures. The child persists in trying until the problem is solved; this builds the child's self-esteem and confidence. Problem-solving skills will be used by the child throughout life. Other goals/objectives that can be targeted at the same time as Goal 4 are listed on the following page.

TEACHING SUGGESTIONS

Activity-Based

Playtime

- Encourage the child to get toys or objects that require problem solving; for example, move a riding toy off of the porch and onto the sidewalk or get a toy from inside a toy box that is covered with several items. (4, 4.1)

Bathing

- Have the child play a game of trying to gather all bath toys in a basket before the water drains out. (4, 4.1)

Throughout daily routines

- During daily routines and activities, observe the child's ability to use different strategies and appropriately modify each successive strategy to attain a solution to the problem by trial and error; for example, the child raises an arm in the direction of cookies that are out of reach, the child then stands on tiptoes in attempt to reach the cookies, and finally the child moves a chair to stand on in order to obtain the cookies. (4, 4.1)

- Encourage the child to independently act on objects and to attempt different strategies when confronted with a problem. If necessary, provide a demonstration and encourage the child to imitate; for example, if the child begins to get upset after attempting to open a box by first shaking the box and then banging on the lid, then demonstrate lifting the lid. Put the lid back in place and observe whether the child lifts off the lid. (4, 4.1)

- Observe the child's attempts to put on or take off clothing, to obtain objects out of reach, to open a paper bag or container with a favorite food, to turn on a water faucet, to open drawers or doors, or to gain attention. Allow the child independence to try activities such as dressing or undressing. If the child gets "stuck," then wait before offering assistance, and give the child the opportunity to solve the problem. (4, 4.1)

- While playing with objects and toys, problems might occur when the child cannot open a book, fit an object into a defined space, or activate a mechanical toy. After trying an unsuccessful strategy, encourage the child to try a different strategy; for example, the child first pushes on the water faucet, then bangs on it; the child tries to shake off a shoe, then taps his or her foot on the ground. (4.1)

Concurrent Goals/Objectives for Cognitive Strand E

Goal 4: Solves common problems

Fine Motor

B:2 Assembles toy and/or object that require(s) putting pieces together

Gross Motor

D:2 Pedals and steers tricycle

Adaptive

C:1 Undresses self

Cognitive

D:1 Imitates motor action that is not commonly used

D:2 Imitates words that are not frequently used

E:1 Retains objects when new object is obtained

E:2 Uses an object to obtain another object

E:3 Navigates large object around barriers

F:1.2 Uses functionally appropriate actions with objects

Social

B:1 Meets observable physical needs in socially appropriate ways

Notes:

- Provide the child with the opportunity to discover and practice new strategies by not intervening and assisting too soon. (4.1)

Environmental Arrangements

- Arrange the environment so that the solution to the problem is easily available; limit the number of alternative strategies; for example, if the child tries to eat applesauce with his or her fingers, then have only a spoon available on the table. If the child tries to fit a square in a round hole, then have several circles available. (4)

- Use situations in which the solution can be found accidentally through manipulation, such as a mechanical toy that the child can activate by accidentally touching a button or switch, by banging on the toy, or by shaking it. (4)

- Set up materials close to the source of the problem. Have a step stool next to the cupboard, or put a string on a soft toy, high on a shelf so it can be pulled down. Make the solutions obvious at first. Model if needed. (4)

- Give the child novel toys and objects (e.g., mechanical toys, kitchen gadgets) that the child does not yet know how to manipulate. Encourage the child to try different strategies to activate the object. If the child repeatedly uses only one strategy unsuccessfully, then demonstrate how to activate the object. Observe whether the child modifies the first strategy to approximate the correct strategy modeled. (4, 4.1)

- If the child tries to get a jack-in-the-box to pop out by pounding on the lid or pulling the handle, then model turning the crank until the "jack" pops out. Close the lid and offer the toy to the child. (4, 4.1)

- If the child twirls or hits a top to get it to spin, then model pushing on the handle several times until the top spins on its own. (4, 4.1)

- Arrange situations so that a second strategy is readily available in the child's immediate environment; for example, place an object on a high shelf in a cupboard. Have a stool available so that after reaching for the object from the ground the child will use the stool to reach the object. (4, 4.1)

Instructional Sequences

- Model problem solving for the child; for example, take the lid off of a container to get a toy. Replace the lid. (4, 4.1)

- Give the child verbal instructions (e.g., say, "Stand on the chair," "Push the button," "Turn it around"). (4, 4.1)

- If the child becomes upset or bored after unsuccessful attempts, then provide assistance by completing part of the action required to solve the problem. Encourage the child to complete the action (e.g., partially remove the lid from a container, partially push a button through the buttonhole). (4, 4.1)

Cognitive

- Provide minimal physical assistance to help the child successfully solve the problem; for example, point to a stool and say, "Let's use this to reach the raisins." Assist the child, as necessary, to move the stool into position and stand on it to reach the raisins. (4, 4.1)

- Physically assist the child to solve a problem; for example, place your hand on the child's hand to help the child remove the lid. (4.1)

TEACHING CONSIDERATIONS

1. Make sure that the solution to the problem is meaningful and motivating for the child.

2. Problems should be slightly beyond the child's current abilities (principle of minimal discrepancy).

3. Make sure that the strategies required to solve the problem are within the child's repertoire (precise fine motor skills should not be required if the child's motor responses are limited).

4. Use materials that are safe for the child to manipulate and that lend themselves to a variety of uses.

5. Arrange the environment so that the child will encounter interesting problems.

6. Arrange problems so that more than one strategy is available as a solution.

7. Assist the child with a sensory impairment to solve problems with an appropriate sensory modality.

Interaction with Objects

GOAL 1 Uses imaginary objects in play

- PS1a The child uses an action associated with a common object, but the object is absent. The focus of the child's play is on the action rather than the imaginary object; for example, the child kicks an imaginary ball, eats an imaginary cookie, or throws an imaginary ball.

- PS1b The child enacts the typical action of a familiar character or animal by using a real object associated with the character or animal; for example, the child sits in baby brother's chair and pretends to cry or takes Mommy's keys and pretends to go bye-bye.

- PS1c The child enacts imaginary events related to daily routine activities; for example, the child pretends to sleep on the bed or drink from an empty cup.

Objective 1.1 Uses representational actions with objects

- PS1.1a The child uses a picture or a toy to represent a real object; for example, the child pretends to peel and eat a plastic banana or makes a barking noise while holding a picture of a dog.

- PS1.1b The child uses a functionally similar object as a substitute for another object to perform a game or action; for example, the child feeds the doll with a bottle and then takes a cup and gives the doll a drink.

Objective 1.2 Uses functionally appropriate actions with objects

- PS1.2a The child differentiates actions on objects according to the response of the object; for example, hard objects bang together; round objects roll, rattle, or shake; and soft objects are good to chew.

Objective 1.3 Uses simple motor actions on different objects

- PS1.3a The child produces a simple, undifferentiated action on all objects (e.g., drops, bangs).

Objective 1.4 Uses sensory examination with objects

- PS1.4a The child explores or plays with parts of his or her own body; for example, the child sucks fingers or watches hands and feet.

- PS1.4b The child explores or plays with objects that satisfy physical needs, such as the nipple on a bottle, a mother's breast, a pacifier, a blanket, or clothing.

IMPORTANCE OF SKILLS

The child acquires knowledge about the world through interactions with people and objects. The ability to use imaginary objects in play demonstrates that the child's actions and thoughts no longer require the physical presence of objects. The child recognizes the connection between the object and the intention of the object. This skill increases the flexibility of the child's actions and thoughts so that the child's play is no longer restricted to objects in the immediate environment. The child discovers that objects differ in function, size, shape, weight, and texture, and the child no longer treats all objects in the same way. The functional use of objects is particularly important to the development of the child's independent movement in the daily environment. Other goals/objectives that can be targeted at the same time as Goal 1 are listed on the following page.

TEACHING SUGGESTIONS

Activity-Based

Playtime

- When the child is playing with toys or objects, introduce an imaginary game; for example, when the child is playing with a stuffed animal, pretend to be in the jungle. When the child is climbing on an outdoor structure, pretend to be climbing a mountain. (1)

- Provide the child with a variety of objects that can be used for multiple purposes, such as blocks, sticks, cans, boxes, string, or cloth. Have a few defined objects available, but provide many objects that can serve multiple purposes; for example, give the child toy cars and encourage the child to use a box as a garage and blocks or string as a road. (1.1)

- Observe the child's functional use of toys and objects. During pretend play, encourage the child to make a toy animal run or to give a doll a bath. During water and sand play, encourage the child to fill a bucket with water or dig a hole with a spoon. During art activities, give the child brushes to paint, crayons to draw, and scissors to cut paper. Have the child play musical instruments (e.g., drums, xylophone, bells, piano) by using the appropriate action with each instrument. (1.2)

- Place a safe object such as a furry musical bear with multiple sensory properties (i.e., an object that is interesting to look at, touch, smell, or listen to) within the child's reach in the crib or play area. Rotate or move objects up and down to provide a variety of sensory explorations. (1.4)

Feeding

- Place food on the child's lips or tongue and observe whether the child moves the lips or tongue or swallows the food. (1.4)

Goal 1: Uses imaginary objects in play

Gross Motor

D:4 Climbs up and down play equipment

Cognitive

D:1 Imitates motor action that is not commonly used

D:2 Imitates words that are not frequently used

E:4 Solves common problems

Social-Communication

C:1.2 Locates common objects, people, and/or events in familiar pictures

D:1 Uses 50 single words

Social

A:2 Initiates and maintains interaction with familiar adult

C:1 Initiates and maintains interaction with peer

Notes:

Cognitive

Throughout daily routines

- When playing with the child, talk about familiar activities such as going to the store, going to bed, or riding in the car. Encourage the child to use imaginary objects to enact common situations; for example, ask the child to give you a bite of an imaginary cookie or help fasten an imaginary seat-belt. (1)

- Throughout typical daily activities encourage the child to use imaginary objects; for example, when dressing, put on imaginary boots and a hat; when going outside to play, take an imaginary dog for a walk; during meal-times, pretend to eat imaginary food. (1)

- During daily activities and routines, encourage the child to independently perform actions with various objects rather than perform the action for the child; for example, encourage the child to put on clothing correctly (e.g., hold up a sock and ask, "Where does this go?"), use feeding utensils correctly during mealtimes (e.g., give the child a spoon and ask, "What do we do with this?"), and use toiletry objects (e.g., soap, towel, toothbrush, comb) during bath time. (1.2)

- Provide a variety of objects and encourage the child to use motor actions on different objects. Encourage the child to strike or kick hanging objects and mobiles, pat or bang toy animals and rattles, or tear or crumple paper and aluminum foil. (1.3)

- Draw the child's attention to interesting objects that are familiar and used frequently in daily routines. Encourage the child to use sensory examination with the objects; for example, show the bottle to the child before placing it in the child's mouth, then encourage the child to pat the bottle during the feeding. Gently touch the child's face or body with a soft blanket at bedtime, then encourage the child to stroke the blanket. (1.4)

- Make noises with objects to the side of the child and observe whether the child turns toward the sound, changes facial expression, or quiets to the sound. The child may look at the object or notice the sound it makes. (1.4)

Environmental Arrangements

- Use mostly real objects in a particular situation but have one critical object be imaginary; for example, use a real pot, spoon, and bowl to cook and serve imaginary soup. Let the child swim in imaginary water after the tub has been drained. Feed the rocking horse imaginary hay from a real bucket. (1)

- Use puppets or stuffed animals to perform imaginary actions. (1)

- Sing familiar songs that require the child to use different actions, such as "Wheels on the Bus," "Baby Bumblebee," or "Row, Row, Row Your Boat." (1)

- Play interactive games. Pretend to be hungry, and ask the child to give you a bottle or cup. Have only one appropriate object available. Interact with the object and encourage the child to imitate, using another object; for example, pretend to talk to the child on the telephone, using the only telephone, and encourage the child to respond by using a block as a telephone. (1.1, 1.2)

- Have available other objects similar to the object to be represented; for example, while pretending to have a snack, substitute seashells for cups and observe whether the child pretends to drink from a shell. (1.1)

- Take a ride using chairs or cushions to represent a car. Have the child close the door, buckle the seatbelt, and steer the car. (1.1)

- Use objects with which the child is familiar and has had previous opportunity to explore and manipulate initially. Present objects that elicit functionally appropriate actions related to an activity that is reinforcing for the child, such as utensils for eating and drinking; hats or mittens to wear for outdoor play; and balls for rolling, kicking, and throwing. (1.2)

- Use contextual language to elicit functional use of an object; for example, if the child is patting a doll with a bottle, then encourage the child to feed the doll by saying, "The baby is hungry." (1.2)

- Use objects that produce an interesting effect with minimal manipulation, such as noise-producing toys, balls and roly-poly toys that move easily when touched, a Busy Box, and mirrors and bright-colored shiny objects that reflect the light when moved. (1.3)

- Present objects with which the child has become familiar through sensory examination. Observe whether the child attempts to act differently on an object by using motor actions; for example, at bedtime the child sucks a favorite blanket then starts to stroke or rub it. (1.3)

- If the child initiates a nondirected movement with hands, arms, or legs, then introduce an object and observe whether the child continues the motor pattern; for example, if the child is making nondirected kicking movements, then put a light blanket over the child's feet and encourage the child to continue to kick the blanket. (1.3)

- Present strong-smelling foods or objects and observe whether the child moves toward or away from the odor. (1.4)

- Play face-to-face interaction games with the child and gradually introduce objects within the game; for example, gently tickle the child, making the child laugh, then tickle the child with a soft toy and observe whether the child looks at or touches the toy. Play "gotcha" using a favorite stuffed animal or doll. (1.4)

- Use objects that produce exaggerated stimulation, such as flashing lights or big, noisy, shiny toys. (1.4)

Cognitive

Instructional Sequences

- Model play using an imaginary object and encourage the child to imitate. (1)

- Play interactive games and model representational actions with objects. Encourage the child to imitate; for example, pretend to eat a sandwich using a block, then offer the child a bite. (1.1)

- Model the functional use of objects and encourage the child to imitate. (1.2)

- Model a simple motor pattern on an object that the child is already exploring in a sensory manner; for example, if the child looks at a piece of aluminum foil, then crumple the foil and encourage the child to imitate. (1.3)

- Model a simple action with an object, then place the object within the child's proximity and observe whether the child acts on the object using sensory examination. (1.4)

- Provide verbal cues related to specific actions, such as "Let's go for a ride in the car: Here's my seat and there's your seat," or "Let's paint this wall: Here's my brush and here's yours." (1, 1.1)

- Hand the child an object and instruct the child to use the object in a representational manner; for example, give the child a kitchen towel to cover a doll and say, "Pretend the towel is a blanket." (1.1)

- Verbally instruct the child to "Give the baby the bottle," or "Comb your hair." Encourage the child to bang a wooden spoon on a cake tin. (1.2, 1.3)

- Give the child verbal assistance (e.g., say, "Look at this," "Can you smell it?" "Touch the bear"). Use an exaggerated and captivating tone of voice and facial expression to make the object interesting to the child. (1.4)

- Physically assist the child to reach objectives; for example, hold an imaginary cup to the child's mouth during a tea party; help the child to brush his or her teeth or comb his or her hair; help the child contact and act on an object, such as a Busy Box; or have the child play an interactive game with you that includes objects. (1.1, 1.2, 1.3, 1.4)

- Physically assist the child to look by gently turning the child's face toward a visual or auditory stimulus. Touch the child's lips or hands with appropriate objects to taste or feel. Wait to see if the child repeats the action. (1.4)

- Combine sensory explorations using a modality that the child prefers, such as vision and sound, and then fade to one sensory modality. (1, 1.1, 1.2, 1.3, 1.4)

Combining or pairing different levels of instructions may be helpful when beginning to teach a new and difficult skill. Fade to less intrusive instructions as soon as possible to encourage more independent performance.

TEACHING CONSIDERATIONS

1. Elicit use of imaginary objects within the context of dramatic play with peers. Encourage social interaction, communication, role playing, and turn taking among peers.

2. Representational use of objects can be easily elicited in the context of pretend play. In pretend play, the child can practice a variety of social, communicative, and cognitive skills. The child gains a better understanding of the environment by reproducing and enacting familiar events.

3. If the child has a motor impairment that restricts movement or manipulation of objects, consider the following teaching guidelines:

   • Engage the child in storytelling and relating of events. Observe the child's ability to relate stories and past events, tell stories about imaginary events, and create fictitious characters and objects.

   • Engage the child in verbal pretend games; for example, show the child an object such as a block, a stick, or a piece of cloth, and ask the child to verbally indicate what else the object could be.

   • Use objects and toys that are easy for the child to hold and activate, such as mobiles and balls.

   • Present stimuli to which the child is able to respond.

4. If the child has a visual impairment, consider the following teaching guidelines:

   • Encourage play-acting by describing actions that the child should make on imaginary figures (e.g., say, "This is a very tall horse. Lift your leg high and jump on!")

   • Describe objects and verbally direct the child in representational actions with them.

   • Use large or bright objects or ones that can be easily recognized by tactile exploration. Make sure that the effect of the action on the object is interesting to the child, such as with a noise-producing object or one that has interesting textures.

5. If the child has a hearing impairment, consider the following teaching guidelines:

   • Model imaginary behaviors for the child. Use total communication.

   • Use visually attractive or easily activated objects.

6. Consult a qualified specialist for techniques for the child with a visual, hearing, or motor impairment.

7. Consider safety with all objects that the child handles.

Cognitive

Early Concepts

GOAL 1   Categorizes like objects

- PS1a   The child acts successively upon objects belonging to a category; for example, when presented with a plate of apple slices and crackers, the child eats the crackers before the apple slices or vice versa.

Objective 1.1   Groups functionally related objects

- PS1.1a   The child groups two functionally related objects; for example, a diaper and a pin or a doll and a blanket.

- PS1.1b   The child functionally relates one object to a succession of similar objects from another class; for example, the child gives each of three dolls a drink, in turn, from a toy cup.

Objective 1.2   Groups objects according to size, shape, and/or color

- PS1.2a   The child groups objects according to size.

- PS1.2b   The child groups objects according to shape.

- PS1.2c   The child groups objects according to color.

Objective 1.3   Matches pictures and/or objects

- PS1.3a   The child groups together two or more similar objects; for example, the child plays with two toy airplanes or the child chooses two spoons from a drawer.

- PS1.3b   The child recognizes a familiar object, person, or event by responding the same way to a similar object, person, or event over time; for example, the child looks into all mirrors and smiles or pushes suspended objects to make them swing.

IMPORTANCE OF SKILLS

The ability to categorize is essential to organizing and making sense of the environment. The grouping of new objects and events within a category allows the child some immediate knowledge about the new object or event. Categorization serves to organize perception of the environment and helps to organize familiar information and assimilate new information.

A first step toward the ability to categorize objects is to recognize that two or more objects are the same. This skill develops visual discrimination of objects and forms, which is necessary for the child to later recognize numbers and letters. The child then learns to relate a set of objects that look and feel different from one another by organizing them on the basis of a common function or use. This implies the ability to abstract a common functional similarity among perceptually different objects. This skill teaches the child to group objects consistently on different dimensions that are perceptually striking, such as size, shape, or color. Categorizing is important for understanding numbers and is fundamental to mathematical skills. Other goals/objectives that can be targeted at the same time as Goal 1 are listed on the following page.

TEACHING SUGGESTIONS

Activity-Based

Playtime

- Encourage the child to help clean up; for example, put Legos in a container, books on a shelf, crayons and paper in a drawer, clothes in a dresser, or groceries on a shelf. Allow the child to help clean up after mealtime and have available objects that can be grouped according to size, shape, or color. (1, 1.1, 1.2, 1.3)

- When playing with peers, encourage the child to distribute a group of objects from one category to each peer; for example, the child gives all of the toy cars to one peer and all of the toy animals to another. (1, 1.1)

- During play, make two roads or two necklaces of two different colors by aligning blocks or stringing beads of the same color. (1.2)

- Participate in activities with the child by pointing out objects and pictures that are the same. Hold toy cars, beads, blocks, or animals next to each other and show the child that they match. Ask the child to find matching objects: "Find the one that matches," or "Give me the one that is the same." (1.3)

- Play lotto games in which the child matches a picture to the same picture on a game board. (1.3)

Feeding

- When preparing a snack, use crackers of different shapes and begin to place square crackers on one plate and round crackers on another. Encourage the child to continue placing crackers on plates. (1.2)

Travel

- While driving, point out different road signs by size, shape, and color. (1.2)

Storytime

- When looking at books, ask the child to point to or find similar objects (e.g., say, "Find more," "Where's another one?"). (1.3)

Concurrent Goals/Objectives for Cognitive Strand G

Goal 1: Categorizes like objects

Fine Motor

A:5.3 Releases hand-held object onto and/or into a larger target with either hand

B:2 Assembles toy and/or object that require(s) putting pieces together

Gross Motor

B:1.2 Regains balanced, upright sitting position after reaching across the body to the right and to the left

Cognitive

B:3.1 Looks for object in usual location

E:1.2 Retains object

F:1.2 Uses functionally appropriate actions with objects

G:2 Demonstrates functional use of one-to one correspondence

Social-Communication

C:2.3 Carries out one-step direction with contextual cues

Social

B:2.1 Responds to established social routine

C:1 Initiates and maintains interaction with peer

Notes:

Throughout daily routines

- During daily activities and routines, give the child an opportunity to put together matching objects or objects belonging to a broad-based category. Encourage the child to select matching socks or shoes or group toy animals, eating utensils, care items, and dolls during and after play. (1, 1.1, 1.2, 1.3)

- When putting away groceries, ask the child to put away all of the canned goods. (1, 1.1)

- During daily routines, provide the child with general verbal cues and observe whether the child groups functionally related objects; for example, you say, "Time to eat," and the child gets a bib and a spoon and goes to the highchair. The adult says, "Let's brush teeth," and the child gets the toothbrush and toothpaste and asks to turn on the water. The adult says, "Time to get dressed," and the child picks out pants, shirt, socks, and shoes. (1.1)

- While folding laundry, have the child help group clothing items, towels, or napkins by color or size. Make differences obvious, such as an adult's big socks and the child's little socks. (1.1, 1.2)

- Show the child pairs of objects that match and pairs that do not match. Show how each pair is the same (matches) or not the same (does not match); that is, during dressing, contrast mom's shoes with child's shoes and brother's pants with child's pants. (1.3)

Environmental Arrangements

- Provide the child with containers for sorting objects into categories when cleaning up. Use baskets or buckets to store personal items, such as a comb, brush, and mirror, or toys such as a road track and cars. Put a picture on the outside of the bucket to denote the objects to be stored. (1, 1.1, 1.2, 1.3)

- Place at least three objects from a broad-based category that look, feel, and are used the same way into a group of completely dissimilar objects; for example, when playing outdoors, place the child's book, paper, and crayons among gardening tools and observe whether the child gathers together the book, paper, and crayons to take indoors. (1, 1.1)

- Present the child with sets of objects that can be fitted together, each differently; for example, have the child fit pop beads together, put beads on a string, and fit puzzle pieces together. (1, 1.2)

- Place at least three identical objects in a group of different objects; for example, ask the child to take three identical cans of soup from the grocery cart that also contains large packages of diapers and gallon jugs of milk. (1, 1.2)

- Place a set of functionally related objects that are of interest to the child among other objects of less interest; for example, place a train, tunnel, and tracks among old newspapers or some cushions. (1, 1.1)

- Make available on the counter a cup, bowl, and spoon among papers, books, and pencils. Ask the child to set the table for lunch. (1.1)

- Have two groups of objects that differ on dimensions in addition to size, shape, and color; for example, after providing a visual model, have the child take the big cups to the kitchen and place the miniature cups in the doll house. Put shiny star stickers on one sheet and opaque circles on another. Place big metal trucks in a toy garage and small wooden train cars on a railway track. (1.1, 1.2)

- Make placemats that match the color of the child's cup and plate. Trace a small circle around the cup and a large circle around the plate on the placemat to give the child a size and color form to match when setting the table. Introduce contrasting placemats and dishes. (1.1, 1.2)

- Cut out different shapes in the lids of plastic containers; for example, cut a circle in one lid, a square in another, and a rectangle in a third lid. Encourage the child to drop blocks through the corresponding holes in the container lids. (1, 1.2)

- When playing with blocks, encourage the child to build towers of different colors or shapes, such as a red tower and blue tower or a square tower and cylindrical tower. During art activities, encourage the child to group shapes, sizes, and colors; for example, use yarn to make different spaces to be filled with "big beans here" and "little beans there." Provide paper for the child to first "paste all of the circles" and then "paste all of the squares." (1.2)

- Give the child a basket of two or three different types of interlocking toys (e.g., pop beads, Legos, Bristle Blocks). Encourage the child to match objects by finding and putting together the same type of interlocking toy (e.g., all of the Legos). (1.3)

- Present objects that are unlike the object to be matched in color, brightness, size, shape, and function; for example, have the child match a shiny red ball from an array of white toy cars and furry toy animals or a banana from an array of crayons and sheets of paper. (1.2, 1.3)

- Limit the number of pictures or objects available so that only one distractor object is present; for example, when presenting a picture of a dog, have available only one picture of another animal in addition to a matching picture. Increase to three or four distractor pictures or objects as the child becomes more proficient in matching. (1.3)

Instructional Sequences

- Model putting like objects together. Encourage the child to include additional like objects in the group one at a time. (1, 1.1, 1.2, 1.3)

- Encourage the child with nonspecific verbal prompts (e.g., say, "What goes with this?" "You need something else," "The baby is hungry," "How will you dry your hands?"). (1.1, 1.2, 1.3)

- Give the child general verbal cues, such as "Put all of the things to eat on this shelf." (1, 1.1, 1.2, 1.3)

- Indicate verbally or point to the location of the group in which the object belongs (e.g., "On the shelf," "In the box"). Physically direct the child to the correct location. (1, 1.1, 1.2, 1.3)

- Physically assist the child to place like objects together; for example, stack large books in one pile and small books in another. (1.2, 1.3)

Combining or pairing different levels of instructions may be helpful when beginning to teach a new and difficult skill. Fade to less intrusive instructions as soon as possible to encourage more independent performance.

TEACHING CONSIDERATIONS

1. The activity should have a purpose. Cleaning up can be integrated in a game; for example, after playing grocery store, one child (sales clerk) picks up all of the coins and the other child (customer) picks up all of the groceries.

2. Arrange the situation so that objects that the child needs are not readily available. Encourage the child to obtain the objects needed for the event; for example, at mealtime, do not set the table and wait for the child to get a spoon, plate, and cup.

3. Be sure that the child understands the task and directions. If necessary, the adult may demonstrate with other objects.

4. When giving verbal instructions, such as, "Show me the same," avoid giving a verbal cue by naming the object; for example, avoid saying, "Where's the horse?" as the child becomes proficient.

5. If the child has a motor impairment, show the child an object and ask the child to point to a corresponding model to identify functional relationships. Use alternate methods of matching objects or pictures, such as looking at similar objects or touching similar objects.

6. If the child has a visual impairment, allow tactile exploration of the objects. Use different textures and shapes (e.g., soft, furry animals and cold, metal cars). Also, use noise-producing objects.

7. If the child has a hearing impairment, use a language modality that ensures the child's understanding of your instructions. If necessary, demonstrate for the child.

8. Consider safety with all objects that the child handles.

Cognitive

GOAL 2   Demonstrates functional use of one-to-one correspondence

- PS2a   The child demonstrates one-to-one correspondence by assigning one of two objects to another person and keeping the other object; for example, the child gives one of two daisies to the father and keeps the other.

Objective 2.1   Demonstrates concept of one

IMPORTANCE OF SKILLS

The development of quantitative knowledge is basic to the acquisition of a range of numerical and quantitative abilities, such as size discrimination, counting, and estimation of relative and equivalent numbers. One-to-one correspondence is the simplest and most direct measure of the equivalence of two sets of objects. This skill is basic to the understanding of the numerical concepts of equal, more, and less. It also enables the child to make judgments of numerical equalities and differences, independent of how objects look, feel, or are arranged. Other goals/objectives that can be targeted at the same time as Goal 2 are listed on the following page.

TEACHING SUGGESTIONS

Activity-Based

Group activities

- During group activities, have one child distribute materials to peers rather than having each child obtain his or her own materials. (2, 2.1)

Playtime

- Encourage the child to engage in pretend play, such as having a tea party or playing school with dolls, in which objects can be distributed to each doll. Have the child play grocery store and exchange a coin for each grocery item. (2, 2.1)

- During playtime, ask the child to pick one book to read, one car to roll, or one baby to rock to sleep. (2.1)

Dressing

- When assisting the child with dressing, be sure to point out, "One sock for each foot," "One mitten for each hand," and "One leg in each pant leg." (2, 2.1)

Goal 2: Demonstrates functional use of one-to-one correspondence

Fine Motor

A:5.3 Releases hand-held object onto and/or into a larger target with either hand

B:2.2 Fits object into defined space

Cognitive

F:1 Uses imaginary objects in play

G:1.2 Groups objects according to size, shape, and/or color

Social-Communication

B:1.2 Points to an object, person, and/or event

C:1.3 Locates common objects, people, and/or events with contextual cues

C:2.3 Carries out one-step direction with contextual cues

Social

C:1.1 Initiates social behavior toward peer

C:2.1 Initiates communication with peer

Notes:

Travel

- Allow the child to help at a grocery store by placing one box of crackers in the grocery cart. Ask the child to select one loaf of bread. (2, 2.1)

Throughout daily routines

- During daily activities and routines, encourage the child to match functionally related objects to two or more other objects, using one-to-one correspondence; for example, when setting the table at mealtimes, provide opportunities for the child to place a cup or utensil next to each plate or give a cracker or piece of fruit to each peer. (2)

Environmental Arrangements

- Look at books with the child and count objects as you point to them. Encourage the child to assist by pointing to the objects while the adult counts. (2)

- Have the child use one-to-one correspondence to fit parts of objects together; for example, encourage the child to fit covers on boxes or toy people into miniature cars. (2)

- Provide arrays of objects in which the number of objects to be assigned is identical to the number of objects or people involved; for example, give the child four napkins to place beside four plates. (2)

- Encourage the child to select the one object out of several similar objects in a familiar situation that is customarily used for a purpose; for example, at changing time ask the child to get one diaper, or at mealtime ask the child to get one plate. (2.1)

- Ask the child to place one object in a container that will hold only one, such as a doll in a doll bed or an egg in an egg cup. (2.1)

- Ask the child to match an object to a visual model by selecting one from several dissimilar objects; for example, have the child search for a matching mitten from several assorted objects. (2.1)

- Have the child indicate an object when only one object is present; for example, ask the child to show one tricycle when only one tricycle is present. (2.1)

Instructional Sequences

- Model assigning one object to each person; for example, model showing, giving, or assigning one item (e.g., napkin, paintbrush) for the child and encourage the child to imitate. Give the child the rest of the napkins or paintbrushes to pass out. (2, 2.1)

- Give the child verbal instructions for each match; for example, say, "Give one crayon to Daddy," and "Give one crayon to Sally." (2, 2.1)

- Verbalize and point successively to each object to which the other object is being assigned; for example, point to each plate on which the child must place a cracker and say, "One cracker here." (2)

- Physically assist the child to assign one item (e.g., place one cup by each plate at the table). (2.1)

TEACHING CONSIDERATIONS

1. The objects to be assigned should be functionally related to the objects or people involved.

2. If the child has a motor impairment, allow the child to use alternate means of demonstrating one-to-one correspondence (e.g., touching, looking).

3. If the child has a visual impairment, increase the intensity and variety of cues. Use bright-colored objects, tactilely different objects, or noise-producing objects.

4. If the child has a hearing impairment, use a language approach such as total communication that ensures the child's understanding of your instruction.

5. When asking the child to indicate one, verbally or visually emphasize one (e.g., by showing one finger) and avoid naming the object. If the object is named, the child may just locate the object rather than focus on the numerical concept.

6. Consider safety with all objects that the child handles.

GOAL 3   Recognizes environmental symbols
          (signs, logos, labels)

Objective 3.1   Labels familiar people, actions, objects, and events in pictures

- PS3.1a   The child indicates recognition (points to, touches, picks up) of familiar people, actions, objects, and events in pictures.

IMPORTANCE OF SKILLS

Common signs, logos, and labels are symbols that indicate places (e.g., rest-rooms, exits, airports), actions (e.g., stop signs), and events (e.g., riding on buses, eating at restaurants). Interpreting the meaning of environmental symbols is an early form of interpreting print symbols and is a bridge to recognizing words and letters. In addition, young children are often quite impressed with their own ability to "read" environmental symbols, increasing their motivation and confidence for reading books. Other goals/objectives that can be targeted at the same time as Goal 3 are listed on the following page.

Cognitive

Concurrent Goals/Objectives for Cognitive Strand G

Goal 3: Recognizes environmental symbols (signs, logos, labels)

Fine Motor

B:4 Orients picture book correctly and turns pages one by one

B:5 Copies simple written shapes after demonstration

Gross Motor

C:1 Walks avoiding obstacles

Adaptive

B:1 Initiates toileting

Cognitive

D:2 Imitates words that are not frequently used

F:1 Uses imaginary objects in play

G:4 Demonstrates functional use of reading materials

G:4.1 Orally fills in or completes familiar text while looking at picture books

Social-Communication

C:2.1 Carries out two-step direction with contextual cues

D:3 Uses three-word utterances

Social

A:3 Initiates and maintains communicative exchange with familiar adult

B:2 Participates in established social routines

C:2 Initiates and maintains communicative exchange with peer

Notes:

TEACHING SUGGESTIONS

Activity-Based

Storytime

- Encourage the child to select a favorite book for shared reading by recognizing the picture on the cover. (3)

- Provide books that have a consistent picture or symbol on every page, such as books in which the child searches for a certain person or figure on each page. Have the child identify and label the item, and wait to see if they will look for it on successive pages without prompts to do so. (3, 3.1)

- Make books that have pictures of children's family members, favorite toys, peers, and so forth. Encourage children to look at and add to the books frequently and to label individual pictures. (3.1)

Travel

- When walking or riding in a vehicle, point out and label environmental symbols that are common at home, in the classroom, and in the community. Encourage the child to recognize and label frequently occurring symbols for restrooms, exits, stop signs, and high interest logos for brand names of food, toys, and favorite locations. (3, 3.1)

Art activities

- Have children dictate labels for the pictures that they draw and paint, and have them "read" the labels back to adults or peers when showing the pictures. (3.1)

- Have a variety of magazines for children to cut out advertisements containing pictures and/or symbols that they recognize. Use the cut-out pictures to make books or collages to "read" to peers and adults. (3, 3.1)

Group activities

- Develop short picture recipes for simple cooking projects. Encourage children to label the pictures and follow the recipe by "reading" the symbols in sequence. (3, 3.1)

- Integrate pictures of children into daily attendance or opening circle. Pair the child's name with each picture to promote recognition of peers' names. (3, 3.1)

Throughout daily routines

- Whenever the child indicates recognition or labels environmental symbols, reinforce the connection with reading. Point out that knowing what symbols mean is "reading" the print or graphic. (3)

- Let children draw and label logos to identify their rooms, cubbies at school, toy boxes, places at snack, and so forth. (3, 3.1)

Cognitive

Environmental Arrangements

- Conduct an inventory of obvious environmental symbols at home, at preschool, at child care, or in the neighborhood. Select two or three symbols that are of especially high interest to the child and are encountered frequently, and emphasize those symbols at every opportunity. Once the child recognizes a few symbols, introduce others. (3, 3.1)

- Use photographs of familiar people and favorite toys as a first step in picture labeling, then introduce unfamiliar photographs; realistic, colored drawings; and line drawings as children become more proficient at labeling pictures. (3.1)

- Label shelves with pictures to indicate where toys, materials, and supplies are kept. Encourage children to recognize and label the right places for putting things away. (3.1)

- Use pictures to label children's cubbies, show the daily schedule in the classroom, preview snack choices, and show activity center options. Encourage discussion and labeling of people, objects, actions, and events in the pictures. (3.1)

- Use graphics or photographs to label centers in the classroom and to indicate whether the centers are open or closed. Encourage children to "read" the center labels when planning activities for the day. (3, 3.1)

Instructional Sequences

- Model reading environmental symbols out loud and explaining their meaning: "That big red sign is a stop sign. A stop sign means that every car has to stop." (3)

- Give the child verbal reminders to look for specific environmental symbols, with cues as to location: "Look across the street for a bus stop sign so we know where to wait for the bus." (3)

- Provide minimal assistance by pointing to or touching the environmental symbol to draw the child's attention. Ask the child what the symbol stands for, and provide a verbal model, if necessary, for labeling. (3)

- Design matching picture cards with environmental symbols on some cards and pictures that represent interpretations of the symbols on others (e.g., cars with traffic signs, bathroom fixtures with restroom signs, fast food with golden arches). (3)

- Teach the child to sort and match pairs of cards, starting with a few high interest pictures and progressing to larger sets of pairs. Be sure to continue pointing out the symbols in the environment and interpreting meaning. (3)

- During shared reading time, take turns labeling familiar pictures in favorite books by asking the child to find specific items. Start with books that have only a few clear pictures of familiar items per page and progress to more pictures per page and more complex scenes. (3.1)

- During shared reading times, ask the child to point out specific familiar items in pictures as you label them. (3.1)

- Use memory game cards to have the child match pictures to other pictures, and find items in the child's environment to teach matching pictures and objects. Start with one target object/picture and two response options (one distractor and one matching picture). Increase the number of choices as the child becomes more proficient at matching. (3.1)

TEACHING CONSIDERATIONS

1. For children whose families have oral traditions, encourage storytelling as an alternative to, or in addition to, reading. Have children identify the people, events, routines, and symbols associated with storytelling in their families. Use tape recordings and have the child identify different voices.

2. If the child has a visual impairment, increase the intensity and variety of environmental support and cues (e.g., large, bright, high contrast pictures; closer proximity to and examination of symbols). Consult a vision specialist for evaluation of the need for large print books, speech output computer software, and/or braille instruction for the child with a visual impairment.

3. If the child has a motor impairment or abnormal muscle tone, consult a physical or occupational therapist about appropriate positioning, related issues, and assistive devices for mobility and literacy. Use teaching materials that are easy to manipulate.

4. If the child has a hearing impairment, consult an audiologist or speech-language pathologist about programming issues, amplification, and assistive devices. Consult with parents for interaction strategies, and increase the intensity and variety of cues (e.g., clearer picture cues, louder verbal cues, more gestures, exaggerated motions, consistent routines for taking walks and identifying environmental symbols).

5. Integrate realistic environmental symbols into dramatic play, oral language, art, writing centers, and literacy centers of the classroom. Encourage and reinforce interpretation of environmental symbols as a first step in reading when discussing early literacy with parents.

6. Be alert for the environmental symbols that are highly salient to young children. Games, toys, card games, clothing, food, vehicles, and special places in the community are all themes that tend to be of special interest.

Cognitive

GOAL 4   Demonstrates functional use of reading materials

Objective 4.1   Orally fills in or completes familiar text while looking at picture books

- PS4.1a Indicates awareness that familiar text is being left out or skipped over while looking at picture books

Objective 4.2   Makes comments and asks questions while looking at picture books

• PS4.2a The child points to objects and answers questions while looking at picture books.

Objective 4.3   Sits and attends to entire story during shared reading time

• PS4.3a The child responds to request to sit and read book with adult.

IMPORTANCE OF SKILLS

Listening, commenting, and asking and answering questions about stories and pictures represent an important connection between oral language and print and provides a framework for acquisition of reading and writing skills. Associating the spoken word with print and graphics promotes understanding that the written word contains a message. Other goals/objectives that can be targeted at the same time as Goal 4 are listed on the following page.

TEACHING SUGGESTIONS

Activity-Based

Storytime

• Schedule regular times for shared reading at home or in the classroom (e.g., naptime, bedtime, storytime), and look at the same books repeatedly. Encourage comments and questions on each page by pausing after turning to each page and before going on to the next page. (4.1, 4.2, 4.3)

• Once the child is familiar with a book/story, purposefully skip favorite passages or pause to see if the child will complete the missing text. (4.1)

• Once the child is familiar with a book/story, have the child "read" it aloud to you, a peer, or a younger sibling. (4)

• Go to the library with the child and check out picture books of his or her choosing. Point out all of the people reading and reading behaviors (e.g., quiet bodies, quiet voices, attention to the books), and suggest that you read books together at the library. (4, 4.1, 4.2, 4.3)

• Make books from children's drawings, having each child draw two or more pictures about a specific topic to tell a story. Write a simple narration for each picture as the child dictates, and ask the child to "read" their book to an adult, a peer, or a group. (4, 4.1)

• Provide books that have clear pictures and address age-appropriate issues, themes, and stories of daily life, such as expressing emotions, toileting,

Goal 4: Demonstrates functional use of reading materials

Fine Motor

B:4 Orients picture book correctly and turns pages one by one

Gross Motor

B:2 Sits down in and gets out of chair

Cognitive

C:2 Reproduces part of interactive game and/or action in order to continue game and/or action

D:1 Imitates motor action that is not commonly used

D:2 Imitates words that are not frequently used

G:3 Recognizes environmental symbols (signs, logos, labels)

G:6 Repeats simple nursery rhymes

Social-Communication

C:1 Locates objects, people, and/or events without contextual cues

C:2 Carries out two-step direction without contextual cues

D:3 Uses three-word utterances

Social

A:3 Initiates and maintains communicative exchange with familiar adult

B:2 Participates in established social routines

C:2 Initiates and maintains communicative exchange with peer

Notes:

Cognitive

sharing, or waiting. Encourage the child to "read" the pictures while narrating the stories. (4, 4.1, 4.2, 4.3)

- Make picture books from photographs of children taken at home, starting with baby pictures and continuing until the present. Have children "read" their books to peers, and encourage peers to comment and ask questions of one another. (4, 4.2, 4.3)

Group activities

- Invite each child in the classroom to bring a favorite book from home and "read" it to the class. (4)

- Take pictures or have children draw pictures of field trips, and make books for the class with narrations of each picture. Have one child "read" the story of the field trip to a group of peers, and encourage others in the group to comment and ask questions. (4, 4.1, 4.2)

- Have an "author's circle" in the classroom, where one child "reads" or tells about a favorite book, including showing the cover, telling the story, describing favorite features, answering questions, and taking comments. (4, 4.1, 4.2, 4.3)

Environmental Arrangements

- Arrange the classroom with a book corner or literacy center that is comfortable, quiet, and supplied with a variety of reading materials, child-size seating, and accessible shelving. (4)

- During storytime, when an adult is reading to children, arrange seating in a semi-circle so that all children are close to the teacher with a clear view of the pictures. (4.1, 4.2, 4.3)

- Begin independent book reading by providing cards or books with one picture and a label per page, then progressing to short, simple stories with one line of text and one picture per page. (4, 4.1, 4.2, 4.3)

- Provide books that have large pictures and pages that are easy for children to manipulate independently (e.g., board books, big books, cloth books, plastic books). Make smaller books with thinner pages available as the child becomes more proficient at using reading materials. (4, 4.1, 4.2, 4.3)

- Provide a variety of accessible reading materials with pictures in the child's environment: picture books, magazines, newspapers, and picture cards with labels. (4, 4.1, 4.2)

- Have specific places marked for sitting on the floor or in child-size chairs during shared reading time. (4.3)

- Use books that have a consistent rhythm and/or rhyming words throughout to facilitate memory and to hold the child's interest. (4, 4.1, 4.2, 4.3)

- Sit next to or behind a child who has difficulty attending to books during storytime, or hold the child on your lap while someone else reads. (4.3)

Instructional Sequences

- Model the functional use of reading materials by showing the child how to look at the picture and talk about it. Point out word labels that go with pictures or run your finger under the text as you read. (4)

- Provide verbal encouragement for children to "read" to adults and one another, taking turns having peers read page by page. Remind each child to listen to the others and to look at the picture(s) and tell the story when it is his or her turn. (4, 4.1, 4.2, 4.3)

- Pause at critical points in familiar books to ask children about what has just happened in the story, what is about to happen, what characters are feeling and doing, why something happened, and so forth. Encourage them to ask questions as well. (4.2, 4.3)

- Provide minimal assistance by directing the child's attention to the picture and begin to describe it. Pause and wait for the child to fill in information or text from the story, telling the child what to say, if necessary. (4, 4.1)

TEACHING CONSIDERATIONS

1. For children whose families have oral traditions, encourage storytelling as an alternative to, or in addition to, reading aloud. Tape record stories and design feltboard figures to show the story as it is narrated.

2. If the child has a visual impairment, increase the intensity and variety of environmental support and cues (e.g., large, bright, high contrast pictures; textured pages; proximity to adult reader). Use books that are easy to manipulate, buy book/tape combinations, or make companion tape recordings for favorite stories. Consult a vision specialist for evaluation of the need for large print books, speech input/output computer software, and/or braille instruction. Consult with parents about successful interaction strategies.

3. If the child has a motor impairment or abnormal muscle tone, consult a physical or occupational therapist about appropriate positioning, related issues, and assistive devices for holding books and turning pages. Consult with parents for successful interaction strategies, and determine a consistent response (eye point, hand motion, etc.) for the child to indicate comments or questions about the story.

4. If the child has a hearing impairment, consult an audiologist or speech-language pathologist about programming issues, amplification, and assistive devices. Consult with parents for interaction strategies, and increase the intensity and variety of cues (e.g., louder verbal cues, more gestures, exaggerated motions, consistent routines for shared reading).

5. Provide quiet and comfortable settings for shared reading activities.

Cognitive

6.   Integrate books and story reading into dramatic play, oral language, art, writing centers, and literacy centers of the classroom. Encourage shared reading and family literacy activities in discussion with parents.

GOAL 5   Demonstrates use of common opposite concepts

Objective 5.1   Demonstrates use of at least four pairs of common opposite concepts

• PS5.1a The child demonstrates use of at least three pairs of common opposite concepts.

Objective 5.2   Demonstrates use of at least two pairs of common opposite concepts

• PS5.2a The child demonstrates use of at least one pair of common opposite concepts.

• PS5.2b The child demonstrates understanding of at least three simple concepts (e.g. stop, hot, big).

IMPORTANCE OF SKILLS

The very first concepts learned are those that are directly relevant to a child's daily life. Opposite concepts are relatively easy to learn because they are pairs of related concepts on the extremes of a continuum. Learning polar opposite concepts (e.g., hot/cold) supports acquisition of more finely graded concepts (e.g., warm, cool, freezing, roasting) and promotes understanding of comparative concepts (e.g., warmer, colder, warmest, coldest). Polar opposites also contribute to language development, providing vocabulary for describing people, actions, objects, and events. Other goals/objectives that can be targeted at the same time as Goal 5 are listed on the following page.

TEACHING SUGGESTIONS

Activity-Based

Playtime

•   Emphasize opposites concerning spatial relationships (e.g., up/down, in/out, top/bottom) in the context of block play, construction activities, and active play. Describe and label children's structures as being tall/short, big/little, or long/short, and ask them to describe their projects to one another using the same terms. (5, 5.1, 5.2)

Concurrent Goals/Objectives for Cognitive Strand G

Fine Motor

A:5 Aligns and stacks objects

B:2 Assembles toy or object that require(s) putting pieces together

Gross Motor

B:2 Sits down in and gets out of chair

C:3 Runs avoiding obstacles

C:4 Walks up and down stairs

D:4 Climbs up and down play equipment

Adaptive

A:5 Transfers food and liquid between containers

B:2 Washes and dries hands

Cognitive

D:2 Imitates words that are not frequently used

E:3 Navigates large object around barriers

G:1.2 Groups objects according to size, shape, and/or color

G:4.1 Orally fills in or completes familiar text while looking at picture books

Social-Communication

C1 Locates objects, people, and/or events without contextual cues

C:2 Carries out two-step direction without contextual cues

D:3 Uses three-word utterances

Social

A:3 Initiates and maintains communicative exchange with familiar adult

C:2 Initiates and maintains communicative exchange with peer

Notes:

Assessment, Evaluation, and Programming System for Infants and Children (AEPS®), Second Edition,
edited by Diane Bricker © 2002 Paul H. Brookes Publishing Co., Inc. All rights reserved.

317

Feeding

- Focus attention on opposite concepts during snack and mealtimes. Have children ask for big/little portions, hot/cold drinks, or full/empty containers. (5, 5.1, 5.2)

Toileting

- Ask the child if they are wet/dry or dirty/clean when checking diapers or pants, and emphasize wet/dirty before changing diapers or if there is an accident and dry/clean after pants are changed or when taking the child to the toilet. (5, 5.1, 5.2)

Travel

- Use opposite concepts to describe travel in vehicles and action play. Encourage the child to talk about going fast/slow, up/down hills, in/out of tunnels, and stopping/going. Play Simon Says and give directions for children to go fast/slow, up/down, or with big/little steps. (5, 5.1, 5.2)

Throughout daily routines

- Opposite concepts that are concrete and immediate in the child's activities will be the easiest to learn. Use polar opposite terms whenever possible during daily activities such as dressing, washing/bathing, toileting, eating, going on outings, and playing. (5, 5.1, 5.2)

- Draw the child's attention to his or her hands and face after meals, snack, painting, outdoor play, or any other time that washing is needed. Have the child label washing water as hot/cold. Have the child feel his or her hands and look in the mirror to see and label *dirty* and again after washing to see and label *clean*. (5, 5.1, 5.2)

- Label clothing, tables, and floors as dirty before and after art or cooking projects and clean after being cleaned up. Ask children to use opposite concepts in describing their activities when cleaning up. (5, 5.1, 5.2)

- Use opposite concepts in assisting children to clean up the room, describing top/bottom shelves, placing an item over/under other items, and for quantities of one/many items in big/little cupboards. (5, 5.1, 5.2)

- Follow the child's interest and attach polar concept labels to fascinating events, people, animals, or toys. Label big/little dogs, loud/soft music, big/little cookies, and fast/slow cars. (5.1)

- For children just beginning to learn opposite concepts, find actions that are meaningful in a social context. Have the child repeat "up" when desiring to be picked up and "down" when wanting to get down. (5.2)

Environmental Arrangements

- Provide a variety of manipulative materials that promote attention to opposite concepts. Rough/smooth textures, large/small items and containers, items with clear bottoms and tops, and dark/light colors. (5, 5.1, 5.2)

- Purposefully present choices that emphasize opposite concepts; for example, ask children if they want to be first or last, have a big or little piece of cake, or want soft or hard mats. (5, 5.1, 5.2)

- Pretend not to understand what the child is asking for until a opposite concept is used to describe the item. Prompt use of the concept by using the opposite: "Oh, I thought you wanted the little one." (5.1, 5.2)

- Select items that are at opposite ends of a continuum; for example, ice cream and hot fudge to illustrate cold/hot or a big book and its smaller companions for big/little. (5.1, 5.2)

- Take a nature walk and have children describe everything that they collect as large/small, rough/smooth, long/short, big/little, or wet/dry. (5, 5.1, 5.2)

- Make a grab bag of items that children must describe by feel, without visual inspection. (5, 5.1, 5.2)

- Play a guessing game where children describe items without naming them, using polar concepts as clues. (5, 5.1, 5.2)

Instructional Sequences

- Model use of polar opposite terms by presenting pairs of concepts together and emphasizing the contrast. Have multiple exemplars for each concept; for example, a variety of big and little blocks of different colors and shapes to emphasize size. (5, 5.1, 5.2)

- Give children verbal cues to use polar concepts. Ask them, "Bring me an empty container, and I'll help you pick up these Legos." (5, 5.1, 5.2)

- Have children sort and match items by size, temperature, or texture. (5, 5.1, 5.2)

- Label polar opposite concepts as children are completing tasks and engaging in activities. Emphasize that children are putting blocks in the box or taking paint jars out of the cupboard, jumping on the bed or crawling under it, or getting under the covers or on the top bunk. (5, 5.1, 5.2)

- Provide minimal assistance by using polar concepts and pointing to the correct items or prompting the correct actions. Point to the dry towel or the top of the shelf; hold children's hands and prompt them to run fast and walk slow with your assistance. (5, 5.1, 5.2)

Cognitive

TEACHING CONSIDERATIONS

1. Consult with parents to identify the polar concepts likely to be most interesting and frequently encountered at home.

2. If the child has a visual impairment, increase the use of tactile cues (e.g., having them handle items). Use materials that are easy to manipulate. Consult a vision specialist for evaluation of the need for high contrast materials and/or braille instruction. Consult with parents about successful interaction and tactile exploration strategies.

3. If the child has a motor impairment or abnormal muscle tone, consult a physical or occupational therapist about positioning, related issues, and assistive devices for holding and manipulating materials. Consult with parents for successful interaction strategies, and determine a consistent response (eye point, hand motion, etc.) for the child to indicate understanding of concepts.

4. If the child has a hearing impairment, consult an audiologist or speech-language pathologist about programming issues, amplification, and adaptive devices. Consult with parents for successful interaction strategies, and increase the intensity and variety of cues (e.g., clearer visual cues, louder verbal cues, more gestures, exaggerated motions, consistent routines for taking walks, hygiene, dressing).

GOAL 6   Repeats simple nursery rhymes

Objective 6.1   Fills in rhyming words in familiar rhymes

- PS6.1a   The child fills in words in familiar sentences ("Your name is _____"; "Let's read a _____"; "Let's go for a _____").

Objective 6.2   Says nursery rhymes along with familiar adult

- PS6.2a   The child indicates interest in hearing/repeating nursery rhymes.

IMPORTANCE OF SKILLS

Nursery rhymes are in essence very short stories that are easy to remember because of rhyming words at the end of each line. Learning rhymes is often the first opportunity children have to compare and analyze the sounds that make up words. Hearing similar sounds at the ends of rhyming words is a precursor to identifying similar features in written words, for example, words that start with the same letter or have the same ending. Perceiving and remembering sounds is an important skill for using letter sounds to sound out and spell words. Other goals/objectives that can be targeted at the same time as Goal 6 are listed on the following page.

Goal 6: Repeats simple nursery rhymes

Fine Motor

B:4 Orients picture book correctly and turns pages one by one

Gross Motor

B:2 Sits down in and gets out of chair

Cognitive

D:2 Imitates words that are not frequently used

G:3 Recognizes environmental symbols (signs, logos, labels)

G:4 Demonstrates functional use of reading materials

Social-Communication

D:3 Uses three-word utterances

Social

A:3 Initiates and maintains communicative exchange with familiar adult

Notes:

Cognitive

TEACHING SUGGESTIONS

Activity-Based

Group activities

- Invite parents into the classroom to share favorite rhymes and songs with the class. If the parents speak a language other than English, then point out that words in other languages rhyme, emphasize rhyming words ahead of time, and interpret the meaning of the rhyme. Encourage children with the same primary language to say the rhyme with the adult. (6, 6.1, 6.2)

- Combine music and movement activities, encouraging children to dance as they sing and repeat simple rhymes such as "The Hokey Pokey," "London Bridge," and "Ring Around the Rosey." Emphasize rhyming words that correspond with actions: putting limbs in and out of the circle and falling down. (6, 6.1, 6.2)

- Determine a word for the day, and ask each child in the group to think of a rhyming word. Use the children's rhyming words as "tickets out," having each child tell you a rhyming word before they go to lunch or outside to play. (6.2)

Bathing

- When changing or bathing the child, repeat rhymes such as "This little piggy" that involve tickling or hugging. Wait for the child to fill in the last word at the end of the rhyme before tickling or hugging. (6.1)

Storytime

- Once the child is familiar with a rhyme, encourage him or her to repeat it aloud to you, a peer, or a younger sibling. (6)

- Encourage the child to say the rhyme along with you by repeating each rhyme a few times. (6.2)

- Once the child is familiar with a rhyme, purposefully leave out the last word of the rhyming phrase and pause to give the child the opportunity to fill in the rhyming word. Repeat the entire rhyme immediately to give the child another chance, if a verbal model is required to fill in rhyming words at first. (6.1)

Travel

- While waiting with children at bus stops or in lines on community outings, play rhyming games and sing/say familiar nursery rhymes. Encourage children to select their favorite rhymes. (6, 6.1, 6.2)

Throughout daily routines

- Sing songs, tell stories, and read books with simple rhyming verses at naptime, bedtime, storytime, when riding in the car, or while waiting for the bus. Encourage children to repeat the rhymes and/or sing or say along with you. (6, 6.1, 6.2)

- Repeat the same rhymes frequently and practice saying familiar rhymes when a related topic comes up in the daily routine; for example, say, "Good night mouse, good night house" while tucking the child into bed at night, or sing "Row, Row, Row Your Boat" when the child is in the bathtub. (6, 6.1, 6.2)

Environmental Arrangements

- Provide books and music that emphasize rhyming and rhythmic, repetitive text, such as a Dr. Seuss book and Mother Goose nursery rhymes. Read the books during shared reading time, and sing the songs during music and movement activity time. (6, 6.1, 6.2)

- Make prop boxes to go along with specific rhymes; for example, miniature plastic monkeys and a bed to illustrate, "Five Little Monkeys Jumping on the Bed." Have children take turns using the props to act out the rhyme as it is repeated, emphasizing rhyming words. (6, 6.1, 6.2)

- Make rhyming books or collages by having children cut out pictures of items that rhyme (e.g., Dan, man, pan, fan, can, ran, tan, van; cat, mat, Pat, bat, fat, flat, sat, rat), pasting them on paper, and "reading" them aloud. (6.2)

- Integrate simple rhyming songs into morning circle and transitions during the day. Sing good morning songs to welcome each child, tunes for picking up toys, and songs for saying good-bye at the end of the day. Encourage children to sing/say the rhymes. (6, 6.1, 6.2)

- Play music at home and in the classroom that contains simple rhymes, especially during times when children are resting, going to bed, or eating quietly. (6, 6.1, 6.2)

- Make tape recordings of parents, other familiar adults, siblings, or peers repeating nursery rhymes and songs. Have the people making the tape repeat each rhyme a few times, beginning slowly and speaking faster each time they repeat the rhyme. Encourage the child to sing/speak along and to make their own tape of the same rhymes. (6, 6.1, 6.2)

Instructional Sequences

- Model short rhymes by saying/singing them twice before having children try to repeat them. (6)

- Break rhymes into smaller segments and teach them to children a few words at a time. After the child learns each segment separately, practice saying them all together. Start slowly and pick up the pace as the child learns the rhymes. (6)

Cognitive

- Say the rhyme and the first part of the word that you want the child to fill in. Wait a few seconds for the child to say the whole word. (6.1)

- Cue the child ahead of time about the rhyming word. Tell the child, "I'm going to say a rhyme, and when I stop you say ____." Check to be sure the child remembers the rhyming word, and then say/sing the rhyme, pausing at the point where the child fills in the rhyming word previously cued. (6.1)

- Use books with pictures that illustrate rhymes. At the end of the rhyme, point at the picture that represents the rhyming word, and wait for children to say the word. (6.1)

- Prompt children to say/sing rhymes along with adults by using your hands and body to indicate rhythm and to accent rhyming words. (6.1, 6.2)

TEACHING CONSIDERATIONS

1. For children who are learning English as a second language, provide songs and rhymes in the first language whenever possible. Parents are a good resource for making tapes and teaching rhymes and songs in the family's native language.

2. If the child has a visual impairment, increase the intensity and variety of environmental support and cues (e.g., large, bright, high-contrast pictures; textured pages; proximity to adult reader). When using books, make sure that they are easy to manipulate, and buy book/tape combinations for rhymes and songs.

3. If the child has a motor impairment or abnormal muscle tone, consult a physical or occupational therapist about the appropriate positioning for oral language activities, related issues, and assistive devices for speech output. Consult with parents for successful interaction strategies, and determine a consistent response (eye point, hand motion, etc.) for the child to indicate knowledge of rhyming words.

4. If the child has a hearing impairment, consult an audiologist or speech-language pathologist about programming issues, amplification, and adaptive devices. Consult with parents for interaction strategies, and increase the intensity and variety of cues (e.g., clearer visual cues, louder verbal cues, more gestures, exaggerated motions, consistent routines for shared reading).

5. Provide quiet and comfortable settings for rhyming activities.

6. Integrate books and songs into dramatic play, oral language, art, writing centers, and literacy centers of the classroom. Encourage shared reading, music, and family literacy activities in discussion with parents.

Social-Communication Area
Birth to Three Years

LIST OF AEPS TEST ITEMS

The Social-Communication Area begins with prelinguistic communicative behaviors and culminates with three-word utterances. Early social-communication development is organized into four strands for this curriculum: prelinguistic communicative interactions; transition to words; comprehension of words and sentences; and production of social-communicative signals, words, and sentences. The title, social-communication, reflects the perspective that communication is social as well as linguistic. Communication occurs between people, and competence in communication represents more than the

Social-Comm

specific skills of production and comprehension (i.e., expression and reception). As the child learns to communicate, he or she becomes more independent of adults and other caregivers and is less likely to express frustration at being misunderstood, misrepresented, and overlooked.

Although the first communication skills seem to appear when the child starts to speak, in reality, the infant begins much earlier to engage in communicative interactions. An infant's earliest cries signal the caregiver to respond, and the cessation of crying communicates that a need has been met. Caregiving activities such as feeding, diapering, and bathing, as well as face-to-face play, provide valuable opportunities for early communication of preference, mood, comfort level, and affection.

Attending to sounds in the environment, and voices in particular, develops into more complex turn-taking interactions by the time a child begins to coo and babble. The production of sound becomes associated quickly with getting the caregiver's attention, showing attention to objects and people, and expressing likes and dislikes. Both the infant and young child send and receive an enormous amount of information long before they are able to produce speech sounds.

The child uses a formal system of communication much earlier than he or she produces recognizable words. Concrete gestures and actions are combined with consistent vocalizations to form the earliest word approximations. Attention to the inflections of speech allows the child to respond appropriately to questions and statements before he or she can answer verbally. In this sense, early communication involves cognition, movement, and social development.

Because early communication is influenced by motor, cognitive, and social behaviors, at times a young child seems to emphasize one area at the expense of developing other skills; for example, it is common for the child to make few gains in language and communication skills while learning to walk. Once walking is mastered, development of communication skills may accelerate.

The rate of gaining skills in social-communication will vary over time in relation to development in other areas. More progress will ultimately be made by following the child's lead and encouraging mastery of new skills in the areas where the child is showing the most interest. The adage that "You can lead a horse to water, but you can't make him drink," has a parallel in teaching communication skills. The best intervention programs cannot be successful unless the child has a reason for communicating and finds the effort rewarding.

It is important to recognize that communication develops primarily in response to and with attention from the child's social environment. The child learns to ask for things by having someone respond to requests that are reasonable. A child learns to show interest in objects and people if the interest is reciprocated. Similarly, the child learns to follow directions by being encouraged and rewarded for doing so. Early communication in its many forms must obtain meaningful results or the child may stop trying to communicate. This means that adults in the social environment must initiate often and respond quickly to the young child who is learning communication skills.

The prelinguistic interactions and comprehension skills addressed in this curriculum are designed to provide the foundations for communicative competence. Many of the activities suggested create the expectation that communication is a functional, generative, and reciprocal enterprise. The use of early caregiving and play routines in the AEPS Curriculum is a purposeful attempt to encourage this approach to teaching and learning communication.

The production of words demonstrates the child's ability to use abstract symbols to refer to concrete objects, events, and people in the immediate environment. The AEPS Test and Curriculum recognize signing and other formal symbol systems as both augmentative and alternative communication systems. Some children only use sign or other symbol systems when they begin to produce words and phrases. Many children quickly replace a gestural or pictorial system with speech after the notion of using symbolic communication is established. Other children continue to use alternative symbol systems as a primary method of communication. The curriculum activities suggested in the production strand are usually appropriate for any formal system of communication.

When the child begins to use words, he or she tends to talk about familiar topics. Early words usually refer to familiar people and favorite objects in the child's environment. Other early topics include familiar actions and favorite games, such as Go and Peekaboo. Words that describe impressive events and objects, such as *hot* and *big*, also appear early. The child learns to talk about the relationships between actions and objects that he or she has observed many times by using words such as *more, mine,* and *no.*

The AEPS Curriculum does not select and sequence specific words because words of interest and relevance will vary from child to child. The child uses words that are important in play and in interactions with caregivers. The occupation and interests of a child's parents bring attention to certain events and objects. Some adults use expressions such as *whoops* and *uh-oh* when interacting with their infants. Other caregivers tend to label things in the environment, such as *milk, baby,* or *dog.* The style of the caregiver's language is reflected in the early words that the child uses; therefore, some children are more expressive and others are more referential.

When the young child begins to use words, he or she establishes meanings different from adult meanings. The child may use a word more narrowly than its true meaning, such as labeling only the family cat as *kitty.* Conversely, the child may generalize words, such as calling any and all men *daddy.* It is important to look for the concept behind the word that is misused rather than just correct the child's usage.

Several factors must be considered in identifying each child's communication needs. Words that serve multiple functions are good choices for early vocabulary because they quickly teach the child the usefulness of language. A word such as *help,* for example, can be rewarded in many different situations for a child who needs assistance with dressing, eating, and operating toys. Some other words with this kind of broad usefulness are *more, look, go, up, down,* and *want.*

It is important to choose words that are used frequently because the child will have more opportunities to hear, learn, and use these words. The child who sees Kris the baby sitter every day and his grandmother only twice a year, for example, will appropriately learn the word *Kris* before *Grandma.* Because familiar objects, events, and people are often preferred by young children, it makes sense to choose labels for these favorites as initial language targets. Words such as *eat, drink, ball,* and *go,* that are common and frequently used, are most functional for young children.

The ease or difficulty of pronouncing words is another factor to consider in selecting early vocabulary. Usually, words that children use are short and easy to pronounce. A child will say *doll* or *baby* and *drink,* but probably will not say *Cabbage Patch Kids* or *raspberry juice.* If a word is important enough to a child, then he or she will find a way to say it, even if it does not sound quite right. As a rule, however, it is wise to select words for the child that are easy to pronounce.

It is also important to identify words that will be rewarded by the child's social environment. Words such as *hi, night-night, bye-bye,* and *please* are well received by caregivers and will bring a pleasant and affectionate response for the young child. Such social amenities are appropriate to many situations and offer opportunities for successful interactions with many different people.

Learning words that represent different parts of speech (e.g., nouns, verbs, adverbs, adjectives, pronouns) allows the child to combine words and become more specific about requests, comments, and directions. The ability to label people, objects, and actions allows the child to express who is doing what or what happened to whom. Other parts of speech provide additional information about possession, description, and negation. Combining words into phrases and sentences provides opportunities to express many different things with the same labels.

Early attempts to combine words may require interpretation by the listener because the conventional rules of grammar are complex. The phrase "Juanita go" can mean "Juanita, let's go," "Juanita went somewhere," or "Juanita, go away!" The context is critical for understanding and responding appropriately to early utterances, and most children who expect a response will persist until the adult hits upon the correct meaning.

The AEPS Curriculum leaves selection of specific target words and phrases to caregivers and interventionists who are familiar with the child's environment, preferences, and interests. Careful selection of target words and phrases, creative and spontaneous use of the activities in the curriculum, and a constant sensitivity to the child's perspective should yield an environment that maximizes language learning. Communication can and should be taught all day and across all activities so that children learn the meaning, form, and function of word and phrase combinations in many settings.

Prelinguistic Communicative Interactions

GOAL 1   Turns and looks toward person speaking

Objective 1.1   Turns and looks toward object and person speaking

Objective 1.2   Turns and looks toward noise-producing object

IMPORTANCE OF SKILLS

The ability to turn and look at people when they are speaking is an integral component of social-communication exchanges. It is an initial listening experience and it allows the child to attend to the speaker, be ready to take a turn, respond, and continue the exchange. Focusing on speakers offers numerous opportunities to learn the language system; much can be learned by listening to and watching more mature users. Early motor movements to search for the sound are often jerky and slow, but they improve with practice. Turning and looking for noise-producing objects offers the child opportunities to integrate motor movements and to use the eyes and ears together to explore new objects and events in the world. This provides a foundation for the desire to communicate. Other goals/objectives that can be targeted at the same time as Goal 1 are listed on the following page.

TEACHING SUGGESTIONS

Activity-Based

Playtime

- While the child is playing, introduce opportunities for him or her to turn and attend to other children and other familiar and unfamiliar voices. (1)

- When the child turns and looks toward you or an object, provide opportunities for the child to look for you in different areas around the room by standing in back, in front, and to the side of the child. Activate a toy (e.g., bell, squeak-toy) so that it produces a noise. Call the child's name. When the child orients to the sound, activate the toy again, and try to engage the child's attention with the toy for several seconds. Gradually increase your distance from the child. (1.1, 1.2)

- Objects such as jewelry (especially bright-colored beads and dangling earrings) and glasses can be moved to attract the child's attention to the speaker's face and voice. (1.1, 1.2)

Concurrent Goals/Objectives for Social-Communication Strand A

Goal 1: Turns and looks toward person speaking

Gross Motor

A:1 Turns head, moves arms, and kicks legs independently of each other

Adaptive

A:1.4 Swallows liquids

Cognitive

A:1 Orients to auditory, visual, and tactile events

B:1 Visually follows object and/or person to point of disappearance

Social

A:1.3 Smiles in response to familiar adult

A:2.2 Responds to familiar adult's social behavior

Notes:

Feeding

- When feeding the child, use the bottle, spoon, or toy to direct the child's attention to your face while you speak. (1.1)

Throughout daily routines

- Throughout the day, when the child is content and alert but is not attending to you, stand a few feet behind or to the side of the child. Call the child's name. When the child looks at you, smile and engage the child for several seconds by talking to him or her. Vary the pitch and melody of your voice as the child attends to help keep the child's interest. (1, 1.1)

- As you enter a room, greet and gain the child's attention by saying, "Hello, Andrea," or "Good morning, Thomas." Watch to see if the child turns and looks toward you. (1, 1.1)

- Provide a range of opportunities during daily routines to engage the child in play with noise-producing objects to practice listening and finding the source of the sound. Radio, television, vacuum cleaner, running water, falling rain, bird, and dog noises are everyday sounds that you can experience with your child. Whenever possible, combine the sound and your presence to help the child focus on both the sound and you. (1.1, 1.2)

- As you encounter noises in the environment, observe the child's reaction and encourage the child to attend to the sound by commenting on it; for example, observe the child when the doorbell rings, the television or radio is turned on, the dishwasher starts, or cars or trucks pass by, and comment on the event. Carefully expose the child to a variety of sounds to reduce startling the child. (1.2)

Environmental Arrangements

- Build on the child's ability to turn and look toward you by systematically varying your position in the room until the child can visually locate you when you are standing in back of, in front of, and beside the child. Gradually increase your distance from the child while remaining in the same room. (1)

- Combine gestures with speech, such as a waving and saying "Hello," or combine a pointing response with speech. (1)

- Use exaggerated vocal and facial expressions as well as interesting, bright, noisy, or novel objects to gain and maintain the child's attention; for example, sing a nursery song, a catchy phrase from a commercial, or a family favorite to gain the child's attention. (1, 1.1)

- Initially, the setting may need to be free of objects and events that compete for the child's attention. Be sure that the person or the toy is an interesting event for the child. Let the child see you first and then step back and begin to speak. (1, 1.1, 1.2)

Social-Comm

- Play a tactile and vocal game such as "goochy goo" by gently touching the child's face to orient him or her to the location of your voice. (1, 1.1, 1.2)

- If the child does not readily respond to most objects, then present objects that you are certain the child desires, and then give the object to the child after the child looks at you. Be sure to talk to the child and say the child's name when you present the object; for example, present an interesting object near your face, and talk to the child. After the child looks toward you, give the object to the child, and comment about it or engage the child's attention with it. (1.1)

- Manipulate bright-colored puppets next to your face while talking to the child. Move the puppets closer to the child to re-engage his or her attention as needed, and then return the puppet next to your face.

- Place musical mobiles on a child's crib or playpen. (1.1, 1.2)

- When the child consistently turns and looks toward the noise-producing object, systematically vary your position in the room until the child can visually locate the object when it is activated behind, in front of, and beside the child. Gradually increase your distance from the child when you activate the object so that the child responds to sounds in a variety of locations. (1.2)

- Use combs and toothbrushes with chimes. Put bells on shoes or socks, or attach bells to the sleeve of the child's shirt. (1.2)

- Wind chimes are colorful and easy to activate when the child is near them. Let the child activate the chimes, and then talk to the child about the noise and the chimes. Attractive objects such as bright-colored or patterned toys and objects with interesting shapes or sizes may be used to gain the child's attention. Wave or wiggle the objects to gain the child's attention. (1.2)

Instructional Sequences

- Show the child an interesting toy or noise-producing object. After the child orients to the toy alone, present the toy close to your face and talk to the child at the same time. Gradually fade the use of the toy until the child orients to just your voice. Increase the distance from which the toy and your voice are presented to encourage the child to respond in a variety of situations. (1, 1.1, 1.2)

- Stand in front of the child and obtain a consistent response before moving a little farther to the child's side each time you speak. If your voice and interactions do not engage the child for more than a few seconds, then present an interesting toy immediately after the child orients. Talk to the child as you present the toy. After the child consistently responds to your voice and the toy, use the toy intermittently to engage the child; then use your voice only. (1, 1.1)

- Present an object in front of or close to the child (but not so close that it is offensive to the child). When the child consistently looks toward the object, present it at different angles. (1.2)

- Gently guide the child's face toward the object and activate it to make noise. You may also move the object slightly to engage the child's interest. (1.1, 1.2)

Combining or pairing different levels of instructions may be helpful when beginning to teach a new and difficult skill. Fade to less intrusive instructions as soon as possible to encourage more independent performance.

TEACHING CONSIDERATIONS

1. A child with a hearing impairment may hear only selected frequencies (high- or low-pitched sounds) or may hear only loud sounds. The child may also be sensitive to certain sounds or intensities (sounds that seem normal to you may be uncomfortably loud to some children; certain frequencies may be painful, or combinations of sounds or too much noise may be uncomfortable).

2. A child with a visual impairment may orient his or her body toward the speaker rather than look at the speaker's face. If the child has some vision, then the speaker should stand close enough for the child to see the face.

3. If a child has restricted range of motion in the head or trunk, objects should be presented in positions other than where the child is visually focused but still within the child's field of vision. Observe the child's gaze to see if he or she consistently localizes to the speaker or noise-producing objects. Consult a qualified specialist for individualized teaching ideas.

4. Be alert to safety precautions for all materials used.

GOAL 2   Follows person's gaze to establish joint attention

Objective 2.1   Follows person's pointing gesture to establish joint attention

Objective 2.2   Looks toward an object

IMPORTANCE OF SKILLS

Attention to one topic or event by two or more people (joint attention) is necessary for meaningful communication. Following a person's gaze to establish joint attention is a more developed skill than responding to a noise-producing object or person because the child no longer needs physical (e.g., toys, a pointed finger) or vocal cues to establish attention. Joint attention allows a common understanding between communicating partners, and it precedes more sophisticated conversational behaviors, such as initiating and maintaining topics, switching topics, or following another person's conversational lead. Following a person's pointing gesture to establish joint attention is a transition step for the child from attention toward a single object, person, or event to attention shared with another person. It is an important first step to identify the object of interest around which an interaction may occur. Other goals/objectives that can be targeted at the same time as Goal 2 are listed on the following page.

TEACHING SUGGESTIONS

Activity-Based

Travel

- Look toward people, pets, or objects while on walks or riding in the car; point out objects of interest (e.g., big trucks, McDonald's, colors, flowers). Encourage the child to look, too. (2, 2.1, 2.2)

Playtime

- Put frequently used and preferred items (e.g., child's ball, truck) in their usual location on a shelf. When it is time to play, look to the familiar location and wait for the child to follow your gaze. Tell the child to find the ball as you look at it. (2)

Storytime

- Look through picture books together. Point to the pictures, and name them for the child. (2.1)

Bathing

- Point to body parts while looking in the mirror or during bath time. (2.1)

Throughout daily routines

- Throughout the day, when you and the child are interacting, turn and look at another person, object, or event in the environment. When the child looks in the direction of your gaze, comment about the person, object, or event to confirm that the child is looking at the object of your attention. (2, 2.1)

- When the child consistently follows your pointing gestures, systematically vary your distance from the child so that the child responds to you when you gesture from different places in the room. Systematically vary the position of the objects, people, or events to which you point so that the child will orient to a variety of points in space. (2.1, 2.2)

Concurrent Goals/Objectives for Social-Communication Strand A

Goal 2: Follows person's gaze to establish joint attention

Fine Motor

A:3 Grasps hand-size object with either hand using ends of thumb, index, and second fingers

Gross Motor

A:2.1 Rolls from back to stomach

B:1.4 Sits balanced without support

Adaptive

A:2.2 Munches soft and crisp foods

A:3.2 Drinks from cup and/or glass held by adult

Cognitive

B:1 Visually follows object and/or person to point of disappearance

C:2.1 Indicates desire to continue familiar game and/or action

E:4.1 Uses more than one strategy in attempt to solve common problem

Social

A:1.2 Responds appropriately to familiar adult's affective tone

A:2.2 Responds to familiar adult's social behavior

Notes:

Social-Comm

- Throughout the day, watch for the child to attend to an object, person, or event; for example, if the child looks at a ball, then give it to the child, and label it as you do so. (2.2)

Environmental Arrangements

- The setting should be free of objects and events that compete for the child's attention because it is difficult to follow a speaker's gaze in a crowded and noisy setting. (2, 2.1, 2.2)

- Ask another person to produce an interesting visual or auditory event immediately after you point to that person or after you have made an obvious shift in gaze; for example, point to the person, and have him or her activate an interesting toy; look at the person, and have him or her engage the child in a social or communicative interaction. (2, 2.1, 2.2)

- Activate a musical toy on a table or bookcase. Engage the child in a game, and then look to the toy. (2)

- As you look toward an object of interest, change the tone of your voice, increase your volume, or use exaggerated facial expressions to help the child change the focus of attention. (2)

- After the child responds consistently, make your gaze and physical movements less obvious. Be sure to comment about the object, person, or event after the child looks at it. If the child does not readily follow your pointing gesture, then follow the child's gaze; point to an object, person, or event within the child's field of vision; and comment on it. Point to objects in positions that become gradually more distant from the child's immediate focus of attention so that the child must follow your pointing gesture to a variety of objects. (2, 2.1)

- The child may not respond if a speaker or object is too far away. Check for an optimal distance, and then vary the distance after the child responds consistently. (2, 2.2)

- Sing songs that require the child to look for peers as you call their names and point. (2.1)

- When the child is involved in an activity, gain the child's attention, and then direct attention back to the activity by pointing. (2.1)

- If the child does not look at objects you present, then follow the child's gaze, and manipulate an object at which the child is looking; for example, if the child looks at a toy bear, then make the bear dance and talk to the child. (2.2)

- Place a toy within the child's visual range. Move the object and wait for the child to relocate it. (2.2)

- Partially wind up a mechanical toy. Wait for the child to look at it before rewinding. (2.2)

- Establish locations for preferred items to be routinely placed so that the child can learn where to look for favorite, reinforcing objects that he or she may want. Allow the child time to look for objects before giving him or her a variety of entertaining toys. (2.2)

Instructional Sequences

- Use auditory events as the source of your change in gazes. Look toward the telephone as it rings, the door as it shuts, or the mobile as the music starts. (2)

- Verbally encourage the child to look at an object. (2, 2.2)

- When the child consistently follows your pointing gesture visually, present the objects to which you are pointing to the side of the child so that he or she must turn and look to follow your pointing gesture. (2, 2.1)

- Present new objects in front of the child by gradually increasing the distance between the child and the object. Point to the object each time before picking it up or giving it to the child to play with. (2.1)

- Present directly in front of the child an object that you are certain the child desires. Point to the object, pick it up, and give it to the child. (2.1)

- Touch the child as an attention-getting signal before you point. Gently guide the child's head to follow your point. (2.1, 2.2)

- Gently guide the child's face toward the object or action of interest. (2, 2.2)

TEACHING CONSIDERATIONS

1. A child with a hearing impairment may hear only selected frequencies (high- or low-pitched sounds) or may hear only loud sounds. The child may also be sensitive to certain sounds or intensities (sounds that seem normal to you may be uncomfortably loud to some children, certain frequencies may be painful, combinations of sounds or too much noise may be uncomfortable).

2. If the child has a visual impairment, use another sensory modality, such as sound, smell, or touch, to establish joint attention; for example, say, "I hear the music box playing. Do you hear it?" or direct the child's attention to the food you are serving by saying, "Oh, this is hot. Let's blow on it so that it doesn't burn you." When the doorbell rings, say, "Someone's at the door. Let's open it."

3. If a child has a restricted range of motion in the head or trunk, objects should be presented in positions other than where the child is visually focused but still within the child's field of vision. Position the child to reduce the amount of effort required to follow the speaker's gaze. Consult a qualified specialist for individualized teaching ideas.

Social-Comm

4. Pay careful attention to the child's reaction to tactile cues. Some children may find them aversive or may be sensitive to the amount or type of touch.

5. Be alert to safety precautions for all materials used.

GOAL 3   Engages in vocal exchanges by babbling

Objective 3.1   Engages in vocal exchanges by cooing

IMPORTANCE OF SKILLS

The purpose of this goal is to establish give-and-take communication between the child and others, which is fundamental to the development of conversational language. A second purpose is to encourage the child to practice a variety of consonant and vowel sounds. Other goals/objectives that can be targeted at the same time as Goal 3 are listed on the following page.

TEACHING SUGGESTIONS

Activity-Based

Quiet time

*   The child may experiment with making sounds when playing quietly or when alone. Pause and provide opportunities for privacy for the child to practice sounds, then join the child's activity. (3, 3.1)

*   Young children are often observed cooing quietly to themselves when they are content and alone (e.g., after waking from a nap). Join the interaction, and follow the child's lead. (3.1)

Dressing

*   After a bath or diaper change, encourage the child to vocalize. Provide time before you join the child's sound play. Mimic the child's sounds rather than expect the child to make the sounds you model. (3, 3.1)

Throughout daily routines

*   During daily caregiving routines (e.g., feeding, diapering, bathing) or when the child is content and alert, stand close to the child, and talk. Use a varied pitch and melody. Make simple consonant–vowel combinations, and repeat them for the child to hear. Pause repeatedly to give the child an opportunity to respond. The child may first respond by quieting, watching you, or increasing activity. Begin talking to the child again when you observe a response. (3, 3.1)

Concurrent Goals/Objectives for Social-Communication Strand A

Fine Motor

A:2 Brings two objects together at or near midline

A:3.2 Grasps cylindrical object with either hand by closing fingers around it

Gross Motor

B:1.4 Sits balanced without support

Adaptive

A:2.1 Bites and chews soft and crisp foods

A:4.3 Accepts food presented on spoon

Cognitive

C:2 Reproduces part of interactive game and/or action in order to continue game and/or action

F:1.3 Uses simple motor actions on different objects

Social

A:1.3 Smiles in response to familiar adult

A:2.2 Responds to familiar adult's social behavior

Notes:

Social-Comm

- Use consonant–vowel combinations as interjections in your speech when appropriate, such as "Bye-bye" when leaving, "Uh-oh" when something drops, "Boo-boo" when an accident occurs, or "Okay" when you are expressing affirmation. (3)

- Provide opportunities for the child to be with other young children who babble or talk. Younger voices may be more interesting and initiate a response more readily. (3)

- Identify the times or activities when the child vocalizes most. Use these times to engage in babbling or cooing activities. (3, 3.1)

Environmental Arrangements

- Sit behind the child looking into a mirror. Watch each other making sounds. Pat the child's mouth as the child makes sounds to show how to turn long vocalizations into intermittent sounds with pauses. Have the child pat your mouth to make the same "stop" sounds. Let the child feel your mouth as you babble. (3)

- Make a tape recording of a young child babbling, and intersperse the babbling with pauses to allow the child to respond. Play the tape for the child during quiet play times. (3)

- Use exaggerated vocal and facial expressions to gain, and maintain the child's attention. Songs and rhymes can be used, too. (3, 3.1)

- Try different vowel and consonant noises, and observe which sounds the child seems to prefer. Repeat what the child says or add a new syllable. It is not necessary for the child to imitate your sounds. (3, 3.1)

- Play tactile and vocal games to make the child laugh or produce a sound; reinforce the child with talking and cuddling. "Pop" and "Boo" are good utterances to include in games. (3, 3.1)

- Try different visual and auditory stimuli (e.g., musical bear) to gain the child's attention. Talk to the child, and remove the stimulus. Present it again when the child makes a sound, and talk to the child as you do so. (3, 3.1)

- The child may not respond if the speaker is too far away. Check for an optimal distance, then vary the distance after the child responds consistently. Let the child see your face and mouth movements. (3, 3.1)

- Include interesting objects in the sound–play activities. The child may vocalize when mouthing, banging, or shaking objects. Imitate the child's actions with objects and sounds. (3, 3.1)

Instructional Sequences

- Imitate the child's sounds as the child babbles. Wait for the child to start again. It may be necessary to build turn-taking interactions. (3, 3.1)

- Touch your fingers to your mouth and make a labial sound such as "Ba" or "Ma." Touch the child's mouth with your fingers as a cue that it is the child's turn. (3)

- Touch the child's fingers to your mouth as you make sounds. Then, touch the child's fingers to the child's mouth as a cue. (3, 3.1)

- As the child makes sounds with an object or while eating, gently guide the object away, take your turn vocalizing, and return the object to the child to repeat sound play. Continue interrupting and taking your turn until the child begins to take turns without your physical guidance. (3.1)

TEACHING CONSIDERATIONS

1. A child with a hearing impairment may hear only selected frequencies (high- or low-pitched sounds) or may hear only loud sounds. The child may also be sensitive to certain sounds or intensities (sounds that seem normal to you may be uncomfortably loud to some children; certain frequencies may be painful, and combinations of sounds or too much noise may be uncomfortable).

2. If the child has a visual impairment, allow the child to use his or her hands to feel the speaker making sounds. Encourage the child to babble in return. A child with a visual impairment may orient his or her body toward the speaker rather than look at the speaker's face. If the child has some vision, then the speaker should stand close enough for the child to see the face. Allow the child to feel you make sounds by holding his or her hands on your lips or throat. Consult a specialist for information on vocal skills for children with visual impairments.

3. If a child has a restricted range of motion in the head or trunk, the speaker should stand close enough to facilitate visual contact with the child. Positioning is also critical to sound production. Consult a qualified specialist for recommendations for positioning and techniques for eliciting sounds from a child with a motor impairment.

Social-Comm

STRAND B

Transition to Words

GOAL 1 Gains person's attention and refers to an object, person, and/or event

- PS1a The child gains a person's attention.

- PS1b The child establishes joint reference to an object, person, and/or event.

Objective 1.1 Responds with a vocalization and gesture to simple questions

- PS1.1a Confirmation function: For example, the adult asks, "May I have the doll?" The child vocalizes and uses "giving" gestures.

- PS1.1b Comment/reply function: For example, the adult asks, "What did you do?" The child vocalizes and uses "showing" gestures.

- PS1.1c Information function: For example, the adult asks, "Where is the ball?" The child vocalizes and uses "pointing" gestures.

- PS1.1d Request function: For example, the adult asks, "Do you want toast?" The child vocalizes and uses "reaching" gestures.

Objective 1.2 Points to an object, person, and/or event

- PS1.2a Confirmation function: For example, the adult says, "There's the ball." The child points to the ball.

- PS1.2b Comment/reply function: For example, the adult asks, "What happened?" The child points to spilled milk.

- PS1.2c Information function: For example, the adult asks, "Where's your teddy?" The child points to the teddy bear.

- PS1.2d Request function: For example, the child points to a bottle. The adult asks, "Do you want your bottle?"

- PS1.2e Attention function: For example, the child points to a sibling jumping in a swimming pool. The adult says, "There's Billy."

- PS1.2f Question function: For example, the child points to a new stuffed animal. The adult says, "What's that?"

- PS1.2g Comment/describe function: For example, the child points to a truck. The adult says, "That's a truck."

Objective 1.3   Gestures and/or vocalizes to greet others

- PS1.3a   Greet function: The child gestures or vocalizes to greet others; for example, when a sibling enters the room, the child vocalizes or uses a waving gesture. The adult enters the room and the child vocalizes or uses an "up" reaching gesture.

Objective 1.4   Uses gestures and/or vocalizations to protest actions and/or reject objects or people

- PS1.4a   Protest function: The child gestures or vocalizes displeasure; for example, the adult puts the child in a crib, and the child cries.

- PS1.4b   Rejection function: The child gestures or vocalizes refusal; for example, the adult puts a bottle to the child's mouth; the child closes his or her mouth and turns away. The adult offers the child a toy; the child pushes the toy away. The adult gives the child a cracker; the child drops the cracker.

    No standard developmental sequence appears to exist for the programming steps included for this goal and associated objectives. Careful observation will help determine the child's current skill level. Begin programming at the child's level of interest.

IMPORTANCE OF SKILLS

Prior to the production of words, most children vocalize or gesture for a variety of communicative functions. Vocalizations and gestures are called *prelinguistic communication signals* because they precede symbolic language. It is important to establish a relationship between a vocalization or gesture from the child and some response from the environment. From this relationship, the child learns that communication signals serve a variety of functions and allow the child to gain a person's attention, refer to an object, person, or event, respond to questions and make requests. Eventually, vocalizations and gestures are shaped into more conventional language forms (i.e., words). Other goals/objectives that can be targeted at the same time as Goal 1 are listed on the following page.

TEACHING SUGGESTIONS

Activity-Based

Playtime

- If the child is reaching for or pointing to a favorite toy, then label it, talk about it, and give it to the child. (1.2)

Social-Comm

Concurrent Goals/Objectives for Social-Communication Strand B

Goal 1: Gains person's attention and refers to an object, person, and/or event

Fine Motor

A:2.3 Reaches toward and touches object with each hand

B:2 Assembles toy and/or object that require(s) putting pieces together

Gross Motor

C:1 Walks avoiding obstacles

Adaptive

A:3 Drinks from cup and/or glass

A:4 Eats with fork and/or spoon

B:1 Initiates toileting

Cognitive

B:3 Maintains search for object that is not in its usual location

C:2 Reproduces part of interactive game and/or action in order to continue game and/or action

D:1 Imitates motor action that is not commonly used

Social-Communication

A:2 Follows person's gaze to establish joint attention

A:3 Engages in vocal exchanges by babbling

Social

A:3 Initiates and maintains communicative exchange with familiar adult

Notes:

- When peers argue over sharing toys, taking turns, or choosing seats, give the child ample opportunity to protest or reject the peer's behavior before intervening. (1.4)

Travel

- During trips to new places, watch the child's gaze, name the objects and events that the child looks at, and model pointing. (1.2)

Bathing

- While bathing, name body parts, and ask the child to point to them. When the child touches a body part, say, "That's right! That's your foot." Repeat with different body parts. (1.2)

Storytime

- While reading a book, name the pictures that the child points to. Take turns pointing to favorite pictures, and add new ones. (1.2)

Throughout daily routines

- As events occur throughout the day, pretend not to notice immediately, giving the child an opportunity to direct your attention; for example, let the telephone ring an extra ring or two, or use a kitchen timer, alarm clock, or doorbell to initiate a response. (1)

- Use gestures with your words; for example, say, "Bye-bye," and wave or say, "Do you want up?" and hold out your hands. These frequent models are easily imitated by the child. (1)

- Ask questions, and respond to the child's vocalizations and gestures in a variety of settings so that the child learns to gain attention in many situations. Watch for the child to indicate interest at the store, in the car, or at playtime with familiar and unfamiliar people. Respond consistently. (1)

- Throughout the day, talk to the child about routine activities, and ask simple questions; for example, while filling the tub with water for a bath, talk to the child about the floating toys you put in the water. Ask the child, "What do you want?" and encourage the child to reach for the toys. Always pause to give the child time to vocalize or gesture before letting the child play with the toys. Ask what the child is playing with to encourage a showing gesture. (1.1)

- When asking questions, use objects, people, or events with which the child is familiar and readily responds; for example, when a sibling is walking through the door, ask, "Where's Billy?" and observe if the child vocalizes or looks toward the sibling. React by smiling, and say, "That's right, there's Billy!" (1. 1)

- Throughout the day, when friends and family members enter or leave a room, wave and say, "Hi," or "Bye." Stand at the door or hold the child to look out the window at people approaching or leaving. Say, "Wave bye-bye," or "Wave hello." Try this in a variety of settings so that the child learns to respond in many situations. (1.3)

- When putting toys away, say, "Bye-bye," and wave to each one. (1.3)

- Allow the child time to communicate his or her likes and dislikes by responding to people and objects before you introduce new ones. Try not to guess who or what the child prefers, but allow the child time to demonstrate preferences. It may be necessary to initially accept minimal responses from the child. (1.4)

- Give the child multiple opportunities to protest or reject by asking, "Do you want?" or "Do you like?" in situations where a rejection is reasonable. Give the child choices of food, clothing, and activities so that it is necessary to reject one option. (1.4)

- If the child protests or rejects activities, food, toys, clothes, or people, then make every effort to respect reasonable responses; for example, say, "Oh, you don't like that"; or stop tickling if a child says, "No," or squirms away. (1.4)

Environmental Arrangements

- Arrange the play area so that desired toys are visible to the child but just out of reach. Wait for the child to use a vocalization or a gesture to gain your attention and refer to a desired toy. Then, give the toy to the child. (1)

- When the child is consistently focusing on objects, people, or events of interest, refrain from offering the desired material until the child uses a gesture or vocalization to gain your attention and refers to the object, person, or event of interest; for example, when giving a snack to peers or siblings, wait until the child uses a vocalization or gesture to gain your attention and refers to the food or the other child eating. Then, give the child the desired snack. (1)

- The child may not attempt to gain your attention if you are too far away. Check for an optimal distance, then vary the distance after the child responds consistently. (1)

- Show the child a noise-producing object such as a musical toy. Activate the toy, and observe the child's response. If the child uses a vocalization or gesture, then give the toy to the child. Wait for the child to use a vocalization or gesture to gain your attention and refer to the object, then re-activate the toy, and give it to the child. (1, 1.1)

- During snack time, give the child just one piece of a favorite finger food. Place the next piece of food outside the child's reach and ask, "What do you want?" When the child looks, vocalizes, and reaches, say, "Here's a pretzel," and give the child the pretzel to eat. (1.1, 1.2)

- Use questions paired with familiar games and activities; for example, cover the child's head with a diaper and say, "Where's baby?" Wait for the child to vocalize or gesture, then uncover and say, "There's baby." Repeat several times. (1.1, 1.3)

- To encourage the child who does not point, offer two items (preferred and nonpreferred). Give the child the nonpreferred item while you hold the preferred item, and wait for a gesture. (1.2, 1.4)

- Hold two objects, one a bright-colored or musical toy and the other a plain toy. Ask the child, "What do you want?" Wait for the child to reach for or point to the desired toy, then give it to the child. (1.2)

- Use rhymes, songs, and fingerplays that incorporate the use of pointing; for example, play "This little piggy" and point to the child's toes. Then, ask the child to point to your toes as you say the rhyme. (1.2)

- Sing hello and good-bye songs to friends in a group. (1.3)

- Have a helper peek from behind a screen and say, "Hello," and wave. Say, "Hello," and wave back. Have the helper go behind the screen, come out again, and say, "Hello," with a wave. (1.3)

- Use books such as *Hello, Kitty* and greet favorite pictures in stories. (1.3)

- It may be helpful to have a sibling demonstrate preferences during snack time. Ask a sibling, "Do you want this?" and have the sibling say, "No," and shake his or her head. Repeat several times varying yes and no answers. (1.4)

- During initial gestural training, practice action games such as Pat-a-Cake and So Big to help the child learn to associate actions with words and events. These games also help the child learn to imitate your actions. (1.4)

- Name a common object that the child consistently responds to, such as a cup. Provide the child with opportunities to express preferences by letting the child make simple decisions that you are willing to abide by. Ask, "Do you want a drink?" "Do you want to get up?" or "Do you want to rock?" Gesture and show objects, if possible, to give the child cues; then pretend to forget the object's name. Hold a cup and say, "Here's your nose." Observe to see if the child vocalizes or gestures, then laugh and say, "No, this isn't your nose. It's a cup!" (1.4)

- Read or make up stories describing children who demonstrate protesting and refusing. (1.4)

Instructional Sequences

- Model gaining a person's attention to refer to an object by pointing or waving at an object or person; for example, say, "Ginny, would you like a cracker?" Also, model refusing by saying, "No." (1, 1.1, 1.2, 1.3, 1.4)

- Systematically introduce the use of time delay and visual cues; for instance, during snack time, show the child a desired snack, establish eye contact, and give an expectant look. Wait for the child to vocalize or use a gesture to refer to the desired food, then give it to the child. (1, 1.1, 1.2, 1.4)

- Gesturing, pointing, and waving are easy to model. Any looking, vocalizing, or motor gesture that can be shaped into a communicative signal should be encouraged and reinforced. Cues should be consistent and redundant, and all opportunities should be used. (1, 1.1, 1.2, 1.3)

- Show the child an interesting toy placed just out of reach and provide a verbal cue, "Show me what you want." Once the child is consistently vocalizing or gesturing to refer to the object, vary the distance between the object and the child. (1, 1.1, 1.2)

- When playing with the child, provide verbal and physical cues; for example, say, "Show me what you want." Then, point to or move the desired toy closer to the child. Gently guide the child's hand toward the toy. While looking at a book, verbally instruct the child to find certain items in pictures. (1, 1.1, 1.2)

- While the child is bathing, name and touch the child's body parts. The child may relate to body parts more easily than objects at this stage of development. Ask the child to point to his or her own foot. If the child does not respond, then gently guide the child's hand to the foot. Repeat with different body parts. (1.2)

- During snack time, offer the child a food that you know he or she dislikes. Wait for the child to show preferences. If the child does not respond, then gently guide the child's hand to push the food aside. (1.4)

Combining or pairing different levels of instructions may be helpful when beginning to teach a new and difficult skill. Fade to less intrusive instructions as soon as possible to encourage more independent performance.

TEACHING CONSIDERATIONS

1. The child's vocalizations need not approximate actual words.

2. Socially appropriate gestures and vocalizations should be modeled and encouraged to facilitate the child's acquisition of conventional and acceptable attention-getting behaviors.

3. A child with a visual impairment may orient his or her body toward the adult rather than look at the adult's face. Adaptations of conventional gestures may be necessary.

4. If the child has a restricted range of motion, the adult should stand in a position other than where the child is visually focused but still within the child's field of vision.

5. A child with a hearing impairment may be acquiring an augmentative or alternative communication system such as a picture or sign system. Consult a qualified specialist for teaching techniques.

6. In all contexts be consistent about requiring a response from the child before giving a desired object, event, or person.

7. The child may not respond if the adult is too far away. Check for an optimal distance, then vary the distance after the child responds consistently.

8. Respond to the child's vocalizations and gestures in a variety of settings so that the child learns to respond across settings.

9. Teach skills in appropriate contexts.

10. Conventional gestures include pushing objects away, shaking the head "no," turning away, and holding a hand up and out. Any vocalization or motor gesture, however, can be shaped into a communicative signal and should be encouraged and reinforced.

GOAL 2   Uses consistent word approximations

Objective 2.1   Uses consistent consonant–vowel combinations

Objective 2.2   Uses nonspecific consonant–vowel combinations and/or jargon

Objective 2.3   Vocalizes to express affective states

Objective 2.4   Vocalizes open syllables

Social-Comm

IMPORTANCE OF SKILLS

Prior to the production of words, most children use consistent speech–sound combinations to refer to objects, people, or events. These communication sounds precede symbolic language and are used to request, protest, inform, and direct attention. It is important to establish a relationship between communication sounds by the child and some response from the environment. From this relationship, the child learns that communication sounds serve a variety of functions.

Vocal development for most children follows a predictable sequence. Vocal experimentation, including their cries, is important because it allows infants to learn precise control of their lips, tongue, and hard/soft palate and how to coordinate respiration, phonation, and resonance for speech. Initially, most infants use vowel sounds with rising and falling intonation in a sing-song fashion (i.e., cooing) as they experiment with their vocal mechanism and relate to their environment. A child's ability to vocalize affect can result in adult's better responding to their needs and improved ongoing interactions with the environment. An adult is better able to interpret and respond to the child's state as the child learns to use different vocalizations and intonational patterns to communicate a variety of emotions.

These skills represent important steps toward successful communication. Over time, the child's sounds become word approximations, and the child uses them consistently to respond to questions, make requests, and refer to the same object, person, or event. Eventually, vocalizations and gestures are shaped into more conventional language forms (i.e., first words). Other goals/objectives that can be targeted at the same time as Goal 2 are listed on the following page.

TEACHING SUGGESTIONS

Activity-Based

Playtime

- Talk to each other on toy telephones, and provide talking toys such as See-N-Say or stuffed animals that "talk." (2.1, 2.2)

- Play repetitious nursery games such as So Big and Seek to encourage approximation of common key words. (2.1)

- Set up a turn-taking game using word approximations and objects; for example, say, "block" and drop a block into a bucket; say, "ball" and roll the ball to the child. Encourage the child to say the word approximation before performing the action. (2.1)

- Play a naming game. Use the names of common objects and people throughout the day. Wait for the child to use the appropriate word combination, then imitate. If the child does not respond, then repeat the model. (2.1)

- Throughout the day, when playing with the child, place desired toys out of reach; for example, if stacking blocks, then give the child one block but place the others out of reach. Wait for the child to use the appropriate word approximation before giving the child another block. Ask the child, "What do you want?" and pause a second time. Encourage any vocalization before giving the child the toy. (2.1, 2.2)

Bathing

- While bathing, encourage the child to touch and name his or her own body parts; for example, touch the child's foot, and say, "What's this?" Give the child time to respond, then model an appropriate vocalization if necessary. (2.1)

- Play touch and name games; for example, while bathing the child, encourage the child to touch and name bath toys; touch the child's rubber duck and say, "What's this?" Give the child time to respond, then model the appropriate vocalization if necessary. (2.2)

Concurrent Goals/Objectives for Social-Communication Strand B

Goal 2: Uses consistent word approximations

Cognitive

B:3 Maintains search for object that is not in its usual location

C:2 Reproduces part of interactive game and/or action in order to continue game and/or action

D:1 Imitates motor action that is not commonly used

D:2 Imitates words that are not frequently used

Social

A:3 Initiates and maintains communicative exchange with familiar adult

Notes:

Social-Comm

Feeding

- During routine activities such as feeding, place a desired object out of reach; for example, place a piece of cracker within the child's field of vision, but out of reach. Pause, and give an expectant look. If the child vocalizes, then imitate the response, and give the child the cracker. (2.2)

Quiet time

- Allow the child to practice making sounds and sound combinations while playing quietly, such as before and after naps, after meals, and after baths or changing. When all physical needs are met, children are more often interested in learning. (2.2)

Throughout daily routines

- When playing with, dressing, or feeding the child, imitate the sounds that the child makes. Respond to any vocalization by repeating and emphasizing the child's sound. Once reciprocal imitation is established, expand upon the child's repertoire by lengthening the sound sequence or adding new sounds. (2.1, 2.2, 2.4)

- Maximize every opportunity to practice the consistent word approximations the child uses. Say, "Hi," and "Bye," when arriving or leaving. Wait for the child to request "more," not just at meals, but when reading books, stacking blocks, or playing games. (2.1)

- Respond consistently to the child's verbalizations, even when those sounds bear little resemblance to words. Be persistent in attempting to identify objects, people, and events to pair with early word approximations. Repeat correct labels for the child. (2.1)

- During routine activities, give the child many opportunities to vocalize and receive desired objects of interest; for example, while bathing, hold a desired float-toy and encourage the child to vocalize to receive the toy. The adult may model the appropriate response. The child's vocalizations do not need to approximate actual words; for example, the adult gives a cracker to the child after the child points to the cracker and says, "Ka." (2.1, 2.2)

- During daily routines and activities, talk to the child in an affectionate tone and make positive comments about the child's appearance, activities, skills and interests. Pause to allow the child to vocalize pleasure or displeasure during the interactions. (2.3)

- During routine and play activities introduce moments of face-to-face interactions with objects between the child and familiar adult. Adult should smile and make comments as he or she introduces a desired object and pair a frown with a vocalization when he or she removes the desired object. When the adult reintroduces the objects, he or she should smile and vocalize to suggest delight. (2.3)

- Talk to the infant as you are caring for him or her by using appropriate inflectional patterns with typical verbalizations paired with simple open vowel patterns (e.g., "Ahh, are you hungry?" "Oh, are you wet?" "Oooo, does something hurt?"). (2.4)

- Coo softly to the child as he or she is being cared for. Cooing consists of producing vowel sounds in a sing-song pattern. (2.4)

- Sing to your child using simple vowel sounds along with words. (2.4)

Environmental Arrangements

- Observe the child's responses toward objects, people, and events to determine those to which the child most readily responds. When the child focuses on the desired object, person, or event, ask the child to vocalize; for example, as a sibling blows bubbles, ask the child, "What's that?" Wait for the child to respond, then model appropriate vocalization, "Pop, pop," if necessary. (2.1)

- Position the child so that your faces are close. Exaggerate facial expressions, move lips slowly and distinctly, change head orientation, and vary pitch and intensity of voice to evoke a positive vocalization from the child. Encourage all vocalizations. (2.1, 2.2, 2.3)

- Use exaggerated vocal expressions when naming interesting objects or pictures; for example, push a brightly painted train on a track and say, "Choo choo." (2.1, 2.2)

- Look through picture books. Point to pictures of common objects and label them. (2.2)

- Expand on the single sounds that the child makes to develop consonant-vowel combinations; for example, if the child says, "Rrr," when pushing a car or truck, then expand it to "Rum-rum." If the child uses "Nnmm" as a request for food, then expand on the single sound to develop the word *more*. (2.2)

- Play Peekaboo, and wait for the child to say "peek" or "boo" before continuing the game. (2.2)

- Exaggerate vocalizations of affect (e.g., frown deeply, and use a sharp voice if you must say, "No"). Encourage the child to imitate the vocalizations. (2.3)

- Play an interactive game that elicits a response from the child. Interrupt the game briefly, and leave the child's visual range. Re-appear when the child vocalizes dissatisfaction and a desire to continue the game. (2.3)

- Use highly motivating objects, such as musical toys, to engage the child's attention. After activating the toy, remove the toy, and introduce it again when the child makes a sound. Make sure you pause long enough to allow the child an opportunity to vocalize. Comment on the toy while modeling vowel sounds, such as, "Oh, look at the _____!" (2.4)

- Position yourself so that you are face to face with the child, and use appropriate facial expression as you repeat the child's vocalizations and model vowel sounds. Use exaggerated vowel sounds to call the child's attention to sound play (e.g., "Ohh," "Ahh"). (2.4)

- Place the child's hands on his or her own mouth and throat as he or she attempts vocalizations. (2.4)

- Break down words to the vowel or consonant–vowel level when playing; for example, when playing Peekaboo, stress the "oo" sound when saying Peekaboo, (draw out 'oo' sound). Say, "Moo – oo," when playing with a toy cow or when pointing to a picture in a book. (2.4)

Instructional Sequences

- Throughout the day, observe the child's responses toward objects, people, or events to determine those to which the child most readily responds; for example, when the child focuses on a desired object, ask the child, "What do you want?" Wait for the child to respond, then model an appropriate vocalization if necessary before giving the child the object. (2.1, 2.2)

- Systematically introduce the use of time delay and visual cues; for instance, during snack time, show the child a desired snack, establish eye contact, and give an expectant look. Wait for the child to vocalize to refer to the desired food, then give it to the child. (2.1, 2.2, 2.4)

- Encourage the child to imitate by responding to the adult's accentuation of vowel sounds. Use the initial sound of a consonant–vowel combination as a cue. (2.1, 2.2, 2.4)

- Model using sounds that you want the child to imitate when you reach for toys, food, or common objects within routines. Be sure you are positioned in front of the child, and begin using simple vocalizations. Pair sounds to regular activities, and use the same sounds within routines to provide consistent models; for example, every time you pick the child up, model, "You want up?" (i.e., when picked up from crib, floor, diaper table). (2.1, 2.2, 2.4)

- Model eye contact, gestures, and vocalizations that allow the child to express interest and pleasure. Adults must be responsive to the child (e.g., exaggerated facial expressions, varying pitch and voice) when the child attempts to communicate any affective state. (2.3)

- Model pairing your own affective tone to strong pleasurable or negative events and stimuli. Tickle, pick up, and talk to the child to encourage vocalizations that express pleasure. Place the child down and firmly state, "All done." Note if the child vocalizes negative affect. (2.3)

- Hug and kiss the child often. Describe what you are doing in a pleasant voice. Verbally encourage the child to vocalize. (2.3)

- Repeat positive or negative affective cues if the child responds inappropriately. (2.3)

- Touch the child's lips as a cue to vocalize after you have modeled a vowel sound. (2.1, 2.2, 2.3, 2.4)

TEACHING CONSIDERATIONS

1. Words that are important to the family and are used throughout the child's environment are words that should be emphasized when practicing this skill.

2. Choose objects, people, and events to which the child most readily responds.

3. A child with a hearing impairment may hear only selected frequencies (high- or low-pitched sounds) or may hear only loud sounds. The child may also be sensitive to certain sounds or intensities (sounds that seem normal to you may be uncomfortably loud to some children; certain frequencies may be painful, and combinations of sounds or too much noise may be uncomfortable). A child with a hearing impairment may be acquiring an augmentative system such as a picture or sign system. Consult a qualified specialist for teaching techniques in this area.

4. Be consistent about requiring a response from the child.

5. For the child with a visual impairment, touch cues may be useful as a beginning step to identify objects by their feel. Use sensory modalities other than visual whenever possible.

6. Children present individual differences in arousal levels. Adapt the intensity of experiences that are used to elicit affective vocalization to avoid over- or understimulation.

7. To the extent possible, make sure that the child is responding to adult's affective cues (e.g., smiling, laughing, crying).

8. If the child has sensory impairments, interact in a mode that is meaningful to the child; for example, if the child has a hearing impairment, then affect should be encouraged through gestures and facial expressions.

9. Use negative affect such as a sharp voice and corrections sparingly.

10. If the child has a restricted range of motion in the head or trunk or other motor impairment, the speaker should be in a position that facilitates visual contact between the child and the speaker. Positioning will also be critical for easy sound production. A child with motor impairments, in particular spastic cerebral palsy, may be unable to easily produce sounds. Latency of response may be an issue for these children. Consult a qualified specialist for recommendations for positioning and techniques for eliciting vocalizations from children with motor impairments.

Social-Comm

Comprehension of Words and Sentences

GOAL 1 Locates objects, people, and/or events without contextual cues

Objective 1.1 Locates common objects, people, and/or events in unfamiliar pictures

Objective 1.2 Locates common objects, people, and/or events in familiar pictures

- PS1.2a Locates common actions and events in familiar books or pictures.

- PS1.2b Locates common objects and people in familiar books or pictures.

Objective 1.3 Locates common objects, people, and/or events with contextual cues

Objective 1.4 Recognizes own name

Objective 1.5 Quiets to familiar voice

IMPORTANCE OF SKILLS

Children learn to associate words with objects, events, and people by repeatedly hearing the words while interacting with the environment. Eventually, the child learns that certain words represent particular objects, people, and events, even if the child does not have the assistance of contextual cues.

Initially, contextual cues aid the child in comprehending the meaning of words. The word *cow* is easily understood if the child is looking at a toy cow in a play barn. Later, the child associates the word cow with an unfamiliar picture of a cow. The purpose of this skill is for the child to associate a referent with its word symbol while looking at unfamiliar pictures.

The child's awareness and response to familiar voices plays a crucial role in the active participation of social interactions and cognitive development. The child learns that certain sounds have meaning when they begin to recognize their own name amidst all other auditory input.

Comprehending words and sentences permits the child to follow directions and interact with the environment. These skills are important to children in understanding what others say and in developing social skills through conversation and an increased awareness of the environment. Other goals/objectives that can be targeted at the same time as Goal 1 are listed on the following page.

Concurrent Goals/Objectives for Social-Communication Strand C

Fine Motor

A:5 Aligns and stacks objects

Gross Motor

C:1 Walks avoiding obstacles

Cognitive

B:3 Maintains search for object that is not in its usual location

C:1 Correctly activates mechanical toy

E:2 Uses an object to obtain another object

F:1.1 Uses representational actions with objects

Social

A:3 Initiates and maintains communicative exchange with familiar adult

C:1.3 Plays near one or two peers

Notes:

Social-Comm

TEACHING SUGGESTIONS

Activity-Based

Storytime

- Look at pictures in books. Name the objects, people, or events and point to them. Ask the child to point to the pictures that you label. Label the item or event several times. (1.1)

- Look through catalogs and magazines to find variations on common objects such as shirts, shoes, tables, or cars. (1.1, 1.2)

- Go to a children's library, and look at familiar and new books in another setting. (1.1, 1.2)

- When looking at unfamiliar pictures, show the child the object, person, or event that the picture represents; for example, if looking at an unfamiliar picture of a shirt, then point to the child's shirt. (1.1)

- Read the same stories many times so that the child can become familiar with the pictures. Let the child choose favorite stories. (1.2)

- Make a photo album or an "All About Me" book with photos of favorite people, toys, and events. Use it as a story or a schedule of activities. (1.2)

Dressing

- Look in the mirror and point to different body parts of the child and yourself. Ask the child to point to the body parts that you name. Label each body part several times. (1.1, 1.3)

Playtime

- Introduce simple puzzles with pictures of objects. Ask the child to find the pieces as you name them. (1.1)

Feeding

- Show the child pictures of favorite foods, and label them several times, then give the child the favorite food to eat. Offer the child variations of the food, such as a sliced banana, and compare it with the picture of a whole banana. (1.1, 1.2)

Throughout daily routines

- During routine activities, such as bathing, ask the child to give you an object that is usually present, such as a washcloth. Then, ask the child to give you an object that is not usually present but is still relevant to the activity, such as a squeeze-toy. (1)

- Ask the child to locate items or events not immediately present; for example, ask, "Where's Daddy?" when Daddy is in the backyard. Observe to see whether the child looks or moves toward the back door. Then, take the child outside to see Daddy. (1)

- Send the child on simple errands to other locations in the general vicinity; for example, ask the child to bring a toy to you, to take a cup to a table in the dining room, or to retrieve shoes from the closet. (1)

- Recurring environmental events, such as the delivery of the mail, garbage pick-up, and sirens from fire trucks and police cars, offer opportunities to search for the source of the sound. Ask your child, "What do you hear?" or "Where is it?" (1)

- Throughout the day, talk to the child about what you are doing by labeling objects, people, or events in the child's environment. Show the child where objects are commonly located (e.g., coats in the closet, toys on the shelf, snacks in the cupboard). Encourage the child to assist you in putting things away. (1.3)

- Capitalize on interesting events by clearly labeling objects, actions, and people that capture the child's attention; for example, if the child drops a toy, say, "Where did the doll go? You dropped the doll." (1.3)

- Use gestures with your words to help the child comprehend the meaning of words; for example, say, "Bye-bye," while waving your hand, or say, "Up," while extending your arms to the child. (1.3)

- Engage in positive interactions with the child and remain in close proximity when calling his or her name to get a reaction and/or his or her attention. (1.4)

- Use the child's name during departures and arrivals, and play games during changing and dressing routines that include his or her name as well as the communication partner's name (e.g., Mary's pants, Mommy's nose). (1.4)

- Respond quickly and consistently to the child's cues for attention or signs of distress; vocalize prior to entering the child's visual field to help him or her learn to identify your voice. (1.5)

- Vocalize and smile during daily routines and activities. Focus the child's attention on your face while vocalizing. Establish eye contact and joint attention, and smile and talk to the child. Move your face into and out of the child's visual field. (1.5)

- When the child vocalizes for attention, respond with verbalizations from a distance to allow the child to experience comfort from a familiar voice; for example, if the child is fussing in his crib, then wait a few moments before providing physical comfort (i.e., picking up the child and cuddling him or her). Talk to the child in comforting tones prior to providing face-to-face interactions. (1.5)

Environmental Arrangements

- The words chosen should represent objects, people, or events with which the child has frequent contact. Frequent opportunities to hear the word in relation to its referent may facilitate comprehension. (1, 1.1)

- Refer to objects, people, or events that are important to and are of functional value to the child. Learning names of common environmental items and events assists the child's adaptation to the environment and should be intrinsically rewarding. (1, 1.1)

- Choose words that have sound combinations that are relatively easy to produce or are already used by the child. Although the objective of this goal is comprehension, production often follows or occurs simultaneously. Selection of easy-to-produce words may enhance production. (1)

- When the child consistently locates common objects in usual locations, vary the locations so that the object is still within the child's view; for example, if a favorite toy is usually on the floor, then place it in the toy box within the child's view, and ask the child to locate it. (1.3)

- When the child consistently recognizes familiar pictures of objects, people, and events, introduce unfamiliar pictures; for example, if the child consistently points to a dog in a favorite picture book, then introduce a picture of a different size or color dog, and ask the child to point to the dog in the new picture. (1.1, 1.3)

- Introduce new characters to familiar stories in homemade books. Add new photos to an album or scrapbook. (1.1)

- Use exaggerated vocal and facial expressions when naming an unfamiliar picture to gain and maintain the child's attention. (1.1)

- Show the child two pictures: a bright-colored picture of an object and a black-and-white picture of the same object. Ask the child to point to the object. Repeat the activity several times with other sets of pictures to determine if the child has a preference for bright-colored or black-and-white pictures. (1.2)

- Put two familiar pictures on a table. Ask the child to give you one of them at a time. Make place mats with familiar pictures of the objects used at mealtime. Place a picture of a plate, cup, and spoon on construction paper and cover it with contact paper. Label items while the child matches objects and pictures. (1.2)

- Observe the child throughout the day to determine which toys are of particular interest to him or her. Offer two objects, one that is known to be desirable and one that is not. Ask the child to point to the desirable toy, and then give it to him or her. (1.3)

- Audiotapes, CDs, and records for children are a good source for repetitive and familiar words and sounds. These can be paired with motor actions to facilitate communication. (1.3)

- When the child is independently playing, interrupt the play by calling out his or her name, and wait for the child to respond. (1.4)

- Call out the child's name to gain his or her attention prior to presenting an object within his or her visual field. This will allow the child to respond to his or her name rather than simply responding to the visual stimulation of the toy. (1.4)

- When the child is sitting or being cradled in the adult's lap, sit in front of a mirror. Attempt to gain and maintain eye contact while looking in the mirror. Use a variety of inflections and vocal patterns to add interest. Have another adult in the area call out the child's name intermittently and observe the child's response. This will encourage localization as well as name recognition. (1.4)

- Exaggerate or reduce pitch and intensity of your voice to evoke a comforting response from the child. (1.5)

- Play interactive games with the child that elicit a social response. Interrupt the game briefly and leave the child's visual field range. Observe whether the child vocalizes for attention when you disappear. Vocalize in response to the child's bid prior to re-entering his visual field. (1.5)

- Have a familiar adult vocalize to the child in a comforting tone from another room while the child is involved in daily routines. Observe the child's reaction when the familiar person enters the room. (1.5)

Instructional Sequences

- Model locating an object, finding a common object in an unfamiliar picture, or finding a familiar person in a photograph. (1, 1.1, 1.2, 1.3)

- Use exaggerated facial and vocal expressions and verbally ask the child to locate objects, people, or events in the environment. Gradually reduce the number of extralinguistic cues used to help the child. (1)

- Combine familiar and unfamiliar pictures. First, ask the child to point to familiar pictures of objects, people, or events after you label them several times. Then, ask the child to point to unfamiliar pictures of objects, people, or events after you label them several times. (1.1)

- When looking through picture books, ask the child to point to familiar pictures of objects, people, or events after you label them several times. (1.2)

- Ask the child to locate familiar objects, people, or events that are within his or her field of vision and relevant to the activity; for example, while bathing the child, ask him or her to give you the soap. Provide models. Give the soap to the child, and then ask for it back. Take turns. Systematically vary the distance that the child is expected to visually search. (1.3)

- Point to or turn your body toward an object, person, or event while asking the child to locate the same. (1.3)

- Gently guide the child's face or body while asking him or her to locate an object, person, or event. (1, 1.1, 1.3)

- Help the child respond to his or her name by adding highly motivating tactile and visual cues only at the moment when his or her name is spoken. These cues will help the child focus his or her attention on his or her name amidst the other auditory input. (1.4)

- Pair auditory and visual cues with communicative behavior; for example, make sure the child is looking at you while using a comforting voice tone. This will help the child associate the voice and face of a familiar person. (1.5)

Combining or pairing different levels of instructions may be helpful when beginning to teach a new and difficult skill. Fade to less intrusive instructions as soon as possible, to encourage more independent performance.

TEACHING CONSIDERATIONS

1. Remember that the primary objective of this goal is comprehension or word recognition. Do not expect the child to produce words or sounds, but encourage any form of expression (e.g., vocalizations, gestures).

2. If the child has a restricted range of motion in the head or trunk area, the speaker should be in a position that facilitates visual contact between the child and the speaker. Latency of response may be noted. Consult a qualified specialist for recommendations for positioning.

3. The words chosen should have sound combinations that are relatively easy to produce or are already used by the child. Although the objective of this goal is comprehension, word production may follow or occur simultaneously. Easy-to-produce words may enhance production.

4. A child with a hearing impairment may be acquiring an augmentative or alternative communication system such as a picture or sign system. Consult a qualified specialist for teaching techniques.

5. A child with a visual impairment may orient his or her body toward the speaker calling his or her name rather than looking at the speaker's face. If the child has a visual impairment, then use other sensory modalities, such as touch or sound, to teach the skill; for example, when calling out the child's name, be within close proximity to enable him or her to reach out toward the speaker's face.

6. Use language and tones that are soothing to the child. Raise or lower and vary your pitch of voice to match the child's needs.

7. Adapt the type of auditory stimulation to the child's mood. Your voice should be soothing to a child who is sleepy or anxious; speak lively to a child who is alert.

8. If the child has a sensory impairment, offer appropriate forms of communication that will enable the child to perceive and understand; for example, allow a child with visual impairments to touch your face to learn how to associate voice with a familiar person. The child may require more tactile cues.

9. A child with a hearing impairment may hear only selected frequencies (high- or low-pitched sounds) or may hear only loud sounds. The child may be sensitive to certain sounds or intensities (sounds that seem normal to you may be uncomfortably loud to some children, certain frequencies may be painful, and combinations of sounds or too much noise may be uncomfortable).

GOAL 2   Carries out two-step direction without contextual cues

Objective 2.1   Carries out two-step direction with contextual cues

Objective 2.2   Carries out one-step direction without contextual cues

Objective 2.3   Carries out one-step direction with contextual cues

- PS2.3a The child participates in verbal and gestural regulatory social routines such as "Come here" or "Sit down."

- PS2.3b The child ceases action when told, "No."

IMPORTANCE OF SKILLS

The ability to understand increasingly complex directions without immediate contextual cues, allows the child to gain independence and participate in useful daily living activities.

Initially, a child learns to follow one-step directions relying on contextual cues (e.g., one-step directions to get his or her coat when it is on a hook in front of him or her). After depending on contextual cues to follow simple directions, a child then follows directions not related to the immediate environment or without contextual cues. These skills allow the child to expand vocabulary and memory and meet needs more independently (e.g., find toys, put on clothing without an immediate cue in the environment). Following directions is an important foundation for future academic activities. Other goals/objectives that can be targeted at the same time as Goal 2 are listed on the following page.

Social-Comm

Concurrent Goals/Objectives for Social-Communication Strand C

Fine Motor

A:5 Aligns and stacks objects

B:5.1 Draws circles and lines

Gross Motor

C:4 Walks up and down stairs

D:3 Catches, kicks, throws, and rolls ball or similar object

D:4.2 Moves under, over, and through obstacles

Adaptive

A:5 Transfers food and liquid between containers

B:1 Initiates toileting

B:2 Washes and dries hands

B:3 Brushes teeth

C:1 Undresses self

Cognitive

B:3 Maintains search for object that is not in its usual location

C:1 Correctly activates mechanical toy

C:2 Reproduces part of interactive game and/or action in order to continue game and/or action

D: 1 Imitates motor action that is not commonly used

E: 2 Uses an object to obtain another object

E:4 Solves common problems

F:1 Uses imaginary objects in play

G:1 Categorizes like objects

Social-Communication

D:1 Uses 50 single words

Social

A:3.2 Responds to communication from familiar adult

B:1 Meets observable physical needs in socially appropriate ways

C:1.2 Responds appropriately to peer's social behavior

C:2.2 Responds to communication from peer

TEACHING SUGGESTIONS

Activity-Based

Playtime

- Play telephone and give the child directions to carry out actions as a fire-fighter, grocer, pilot, or teacher. (2, 2.1, 2.2, 2.3)

- Play hide-and-seek games. Hide objects, and give the child directions to find them, or tell the child where to hide an object, and ask another child to find it. (2.1, 2.2, 2.3)

- Play tea party together with real or toy dishes. Give simple directions for setting the table, passing snacks to friends, and cleaning up afterward. (2.1, 2.3)

- Action records and tapes can be found in toy stores or bookstores or borrowed from the library. They provide many opportunities for following directions. (2, 2.1, 2.2, 2.3)

Toileting

- During adaptive routines, encourage the child to locate necessary objects and retrieve them for you: "Get your dry pants from the bedroom, and bring them to the bathroom." Initiate independent activities, such as, "Go to the bathroom, and go potty." (2, 2.1, 2.2)

Bathing

- During bath time, direct the child to wash one or two body parts; for example, say, "Wash your hands and face." (2.1, 2.3)

Throughout daily routines

- During routine activities, talk about what you are doing. Label the materials used or the actions taking place. Periodically give the child simple requests to carry out that are related to the activity; for example, when playing with blocks, ask the child to get a storybook from another room to use as a platform for the blocks. (2, 2.2)

- At the playground, give the child directions while playing ball or climbing on equipment. Set up simple obstacle courses and use directions to guide the child over, under, around, and through. (2, 2.1, 2.2, 2.3)

- Watch children's television shows and videos together. Encourage the child to participate in the actions and activities in programs. (2.1, 2.3)

- During routine activities, such as snack time, give the child simple requests to carry out that are related to the activity; for example, ask the child to go to the table and sit down. (2.1, 2.3)

- During routine activities, such as dressing, ask the child to cooperate by raising an arm or standing up straight. (2.3)

Environmental Arrangements

- Arrange the environment to help the child focus on the activity. The setting should be relatively quiet and free from objects and events that compete for the child's attention. The child might not respond if a speaker is too far away. Check for an optimal distance, then vary the distance after the child responds consistently. (2)

- Give the child a one-step and then a two-step direction to carry out, using other children in the group as models; for example, during snack time, ask each child to get something needed for a snack and bring it to the table. (2, 2.2)

- Observe the child throughout the day to determine which toys are highly desirable. Ask the child to look for that toy when it is not present in the immediate environment. Say, "Go to your bedroom and get teddy." (2, 2.2)

- Use exaggerated facial and vocal expressions to gain and maintain the child's attention. (2, 2.1, 2.2, 2.3)

- Read action stories and have the child participate along with the characters. (2.1)

- Use flannelboard characters to tell stories. Give directions to the child that match the story. (2.1)

- Play games and give directions on playground equipment that give cues to the action intended; for example, "Go under the tire and around the merry-go-round." (2.1)

- Read books such as *Pat the Bunny* that include actions. (2.2)

- Listen to and sing songs in which the child can follow directions to perform motor actions. Use the tune "Here We Go 'Round the Mulberry Bush" and add your own lines, such as, "This is the way we eat our soup," " . . . comb our hair," or ". . . brush our teeth." (2.2)

- Play "Give me" when the child extends toys to show you; for example, if the child extends a toy boat during bath time, then say, "Give me the boat." When the child releases the toy, say, "Thank you," and give it back. (2.3)

- Place particularly desirable toys just out of reach but within the child's field of vision. Ask the child to find the toy. (2.3)

- Use gestures when giving the child a direction; for example, point to the child's foot and say, "Get your socks." (2.3)

Instructional Sequences

- Model carrying out directions and comment as you do so. (2, 2.1, 2.2, 2.3)

- Include familiar actions and objects in directions; then use new objects with old actions or old objects with new actions. (2)

- Use exaggerated facial and vocal expressions when asking the child to locate objects, people, or events in the environment, and gradually reduce the number of extralinguistic cues used to help the child. (2)

- Systematically vary the distance that the child is expected to visually search. First, ask the child to locate a familiar object, person, or event that is within the child's field of vision. Then, ask the child to locate a familiar object, person, or event that is outside the child's field of vision. (2)

- Point or use gestures when giving the child a direction to carry out. (2, 2.1, 2.2, 2.3)

- Gently guide the child toward a requested object; for example, guide the child toward the chairs and say, "Go get a chair and sit down for circle." (2, 2.1, 2.2, 2.3)

TEACHING CONSIDERATIONS

1. Carrying out directions should have functional value for the child, assist the child's adaptation to the environment, and have some intrinsically rewarding features.

2. A child with a hearing impairment may hear only selected frequencies (high- or low-pitched sounds), or may hear only loud sounds. The child may also be sensitive to certain sounds or intensities (sounds that seem normal to you may be uncomfortably loud to some children, certain frequencies may be painful, and combinations of sounds or too much noise may be uncomfortable).

3. If the child has a restricted range of motion in the head or trunk area, the speaker should be in a position that facilitates visual contact between the child and the speaker. Responses may be delayed.

Production of Social-Communicative Signals, Words, and Sentences

GOAL 1   Uses 50 single words

Objective 1.1   **Uses five descriptive words**

Objective 1.2   **Uses five action words**

Objective 1.3   **Uses two pronouns**

Objective 1.4   **Uses 15 object and/or event labels**

Objective 1.5   **Uses three proper names**

IMPORTANCE OF SKILLS

It is important that children learn to use words to convey thoughts, wants, and needs in order to control and learn from their environments. Using words to communicate helps promote social skills and affords the child greater interaction with the environment. The child's early repertoire includes descriptive and action words that describe pronouns, object and/or event labels, and proper names; for example, the child sees a steaming kettle on the stove and says, "Hot," or a large ball and says, "Big." The child may hand a box of animal crackers to an adult and say, "Open," or throw a ball and say, "Catch." The child will also look at a photograph and say, "Me," or point to another and say, "You." When labeling an event or object the child sees a cat and says, "Kiki," sees a child swinging and says, "Swing," or looks at a parent and says, "Mama." Before children produce their first words, they use consistent speech–sound combinations to refer to objects, people, or events. A sound combination is considered a word if the child spontaneously produces it, the form is consistent, and it refers to the same object, person, or event. Other goals/objectives that can be targeted at the same time as Goal 1 are listed on the following page.

TEACHING SUGGESTIONS

Activity-Based

Playtime

- When playing with push- or pull-toys, model the appropriate action word when the child is performing the action, and encourage the child to imitate. (1.1, 1.2)

- Playing ball games provides opportunities for practicing action words such as *throwing, catching, passing, rolling, bouncing, hitting,* and *kicking.* (1.1, 1.2)

Concurrent Goals/Objectives for Social-Communication Strand D

Fine Motor

A:5.2 Places and releases object balanced on top of another object with either hand

B:2 Assembles toy and/or object that require(s) putting pieces together

Gross Motor

C:4 Walks up and down stairs

D:3 Catches, kicks, throws, and rolls ball or similar object

B:2 Sits down in and gets out of chair

Adaptive

A:4 Eats with fork and/or spoon

A:5 Transfers food and liquid between containers

B:2 Washes and dries hands

B:3 Brushes teeth

C:1 Undresses self

Cognitive

B:3 Maintains search for object that is not in its usual location

C:1 Correctly activates mechanical toy

C:2 Reproduces part of interactive game and/or action in order to continue game and/or action

D:1 Imitates motor action that is not commonly used

D:2 Imitates words that are not frequently used

E:2 Uses an object to obtain another object

E:4.1 Uses more than one strategy in attempt to solve common problems

F:1.1 Uses representational actions with objects

G:1.2 Groups objects according to size, shape, and/or color

Social-Communication

A:3 Engages in vocal exchanges by babbling

C:1 Locates objects, people, and/or events without contextual cues

Social

A:3 Initiates and maintains communicative exchange with familiar adult

B:2.1 Responds to established social routines

C:1.2 Responds appropriately to peer's social behavior

C:2.2 Responds to communication from peer

Assessment, Evaluation, and Programming System for Infants and Children (AEPS®), Second Edition,
edited by Diane Bricker © 2002 Paul H. Brookes Publishing Co., Inc. All rights reserved.

Social-Comm

- Playing Simon Says includes many actions: jump up, sit down, clap your hands, shake your leg, wave, and roll. (1.1, 1.2)

- Play with boy and girl puppets. Have them perform actions and ask questions such as, "Who did that?" (1.3)

- Play the naming game. Describe and comment on objects and events in the environment throughout the day. Talk to the child, and label toys as the child plays with them, or talk about what is happening around the house. Encourage the child to imitate your talking. (1.4)

- Play a turn-taking game where you label an item and perform an action, and the child repeats it; for example, put a block on a stack for a tower and say, "Block." Give the child a turn. Or, put a cookie on a plate and say, "Cookie." Give the child a turn. (1.4)

- Give names to the child's favorite stuffed animals. When the child is playing with one of them, refer to it by name. (1.5)

Storytime

- Look at books with the child and describe the pictures; for example, point to a doll and say, "Sleepy baby," or point to a kitten, and say, "Little kitty." Encourage the child to label pictures. (1, 1.1, 1.2, 1.4)

- Show the child a photograph of yourself, and say, "Who's this?" Model if necessary. (1.3, 1.5)

Nature

- Activities can be designed to help teach a related group of action words. Planting a garden (or pretending) provides opportunities to practice action words such as raking, digging, hoeing, planting, watering, or covering. Similar groups of words can be developed from cooking, art, exercise, and block activities. (1.1, 1.2)

Dressing

- Have the child look in a mirror, and ask, "Who is that?" Point to yourself, the child, or peers. Look in a mirror, and take turns pointing out body parts. (1.3, 1.5)

Throughout daily routines

- Provide frequent opportunities for the child to interact with peers to use descriptive words, action words, pronouns, proper names, and object and event labels. (1, 1.1, 1.2, 1.3, 1.4, 1.5)

- Throughout the day, observe the child's responses toward objects, people, and events to determine those to which the child most readily vocalizes. Use descriptive words to expand on what the child says; for example, if the child touches his or her toe in the bathtub and says, "Toe," then say, "Big toe, little toe," pointing to the different sizes. (1, 1.1, 1.2, 1.3, 1.4, 1.5)

- Clean out the toy box and sort items. Put the big balls together, red blocks together, and doll clothes together. Sorting and describing activities fit well with the daily routines of laundry, grocery shopping, and getting the mail. Emphasize descriptive words and labels while doing this activity. (1, 1.1, 1.2, 1.3, 1.4, 1.5)

- Throughout the day, during the child's daily routines, model developmentally appropriate descriptive words, such as *big, little, hot,* and *dirty;* for example, when changing the child's diaper, say, "Dirty diaper," or when cooking, tell the child, "Don't touch, hot!" (1, 1.1)

- Allow the child to help take care of the family pet. Let the child feed the pet: open the box of food, pour the food, and give it to the pet to eat. Some pets can be combed, walked, rubbed, petted, chased, or tickled. Pets provide opportunities for labeling objects and actions. (1.1, 1.2)

- Throughout the day, talk about what the child is doing, and label the actions; for example, when the child is eating, say, "Eat," or when the child is drinking, say, "Drink." Encourage the child to imitate. (1.1, 1.2, 1.4)

- If the child uses an action word spontaneously, then respond immediately with an appropriate consequence; for example, if the child says, "Help," and gestures toward a box of crackers, then say, "Oh, you want a cracker," and give one to the child. (1.1)

- When the child is introduced to a new experience or environment, talk about it ahead of time. While you are in the new environment, point out both familiar and new objects and actions. Continue talking about the activity, objects, and people when you return home. (1.1, 1.2, 1.3, 1.4)

- While on outings or looking at picture books with the child, point to people or objects and say, "Look at this," or "He's funny." Model several times. (1.3)

- When the child comments on the activity or action of another child, expand the utterance; for example, if the child says, "Roll," then the adult says, "That's right, he rolled the ball." (1.2, 1.3)

- When interacting with the child during routine activities, imitate the child's words or word approximations. (1.4)

- Throughout the day, use the names of siblings or neighborhood children several times. Call peers by their names, and ask the child to "Go get Billy," "Come sit by Juan," or "Give Jenny a book." (1.5)

Environmental Arrangements

- Watch television together. Many programs for children are designed to encourage language development. Point out what is happening, talk about the action as it occurs, laugh and enjoy the entertainment, and ask questions about what you see. (1)

Social-Comm

- Present two toys or stuffed animals, one plain and one brightly colored. Ask the child, "Which one do you want, this one or the pretty one?" Use an exaggerated pitch and intonation on the targeted word. If the child does not respond, then model and present the bright-colored animal. (1, 1.1)

- Hold several crayons or markers just out of the child's reach. Ask the child, "Which one do you want?" Pause, then model if necessary, and give the child the marker. (1, 1.1)

- Make or find a picture book with pairs of opposite words, one on each page; for example, look at one page and say, "This ball is big"; then turn the page and say, "This ball is . . ." Pause and give the child an opportunity to respond. Model if necessary. (1, 1.2, 1.4)

- Make a mailbox, and sort letters by size and color, naming them out loud. (1, 1.1, 1.4)

- Arrange for the child to participate in small group activities with peers whose language is slightly advanced. Facilitate peer models of descriptive words during activities, and encourage the child to imitate. (1, 1.1, 1.2, 1.3, 1.4, 1.5)

- Play with dolls and stuffed animals. Have them perform common actions such as sitting, sleeping, or eating. Ask the child what the baby is doing. (1.1, 1.2)

- Bounce the child up and down on your knee and say, "Bounce, bounce." Pause and wait for the child to vocalize a word, then continue the action. (1.1, 1.2)

- Play ball with the child. Take turns kicking, throwing, catching, rolling, and hitting. Label the actions. (1.1, 1.2)

- Present a plate of cookies to the child and hold it just out of reach. Ask the child, "Who wants one?" Offer the cookie when the child says, "Me," or "I do." Model, "I want a cookie," if necessary. (1.3)

- Play games such as "Button, button, who has the button?" or "Who's wearing . . .?" (1.3, 1.5)

- Play a turn-taking game with the child using a ball, beanbag, or similar toy. (1.3)

- Observe the objects that the child interacts with frequently throughout the day. Model these labels, and encourage the child to imitate. (1.4)

- Observe the child throughout the day to identify which toys the child prefers. Hold a desired toy just out of reach, and ask, "What do you want?" Pause, and give the child an opportunity to respond; model if necessary. (1.4)

- Make a family photo album. Name the person on one page, then turn the page and pause, giving the child an opportunity to name the next person. (1.5)

- Have more than one photo of the same sibling, parent, or peer. Label the first picture, and ask the child to name subsequent pictures. (1.5)

- Use exaggerated pitch and intonation when calling family members to dinner. "Bobby, time to eat." Ask the child to call to the family member. (1.5)

Instructional Sequences

- Model using descriptive and action words; for example, when playing in a sandbox, hold the child's hand up and say, "Dirty." Pause, and give an expectant look. When playing with a ball, say, "Roll," and "Catch," each time it is your turn. Pause, and give an expectant look. Encourage the child to imitate. (1, 1.1, 1.2)

- Give the child a model and a directive to repeat; for example, say, "Hot! Tell me 'hot'. Say 'bounce', 'men,' 'cookie,' 'Hi, Daddy.' " (1, 1.1, 1.2, 1.3, 1.4, 1.5)

- Model using pronouns, labeling objects and events, and using proper names. When offering the child a cookie from a plate of cookies, say, "I want this one." Pause, and give an expectant look. When a cat enters the room, say, "Kitty," or when the dog barks, say, "Bow-wow." Pause, and give an expectant look. When a sibling enters the play area, say, "Hi, Ricardo!" Pause, and give an expectant look. (1.3, 1.4, 1.5)

- Give a partial sound (or word) cue. Say the first sound (or word) of the utterance; for example, while rolling a big ball to the child, say, "This ball is b–." Encourage the child to complete the utterance, and then repeat. (1, 1.1, 1.2, 1.3, 1.4, 1.5)

- Ask a simple question and answer it. Repeat the question; for example, when the family dog is eating, ask, "What's Ranger doing? He's eating." Encourage the child to answer the question. (1, 1.1, 1.2, 1.3, 1.4, 1.5)

- Combining or pairing different levels of instructions may be helpful when beginning to teach a new and difficult skill. Fade to less intrusive instructions as soon as possible to encourage more independent performance. (1, 1.1, 1.2, 1.3, 1.4, 1.5)

TEACHING CONSIDERATIONS

1. If sensory or motor difficulties interfere with normal speech production, augmentative or alternative communication systems (e.g., signing, communication boards) may be appropriate. Consult a qualified specialist for teaching techniques.

2. A child with a hearing impairment may hear only selected frequencies (high- or low-pitched sounds) or may hear only loud sounds. The child may also be sensitive to certain sounds or intensities (sounds that seem

Social-Comm

normal to you may be uncomfortably loud to some children, certain frequencies may be painful, and combinations of sounds or too much noise may be uncomfortable).

3.   If the child has a restricted range of motion in the head or trunk area, the speaker should be in a position that facilitates visual contact between the child and the speaker. Positioning is also critical to sound production. Response delays may be noted. Consult a qualified specialist for recommendations for positioning and techniques for eliciting sounds from the child with a motor impairment.

4.   Young children acquiring more than one language simultaneously initially learn vocabulary without distinguishing between languages. The number of words in a child's vocabulary includes the total number of words or word approximations the child is using in both languages. This principle holds for toddlers learning English as a second language, as well as for children from bilingual and multilingual homes. Typically developing children do not reliably and consistently sort languages into separate systems until they acquire cognitive skills of categorization and classification, usually after the third birthday.

GOAL 2   Uses two-word utterances

Objective 2.1   Uses two-word utterances to express agent–action, action–object, and agent–object

• PS2.1a   The child uses a two-word utterance to express agent–action.

• PS2.1b   The child uses a two-word utterance to express action–object.

• PS2.1c   The child uses a two-word utterance to express agent–object.

Objective 2.2   Uses two-word utterances to express possession

Objective 2.3   Uses two-word utterances to express location

Objective 2.4   Uses two-word utterances to describe objects, people, and/or events

Objective 2.5   Uses two-word utterances to express recurrence

Objective 2.6   Uses two-word utterances to express negation

IMPORTANCE OF SKILLS

Once the child has learned to produce single words that serve a variety of communicative functions, the child begins to combine words into two-word utterances or phrases. This improves the child's ability to communicate and convey thoughts, wants, and needs. It also promotes social skills and interaction with the environment. The purpose of this skill is for the child to use a variety of two-word utterances to express different meanings; for example, the child sees the dog eating and says, "Doggie eat" (agent–action); the child holds out his or her arms and says, "Throw ball" (action–object); or the child watches the dog chewing a bone and says, "Doggie bone" (agent–object). The child may look at his or her shoe and say, "My shoe" (possession). The child may point to his or her father and say, "There's Daddy" (location). The child may see a favorite toy and say, "Red car" (descriptive-object). The child holds up a cup and says, "More milk" (recurrence). The child holds up his or her hand and says, "No juice" (negation). These two-word expressions provide a basis for future communication that becomes increasingly complex. Other goals/ objectives that can be targeted at the same time as Goal 2 are listed on the following page.

TEACHING SUGGESTIONS

Activity-Based

Playtime

- Play with bubbles together. Blow, pop, step on, and wave at the bubbles. Label with two words, "Blow bubble" or "Bubble pop." (2.1)

- When the child is playing with a favorite stuffed animal, give the child directions; for example, say, "Make teddy sit," or "Feed teddy." Encourage the child to give two-word instructions while you manipulate the animal. (2.1)

- Work on puzzles or shape-sorting activities together. Encourage the child to talk about where you are putting the pieces. (2.3)

- Play a tickle game or any rough-house activity that the child enjoys. Stop, and wait for the child to ask for "more tickle" or to "do again." (2.5)

Art activities

- During a finger-painting activity, encourage the child to make hand- or footprints. When they are dry, see if the child can find his or her print and tell peers about it. (2.2, 2.3)

- While drawing and coloring, use different colors to make big circles, long lines, fat marks, or happy faces. Encourage the child to describe the different shapes and colors. (2.4)

Storytime

- Look at picture books with the child, and encourage her to describe the pictures; for example, point to a picture, and ask, "What do you see?" (2.4)

- Talk about objects that you see more than once; for example, when looking at a farm animal book, say, "Look, more chicks!" Encourage the child to imitate. (2.5)

Social-Comm

Concurrent Goals/Objectives for Social-Communication Strand D

Goal 2: Uses two-word utterances

Fine Motor

B:2 Assembles toy and/or object that requires(s) putting pieces together

B:3 Uses either index finger to activate objects

B:5 Copies simple written shapes after demonstration

Gross Motor

C:2 Stoops and regains balanced standing position without support

C:3 Runs avoiding obstacles

C:4 Walks up and down stairs

D:1 Jumps forward

D:2 Pedals and steers tricycle

D:3 Catches, kicks, throws, and rolls ball or similar object

D:4 Climbs up and down play equipment

Adaptive

A:5 Transfers food and liquid between containers

B:1 Initiates toileting

B:2 Washes and dries hands

B:3 Brushes teeth

C:1 Undresses self

Cognitive

B:3 Maintains search for object that is not in its usual location

D:1 Imitates motor action that is not commonly used

D:2 Imitates words that are not frequently used

E:2 Uses an object to obtain another object

E:3 Navigates large object around barriers

E:4 Solves common problems

F:1 Uses imaginary objects in play

G:1 Categorizes like objects

G:2 Demonstrates functional use of one-to-one correspondence

Social-Communication

C:2 Carries out two-step direction without contextual cues

Social

A:3 Initiates and maintains communicative exchange with familiar adult

B:1 Meets observable physical needs in socially appropriate ways

B:2.1 Responds to established social routine

C:1 Initiates and maintains interaction with peer

C:2 Initiates and maintains communicative exchange with peer

Assessment, Evaluation, and Programming System for Infants and Children (AEPS®), Second Edition,
edited by Diane Bricker © 2002 Paul H. Brookes Publishing Co., Inc. All rights reserved.

Feeding

- During snack time, when the child indicates a desire for an item, expand the sentence; for example, if the child holds up a cup and says, "Milk," then say, "Oh, you want more milk." (2.5)

- During snack time, comment about what the child has eaten; for example, when the child finishes his or her juice, say, "No more," or when all of the crackers have been eaten, say, "All gone." (2.6)

Group activities

- During small group activities, comment about the materials being used by the child or those you are passing out; for example, say, "That's Tommy's paintbrush" or "Here's Cindy's crayon." Encourage the child to comment. (2.2, 2.3)

Throughout daily routines

- Provide frequent opportunities for the child to interact with peers who use two-word or longer utterances to express possession, location, descriptions, recurrence, and negation. (2.1, 2.2, 2.3, 2.4, 2.5, 2.6)

- Comment on and describe what you are doing throughout the day. Whenever possible, use two-word combinations that the child can already say. (2, 2.1)

- When the child uses word approximations for labels and actions, expand on what he or she says; for example, if the child points to the family pet and says, "Doggie," then say, "Doggie bark," "Doggie sleeping," or "Pet doggie." (2.1)

- Throughout the day, within the context of activities, ask occasional questions about ownership of objects. Say, "Whose _____ is this?" Model the response if necessary. (2.2)

- While sorting laundry, categorize clothing by ownership, (e.g., "Joey's shirt," "Mom's socks," and "Susie's pants"). Encourage the child to imitate. (2.2)

- Point out actions and locations while driving together in a car or van. "Where is the garbage truck?" "Can you see the park? Show me where," and "What is on that roof?" (2.2, 2.3)

- Throughout the day, observe the child's response toward objects, people, and events to determine those to which the child most readily vocalizes. Use descriptive words to recast the child's utterance; for example, if the child says, "Truck go," then say, "I see the red truck go." (2.4)

- Ask yes and no questions whenever appropriate. Expand whenever possible. Allow the child to make choices and honor the child's preferences. (2.5, 2.6)

Social-Comm

- When the child uses a gesture or word to express negation, expand the child's utterance; for example, if the child holds up his or her hand to reject a cookie and says, "No," then say, "No cookie." (2.6)

Environmental Arrangements

- Arrange for the child to participate in small group activities with peers whose language is slightly advanced. Facilitate peer models of agent–action, action–object, and agent–object utterances during activities, and encourage the child to imitate them. (2, 2.1, 2.2, 2.3, 2.4, 2.5, 2.6)

- Make a photo album, and use pictures of the child and peers. Sit with the child in your lap, and encourage the child to describe the pictures. Any two-word combinations should be encouraged. (2, 2.1)

- Put the child's favorite toy just out of reach. Pause and wait for the child to request the toy, modeling if necessary, and then give the child the toy. (2, 2.1)

- Toy sets such as a barnyard, garage, or circus train offer many opportunities to combine words while playing. (2, 2.1)

- Tell a story using stuffed animals, and have the animals act out the plot. If telling a familiar story, then pause, and encourage the child to tell what happens next; then use the animals to act out the child's two-word utterances. (2, 2.1)

- Use photos to label the cubbies so that children can describe what goes inside. (2.2)

- Make a "Family Area" where pictures of the child's family members are hanged. Ask the child to tell peers about the pictures. (2.2)

- During an art activity, "accidentally" pick up something that the child is working on and say, "Here's my hat" or say, "I wonder where I put the crayons." (The "confused" adult is a great technique to use during any activity.) (2.2, 2.3)

- Play "police" and encourage the child to direct traffic. (2.3)

- Play a "treasure hunt" game. Hide a favorite toy, and give the child various directions on how to find it: "Look under the table" and "Now, look in the box"; then have the child hide a toy and give directions to another child. Model when necessary. (2.3)

- Present two objects that are the same except for one attribute, such as size or color. Say, "Which one do you want, the big cookie or the little cookie?" Use exaggerated pitch and intonation. If the child does not respond, then model, and present one of the items. (2.4)

- Play a fishing game with cutout fish of different colors, sizes, and textures. Have the child describe the catch. (2.4)

- Hold several colors of crayons or markers just out of the child's reach. Ask the child, "Which one do you want?" Pause, then model if necessary before giving the child the marker. Many objects can be within visual range, yet out of reach, making it necessary for the child to label and request them. (2.4)

- Many toys can be manipulated so that the child asks for "more." Wind up the toy only a little so that it winds down quickly. Give only one piece of tape or a small amount of paint at a time. The child can ask for "More music," or to "Turn it again," or for "More paint." (2.5)

- When playing with blocks, ask the child to build a tower like yours, but give the child only one block. Have more blocks just out of the child's reach, give an expectant look, and ask, "What do you want?" (2.5)

- Play action games with the child, such as pulling the child in a wagon. Stop, and wait for the child to say, "Go again" or "More wagon." Model if necessary before resuming action. (2.5)

- Playground equipment (e.g., slides, swings, merry-go-rounds) may provide opportunities for requesting "more." (2.5)

- During snack time, give the child one cracker, and put others just out of reach. Wait for the child to ask for more before giving the child another cracker. Model if necessary. (2.5)

- When the child makes a choice, give the opposite object, and wait for the child to reject it. (2.6)

- Occasionally, make absurd statements to the child during an activity; for example, when looking at a picture of a boy eating an ice cream cone, say, "Look, the horse is eating ice cream." (2.6)

Instructional Sequences

- Model using two-word expressions for possession, location, description, recurrence, and negation; for example, the child points to a cookie, and the adult says, "Want cookie?" Pause, and give an expectant look. Encourage the child to imitate. (2, 2.1, 2.2, 2.3, 2.4, 2.5, 2.6)

- Give a partial sound (or word) cue. Say the first sound (or word) of the utterance; for example, when looking at a picture of a horse in a picture book, the adult says, "Ride," and pauses and waits for the child to respond. Encourage the child to complete the utterance and then repeat the phrase. (2.1)

- Ask a simple question, and answer it. Repeat the question. Provide guidelines for the child; for example, the adult asks, "What do you see?" and answer, "I see a baby." Then, the adult repeats, "What do you see?" Encourage the child to answer the question. (2, 2.1, 2.2, 2.3, 2.4, 2.5, 2.6)

TEACHING CONSIDERATIONS

1. If sensory or motor difficulties interfere with normal speech production, augmentative or alternative systems (e.g., signing, communication boards) should be introduced. Consult a qualified specialist for teaching techniques.

2. A child with a hearing impairment may hear only selected frequencies (high- or low-pitched sounds) or may hear only loud sounds. The child may also be sensitive to certain sounds or intensities (sounds that seem normal to you may be uncomfortably loud to some children, certain frequencies may be painful, and combinations of sounds or too much noise may be uncomfortable).

3. If the child has a restricted range of motion in the head or trunk area, the speaker should be in a position that facilitates visual contact between the child and speaker. Positioning is also critical to sound production. Response delays may be noted. Consult a qualified specialist for recommendations for positioning and techniques for eliciting sounds from the child with a motor impairment.

4. Young children acquiring more than one language simultaneously initially learn vocabulary without distinguishing between languages. The number of words in a child's vocabulary includes the total number of words or word approximations the child is using in both languages. This principle holds for toddlers learning English as a second language, as well as for children from bilingual and multilingual homes. Typically developing children do not reliably and consistently sort languages into separate systems until they acquire cognitive skills of categorization and classification, usually after the third birthday.

GOAL 3   Uses three-word utterances

Objective 3.1   Uses three-word negative utterances

Objective 3.2   Asks questions

Objective 3.3   Uses three-word action–object–location utterances

Objective 3.4   Uses three-word agent–action–object utterances

IMPORTANCE OF SKILLS

Shortly after two-word expressions are part of a young child's speech, three-word utterances develop. The ability to produce three-word utterances is important for children to more effectively control the environment with words and to help them cope more successfully with increasing social demands. These three-word utterances include the use of agent–action–object (e.g., "I blow bubble"), action–object–location (e.g., "Put baby here"), questions (e.g., "Where my coat?"), and negative utterances (e.g., "No do that"). These expressions provide a basis for future communication that becomes increasingly complex. Other goals/objectives that can be targeted at the same time as Goal 3 are listed on the following page.

TEACHING SUGGESTIONS

Activity-Based

Playtime

- Play blindfold or other games, such as Twenty Questions, in which the child must feel an object or ask questions and guess what it is. Encourage comments such as, "It's not hard," "It's not a book," or "It's not a shoe." You may need to give suggestions to help the child guess. (3.1, 3.2)

- Play beside the child, commenting about or describing the location of play materials; for example, when playing with trucks and cars, say, "Drive under the bridge" or "Move that here." (3.3, 3.4)

- Play circus either with peers in a pretend situation or with toy animals and performers. Have the child announcer give directions to the other children and animals, such as, "Stand the lion up" or "Jump through the hoop." (3.3)

- When playing with dolls or stuffed animals, give the child directions, such as, "Make the teddy bear go to sleep" or "Make teddy sing a song." Give the child the opportunity to give you directions. (3.4)

Storytime

- When looking through picture books, comment about the location of objects and people. Pause, and give the child an opportunity to comment. Expand the child's utterance when possible; for example, if the child points to a dog and says, "Doggie run," then say, "That's right, the doggie runs into his house." (3.3)

Nature

- Plant a garden (real or pretend), and talk about the activity: "Mom digs holes," "Shovel fell down," and "Seeds lying on the dirt." (3.4)

Quiet time

- At quiet time, encourage the child to recall the events of the day using three-word utterances. (3.4)

Throughout daily routines

- Provide frequent opportunities for the child to interact with peers who use three-word negative utterances, questions, action–object–location, and agent–action–object three-word phrases. (3, 3.1, 3.2, 3.3, 3.4)

Concurrent Goals/Objectives for Social-Communication Strand D

Goal 3: Uses three-word utterances

Fine Motor

B:2 Assembles toy and/or object that require(s) putting pieces together

B:3 Uses either index finger to activate objects

B:5 Copies simple written shapes after demonstration

Gross Motor

C:2 Stoops and regains balanced standing position without support

C:3 Runs avoiding obstacles

C:4 Walks up and down stairs

D:1 Jumps forward

D:2 Pedals and steers tricycle

D:3 Catches, kicks, throws, and rolls ball or similar object

D:4 Climbs up and down play equipment

Adaptive

A:5 Transfers food and liquid between containers

B:1 Initiates toileting

B:2 Washes and dries hands

B:3 Brushes teeth

C:1 Undresses self

Cognitive

D:2 Imitates words that are not frequently used

E:2 Uses an object to obtain another object

E:3 Navigates large object around barriers

E:4 Solves common problems

F:1 Uses imaginary objects in play

G:1 Categorizes like objects

G:2 Demonstrates functional use of one-to-one correspondence

Social-Communication

C:2 Carries out two-step direction without contextual cues

Social

A:3 Initiates and maintains communicative exchange with familiar adult

B:1 Meets observable physical needs in socially appropriate ways

B:2.1 Responds to established social routines

C:1 Initiates and maintains interaction with peer

C:2 Initiates and maintains communicative exchange with peer

- Provide the child opportunities to use negative terms throughout the day. Provide immediate consequences when possible; for example, when the child indicates a dislike for a certain food by saying, "Don't want this," allow the child to choose another food. (3.1)

- During small group activities, comment about the materials, and describe the child's actions; for example, during art activities, say, "Mark's not putting a nose on his face" or "Mary doesn't like the blue hat." (3.1)

- Throughout the day, encourage the child to express likes and dislikes by offering many choices. (3.1)

- Several times throughout the day within the context of activities, ask the child simple questions that contain "Wh–" words, such as *what* and *where*. (3.2)

- Observe the child's ability to ask simple questions or use rising intonation. Expand or recast the child's utterance; for example, if the child says, "Doggie go," then using rising intonation, say, "Where did the doggie go?" (3.2, 3.4)

- Encourage curiosity by introducing unique or novel objects and events. Encourage the child to ask questions. (3.2, 3.3)

Environmental Arrangements

- Arrange for the child to participate in small group activities with peers whose language is advanced. Facilitate peer models of three-word negative utterances during activities, and encourage the child to imitate. (3.1)

- Throughout the day, observe the child's responses toward objects, people, and events to determine those to which the child most readily responds. Choose two objects, one known to be particularly desirable and one that is not. Offer the object that is not particularly desirable to the child first, holding the desirable object just out of reach. Pause, and give an expectant look. If the child does not respond, then model a desired response, and give the child the desired toy. (3.1)

- When dressing the child, point to a body part, and pretend to forget its name; for example, point to the child's head, and say, "Okay, now put your sock on your tummy." Make absurd statements or give directions likely to elicit negative responses; for example, tell the child, "Climb inside the milk carton to see if it's all gone." (3.1)

- During large or small group activities, encourage the child to ask questions by giving the child only some of the materials needed to complete a task; for example, offer the child a piece of paper, but do not offer a crayon or marker. Pause, and give an expectant look. (3.2)

- It might be helpful to use a peer to demonstrate asking questions during small group activities; for example, put several objects in a bag, and ask the peer to feel the objects and ask simple questions. (3.2)

Social-Comm

- Use exaggerated pitch and intonation when commenting on the location of objects and people. (3.3)

- Set up a situation in which the child is given a direction to locate an object that is hidden or difficult to find; for example, hide the plastic spoons, and ask the child to find them. Pause, and give the child an opportunity to ask where to look. (3.2)

- During snack time, put the container of juice just out of reach but within the child's field of vision. Pretend to have misplaced the juice and say, "Where did I put the juice?" Pause, and give the child an opportunity to respond, then model if necessary. (3.3)

- Play Treasure Hunt. Hide an object, and give the child directions on how to find it; for example, say, "Look under the blanket" or "Look in the box." Then, have the child hide a toy and give directions to another child. Model when necessary. (3.3)

- Make an "All About Me" book with the child, using photos of the child, family members, and peers. Sit with the child, and encourage the child to describe the pictures. Any three-word utterance should be encouraged. (3.4)

Instructional Sequences

- Model three-word negative expressions, asking questions and using action–object–location and agent–action–object utterances; for example, hide a familiar object, and search for it with the child. Say, "Teddy's not here" or "Can't find teddy." Pause, and give an expectant look. Take turns asking, "What's that?" When playing ball, say, "Push ball here." When beside the child, describe a car or truck, "Truck bumps the car." Encourage the child to imitate. (3.1, 3.2, 3.3, 3.4)

- Give the child a model and a directive to repeat; for example, after bringing the cat indoors, say, "Don't go out. Tell the kitty 'Don't go out.' " (3.1, 3.3, 3.4)

- Ask a simple question and answer it. Repeat the question. Provide guidelines for the child; for example, if the child does not like carrots, then at snack time ask, "Do you want a carrot?" Encourage the child to answer the question with a three-word utterance. (3.1, 3.2, 3.3, 3.4)

- Have the child repeat a question. Tell the child, "Say, 'Where's my coat?' " (3.2)

- Give a partial sound (or word) cue. Say the first sound (or word) of the utterance; for example, hide the teddy bear, and say, "Teddy all _____." Encourage the child to complete the utterance and then repeat the entire utterance. (3, 3.1, 3.2, 3.3, 3.4)

TEACHING CONSIDERATIONS

1. If sensory or motor difficulties interfere with normal speech production, augmentative or alternative systems (e.g., signing, technological devices) should be introduced. Consult a qualified specialist for teaching techniques.

2. A child with a hearing impairment may hear only selected frequencies (high- or low-pitched sounds) or may hear only loud sounds. The child may also be sensitive to certain sounds or intensities (sounds that seem normal to you may be uncomfortably loud to some children, certain frequencies may be painful, and combinations of sounds or too much noise may be uncomfortable).

3. If the child has a restricted range of motion in the head or trunk area, the speaker should be in a position that facilitates visual contact between the child and the speaker. Positioning is also critical to easy sound production. Latency of response may be noted. Consult a qualified specialist for recommendations for positioning and techniques for eliciting sounds from the child with motor impairments.

4. Young children acquiring more than one language simultaneously initially learn vocabulary without distinguishing between languages. The number of words in a child's vocabulary includes the total number of words or word approximations the child is using in both languages. This principle holds for toddlers learning English as a second language, as well as for children from bilingual and multilingual homes. Typically developing children do not reliably and consistently sort languages into separate systems until they acquire cognitive skills of categorization and classification, usually after the third birthday.

Social-Comm

AEPS™

Social Area
Birth to Three Years

LIST OF AEPS TEST ITEMS

Social

Social behaviors are so pervasive in the lives of infants and young children that it is difficult to imagine motor, adaptive, cognitive, or communication skills without a social component. The skills and behaviors included in the Social Area focus on interactions that provide the context for developmental skills in other areas. The Social Area is organized into three strands of related social activity: interaction with familiar adults, interaction with environment, and interaction with peers.

An infant is born totally dependent on a caregiving adult for health, safety, and sustenance. A relationship that begins as a physiological necessity soon develops into a social and emotional bond between parent and child. Early in life, most infants respond differently to familiar adults than they do strangers. This is not surprising, as the familiar adult typically provides food, comfort, entertainment, and security for the young child.

It is in the context of this first relationship with a familiar adult that the infant is introduced to the rules of social response, initiation, and interaction. Infants are more attentive and responsive to features of the human face than to any other visual array in the first months of life. There is considerable evidence that the voice and smell of the primary caregiver are recognized by very young infants.

Infants learn early that crying will summon a caregiver to relieve discomfort. Soon, the child learns more sophisticated methods of gaining the adult's attention, such as smiling or vocalizing. Developing mobility skills allows the child to seek proximity by crawling or walking after the familiar adult. Each developmental advance in the areas of cognition, motor control, and communication is used by the growing child as a means to a social end.

The importance of interacting with familiar adults, and the range of skills developed and perfected in this social arena, cannot be overstated. Many early childhood programs have developed curricula that capitalize on parent–infant interaction for both the content and context of intervention. The young child who has shared affection and mastered interaction with a familiar adult has a strong foundation for expanding social skills to peers and other adults.

Although parents and caregivers are usually the first and most salient adults in the lives of young children, they are not the only adults in their lives. With the increase in two-career families and single-parent families, children age 3 years and younger are often in child care situations. Child care providers, baby sitters, older siblings, neighbors, and extended family members may all be familiar adults for young children. When planning intervention and following curriculum suggestions in the Social Area, it is helpful to begin by identifying all familiar adults and including them in the child's program.

The crux of a successful social interaction is a pleasurable activity; this will vary from child to child. It is important for interventionists to be thoroughly familiar with each child's sensory and object preferences, idiosyncratic response styles, and daily environments. The suggestions in the curriculum are general guidelines and they may be inappropriate for some children; for example, tickling to elicit social smiles will do more harm than good to an infant who is tactilely defensive. Interested involvement in the child by caregivers is the best insurance against creating stressful demands and making social intervention aversive for the child.

Routine events in the child's environment provide a ready source of opportunities for learning socially appropriate behaviors. The infant learns to associate specific events with caregiving and play routines. The sound of water, for instance, might alert the child to bath time. Eventually, the child begins to anticipate the sequence of events that make up a routine. Putting on a jacket tells the child that it is time for a walk or drive; setting the table signals the beginning of a mealtime routine.

Social

Many accepted social conventions are grounded in the simple, daily routine events learned in childhood; for example, "Wash your hands before coming to the table and after using the bathroom," "Take off your muddy shoes at the door," and "Go to the bathroom before you get in the car." Interventionists must be sensitive to the diversity in cultural practices when specifying appropriate social routines for mealtime, bedtime, outings, and family occasions. A thorough familiarity with each child's social and ethnic environment can help prevent culturally inappropriate expectations, conflicting demands, frustration, and confusion for family members and the child.

The child first masters the necessary adaptive skills and later becomes aware of the socially appropriate way of doing things. Before long, the expectation emerges that the child will recognize and conform to accepted social norms. This social requirement goes beyond simply performing an adaptive skill. Social expectations and feedback are generally conveyed through facial expressions and other subtle cues that the child may miss completely. Adults who care for the young child are responsible for making the child aware of proper behavior.

An adult's first response is often to tell the child that his or her behavior is not appropriate: "Don't grab your brother's glass," "Don't eat food from the floor," or "Don't come in Grandma's house with wet bathing suits." This approach often stops the behavior in question but may leave the child wondering what to do instead. When instructing a child in socially appropriate ways to meet needs, it is important to be specific about acceptable alternatives to objectionable behavior: "If you are thirsty, then get a glass from the counter," "If you are hungry, then let's get a snack from the fridge," "If you are cold, then dry off, and come in to get dressed."

Interaction with peers is a constellation of skills that develops gradually in the first 3 years of life. The young infant seems not to notice the difference between peers and inanimate objects but will clearly respond to an older child's voice. Two babies playing together may pull and grab at each other unintentionally at first; this behavior will evolve into social play as the babies get older.

It is an important step when a child becomes more independent and socially self-sufficient. The normal socialization process is a progressive movement away from the caregiver as a provider of social stimulation and regulation. The child develops resources for self-entertainment and sustained independent play in the presence of peers.

As the child grows, he or she begins to observe and imitate peers. The child uses his or her voice to gain another's attention, to play near peers, and to play with the same toys as peers. Eventually, the child maintains communicative interchanges with peers and engages in cooperative play. The young child exhibits the most sophisticated social skills in the presence of familiar peers and in familiar settings.

The range of social styles in young children is broad, and each child should be allowed to develop interaction skills that match his or her temperament. One child will respond and initiate eagerly, even with unfamiliar peers, whereas another child will need to be more familiar with his or her environment to be comfortable and will require more time before interacting. By the time the child is 3 years old, the peer group usually becomes an important social arena, and the child seeks playmates.

Social skills are inherent in almost all activities of early childhood. The lives of infants and young children are organized by adults and shared by peers. The routines of school, home, and community provide the setting for experiences that promote growth in all areas of development. Social competence can make up for skill deficits in other areas, improve the quality of relationships among children, enhance relationships between children and adults, and provide self-created learning opportunities for the young child.

Teaching in the Social Area presents a valuable, if somewhat elusive, challenge for early interventionists. The interventionist's role is to provide appropriate and varied social opportunities and constant encouragement for each child to become a competent social participant.

Social

Interaction with Familiar Adults

GOAL 1   Responds appropriately to familiar adult's affect

Objective 1.1   Displays affection toward familiar adult

- PS1.1a   The child returns affection modeled by adult.

- PS1.1b   The child repeats affectionate response toward familiar adult.

Objective 1.2   Responds appropriately to familiar adult's affective tone

- PS1.2a   The child responds with socially appropriate affect to familiar adult's negative affective tone.

- PS1.2b   The child responds with socially appropriate affect to familiar adult's positive affective tone.

Objective 1.3   Smiles in response to familiar adult

- PS1.3a   The child reacts differently to familiar versus unfamiliar adults.

- PS1.3b   The child stops crying in response to a familiar adult (e.g., approach, vocalization, smile, appearance).

IMPORTANCE OF SKILLS

Responding appropriately to caregiver's affective behaviors signifies the child's growing recognition of familiar individuals and establishment of meaningful and lasting social relationships. These social responses are critical to the child's active participation and interactions with all others. Interactions between infant and adult are based on a pattern of dialog of mutual influences, regulating the behavior of each and influencing the infant's ability to perceive the emotional quality of adult behavior. The child's appropriate affective response is both rewarding to the caregiver and serves to communicate attachment. The emphasis of these skills is on the child's ability to use socially appropriate signals toward familiar adults. These items address the child's spontaneous expression of affect, rather than the child's ability to initiate affective interactions. Other goals/objectives that can be targeted at the same time as Goal 1 are listed on the following page.

Concurrent Goals/Objectives for Social Strand A

Goal 1: Responds appropriately to familiar adult's affect

Gross Motor

G:1 Turns head, moves arms, and kicks legs independently of each other

Cognitive

C:2 Reproduces part of interactive game and/or action in order to continue game and/or action

D:1 Imitates motor action that is not commonly used

Social-Communication

B:1.3 Gestures and/or vocalizes to greet others

Notes:

Assessment, Evaluation, and Programming System for Infants and Children (AEPS®), Second Edition,
edited by Diane Bricker © 2002 Paul H. Brookes Publishing Co., Inc. All rights reserved.

Social

TEACHING SUGGESTIONS

Activity-Based

Playtime

- Engage in interactive games and activities such as Peekaboo. Smile, laugh, and talk to the child. Encourage the child to respond with a similar socially appropriate affect (e.g., the child reproduces part of an interactive game, smiles, and coos). Encourage the child to initiate affectionate responses toward the adult by hugging, kissing, patting, touching, and reaching toward the adult. (1, 1.1)

- Engage in activities that are rewarding to the child; for example, give the child favorite snacks, play with favorite toys, play simple games requiring interactive responses like rolling a ball back and forth, or tell favorite stories. (1.2, 1.3)

Quiet time

- At quiet times, rock and sing with the child. Encourage the child to join in the activity by vocalizing and cuddling. (1, 1.1, 1.2, 1.3)

Throughout daily routines

- During daily routines and activities, engage in positive face-to-face interactions with the child. Children learn to be affectionate through imitation. Talk to the child in an affectionate tone and make positive comments about the child's appearance, activities, skills, interests, and qualities. (1.1, 1.2, 1.3)

- Use feeding, dressing, bathing, and playing to introduce affectionate verbal, tactile, and visual interactions; for example, count, kiss, and play "This little piggy" with toes and fingers while dressing; blow "raspberries" on the child's tummy; wash or rub lotion on arms, legs, and tummy while naming body parts; use terms of endearment with reference to the familiar adult: "Mama's helper," or "Daddy's boy." Comment on what the child is doing, on events that are occurring, or on objects that are present. Use short vocalizations, allowing time for pauses. Vary pitch, melody, and facial expressions to reflect a variety of affective tones. (1, 1.2)

- Use a clear negative (but not harsh) tone and gesture when correcting or reprimanding the child; for example, if the child is reaching for a dangerous object, then frown, shake your finger, and say, "Stop!" and note whether the child frowns or fusses and stops the behavior. (1, 1.2)

- Respond quickly and consistently to the child's bids for comfort or attention. Match your responses to the child's needs; for example, if the child is in discomfort, then your response should recognize the child's need for comfort and soothing; if the child needs your attention, then the response should acknowledge the request and focus on the need. (1, 1.2)

- Pair affectionate interactions with consistent daily routines; for example, make a goodnight kiss part of bedtime routine; use hugs for morning waking, after child care, or bedtime.

- Engage in activities that involve affectionate physical contact throughout the day; for example, read or tell stories with the child on the adult's lap; snuggle during bottle or breast-feeding and before and after sleeping. Once the routine is established, give the child opportunities to initiate. (1, 1.1, 1.2)

- Watch as a familiar adult enters the child's visual range. Encourage the child to reach to be picked up or to hug and kiss the adult after being picked up. (1.1, 1.3)

Environmental Arrangements

- Engage in body play, such as face-to-face interactions, rough-and-tumble play, bouncing the child on your lap, or running after and catching each other. (1, 1.1)

- Exaggerate expressions of affect (e.g., laugh, hug, and kiss the child; frown deeply, and use a sharp voice if you must say, "No" or "Stop"). (1, 1.2)

- Point out and label positive and negative affect in daily interactions with familiar adults. "Look, the baby's crying. He must be sad." (1, 1.2)

- Exaggerate facial expressions; laugh and talk in an affectionate tone to make the interaction lively and exciting to the child. Stop, and wait for the child to initiate hugging, touching, or kissing, and then continue the game. Move lips, change head orientation, and vary pitch and intensity of voice to evoke a smile from the child. (1.1, 1.3)

- Respond to and elaborate on the child's own affective tone and behaviors; for example, if the child smiles or initiates motor movements that indicate interest in the appearance of a pet dog, then comment on the dog in a positive, excited tone, and observe whether the child responds by laughing and waving arms. Observe the child when in proximity to other children who are crying, and see if this causes the child to cry or express discomfort as well. (1.2)

- Engage the child in activities that are likely to elicit a positive affect. Observe whether the child responds accordingly; for example, when making funny faces or tickling the child, observe if the child smiles. (1.3)

- Play an interactive game that elicits a response from the child. Interrupt the game briefly, and leave the child's visual range. Observe whether the child smiles when you re-appear. (1.3)

- Remove competing objects from the child's immediate environment during face-to-face interactions so that the child focuses attention on social rather than nonsocial stimuli. (1.3)

Social

Instructional Sequences

- Model an affectionate response as an example for the child; for example, hug the child's sibling or pat the child's father on the shoulder. (1, 1.1)

- During play with dolls or stuffed animals, model giving a kiss, hug, back-rub, or tickle. Ask the child to do the same, "Now you give your baby a hug." Physically assist the child if necessary. (1.1)

- Model pairing your own affective tone to strong pleasurable or negative events and stimuli. Tickle, pick up the child, and talk to the child in a positive tone. Observe if the child increases activity, smiles, or vocalizes. Cease interaction, put the child down, and quietly say, "All done." Observe if the child calms or fusses. (1.2)

- Model smiling at the child and respond (e.g., exaggerate facial expressions, vary pitch of voice) when the child attempts any change in facial expression that is positive and could lead to a smile. (1.3)

- Comment on affect when it is appropriate. "Mommy and Jesse are so happy today," or "Daddy and Jesse are sad that Grandpa had to go home." (1, 1.1, 1.2, 1.3)

- Ask the child to hug, kiss, or touch a familiar adult; for example, "Give Mommy a kiss good night." Describe what you are doing in a pleasant voice. Verbally encourage the child to respond. (1.1, 1.2)

- Repeat positive or negative affective cues if the child responds inappropriately. (1, 1.2)

- Lead the child into affectionate interactions by asking if the child wants a kiss or hug. Physically encourage the child to hug. (1.1, 1.2)

- Gently stroke the child's face near his or her mouth to encourage a smile, being cautious not to elicit a rooting reflex. (1.3)

Combining or pairing different levels of instructions may be helpful when beginning to teach a new and difficult skill. Fade to less intrusive instructions as soon as possible to encourage more independent performance.

TEACHING CONSIDERATIONS

1. Cultural and individual differences may affect the appropriate frequency, intensity, and form of a child's expression of affection. In particular, the appreciation of physical contact varies greatly according to cultures and individuals.

2. Expressions of affection may vary if a child has a sensory impairment; for example, a child with a visual impairment may respond affectionately with a whole body response; a child with a hearing impairment may convey affection through facial expressions and gestures; a child with low or

high muscle tone may lack differentiation in facial expression; and a child with a severe motor impairment may respond to an adult's affection or affectionate tone with a quiver, a vocalization, or a gaze. Be sensitive to subtle changes in expression and to idiosyncratic expressions of affect.

3. Try not to reject the child's approximations of affection. Open-mouth or sloppy kisses are to be expected.

4. Provide overall body affection, being careful not to ignore body parts that have disabilities.

5. Make sure that the child is responding to the affective quality of the social interaction and not to sensory stimulation or nonsocial events.

6. The child may present individual differences in arousal levels. Adapt the intensity of affective tone to each individual child to avoid over or understimulation.

7. Use negative affect, such as a sharp voice and corrections, sparingly and with caution.

8. Ideally, the child is in a quiet and alert state in order to attend to the external environment.

9. Individual differences may be present in social responsiveness and in preferences for specific stimulation. Vary the intensity, frequency, and type of social behaviors toward the child.

GOAL 2   Initiates and maintains interaction with familiar adult

- PS2a   The child interacts with a familiar adult in a turn-taking pattern; for example, the child alternates gazing at and gazing away from an adult; the child waves his or her arms and kicks his or her legs while the adult is looking at the child and then quiets when the adult vocalizes to the child.

- PS2b   The child responds to a familiar adult's social behavior by maintaining and/or continuing the interaction; for example, the child knocks down a block tower that the adult built and waits for or helps the adult rebuild the tower.

- PS2c   The child responds in an attempt to prolong positive interaction; for example, the child protests when his or her mother leaves the room and reaches out his or her arms to be picked up again.

Objective 2.1   Initiates simple social game with familiar adult

- PS2.1a The child assumes an active role in drawing the attention of or getting close to a familiar adult to continue a social game; for example, the child crawls after father, tugs at grandma's clothes, or climbs into mother's lap.

- PS2.1b When a familiar adult initiates a simple social game, the child responds by performing an action that is part of the game; for example, the adult says, "So big,"

Social

and the child raises his or her arms; the adult places a blanket over the child's head, the child pulls the blanket off, and the adult says, "Peekaboo!"

Objective 2.2   Responds to familiar adult's social behavior

- PS2.2a The child shows interest in familiar adult's social behavior; for example, the child looks at the adult when the adult plays Peekaboo, and smiles when the adult peeks around the corner.

Objective 2.3   Uses familiar adults for comfort, closeness, or physical contact

- PS2.3a The child can be comforted by a familiar adult.

- PS2.3b The child differentiates between familiar and unfamiliar adults for comfort, closeness, or physical contact.

IMPORTANCE OF SKILLS

The child's ability to trust and depend on his or her familiar adult caregivers for security and comfort is fundamental to social, emotional, and cognitive development. Through a variety of repeated interactions, such as sharing, alternating, and reversing role relationships, the child learns the rules of the social and cultural community. Simple social games involving tactile and physical stimulation are some of the earliest forms of social interaction between a child and an adult. Within the context of interactions, the child learns about the properties of objects and actions in the physical world. The child's responsiveness reinforces the adult's initiations and stimulates the adult to maintain the interaction. The child's growing ability to participate in and maintain interactions is important to the development of language, as it provides a basis for the turn-taking pattern underlying a number of conversational pragmatic skills. Other goals/objectives that can be targeted at the same time as Goal 2 are listed on the following page.

TEACHING SUGGESTIONS

Activity-Based

Playtime

- Present the child with toys and/or objects that are more likely to elicit an interaction, such as a ball, toy telephone, or a cloth for Peekaboo. (2, 2.1, 2.2)

- Provide the child opportunities to play simple social games, such as "Gonna get you" or Peekaboo. (2.1, 2.2, 2.3)

Goal 2: Initiates and maintains interaction with familiar adult

Fine Motor

A:5.2 Places and releases object balanced on top of another object with either hand

Gross Motor

D:3 Catches, kicks, throws, and rolls ball or similar object

Adaptive

A:4.3 Accepts food presented on spoon

B:3.1 Cooperates with teeth brushing

Cognitive

B:2.1 Locates object and/or person hidden while child is watching

C:2 Reproduces part of interactive game and/or action in order to continue game and/or action

D:1.1 Imitates motor action that is commonly used

F:1.2 Uses functionally appropriate actions with objects

Social-Communication

A:3 Engages in vocal exchanges by babbling

B:1 Gains person's attention and refers to an object, person, and/or event

Social

A:1 Responds appropriately to familiar adult's affect

B:1 Meets observable physical needs in socially appropriate ways

Notes:

Assessment, Evaluation, and Programming System for Infants and Children (AEPS®), Second Edition,
edited by Diane Bricker © 2002 Paul H. Brookes Publishing Co., Inc. All rights reserved.

Social

401

- Engage frequently in eye contact with the child; smile and talk often. Remain in close proximity to the child while engaging in other activities. Respond immediately if the child initiates simple social games. (2.1)

- When the child uses an action or vocalization from a social game, imitate the child, and expand the game; for example, if the child claps hands, then clap your hands, and say, "Pat-a-Cake." (2.1, 2.2)

Storytime

- Structure time daily for positive personal one-to-one interactive activities between child and familiar adult; for example, child and caregiver may sit together and look through or read a book or sit together and plan or talk about their day, or take a ride together. (2.2, 2.3)

Throughout daily routines

- Engage in positive interactions with the child during daily activities and routines. Establish eye contact and joint attention, and smile and talk to the child. The adult does not need to engage in direct interaction with the child but must remain in close proximity while looking at the child or engaging in some other activity. (2, 2.1)

- When the child requests assistance with play or caregiving activities, respond by giving only partial assistance so that the child is likely to initiate a request for more help. (2, 2.1, 2.2)

- To facilitate social behavior, expand and elaborate on the child's own behaviors; for example, if the child pats the adult's arm, then pat the child's hand. Encourage the child to pat the adult again or indicate an interest in continuing. If the child focuses attention on an object, then get the object, and hand it to the child. (2, 2.3)

- Provide opportunities throughout the day for the child to seek or request comfort, closeness, or physical contact from familiar adults. (2.3)

Environmental Arrangements

- When a child approaches a familiar caregiver with arms up to be held, the caregiver should quickly comment on the communication and ask the child if they want to be held, thus providing an opportunity for the child to maintain the interaction. (2, 2.1, 2.2, 2.3)

- Respond to the child by acting upon a shared object; for example, the child gives the adult a wind-up toy, and the adult activates the toy. When the toy stops, the child tries to wind up the toy, and the adult smiles and claps his or her hands to praise the child. (2.1)

- Adapt toys to present problems that children must request help to solve; for example, present a clear covered tub of toys for which the child must request help to remove the lid. (2.1)

- Lead or set the child up to initiate a social game; for example, during dressing, put a T-shirt over the child's head and wait for it to be pulled away. Say, "Oh, you want to play Peekaboo?" Repeat the activity. (2.1)

- In response to the child's initial behavior, have the adult provide a response that is likely to stimulate the child to maintain the interaction; for example, if the child puts a cloth over his or her head, then the adult removes the cloth and says, "Peekaboo"; the adult then puts the cloth over the child's head, the child removes the cloth, and the adult smiles and says, "Peekaboo"; or the child hands a bottle to the adult, the adult pretends to suck and hands the bottle back to the child, the child sucks the bottle, and the adult smiles and makes sucking movement with lips; or the child gives the adult a cracker, the adult places it out of the child's reach, the child gestures for the cracker, and the adult gives the cracker back to the child. (2.1, 2.2)

- Engage in face-to-face interaction with the child. Have available objects that are commonly used in social games, such as cloths to play Peekaboo, a ball to roll back and forth, and hand-size objects to play give and take. Encourage the child to initiate a social game. If necessary, the adult may draw the child's attention to an object by pointing to or manipulating the object. (2.1, 2.2)

- Place the child in a situation or a position associated with the rules of a social game; for example, hold the child on your knees, and encourage the child to play "horsy"; sit in front of the child on the floor, and encourage the child to play Pat-a-Cake; run with the child, and encourage the child to initiate "Gonna get you"; or sing a song related to finger games. (2.1, 2.2)

- Provide opportunities for the child to request, comfort, contact, or closeness; for example, sing songs that incorporate holding hands or lifting the child, such as "Ring Around the Rosy" or "London Bridge"; mention occasionally during the day that you could use a hug or you'd sure like to sit with the child. (2.3)

Instructional Sequences

- Model repeating or elaborating on a response or pair the response with additional cues if the child does not continue the interaction; for example, the child raises his or her arms over his or her head; the adult says, "So big"; the adult raises his or her own arms; and the child raises his or her arms again. (2.1, 2.2)

- Model playing a game with the child's peer or another adult. Encourage the child to join in the game. (2.1, 2.2)

- Model social behaviors that involve a combination of auditory, visual, tactile, and physical cues; for example, play "horsy" with the child while singing a favorite song; play Peekaboo using bright-colored cloth and calling the child's name. (2.2)

- Ask the child to continue an interaction by repeating the same behavior; for example, tell the child, "Your turn," or "Do it again." (2.1)

- Ask the child to initiate a simple social game. Use verbal cues to prompt the child to respond. For example, "Let's play Pat-a-Cake," "Roll the ball," "Give me a kiss/hug," "Push the ball," or "Wave bye-bye." (2.1, 2.2)

- Provide physical cues to the child; for example, hand the child a blanket to place over the head, push hands together to play Pat-a-Cake, push a hand to contact a ball to make it roll, or hold arms out to offer comfort. (2.1, 2.2, 2.3)

TEACHING CONSIDERATIONS

1. Avoid continuous stimulation and interaction with the child. Allow for pauses and silences to give the child the opportunity to initiate or maintain the interaction.

2. Adapt the pace of the interaction to the individual child and his or her state. Some children are stimulated by a fast pace, whereas others may need more time to process a response and to reinitiate an interaction. Also, avoid, strong tactile and physical stimulation after feedings or when the child is sleepy or overstimulated.

3. Make sure that the child has the opportunity to engage in social games and knows the actions and rules of the games you want him or her to initiate.

4. A child with a sensory impairment may use signals that are difficult to read; for example, a child with a visual impairment may use hands to explore an adult's face, search for an object, or seek comfort. Encourage sensory modalities other than visual, such as laughing or clapping, in your interaction with the child. A child with a hearing impairment may initiate a simple game with facial expressions or gestures.

5. A child with a motor impairment may move only one hand or his or her whole body to initiate Pat-a-Cake or may move his or her head while gazing at a person or object to establish physical contact or to initiate a game. This child's responses may be subtle and/or hard to interpret.

6. Engage in social behaviors that are developmentally appropriate for the child; for example, younger children are more likely to respond to tactile and physical stimulation, such as a game of Peekaboo or a give-and-take game, whereas older children may prefer more complex motor games, such as playing ball.

GOAL 3   Initiates and maintains communicative exchange with familiar adult

- PS3a   The child responds to communication from a familiar adult and maintains the interaction; for example, the adult asks the child to tell about pictures in a book, and the child makes vocalizations about the pictures; then the adult supplies words for the pictures, and the child vocalizes again or points to the picture.

- PS3b   The child interacts with a familiar adult in a vocally similar manner by matching the patterns of vocal exchanges; for example, the child gurgles when the adult stops vocalizing; the child varies the length of vocalizations as a function of the length of the adult's verbalizations; or the child changes the rhythm of vocalizations when the adult sings to the child.

Objective 3.1   Initiates communication with familiar adult

- PS3.1a The child uses behaviors similar to communication skills; for example, while lying awake in the crib, child uses vocalizations, gestures, and expressions that are similar to those used to communicate with another.

Objective 3.2   Responds to communication from familiar adult

- PS3.2a The child shows interest in communication from a familiar adult; for example, the child stops crying when the adult talks soothingly, increases motor action when the adult speaks playfully, looks at adult who is talking, and watches adult as he or she sings.

IMPORTANCE OF SKILLS

By responding to communication from an adult, the child demonstrates a gradual increase in understanding. This skill enables the child to learn about communication as a system of signals that includes gestures, vocalizations, and verbalizations. From these early interactions, the child gradually learns to communicate intentionally, using a conventional system of gestures or language. First intentional communication can include a variety of gestures, vocalizations, and words to achieve desired goals, make comments, protest and reject, and convey needs. The ability to actively engage in a sequence of communicative exchanges is basic to social, emotional, social-communicative, and cognitive development. By communicating with others through a variety of means, the child learns about the social and cultural rules of the community, establishes relationships with others, expresses emotions and needs, and learns about properties of the physical environment. Other goals/objectives that can be targeted at the same time as Goal 3 are listed on the following page.

TEACHING SUGGESTIONS

Activity-Based

Playtime

- Play games involving tactile and kinesthetic stimulation that may induce the child to vocalize; for example, play "Gonna get you" and observe whether the child protests when the adult suddenly stops chasing or hides.

Social

Goal 3: Initiates and maintains communicative exchange with familiar adult

Gross Motor

D:3 Catches, kicks, throws, and rolls ball or similar object

Cognitive

C:2.1 Indicates desire to continue familiar game and/or action

D:2.2 Imitates words that are frequently used

E:4 Solves common problems

F:1.2 Uses functionally appropriate actions with objects

Social-Communication

A:3 Engages in vocal exchanges by babbling

B:1 Gains person's attention and refers to an object, person, and/or event

B:2 Uses consistent word approximations

C:1.2 Locates common objects, people, and/or events in familiar pictures

C:2.3 Carries out one-step direction with contextual cues

D:1 Uses 50 single words

Social

A:2 Initiates and maintains interaction with familiar adult

B:1 Meets observable physical needs in socially appropriate ways

Notes:

When the child puts a cover over his or her head to play Peekaboo, the adult exclaims, "Where are you?" and the child answers, "Here," or uncovers his or her face. (3, 3.1, 3.2)

- Play interactive games with and without objects. Encourage the child to label or point to objects. Ask for help in activating toys; hold up objects. (3.2)

Storytime

- During storytime or before going to bed, present the child with several books. Wait to see if the child picks a story and asks you to "read this one." If the child doesn't initiate, then ask, "What book shall we read?" Engage the child in conversation about the story and pictures. (3, 3.1, 3.2)

Travel

- Arrange situations where communication is meaningful; for example, returning home after a walk with Daddy, the child runs toward his or her mother and says, "Quack, quack." The mother comments, "Did you see the ducks?" The child nods head, the mother smiles and comments, "Were the ducks at the park?" (3, 3.1)

Throughout daily routines

- Engage in positive interactions with the child during daily activities and routines. Establish eye contact frequently; smile and play with the child. Wait for the child to initiate or maintain a communicative exchange by directing gestures, signs, vocalizations, and verbalizations toward the adult for two or more consecutive exchanges; for example, the adult watches the child play in the sand, the child looks up at the adult and gestures, and the adult moves closer to the child and asks, "What's that?" The child answers by gesturing, verbalizing, or vocalizing. (3, 3.1)

- Respond to the child's requests for interaction when he or she brings a book to look at, a shoe to put on, or a cup to put juice in. Label the child's request and your own actions. (3.1)

- Seize the opportunity to elaborate and expand on the child's communication or knowledge; for example, respond with words to the child's word approximations or provide information on properties of objects so as to expand the exchange. Be sure not to pre-empt the interaction with your responses. (3, 3.1)

- During familiar daily routines such as bath time, storytime, or snack time, present objects such as toys, books, or fruit (apples and bananas), and wait for the child to initiate a choice. (3.1, 3.2)

- Model conversations with other adults or peers. Wait for the child to initiate communication by participating in the conversation or by trying to gain the adult's attention. Encourage the child to greet and interact with other familiar adults. (3, 3.1)

- Ask the child questions about actions, events, and objects; for example, the child drops a spoon from the table; the adult asks, "What did you do?" The child answers by looking down to the floor and pointing. (3.2)

Environmental Arrangements

- In response to the child's initial communication, select a response that is likely to stimulate the child to maintain the interaction; for example, if the child points to a cracker, then ask, "What do you want?" and wait for the child to gesture, vocalize, or verbalize. (3, 3.1)

- When playing interactive games with the child, interrupt the game, and wait for the child to ask to continue the game or indicate a desire to continue; for example, the adult stops rolling the car, the child points to the car, the adult looks at the child and asks, "What do you want me to do?" The child answers, "Go," moves the adult's hand to the car, or makes car noises. (3, 3.1)

- Participate in sequential activities, such as getting dressed or making a sandwich. Interactions can follow the logical routine. If necessary, change the logical sequence, put the shoe on without the sock, and wait for child to initiate, then continue. (3.1)

- Communicate about objects and events in the child's immediate environment. (3.1, 3.2)

- Place favorite toys and snacks out of the child's reach. Wait for the child to initiate a communicative behavior with a familiar adult in order to obtain the object. (3.1)

- Put a desired object inside a difficult-to-open container, such as a clear plastic jar, and wait for the child to request assistance. (3.1)

- Introduce novel objects or unusual events; for example, while the child is placing blocks in a box, hand the child a toy animal, and wait for the child to express surprise ("Oh") or label the animal. (3.1, 3.2)

- Provide small amounts of materials such as only one or two blocks or just a swallow of juice to encourage the child to initiate a request for "more" before you provide more. (3.1)

- Be sure to take turns talking with the child. After the adult talks, there should be a pause for the child to initiate a communicative behavior to re-establish the interaction. (3.1)

- Play "Where is the _____?" game; for example, the adult names an object, and the child points to it. This game is easy to incorporate when looking at books or photos and can accommodate the child's level of response and beginning initiation skills. (3.2)

- Ask the child questions that can be answered using familiar words or gestures that have been recently produced by the child; for example, after observing the child, point to an airplane, ask the child, "Where's the air-plane?" or "What's that?" (3.2)

Instructional Sequences

- Model repeating or elaborating on the child's response. Pair the response with additional cues if the child does not continue the communication; for example, the child points to the doll, and the adult says, "Baby." If the child does not respond, then the adult repeats, "Baby, put the baby to bed." Wait for the child to repeat "baby" or follow the directions. (3, 3.1)

- Model initiating communication to familiar adults, then give the child the verbal direction to initiate communication. Say, "Let's go tell your dad you're ready to go home," or "Let's go say 'hello' to Aunt Molly." Initiate the interaction, and then give the child a turn to initiate. (3.1)

- Model pairing auditory, visual, and tactile cues with the communicative behavior; for example, tell the child to look at a llama while exaggerating the pitch of your voice and facial expression and pointing to the animal. (3.2)

- Model the response and verbally encourage the child to imitate; for example, ask the child the name of an object. Label the object if necessary, and ask the child to repeat the name of the object. (3.2)

- Ask the child to continue the conversation; for example, the child points to an object, and the adult labels the object. If the child does not respond, then tell the child, "Your turn," "Show me again what you want," or ask, "Is this what you want?" (3, 3.1, 3.2)

- Assist the child to initiate by saying, "Your turn to say 'Hi' to Aunt Molly." Encourage other adults to wait for the child to initiate. (3.1)

- Physically assist the child if an appropriate response can be given with a gesture; for example, the child holds up keys and says, "Ke-ke"; adult says, "Yes, those are your keys. Where do the keys go?" When the child does not respond, the adult moves the child's hand toward the keyhole. (3, 3.1, 3.2)

- Gently physically assist the child toward a gesture; for example, say, "Time to go; wave 'bye-bye,'" and assist the child in raising his or her hand to wave good-bye. (3.2)

TEACHING CONSIDERATIONS

1. Adapt the pace of the interaction to the individual child. Some children prefer a faster pace, whereas others need more time to process a response and re-initiate communication. The child's mood may also require changing the type of the interaction. If a child is sleepy or nervous, then talk soothingly; if a child is awake and alert, then speak in a lively manner.

2. A child with a sensory impairment may use signals that are difficult to read; for example, a child with a hearing impairment may also use gestures and signals to communicate; a child with a visual impairment may respond to tactile and auditory communication from the adult.

3. A child with a motor impairment may have difficulty articulating words clearly and may use nonconventional gestures and signals, such as eye gaze or body orientation, to engage an adult in social interactions.

4. Avoid continuous stimulation and interaction with the child. Allow pauses and silences to give the child the opportunity to initiate or maintain the communicative exchange.

5. Provide a stimulating environment, and allow the child to actively explore objects and independently initiate actions so that he or she will have reason and motivation to communicate.

6. Use language and gestures that are developmentally appropriate for the child. Use short phrases, raise and vary the pitch of your voice, and make large and visible gestures.

7. Engage in communication that is appropriate to the context; for example, wave bye-bye when departing, talk about the object the child is playing with, and ask questions related to what the child is doing.

Interaction with Environment

GOAL 1   Meets observable physical needs in socially appropriate ways

- PS1a   The child shows awareness of external physical needs such as being cold, hot, dirty, wet, or hurt. The child manifests discomfort by frowning or whining when wearing dirty or wet clothes.

Objective 1.1   Meets internal physical needs of hunger, thirst, and rest

- PS1.1a   The child signals awareness of physical needs of hunger and thirst. The child grabs a bottle and starts to suck rapidly; the child smiles and waves arms when food is presented.

Objective 1.2   Uses appropriate strategies to self-soothe

- PS1.2a   The child accepts pacifier, own thumb, or adult's finger for nonnutritive sucking.

- PS1.2b   The child can be soothed by familiar adult caregiver.

IMPORTANCE OF SKILLS

These skills are important steps in building the child's independent functioning in the daily environment. The child learns to use socially appropriate strategies to cope with stressful events. The child recognizes the basic physical needs of hunger and thirst and learns to use socially appropriate ways to meet these needs. This leads the way to the child's ability to meet a variety of physical needs defined by the social group. These skills both foster independence as the child acts to take care of his or her own needs and enhance the integration and acceptance of the child by other members of the social community. The child develops a group identity by recognizing the social attitudes of other individuals and reproducing behaviors to meet standards set by the community. Other goals/objectives that can be targeted at the same time as Goal 1 are listed on the following page.

TEACHING SUGGESTIONS

Activity-Based

Feeding

- When the child is hungry or thirsty, wait to see if the child uses socially appropriate ways to meet those needs. (1.1)

- At mealtimes, let the child help place food on the table. Do not place food directly on the child's plate, but wait for the child to request food or a drink before serving. Between meals, encourage the child to request food or a

Concurrent Goals/Objectives for Social Strand B

Goal 1: Meets observable physical needs in socially appropriate ways

Fine Motor

B:1 Rotates either wrist on horizontal plane

Gross Motor

C:1 Walks avoiding obstacles

Adaptive

B:1 Initiates toileting

B:2 Washes and dries hands

C:1 Undresses self

Cognitive

E:4 Solves common problems

F:1.2 Uses functionally appropriate actions with objects

Social-Communication

B:1 Gains person's attention and refers to an object, person, and/or event

D:1 Uses 50 single words

Social

A:3.1 Initiates communication with familiar adult

Notes:

drink or go to the cupboard or refrigerator to get food or a drink. Use general questions such as, "What do you want?" (1, 1.1)

- Provide plastic cups and a stool at the sink or drinking fountain for the child to get a drink independently. (1, 1.1)

Dressing

- Wait briefly for the child to ask for additional clothes when cold or to take off clothes when hot or when he or she needs a change of pants. (1.1)

Throughout daily routines

- During daily activities and routines, encourage the child to use socially appropriate ways to meet a variety of external physical needs. When playing with water, sand, or paint or when eating food, the child may soil hands or clothes. If the child shows discomfort or displeasure, then assist in labeling the discomfort by asking, "What's wrong?" "What's the matter?" or "What would make you feel better?" Give the child a chance to initiate hand washing or a clothing change. (1, 1.1, 1.2)

- Encourage the child to ask for help to wipe a runny nose, to clean a scrape and put on a bandage, or to be held if hurt. Use general cues and questions to draw the child's attention to solutions for meeting physical needs; for example, ask, "Do you need help?" "What should you do now?" or "What would make you feel better?". (1, 1.2)

- Establish "rules" for meeting needs appropriately, such as washing hands before a snack or going to the potty before leaving home. Maintain a consistent routine. Once the child is familiar with these rules, ask questions such as, "What do we need to do before _____?". (1.1)

- Give the child a choice in identifying strategies that will help him or her manage stressful events; for example, ask the child, when he or she is upset, if he or she would rather sit with someone or rest alone. (1.2)

Environmental Arrangements

- Leave the child's coat on briefly when entering a hot room or delay putting on coat and mittens to go out in the cold to see if the child will ask for them. (1, 1.1)

- Practice washing with dolls during pretend tea parties. (1, 1.1)

- Make available objects/people the child might need; for example, place dry clothes on a nearby stool if the child is playing with water; move physically closer if the child falls and scrapes his or her knee; and set out tissue for a child who has a runny nose. (1, 1.1, 1.2)

- Make the child's favorite foods and drink visible; for example, place cookies on open shelves near the snack table and place a bottle of juice on the

Social

sofa near the child's play area; cut up fruit and keep it on low shelves of the refrigerator. (1.1)

- Design activities with materials such as glue, sand, or water that are generally unappealing to have on hands or clothes. (1.1)

- Take the child into settings related to meals and foods; for example, take the child to self-service restaurants and let the child go to a counter to get some food. In grocery stores, ask if the child wants anything available in the displays. (1.1)

- Plan for snacks or meals to take place later than usual. Give the child an opportunity to request or obtain food or liquid at the regular time. (1.1)

- Make an appealing event contingent upon meeting a physical need in a socially appropriate way; for example, allow the child to eat only after his or her hands have been washed or his or her nose has been blown. Allow the child to get a favorite bedtime toy only after the child has sat on the potty or had his or her diaper changed. Allow the child to go outdoors only after putting on his or her coat and mittens. (1.1, 1.2)

- Set up areas in the environment where a child can have quiet time alone or work/play independently. (1.2)

Instructional Sequences

- Provide the child with a visual model or cue. Have a sibling model removing wet clothing. If the child needs to blow his or her nose, then model blowing your nose with a tissue. Model going to the refrigerator and taking out a bottle of juice. Give the child an opportunity to do the same. (1, 1.1)

- Give verbal cues or directions that propose ways to meet needs: "Get a diaper and I'll change your pants," "Do you need a tissue/bandage/washcloth?" or "Would you like to find a quiet place to rest?". (1, 1.1, 1.2)

- Use verbal cues or directions that label needs: "Are your hands dirty?" "Are you wet?" "You must be cold," or "Does your tummy ache?". (1, 1.1, 1.2)

- Give verbal cues that assist the child in managing stressful events: "Having a hard time with your buddy leaving? Maybe you could wave good-bye to him when he gets on the bus," or "Ooh, that looks like it must hurt. Would you like to put something on it to help it feel better?". (1.2)

- Physically assist the child to meet evident needs. Get dry clothes or assist the child to wash and dry hands. (1, 1.1)

- Physically assist the child by guiding him or her to the cupboard or by touching a cup, indicating to the child to hold up the cup. (1.1)

Combining or pairing different levels of instructions may be helpful when beginning to teach a new and difficult skill. Fade to less intrusive instructions as soon as possible to encourage more independent functioning.

TEACHING CONSIDERATIONS

1. Make sure that the child is aware of the location of relevant objects such as food and drinks.

2. If the child has a sensory impairment, make sure that the child has the means to adequately meet needs; for example, if the child has a visual impairment, have available food and drinks that have a strong smell, such as fresh bread or steaming hot chocolate. If the child has a hearing impairment, visually demonstrate the location of relevant objects such as food and drink.

3. Learn the child's method for self-soothing, and help him or her use it. Provide a place in the environment where he or she can use the strategies more independently.

4. If the child has a motor impairment, make sure the child has the means to adequately meet needs; for example, if the child uses a walker, have clean clothes, tissues, and toys available within a reasonable distance. Encourage the child to request help.

5. Consider safety with any objects that the child handles such as breakable containers, hot foods, or foods on which a child can choke. Place only appropriate foods and drinks within the child's reach.

GOAL 2   Participates in established social routines

- PS2a   Child performs at least one response associated with a variety of established social routines.

Objective 2.1   Responds to established social routines

IMPORTANCE OF SKILLS

The ability to independently perform a sequence of responses to established social routines demonstrates the child's awareness of a specific social structure; for example, the child gets his or her own jacket when he or she wants to go outside to play, or the child undresses him- or herself when it is bath time. The ability to participate and share in social events and routines enables the child to see him- or herself as part of a group and to gain control and independence by following socially approved rules. Other goals/objectives that can be targeted at the same time as Goal 2 are listed on the following page.

Social

Goal 2: Participates in established social routines

Fine Motor

B:1 Rotates either wrist on horizontal plane

Gross Motor

C:4.3 Gets up and down from low structure

Adaptive

A:5 Transfers food and liquid between containers

B:1 Initiates toileting

B:2 Washes and dries hands

B:3 Brushes teeth

C:1 Undresses self

Cognitive

E:4 Solves common problems

G:2 Demonstrates functional use of one-to-one correspondence

Social-Communication

C:1.3 Locates common objects, people, and/or events with contextual cues

C:2.1 Carries out two-step direction with contextual cues

Social

A:3.2 Responds to communication from familiar adult

B:1 Meets observable physical needs in socially appropriate ways

Notes:

TEACHING SUGGESTIONS

Activity-Based

Bathing

- When running bath water, first tell the child that it is bath time, then give the child the cue to get a towel and bath toys, remove his or her clothes, and climb into the bathtub. Decrease the cues as the child's participation increases. (2, 2.1)

Feeding

- At mealtime, give a general cue to indicate the start of the meal and wait for the child to come to the kitchen, sit at the table, and pick up a spoon. (2.1)

Dressing

- When it is time to get dressed, first tell the child, then give the child the cue to go to the bedroom and get clothes. Decrease the cues as the child's participation increases. (2, 2.1)

Playtime

- When playing, encourage the child to get materials, bring them to the play area, and begin an activity. (2, 2.1)

Throughout daily routines

- During daily activities and routines, allow opportunities for the child to independently perform a series of responses to established social routines. Give the child one general verbal or contextual cue, and wait for the child to perform actions to complete a routine; for example, when the adult announces that it is time to leave the house, the child gets his or her coat, goes to the door, runs to the car, and gets in the car seat. (2, 2.1)

- At bedtime, wait for the child to get a favorite, blanket, a book, a drink, and a kiss goodnight from the adult. (2)

- Be sure that the child has the opportunity to perform independently the series of responses associated with a social routine. Place relevant objects within the child's reach, use child-size furniture, and so forth. (2)

Environmental Arrangements

- Provide general verbal or contextual cues for each step of the sequence of actions of the social routine; for example, begin to set the table for dinner and encourage the child to bring his or her favorite cup to the table, then announce, "Dinner is ready," and encourage the child to sit at the table. (2, 2.1)

- Arrange for numerous social routines that are especially reinforcing to the child, such as favorite meals, outings to interesting locations, or favorite activities. (2, 2.1)

- Begin with social routines within which the sequence of actions can be performed in the same location or with the same objects; for example, give verbal or contextual cues for the child to take off pants and sit on the potty, to wash and dry hands, or to undress and go to bed. (2, 2.1)

- Make an event that is especially interesting to the child contingent upon the completion of a social routine; for example, have the child wash and dry hands before eating ice cream; have the child undress and climb into bed before hearing a favorite bedtime story. (2, 2.1)

- Vary the type, length, and complexity of the social routines. (2, 2.1)

Instructional Sequences

- Have peers provide visual models of social routines for the child to follow. (2.1)

- Demonstrate an entire routine, and ask the child to do it with you. (2)

- Ask the child to continue a typical routine once you begin it; for example, an adult gets out clean clothes, the child removes his or her pajamas, and the adult asks, "What do you do next?" The child then begins to dress. (2, 2.1)

- Give the child specific verbal instructions for each step of the routine; for example, when it is mealtime, tell the child, "Go to your chair." After the child arrives at the chair, say, "Put on your bib." (2.1)

- Physically assist the child with the actions associated with the social routine; for example, assist the child to the chair after saying, "It's time for dinner." (2.1)

TEACHING CONSIDERATIONS

1. Allow time for the child to respond independently.

2. Make sure that verbal and contextual cues, as well as the responses required, are developmentally appropriate.

3. If the child has a sensory impairment, make sure that he or she has the means to respond to the event; for example, direct the child with a visual impairment to the relevant objects, and demonstrate the availability of relevant objects for the child with a hearing impairment.

4. Consider safety when the child handles foods and objects.

STRAND C

Interaction with Peers

GOAL 1 Initiates and maintains interaction with peer

- PS1a The child responds to and maintains interaction with peer; for example, the child is holding a ball, a peer takes the ball, and the child reaches for the ball until the peer hands it back.

Objective 1.1 Initiates social behavior toward peer

Objective 1.2 Responds appropriately to peer's social behavior

- PS1.2a The child shows interest in a peer's social behavior; for example, the child looks at a toy offered by the peer or waves arms and smiles while watching a peer on a swing.

Objective 1.3 Plays near one or two peers

- PS1.3a The child plays near one or two peers in the presence of a familiar adult; for example, the child plays with Legos in the proximity of the teacher who is reading a story to a peer.

Objective 1.4 Observes peers

- PS1.4a The child observes peers or siblings; for example, the child watches older sibling playing with a friend.

Objective 1.5 Entertains self by playing appropriately with toys

- PS1.5a The child plays appropriately with toys with adult assistance.

IMPORTANCE OF SKILLS

Initiating and maintaining a social interaction with a peer is a basic skill for the development of friendships. In a relationship, each person's behavior has an influence on the other. Friendships grow as children learn to understand each other and communicate and interact constructively. Peer interaction is an egalitarian experience, providing the child with the give and take essential to socialization, communication skills, and moral development. Initially, the focus in interactions is on the manipulation of objects or activities. Social behaviors such as exchanging objects, imitating actions, and building structures together are ways that children intentionally interact with each other. The observation of peers is also important because peers can serve as models for the child in a variety of social and cognitive behaviors. A first step toward participation in social play with peers is solitary play, in which the child learns to play independently. Other goals/objectives that can be targeted at the same time as Goal 1 are listed on the following page.

TEACHING SUGGESTIONS

Activity-Based

Playtime

- Provide settings where the child has the opportunity to interact with peers; for example, take the child to child care, take the child to the playground, and invite peers to the child's home. Encourage the child to develop an interest in peers by watching them play. Provide free-play time in the classroom. (1, 1.1, 1.2, 1.3, 1.4, 1.5)

- Provide toys such as balls, blocks, beanbags, puppets, musical toys, and doll houses that encourage interactions and offer opportunities for exchanging and sharing. Encourage children to play together by directing interactions to peers; for example, if a child asks an adult for help or shows you an object, then say, "Maybe Mara could help you," or "Jamal might like to see your doll." Have enough toys for children to use without conflict but not too many to discourage interaction. (1, 1.1, 1.2, 1.3)

- Place the child in situations where peers are present. Observe which peers the child prefers. Allow the child to initiate social interactions with a peer and maintain two or more consecutive exchanges without interruption or assistance; for example, the child offers a toy cup to a peer, the peer takes the cup, puts it on a saucer, and pretends to pour some tea. The child takes the cup back, pretends to drink, and asks the peer for more. The peer pretends to pour more tea, but refuses to relinquish the cup. Avoid the presence of too many adults. Wait for the child to initiate a social behavior toward a peer by looking and smiling, offering or showing a toy, and helping to complete a task. Encourage the child to approach other children and remain near them when playing independently with a toy or object. (1.1, 1.2, 1.3, 1.4)

- Encourage the child to entertain him- or herself appropriately. Provide a variety of age-appropriate toys. Set the child up with a toy or activity while an adult is nearby but otherwise engaged. Help the child entertain him- or herself by joining in daily activities that the child especially enjoys; for example, let the child dig holes in the garden, sweep the leaves, or play with soap bubbles and bath toys in the bathtub. (1.5)

Throughout daily routines

- Encourage activities with peers that require more than one step for completion, such as finishing large puzzles, building a tall tower with blocks, or preparing food. Show the child an activity that produces a visible effect

Concurrent Goals/Objectives for Social Strand C

Goal 1: Initiates and maintains interaction with peer

Fine Motor

A:5 Aligns and stacks objects

B:2 Assembles toy and/or object that require(s) putting pieces together

---

Gross Motor

C:3 Runs avoiding obstacles

D:1.1 Jumps up

D:3 Catches, kicks, throws, and rolls ball or similar object

D:4 Climbs up and down play equipment

Cognitive

C:2 Reproduces part of interactive game and/or action in order to continue game and/or action

D:1.1 Imitates motor action that is commonly used

E:3 Navigates large object around barriers

F:1 Uses imaginary objects in play

G:2 Demonstrates functional use of one-to-one correspondence

Social-Communication

B:1 Gains person's attention and refers to an object, person, and/or event

B:2 Uses consistent word approximations

D:1.4 Uses 15 object and/or event labels

Social

B:2.1 Responds to established social routines

Notes:

Social

or has a purpose meaningful to the child; for example, ask the child to draw a picture for Grandma or prepare a "snack" for Daddy with playdough. (1.1, 1.2, 1.3, 1.5)

- Encourage the child to respond to peers in a socially appropriate way by pointing out positive aspects of peers' actions; for example, say, "That was nice of Evan to give everyone crackers." (1.2, 1.4)

- Allow the child opportunities to observe peers play. During free play at school, encourage the child to walk around the room to watch peers play. Say, "Let's go see what Jamie is doing." During daily activities, make sure the child has access to other peers and has free time to observe others during snack, toileting, dressing, or playing. (1.1, 1.3, 1.4)

Environmental Arrangements

- Give peers verbal cues to use in response to another child's initiation; for example, the child walks over and sits close to a peer, and you tell the peer to offer a toy to the child. (1.1, 1.2)

- Encourage the group of children to participate in activities that require collaboration, such as constructing with large blocks, painting on a large sheet of paper, or setting the table for meals. Arrange a room partitioned by play areas to bring children into closer proximity for interaction. Provide materials that go together to stimulate the child to ask a peer for objects; for example, give the peer all of the dolls and the child all of the doll clothes. Encourage activities that increase the likelihood that the child will be asked for help by peers. Ask a peer to ask the child for help in moving a table. (1.1, 1.2, 1.3)

- Encourage the child to participate in activities with preferred peers or peers who have been observed to be particularly sociable and friendly. Initially, limit the size of the group of peers. Have a sibling interact with the child and peers. For quiet children, arrange quiet activities ahead of time to avoid too much noise or confusion, which may reduce peer interaction. (1.1, 1.2, 1.3)

- Encourage the child to share or exchange objects; for example, children can paint together, exchanging colors with each other. Give objects to the child to "deliver" to a peer. Say "Give Bill a cup," or "Give Ann a spoon." (1.1, 1.2, 1.3)

- Comment on the peer's response to the child's initiation to encourage another exchange; for example, after the child puts a blanket over the peer and the peer takes it off, say, "Fred took off the blanket." (1.1, 1.3)

- Give the child an object or toy similar to that used by peers, and encourage the child to observe and imitate peers; for example, while peers are engaged in sand play, hand the child a bucket and shovel and ask, "Can you dig, too?" (1.1, 1.3, 1.4)

- Set up dramatic play roles that require the child to initiate and maintain interactions (e.g., bus driver, shop keeper, taxi driver). Keep the adult–child ratio low and encourage unstructured child-oriented activities. Have the child play with slightly younger peers or participate in activities at which the child is proficient; this provides the opportunity for the child to help others. (1.1, 1.3, 1.4)

- Encourage older peers to talk to the child and offer objects to help maintain proximity. (1.2, 1.3)

- Introduce one novel item for peers to play with and learn to manipulate, such as a turkey baster during water play. Design activities so that a peer's action produces an interesting and immediate effect, such as pulling a chain or flipping a switch for lights, bouncing or rolling balls to knock blocks over, or sliding down a slide. (1.3, 1.4)

- Select a range of objects to allow the child to use a variety of modes of exploration: simple toys that are easily activated by motor actions and provide sensory stimulation (e.g., rattles, drums, bells); mechanical toys (e.g., dump trucks, wind-up toys); construction toys (e.g., Legos, blocks); miniature objects (e.g., dolls, animals); materials (e.g., paint, water, playdough, sand); and books, paper, and crayons. (1.5)

Instructional Sequences

- Model initiating and maintaining interactions; for example, the child places a block to build a tower, and the peer places a second block. If the child does not continue, then place a third block, and hand the child another block. (1, 1.1, 1.2)

- Show the child how to respond to a peer's social behavior; for example, wave back to a peer. (1.2)

- Demonstrate the use of a toy, and ask the child to imitate by acting independently on the toy. (1.5)

- Encourage the child to entertain him- or herself by systematically increasing the amount of time the child plays independently and the distance that the child plays from the adult. Model observing peers in an interesting activity. Direct the child's attention to peers by pointing toward a group of children playing; describe their actions. (1.4, 1.5)

- Give the child specific verbal instructions to initiate or maintain the interaction; for example, after the child approaches the peer and the peer greets the child, tell the child to say, "Hello." (1.1, 1.2)

- Give specific and nonspecific verbal cues to encourage social behavior; for example, "Jason doesn't have anything to play with," or "Sarah's here!" Give the child verbal directions to play in proximity to peers. (1.1, 1.2, 1.3)

- While at a distance from the child, verbally encourage him or her to play. Observe the child, and comment on the child's actions. (1.3, 1.5)

Social

- Verbally encourage the child to watch peers, first by instructing the child to look at them, and then by commenting on peers. Ask the child to tell you what peers are doing. (1.1, 1.2, 1.3, 1.4)

- Physically assist the child; for example, the child looks at the peer and claps his or her hands; the peer imitates. If the child does not continue clapping, then gently press the child's hands together in a clapping motion; gently place the child's hand in the peer's hand after the peer extends his or her hand in an offer to take the child to the playground; have the child sit and play on the lap of an adult who is near one or two peers; place the child in the middle of peers playing in the sandbox; demonstrate the use of a toy and physically assist the child to activate the toy. (1.1, 1.2, 1.3, 1.4, 1.5)

Combining or pairing different levels of instructions may be helpful when beginning to teach a new and difficult skill. Fade to less intrusive instructions as soon as possible to encourage more independent performance.

TEACHING CONSIDERATIONS

1. Ensure that the child feels at ease within the setting or activity. Some children might prefer quiet, sedentary activities; others might prefer noisy activities involving movement. A child may not enjoy large group or noisy activities and may not respond to a peer's social behavior within such activities but may adequately respond to a single peer's approach. Encourage two or three members of a group to pull away and play near the child. Do not intervene with the child who becomes involved independently after initial observation.

2. Provide the child the opportunity to initiate and maintain interactions. Avoid the presence of domineering peers or of too many adults. Activities should be child directed rather than adult directed.

3. A child with a sensory or visual impairment might present social behaviors that are difficult for peers to read. Help peers interpret the child's initiations; for example, a child with a visual impairment sits close to a peer; the peer greets the child; and the child touches the peer's face. Explain to the peer that the child cannot see well and is exploring his or her face; this will help the peer feel comfortable with the tactile contact. Use visual, tactile, and auditory cues; for example, use bright, noisy objects or objects that have interesting tactile characteristics for a child with visual impairment. Provide toys or objects that are colorful and visually appealing for those with hearing impairment.

4. Remember that sharing toys does not come easily to most toddlers. Many legitimate interactions may be initiated and maintained in conflicts over toys and materials. Adult assistance and/or supervision may be required. Encourage the child to negotiate with others. Appropriate responses also include reactions to negative behaviors, such as moving away from a peer who is hitting or yelling or shaking his or her head when a peer offers an

object grabbed away from another child. Do not engage the child continuously in activities; allow the child some time to be an observer.

5.   Provide situations in which the child can maintain interest in activities. If possible, have the child play with peers whose development is slightly above the child's. Their ages should be similar enough to allow the child to identify with a peer group, but the peers should have slightly advanced social skills to serve as models of constructive social interactions.

GOAL 2   Initiates and maintains communicative exchange with peer

- PS2a   The child responds to communication from a peer and maintains the interaction for two or more turns; for example, a peer asks the child for an object, "Car?" The child answers, "No!" and the peer responds, "Mine!" The child insists, "My car."

Objective 2.1   Initiates communication with peer
Objective 2.2   Responds to communication from peer

- PS2.2a   The child shows interest in communication from peers; for example, the child looks at the peer when the peer asks a question.

IMPORTANCE OF SKILLS

Communication is basic to social interaction. The child learns to communicate messages and meanings about objects, people, and events. The ability to initiate and maintain a communicative exchange with a peer demonstrates that the child can use basic conversational skills, focusing and expanding on a topic and adjusting to topic changes. The child learns to share feelings, ideas, and facts with peers. A child's early interactions with peers involve manipulation of objects and activities. Later, the child receives verbal communication from a peer and responds. Other goals/objectives that can be targeted at the same time as Goal 2 are listed on the following page.

TEACHING SUGGESTIONS

Activity-Based

Playtime

- Use dramatic play such as dress-up, playing house, or playing doctor to encourage communicative exchanges with peers. (2, 2.1, 2.2)

- Provide interesting toys, materials, and environments and wait for the child to initiate and maintain a communicative interaction with a peer for two or

Social

Concurrent Goals/Objectives for Social Strand C

Goal 2: Initiates and maintains communicative exchanges with peer

Fine Motor

A:5 Aligns and stacks objects

B:2 Assembles toy and/or object that require(s) putting pieces together

Gross Motor

C:3 Runs avoiding obstacles

D:3 Catches, kicks, throws, and rolls ball or similar object

D:4 Climbs up and down play equipment

Cognitive

E:4 Solves common problems

F:1 Uses imaginary objects in play

G:2 Demonstrates functional use of one-to-one correspondence

Social-Communication

B:1 Gains person's attention and refers to an object, person, and/or event

C:1.3 Locates common objects, people, and/or events with contextual cues

C:2.3 Carries out one-step direction with contextual cues

D:3 Uses three-word utterances

Social

B:2 Participates in established social routines

C:1 Initiates and maintains interaction with peer

Notes:

more consecutive exchanges; for example, take children on a field trip to pick strawberries and encourage interactions during the activity. The child might ask a peer, "Taste berry?" The peer responds, "Yummy," the child looks at his or her hands and says, "Messy," and the peer responds, "Messy." When the child plays in a sandbox, encourage the child to initiate communication with a peer by asking for a shovel; for example, say, "Ask Rosa," or "Tell Jamal." (2)

- Encourage children to play verbal and/or vocal activities, such as telephone, house, school, store, or singing so that the primary interactions are verbal. (2, 2.1, 2.2)

- Provide opportunities for the child to play with peers who communicate verbally or with gestures. Wait for the child to respond to peer's communication by gesturing or verbalizing; for example, when playing dollhouse, the peer tells the child, "You're going to be the baby," and the child answers, "No." Refrain from intervening unless the children are quarreling. (2.2)

Group activities

- Ask children to sing with you. Stop singing, and encourage the children to continue singing without you. (2.1, 2.2)

Throughout daily routines

- If the child engages in one communicative exchange, then encourage more discussion on the same topic; for example, if the child says, "Me eat," and another child says, "Me, too," then ask what they are eating and how it tastes. (2.1)

- Interpret the child's response to peers, if necessary, without pre-empting the interaction. Redirect the interaction back to the child; for example, say, "Maybe Patrick has an idea for who would like to be the baby, if he doesn't want to." (2.1, 2.2)

Environmental Arrangements

- Give peers verbal cues to respond to the child's initiation; for example, tell the peer, "Alex asked if you want a crayon; tell him if you do." (2, 2.1, 2.2)

- Have children engage in an activity involving two or more sequences of events to facilitate maintaining communication for two or more consecutive exchanges; for example, have two children share a book and take turns commenting about pictures. Encourage the child to comment about pictures; for example, the child may say, "Look, doggie," and the peer continues, "Doggie lick." The child turns a page and says, "Boy laughing," and the peer answers, "Good doggie." Ask children to describe what they see. (2, 2.1, 2.2)

- Introduce changes or novel elements, and wait for the child to comment about them to a peer; for example, while the child and a peer are playing with a ball, substitute a rubber toy. Make a surprised expression, and shrug your shoulders; wait for the child to comment. (2, 2.1)

- Encourage an older peer to assist the child to perform a task or activity by giving simple verbal instructions. Encourage the child to ask questions. Have the peer tell the child, "Put on your shoes," and observe whether the child asks for help. (2, 2.1)

- Provide children with interesting toys and materials, and allow them to play freely without adult intervention. Communication should occur as a result of wanting to obtain toys, exchange materials, collaborate on the construction of an object, or assign roles in pretend play. (2, 2.1, 2.2)

- Design dramatic play such as shopping in which peers exchange objects and money. Practice with the children until they become familiar with the exchanges, and then allow the children to interact independently. (2, 2.1, 2.2)

- Encourage children to engage in activities that require collaboration; for example, place one child in a wagon and have a peer push the wagon. Wait for the peer to ask child, "Ready to go?" and for the child to answer, "Go." (2, 2.1, 2.2)

- Assign the child the role of leader within a simple, familiar game or activity to encourage the child to initiate communication with peers by giving instructions; for example, have the child play the leader in "Follow the Leader" or "Simon Says." Encourage the child to tell other children what to do. (2.1)

- Encourage a peer to play with objects or engage in activities of interest to the child to encourage the child to interact or participate in the activity; for example, suggest that an older sibling go for a walk with the dog and wait for the child to ask to go along with the sibling. (2.1, 2.2)

- Sing songs and play games that require turn taking and peer responses such as "Ring Around the Rosy." (2.1, 2.2)

Instructional Sequences

- Provide visual or tactile cues to accompany communicative exchanges; for example, model identifying animals in pictures. Hand the pictures to the children. Pause, and wait for the children to take turns identifying the pictures. (2, 2.1, 2.2)

- Give the child verbal instructions and models to maintain the interaction; for example, after the peer accepts the child's invitation to go for a walk, instruct the child to "Tell Joey where we are going"; after the child approaches and says, "Hello," encourage the peer to answer. (2, 2.1)

- Provide physical assistance to help a child approach a peer and offer a greeting. Hold your hand out to the child, and say, "Let's go say hi to Simon." (2.1)

- Have peers model communicative exchanges with other children. Ask the child to imitate. Say, "Show Alison how to ask for a cracker," then tell Alison it is her turn to ask. (2.2)

- Instruct the child to ask a question, greet a peer, explain a behavior, or describe an object or activity to a peer; for example, say, "Ask Jason for the block." (2.1, 2.2)

- If the child does not respond to the peer's communication, then verbally direct the child to answer or first provide a model by answering the peer and asking the child to imitate; for example, tell the child, "Jacob said, 'Hi!'" If the child does not respond, then instruct the child, "Say, 'Hi,' to Jacob." (2.1, 2.2)

TEACHING CONSIDERATIONS

1. Ensure that the child feels free to engage in communicative interactions. Provide an environment of stimulating language to foster interactions among children.

2. The child may have difficulty synchronizing communicative attempts with those of peers. Assist peers in allowing the child enough time to respond.

3. A child with a sensory impairment may present communicative behaviors that are difficult for peers to read. Help peers interpret the child's communication; for example, the child with a severe motor impairment might glance or nod toward a peer to initiate an interaction.

4. A child with a sensory impairment might have difficulty understanding a peer's response. Help the child interpret the peer's behavior; for example, a child with a severe visual impairment might not be aware that a peer responded to the child by coming near.

5. If the child has a hearing impairment, give visual and tactile cues that help orient the child to a peer's activities.

6. If necessary, translate for a peer the signs used by a child with a hearing impairment.

Social

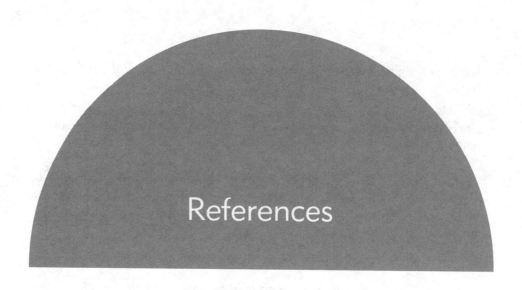

References

Feldman, T. (2002). *Hello kitty hello friends.* New York: Abrams.
Kunhardt, D. (2001). *Pat the bunny.* New York: Golden Books.

APPENDIX

A

Routine Activity Format I

An Activity Targeting Goals/Objectives
from Multiple Developmental Areas

INTRODUCTION

This appendix presents one routine activity format that caregivers and interventionists may wish to consider when designing intervention efforts for individual or groups of children. The seven activities that are included may be used as models for the development of additional plans or can be modified to meet the needs of individual or particular groups of children.

The purpose of this activity format is to assist caregivers and interventionists in using a variety of routine activities to target specific goals/objectives across many developmental areas. Routine activities are those that typically occur within a child's day (e.g., bedtime, snack time, time at the playground) and provide valuable opportunities for children to learn and practice targeted goals/objectives; for example, during snack time, an interventionist might be able to provide opportunities for a child to practice gross motor (e.g., sits down in and gets out of chair), adaptive (e.g., transfers food and liquids between containers), and cognitive (e.g., demonstrates functional use of one-to-one correspondence) skills. This routine activity format is advantageous in providing opportunities to work on multiple skills for an individual child or for groups of children within the context of one routine activity. The following components are contained in Routine Activity Format I:

- Name of the activity
- Six areas of development that specify
  - AEPS goal/objective
  - What to do during the activity
  - Materials needed for the activity

In addition to using the seven activities contained in this appendix, it may be valuable to create routine activities specific to your environment, individual children, and families. An analysis of routine activities in the home and/or child care setting can reveal a variety of routines that provide practical opportunities to target children's goals/objectives. In selecting routine activities for embedding children's targeted goals/objectives, choose activities and materials that are interesting and fun for the child and that occur at appropriate teaching times for caregivers and personnel; for example, families who have tight timelines for getting to work may find it difficult to use breakfast as a teaching time. Through careful observations and working closely with caregivers, appropriate routine activities can be identified that offer numerous opportunities for children to practice targeted goals/objectives from multiple developmental areas.

Routine Activity: Bathroom

FINE MOTOR AREA

Goal/Objective	What to Do	Materials
Rotates either wrist on horizontal plane (B:1)	Encourage child to open the door to the restroom and/or flush toilet after toileting.	

GROSS MOTOR AREA

Goal/Objective	What to Do	Materials
Sits down in and gets out of chair (B:2)	Provide potty chairs or stools in front of toilets, and encourage the child to get on and off of potty chair or toilet seat. Use caution with adult-size toilets.	Potty chairs, stools, ladder-style adaptive toilet seats with handles

ADAPTIVE AREA

Goal/Objective	What to Do	Materials
Washes and dries hands (B:2)	Model washing and drying hands, and have children imitate the steps (e.g., turn on water, put soap on hands, rub hands together, "make bubbles," rinse hands, "rinse off bubbles," turn off water, dry hands). Make up a fun hand-washing song to accompany the activity.	Bar soap, small bars of hotel soap, liquid soap dispenser, towels

COGNITIVE AREA

Goal/Objective	What to Do	Materials
Imitates motor action that is not commonly used (D:1)	During or after hand washing, sing songs or play games in front of the mirror that include novel actions and/or signs (e.g., "Wheels on the Bus," "Itsy, Bitsy Spider," "Simon Says"). Use hands and face to make funny images.	Bathroom items, wall mirrors

SOCIAL-COMMUNICATION AREA

Goal/Objective	What to Do	Materials
Carries out two-step direction without contextual cues (C:2)	During toileting or hand washing, talk to the child about what you are doing. Initiate independent activities by saying, "Time to turn off the water and dry your hands."	Bathroom items

SOCIAL AREA

Goal/Objective	What to Do	Materials
Initiates social behavior toward peer (C:1.1)	Encourage the child to invite several other children to wash hands or make funny faces in front of the mirror.	Bathroom items, wall mirror

433

Routine Activity: Playground

FINE MOTOR AREA

Goal/Objective	What to Do	Materials
Rotates either wrist on horizontal plane (B:1)	Give the child plastic jars with screw-on lids and encourage him or her to find leaves, rocks, or other items to put in the jars. Remind the child to open and close jars with each item.	Plastic jars with lids, leaves, rocks, sea shells, small toys, and so forth

GROSS MOTOR AREA

Goal/Objective	What to Do	Materials
Jumps forward (D:1)	Blow bubbles and encourage the child to pop them by jumping on them.	Bubble solution, bubble wand

ADAPTIVE AREA

Goal/Objective	What to Do	Materials
Transfers food and liquid between containers (A:5)	Make birthday cakes in the sandbox! Pour and transfer sand into mixing bowls and/or cake pans. Use twigs for birthday candles.	Sand, mixing bowls, serving spoons, small pitchers, twigs

COGNITIVE AREA

Goal/Objective	What to Do	Materials
Navigates large object around barriers (E:3)	Set up an obstacle course, and encourage the child to push strollers, pull wagons, or ride push-toys or tricycles around obstacles.	Obstacles such as traffic cones, chairs, sand bags, and strollers; tricycles, wagons, push-toys

SOCIAL-COMMUNICATION AREA

Goal/Objective	What to Do	Materials
Carries out two-step direction without contextual cues (C:2)	Set up a small obstacle course for dolls or action figures. Model how to play "obstacle course" with the dolls while incorporating two-step directions.	Obstacles (e.g., chairs, large blocks, hoops)

SOCIAL AREA

Goal/Objective	What to Do	Materials
Respond appropriately to peer's social behavior (C:1.2)	Encourage the child to play interactive games such as ball, London Bridge, or Duck, Duck, Goose.	Balls, bean bags

Routine Activity: Snack time

FINE MOTOR AREA

Goal/Objective	What to Do	Materials
Grasps pea-size object with either hand using tip of the index finger and thumb with hand and/or arm not resting on surface for support (A:4)	Encourage the child to pick up pea-size foods during snack.	Pea-size food items such as raisins, grapes, peanuts, pistachios

ADAPTIVE AREA

Goal/Objective	What to Do	Materials
Transfers food and liquid between containers (A:5)	Provide opportunities for the child to participate in pouring and transferring food.	Pitcher (preferably 2-cup size, plastic, lightweight), serving bowl, spoon, large serving spoon

SOCIAL-COMMUNICATION AREA

Goal/Objective	What to Do	Materials
Carries out two-step direction without contextual cues (C:2)	Ask the child to get items needed for snack and to put them on the table. Have the child help with cleanup after snack, incorporating two-step directions.	Table, snack items (e.g., serving dish, pitcher, condiments)

GROSS MOTOR AREA

Goal/Objective	What to Do	Materials
Sits down in and gets out of chair (B:2)	Provide child-size chairs at the snack table, and ask children to sit down after washing hands.	Child-size chairs, table

COGNITIVE AREA

Goal/Objective	What to Do	Materials
Demonstrates functional use of one-to-one correspondence (G:2)	Ask the child to assist with setting the table. The child can place cups, napkins, and/or utensils next to each plate.	Table, plates, cups (preferably nonbreakable), napkins, eating utensils

SOCIAL AREA

Goal/Objective	What to Do	Materials
Initiates and maintains interaction with peer (C:1)	Encourage the child to ask other children to pass serving bowls to each other. Model and encourage appropriate etiquette (e.g., please, thank you, you're welcome).	Serving bowls with food in them

435

Routine Activity: Bedtime

FINE MOTOR AREA

Goal/Objective	What to Do	Materials
Fits object into defined space (B:2.2)	Have child put shoes into specific space.	Cubby or shoe rack

ADAPTIVE AREA

Goal/Objective	What to Do	Materials
Takes off shoes (C:1.5)	Encourage child to remove shoes. If child does not initiate, then offer a reminder.	Shoes

SOCIAL-COMMUNICATION AREA

Goal/Objective	What to Do	Materials
Locates common objects, people, and/or events in familiar pictures (C:1.2)	Read a book before bed/nap. Look at pictures of common objects in books. Name the objects, people, or events as you point to them. Ask child to point to pictures that you label.	Book, photo album, magazine

GROSS MOTOR AREA

Goal/Objective	What to Do	Materials
Walks without support (C:1.1)	Have child carry items to the sleep area.	Book, blanket, pillow, sleeping pad

COGNITIVE AREA

Goal/Objective	What to Do	Materials
Uses more than one strategy in attempt to solve common problem (E:4.1)	Put bedtime items out of reach or behind an obstacle. Observe child's ability to obtain necessary items.	Shelves, drawers, bedtime items (e.g., books, blanket)

SOCIAL AREA

Goal/Objective	What to Do	Materials
Displays affection toward familiar adult (A:1.1)	Tuck the child into bed when it is time to go to sleep. Talk to the child in an affectionate tone and make positive comments about child's skills, activities, and interests.	Comfortable sleeping space, blankets, books

Routine Activity: Diaper and potty time

FINE MOTOR AREA

Goal/Objective	What to Do	Materials
Releases hand-held object onto and/or into larger target with either hand (A:5.3)	After washing hands, encourage child to drop paper towel into wastebasket.	Paper towels, wastebasket

GROSS MOTOR AREA

Goal/Objective	What to Do	Materials
Stoops and regains balanced standing position without support (C:2)	Place stack of diapers low to ground. Ask child to retrieve a clean diaper.	Diapers

ADAPTIVE AREA

Goal/Objective	What to Do	Materials
Indicates awareness of soiled and wet pants and/or diapers (B:1.2)	As you change child's diaper, clearly label it as wet or soiled. Have child repeat the label with an appropriate sign, gesture, or word.	Child's wet or soiled diaper

COGNITIVE AREA

Goal/Objective	What to Do	Materials
Uses an object to obtain another object (E:2)	Put diaper wipes just out of reach of child. Provide a stool nearby for child to climb on to reach the wipes.	Diaper wipes, stool

SOCIAL-COMMUNICATION AREA

Goal/Objective	What to Do	Materials
Locates common objects, people, and/or events with contextual cues (C:1.3)	Ask child to find items integral to diapering/potty (e.g., ask child to give you the wipes or a clean diaper).	Items necessary for diapering/potty (e.g., diapers, wipes, towel)

SOCIAL AREA

Goal/Objective	What to Do	Materials
Initiates and maintains communicative exchange with familiar adult (A:3)	Establish eye contact frequently. When child initiates an exchange with gestures or words, reply to maintain the exchange.	Respond with answers that maintain exchange (e.g., "What's that?" "What's next?")

Routine Activity: Floor play or blanket time

FINE MOTOR AREA

Goal/Objective	What to Do	Materials
Simultaneously brings hands to midline (A:1)	Place a finger in each of the child's palms, and allow the child to grasp them. Slowly move your fingers to midline while the child is still holding them. Pair movements with made-up chants such as, "hands together—hands apart." Hang or dangle objects or toys within the child's visual field and at the child's midline.	Floor gym, variety of textured developmentally appropriate toys/objects (e.g., fabric and plastic blocks, different pieces of fabric, rattles, bells, soft books, stuffed animals)

GROSS MOTOR AREA

Goal/Objective	What to Do	Materials
Turns head, moves arms, and kicks legs independently of each other (A:1)	Place child on lap, over your knees, or on a large therapy ball and bounce him or her while singing songs such as, "Bouncing Up and Down in the Little Red Wagon"; pause after singing one verse, and wait for child's response. Place child on activity blanket.	Large therapy ball, activity blanket with variety of textures and attached objects

ADAPTIVE AREA

Goal/Objective	What to Do	Materials
Drinks from cup and/or glass held by adult (A:3.2)	Offer drinks from a cup.	Cup with lid, water, milk, soy milk, juice

COGNITIVE AREA

Goal/Objective	What to Do	Materials
Visually follows object and/or person to point of disappearance (B:1)	Call a pet over to child when child is attending to pet; activate a battery-operated stuffed animal or toy; play "Going to get you" game and hide behind a sofa or blanket; roll a ball or car under furniture and play "I'm going to get it" game.	Pets (if part of the family), variety of battery-operated toys or stuffed animals, balls

SOCIAL-COMMUNICATION AREA

Goal/Objective	What to Do	Materials
Follows person's pointing gesture to establish joint attention (A:2.1)	Outside on grass, point to nearby objects such as flowers, birds, clouds, and comment on them. Inside, point to people who enter room. Look through picture books, point to pictures, and name them.	Naturally occurring objects, events, or people in the environment; fabric, plastic, or cardboard books with variety of pictures of objects and people

SOCIAL AREA

Goal/Objective	What to Do	Materials
Displays affection toward familiar adult (A:1.1)	Look at books with the child on your lap. Engage child in interactive songs such as, "Row, Row, Row Your Boat." Hold hands and pretend to row back and forth when singing this song.	Select books such as *Pat the Bunny*.

Routine Activity: Mealtime

FINE MOTOR AREA

Goal/Objective	What to Do	Materials
Turns object over using wrist and arm rotation with each hand (B:1.1)	Allow and encourage child to feed self with a spoon.	Spoon, food

ADAPTIVE AREA

Goal/Objective	What to Do	Materials
Brings food to mouth using utensil (A:4.1)	Provide a fork or spoon with food that can be scooped; encourage child to bring filled utensil to mouth.	Fork or spoon, food that can be scooped (e.g., applesauce, yogurt)

SOCIAL-COMMUNICATION AREA

Goal/Objective	What to Do	Materials
Carries one-step direction with contextual cues (C:2.3)	Give simple directions for setting the table, passing snacks to peers, and cleaning up afterward.	Napkins, utensils, cups, food items, sponge

GROSS MOTOR AREA

Goal/Objective	What to Do	Materials
Moves up and down stairs (C:4.2)	Place a step-stool by the sink for washing hands prior to eating.	Step-stool

COGNITIVE AREA

Goal/Objective	What to Do	Materials
Imitates words that are frequently used (D:2.2)	Label foods and objects while eating.	Food and objects at meal location (e.g., cracker, juice, napkin)

SOCIAL AREA

Goal/Objective	What to Do	Materials
Meets internal physical needs of hunger, thirst, and rest (B:1.1)	Wait for the child to request food before or during serving.	Food and drink prepared for serving

APPENDIX

B

Routine Activity Format II

Multiple Activities Targeting Goals/Objectives from

One Developmental Area

INTRODUCTION

This appendix presents a routine activity format that caregivers and interventionists may wish to consider when designing intervention efforts for individuals or groups of children. The included example contains ideas for all goals/objectives contained in Strand B of the Fine Motor Area across four different settings: Mealtime, Bathroom time, Outside time, and Playtime. This activity format may be useful as a model for developing routine activities focused on goals/objectives from a single developmental strand within one area.

The purpose of this activity format is to assist caregivers and interventionists in thinking about and planning intervention strategies for children over time. In addition, it may be used for groups of children with varying developmental competencies in one general area; for example, the routine activity included here that focuses on Strand B: Functional Use of Fine Motor Skills from the Fine Motor Area might be useful for planning over an extended period of time for a child with a motor delay. Using this activity format for strands within the Social-Communication Area may be useful when developing intervention strategies for a group of children within a setting where the primary focus is on developing speech and language skills.

The settings included in Routine Activity Format II are those that typically occur within a child's day (e.g., mealtime, potty or diapering), thus providing valuable opportunities for children to learn and practice targeted goals/objectives; for example, items contained in Strand G: Early Concepts from the Cognitive Area can be integrated in settings such as mealtime, by having the child assign one napkin or fork to each place setting; diapering, by saying simple nursery rhymes while changing a diaper and having the child recite them along with you; and bedtime, by asking the child to pick out a book to read with you before going to sleep. The following components are contained in Routine Activity Format II:

- AEPS area, strand, and title
- The AEPS goals/objectives included in the strand
- Routine activities that offer suggestions for embedding the goal/objective

Through careful observations and working closely with caregivers, a variety of settings can be identified that offer numerous opportunities for children to practice targeted goals/objectives from one developmental area. In selecting routine activities for embedding children's targeted goals/objectives, choose settings and materials that are interesting and fun for the child and that occur at appropriate teaching times for caregivers and personnel; for example, an interventionist who is working with a large group of children during lunchtime without assistance may find it difficult to use this setting as a teaching time. An analysis of routine activities in the home and/or child care setting can reveal a variety of settings and activities, providing practical opportunities to target goals/objectives that are designed to meet the needs of individual children and families.

AEPS Birth to Three

Fine Motor Area, Strand B: Functional Use of Fine Motor Skills, Goal 1, Objective 1.1

Goal 1	Routine Activities			
	Mealtime	Bathroom time	Outside time	Playtime
Rotates either wrist on horizontal plane	• Encourage child to remove lids on jars. • Provide jars with the lids already loosened. Gradually make the task more challenging by screwing the lid a quarter turn. • Allow child to make juice by twisting an orange half on a squeezer. • Encourage child to participate in cleaning activities with you, such as washing the table with a sponge or emptying water from cups into the sink.	• Encourage child to flush the toilet. • Close doors to encourage child to turn doorknobs when entering or leaving the room.	• Encourage child to manipulate the handle of a drinking fountain independently. Child may drink from the fountain or simply watch the effect.	• Encourage child to play with toys, such as a Busy Box, that have knobs that can be turned by rotating the wrist. • Play games with cards. Show child how to deal cards and turn them face up. • Provide toys with large, easy-to-manage wind-up mechanisms (e.g., alarm clock, toy train, toy radio). Systematically introduce smaller mechanisms as child begins to develop wrist rotation.

443

Routine Activities

Objective 1.1			
Turns object over using wrist and arm rotation with each hand	**Mealtime**	**Bathroom time**	**Outside time**	**Playtime**

Mealtime	Bathroom time	Outside time	Playtime
• Allow and encourage child to feed him- or herself with a spoon and/or cup. • Allow child to shake or dump the contents of a container into a bowl during baking activities. • Allow child to make juice by twisting an orange half on a squeezer.	• Encourage child to wash and dry own hands, turning the hands back and forth under the water and rubbing soap on the palms and backs of hands.	• Allow child to play with containers in sand, water, dirt, or cornmeal. Encourage child to dump the contents of one container into another.	• Play at feeding dolls and stuffed animals; have peers "pretend" to eat food or drink liquids. • During preparation for activities, have child dump crayons, stickers, brushes, blocks, or peg people out of storage containers. • Encourage child to turn pages of a book when reading a story with an adult.

Fine Motor Area, Strand B: Functional Use of Fine Motor Skills, Goal 2, Objectives 2.1 and 2.2

	Routine Activities			
Goal 2	Mealtime	Bathroom time	Outside time	Playtime
Assembles toy and/or object that require(s) putting pieces together	• Plan for a special meal (e.g., birthday, holiday) that includes candles and cloth napkins. Have the child help prepare the table by putting candles in a candle holder and napkins in napkin rings.	• Give the child a travel style toothbrush that requires putting pieces together.	• Provide a building or work-space outside that includes toys that can be assembled or put together; for example, bench with wooden pegs and hammer, interlocking wooden tracks, or plastic screws and nuts.	• Establish a routine for the child to put objects away in containers after play; for example, put crayons in a box, peg people in a bus, plastic eggs in egg cartons, or toy milk bottles in a carrier. • Have child complete the assembly of a toy with the last piece; for example, show child how to put the harness on a Fisher-Price horse and attach the wagon, and then have child put the toy person in the wagon for a ride. Systematically in-crease the number of pieces that the child contributes. • Use bristle blocks or Duplos that easily stay together. • Provide puzzles that have shapes of pieces drawn underneath, or trace the shapes yourself.

Objective 2.1

Fits variety of shapes into corresponding spaces

Routine Activities

Mealtime	Bathroom time	Outside time	Playtime
• Talk about things that fit together or into one another as you cook (e.g., lids on pots, bread in toaster). • Provide two or three different sizes of pots with fitting lids. Provide Tupperware containers of different shapes and sizes with lids. Encourage child to fit lids to corresponding containers.	• Talk about things that fit together or into one another as you bathe child (e.g., plug in drain, peg man in bath toy). • Begin with hand-size pieces and gradually choose smaller items; for example, first have child put a cup back in the holder after brushing his or her teeth, then have child put away the cup and the toothbrush in the corresponding places in the holder.	• Talk about things that fit together or into one another as you dress child to go outside (e.g., button in hole, shoe on foot).	• Show how magic marker caps fit on the ends of the markers, and have child help put them away. • Give child coins to put in piggy bank. • Provide simple puzzles or form boards with fitting pieces. Pieces do not need to interlock. • Provide games such as pegs and pegboards, clothespins and jar, toy people and vehicles, or Nerf basketball and hoop. • Use thick puzzle pieces that are easy to hold and manipulate on a shallow form board. Use puzzle pieces with handles or glue on handles (e.g., thread spools).

446

Routine Activities

Objective 2.1— (continued)	Mealtime	Bathroom time	Outside time	Playtime
Fits variety of shapes into corresponding spaces				• Begin with circles, then progress to shapes that will fit into corresponding holes in more than one way (e.g., square, triangle, cross). • Use color cues to help child distinguish shape differences (e.g., circles are red on the board, squares are blue). • Use objects that can be easily activated (e.g., shapes for shape sorters, forms with knobs for form boards, plastic eggs for egg cartons). • When introducing shapes and shape sorters or form boards, present them in completed form, and let child remove and replace pieces to explore.

Routine Activities

Fits object into defined space

Mealtime	Bathroom time	Outside time	Playtime
• Serve appealing finger food at snacks and meals. Encourage child to give you a bite (e.g., "Oh, that looks good. Can I have a bite?"); see if child fits a bite of food into your mouth.	• When introducing objects to child (e.g., soap, toothbrush), present them so that the object is already in a defined space; child must remove the object to explore it and then return it to its space (e.g., soap to soap dish, toothbrush to holder).	• Encourage child to assist with activities that put objects into defined spaces, such as mail in a mailbox, dirt in planter pots, or utensils in drawers. • Provide dump trucks, buckets, wagons, or toy shopping carts that can be filled with small objects. • Arrange objects to produce an effect when one object is activated; for example, water splashes when an object is dropped into a bucket of water.	• Provide numerous containers for child to play with in functional ways; for example, have separate containers for cars, dolls, balls, and blocks. • Use large receptacles for objects, such as blocks in a shoebox. Decrease the size of objects and receptacles systematically to a drinking cup size. • Begin with two objects that can fit together only one way (e.g., two nesting blocks, doll and cradle, toy car and garage, telephone and receiver). Systematically introduce more and varied combinations as child begins to fit objects into spaces. • Use objects that can be easily manipulated (e.g., hand-size pieces that fit only one or two ways).

Fine Motor Area, Strand B: Functional Use of Fine Motor Skills, Goal 3, Objective 3.1

	Routine Activities		
Goal 3	**Mealtime**	**Bathroom time**	**Outside time**	**Playtime**

Goal 3	Mealtime	Bathroom time	Outside time	Playtime
Uses either index finger to activate objects	• Encourage child to poke index finger in cookie dough or soft bread dough. • Put finger food, small blocks, or toys into egg cartons or other small containers so that items can only be accessed using the index finger.	• Show child how to wash his or her belly button and between toes using the index finger during a bath.	• Give child the opportunity to activate familiar objects in the environment with an index finger; for example, allow child to turn on and off lights, press elevator buttons, turn the television or radio off, or press doorbells.	• Have child poke at holes punched in paper, poke holes into shaving cream or playdough, point at pictures in books, or dial a play telephone with the index finger extended. • When child pats pictures or mirror images, model pointing in return and encourage child to point, too. • Engage child in play with a Busy Box or other toy with buttons that produce an effect. • Provide various toys for child to explore that provide highly salient feedback in response to fine motor movement.

Routine Activities

Mealtime	Bathroom time	Outside time	Playtime
			• Give child pull-toys that are extended with the string first. (Remove the ring or handle from the string so that child must manipulate the string to activate the object.) • Provide finger paints and show child how to "write" with the index finger. • Put shiny or interesting toy rings or finger puppets on child's index fingers and encourage child to wiggle the fingers to make them move.

Goal 3— *(continued)*

Uses either index finger to activate objects

450

Routine Activities

Objective 3.1	Mealtime	Bathroom time	Outside time	Playtime
Uses either hand to activate objects	• Give child many opportunities to activate familiar objects in the environment. Encourage child to push open doors and cupboards and pull open drawers. • Let child activate appliances such as the vacuum, toaster, or faucet that require use of the entire hand. • Allow child to push the large buttons on vending machines to receive food or drink.	• Use pump dispensers for soap and lotion, and let child do the pumping.		• Engage in interactive play with blocks, vehicles, balls, and other hand-size objects. • Provide opportunities for child to explore various toys that provide highly salient feedback when activated. Show the child how to activate a Busy Box, musical toys such as a tambourine or jingle bells, or a Happy Apple toy. • Provide materials (e.g., clay, finger paint) that lend themselves well to patting, slapping, pushing, and pulling; for example, show child how to pop bubbles, flatten clay, finger paint, or push floating toys.

AEPS Birth to Three

Fine Motor Area, Strand B: Functional Use of Fine Motor Skills, Goal 4, Objectives 4.1 and 4.2

	Routine Activities			
Goal 4	**Mealtime**	**Bathroom time**	**Outside time**	**Playtime**
Orients picture book correctly and turns pages one by one	• Take picture books along when eating out at a restaurant. While waiting for the food to arrive, have child look at the book with you, turning each of the pages one by one.	• During bath time, include plastic waterproof picture books as part of the bath toys. Ask child about pictures in the book. "Can you find the whale?" "Let's see what's on the next page."	• Bring picture books on an outing to the beach, lake, or park. During quiet time or before or after snack, have child get the books from the backpack to look at. Take turns turning the pages with child.	• Set up a "library" in the play area. Have picture books available in bookshelves or racks. When child chooses a picture book, say, "Can I see the book you picked?" Have child show you the pictures while turning the pages one by one.
Objective 4.1 Turns pages of books	• Prepare a snack with child using a children's cookbook. Have child turn the pages of the book to choose a snack to make.	• Keep a bucket or stack of picture books in the bathroom that relate to bathroom activities, such as washing hands, brushing teeth, and toileting. Present a book to child while sitting on the potty. Comment on the pictures as child turns the pages.	• Take a bus ride to the library. While waiting for the bus, read a book to child. Encourage child to turn the pages; for example, say, "Okay, let's see what happens next."	• Provide books that have an accompanying audiotape. The audiotape will have a sound cue to indicate page turning in concert with the story.

452

Objective 4.2

Turns/holds picture book right side up

Routine Activities

Mealtime	Bathroom time	Outside time	Playtime
• Take pictures of child at snack. Have child orient the pictures right side up and lay them out in sequence (e.g., setting the table, eating, cleaning up).	• Before bedtime, have child brush teeth and then pick out a bedtime book to read.	• Take a sketch pad on a walk outside. Draw pictures of trees, houses, cars, and people. Write a simple narration for each picture as child dictates, and ask child to orient the pictures right side up and stack them in order before stapling the pages together.	• During playtime, provide paper and crayons for making a picture book. Have child show you the picture book once it is completed.

AEPS Birth to Three

Fine Motor Area, Strand B: Functional Use of Fine Motor Skills, Goal 5, Objectives 5.1 and 5.2

Goal 5	Routine Activities			
	Mealtime	Bathroom time	Outside time	Playtime
Copies simple written shapes after demonstration	• Make pudding prints or whipped cream art on the tabletop and copy each other's designs.		• Point out shapes in the natural environment (e.g., wheels are circles, clocks are circles, windows are rectangles), and trace the shapes with your finger.	• Take turns drawing pictures with shapes on magic slates, chalkboard, or paper. Use circles for faces, squares for houses, or triangles for pizza slices. • Use shapes in flannel-board play or art activities, giving child an opportunity to feel, copy, and match them. • Give child a template or piece of cutout cardboard that will guide the writing implement around the desired shape. • Draw dot-to-dots of shapes for child to trace.

454

Routine Activities

Goal 5— (continued)	Mealtime	Bathroom time	Outside time	Playtime
Copies simple written shapes after demonstration				• Engage child's attention by making dots on the writing surface. The auditory component (tapping) of this action usually captures child's interest. Begin with large exaggerations of desired shapes and gradually diminish the size. • Encourage child to make circles, crosses, and triangles with his or her index finger in sand, flour, dirt, or finger paint. • Hang child's work on display to encourage the activity.

Routine Activities

Mealtime	**Bathroom time**	**Outside time**	**Playtime**
• Make lines and circles in clay or cookie dough and "feel" the configuration.	• Use soap crayons in the bath, and take turns drawing lines and dots.	• While playing outside, encourage child to make lines and circles with his or her index finger or with sticks in the sand, dirt, or mud. • Point out shapes in the environment (e.g., wheels are circles, clocks are circles, plates are circles) and trace around them with your finger. • "Paint" with water on the sidewalk, making long lines and big circles.	• Provide crayons or markers for drawing. Take turns drawing lines and circles with different colors.

Objective 5.1

Draws circles and lines

Routine Activities

	Mealtime	Bathroom time	Outside time	Playtime
Objective 5.2 **Scribbles**	• Hang large sheets of paper on a wall for child to color (e.g., paper grocery sacks cut open work well).		• Encourage child to engage in activities with marking tools, such as painting with paint brushes or drawing in dirt with sticks.	• Color together on plain paper or in coloring books without attention to "staying in the lines." • Wrap toys in paper and allow child to "decorate" the packages. • While you write letters or pay bills, give child paper and crayons to use to imitate your activity. • Provide child with a large space to write on; gradually decrease the space to the size of writing paper. • Offer child a picture of his or her favorite object to point to with a writing implement. Move the paper around beneath child's poised writing implement to create a mark. Call attention to the mark, then wait for child's response.

APPENDIX

C

Planned Intervention Activities

INTRODUCTION

Appendix C contains five planned intervention activities that can be used with individuals or with small or large groups of children, which are particularly useful for developing activities in center-based and child care programs; however, interventionists may also find this format helpful when assisting caregivers in the selection of activities for the home and family settings.

Planned intervention activities should be designed to meet two important criteria. First, they should be activities that children find meaningful, interesting, and engaging; for example, when offered the activity, children should show genuine enthusiasm rather than being required to participate. Second, they should offer multiple opportunities to learn and practice targeted goals/objectives. Achieving this second criterion will require thought and preplanning. Although planned activities can occur—and often do—apart from daily activities, they can also be meaningfully embedded into daily activities.

The planned intervention activities in this appendix consist of a sequence of nine components that facilitate thoughtful preplanning to embed goals/objectives for individuals and groups of children. The plans follow an activity from setup to closing in order to maximize the number of opportunities to practice target skills. The nine components and a brief description follow:

1. *Activity name*

2. *Materials,* includes materials that are needed for the activity

3. *Environmental arrangements,* includes suggestions for setting up the activity and materials in a way that enhances opportunities for children to acquire targeted goals/objectives within the activity

4. *Description of activity*

    * *Introduction,* includes setup of the activity and provides a brief preview of the activity before it begins

    * *Sequence of events,* suggests a sequence of actions that may facilitate the activity. Although the suggested *sequence of events* may prove successful in most situations, variations should be expected. Following the child's lead within the activity is advisable, as long as IFSP/IEP goals/objectives continue to be addressed.

    * *Closing,* informs the child that the activity is about to end and provides an opportunity to recap the activity with the child. This can be helpful in reinforcing the learning experience and supporting a smooth transition to the next activity.

5. *Opportunities to embed children's goals/objectives,* includes a list of specific AEPS goals/objectives that are likely to be integrated within the ac-

---

The terms *teacher* and *interventionist* are used in these activities, but it is assumed that teacher and interventionist are interchangeable with parent, caregiver, assistant teacher, or other adults in the classroom who are running the activities.

tivity. Goals/objectives can be included that are specific to an individual child, or general groups of items from particular strands within areas may be included for groups of children.

6. *Planned variations,* suggests additional materials, steps, or actions that are appropriate for the activity and that vary learning opportunities for children; for example, during snack time, instead of working on one-to-one correspondence in which children set the table and assign one napkin to each bowl, a variation could include having children exchange items with each other to facilitate peer interactions.

7. *Vocabulary,* provides a list of specific words and/or categories of words that can easily be incorporated within the activity

8. *Peer interaction strategies,* provides suggestions that are specific to encouraging interaction among peers; for example, the Circle Time activity suggests selecting songs that require partners such as "Row, Row, Row Your Boat" as a strategy to encourage peer interaction.

9. *Parent/caregiver input,* elicits feedback from caregivers that might make the activity more relevant for the child; for example, the caregiver might suggest some of the child's favorite songs that are sung at home for the Circle Time activity, or parents might be invited to attend the child's preschool when the Birthday Party activity takes place. In addition, interventionists can send home materials or information about activities that take place during the child care setting that may be useful at home; for example, a tape of songs that are sung during the Circle Time activity can be made and sent home with children.

The activities included in this appendix may be modified to meet the needs of individual children and families by incorporating specific child goals/objectives or might serve as a model for developing a "bank" of activities to be used in your program setting. Utilizing planned intervention activities supports successful intervention efforts by ensuring that opportunities are arranged to practice targeted IFSP/IEP goals/objectives within activities that are fun and meaningful for children.

SNACK TIME

Materials

- Plates, cups, serving bowls, napkins
- Appropriate eating utensils (spoon, fork, knife)
- Food items
- Beverage in a pitcher

Environmental Arrangements

This activity takes place at the snack tables. Children and teachers sit around the snack tables; a plate, a cup, a napkin, and a eating utensil (if appropriate) is available for each child and teacher. Food is available in serving bowls but unreachable to the children.

Description of Activity

Introduction

- Before snack, one or two children can assist in setting the table by placing one plate, one cup, one napkin, and appropriate eating utensil(s) at each place. (These helpers should wash their hands before assisting.)
- Children wash hands before coming to snack table(s).
- Teachers sit with children at table(s) and label what kind of food is available while modeling signs for the different food items.

Sequence of Events

- Teacher asks children what kind of food they would like first.
- Children are asked to name items by either signing or speaking.
- Children are also encouraged to communicate "please" by signing or speaking.
- Serve children a small portion of the food that they select or they may serve themselves, depending on their developmental skill level. Encourage children to communicate "thank you" by signing or speaking.
- Children eat their snack with appropriate utensils, use napkins when appropriate, and drink from their cup.
- Teachers model signs and words when interacting with other children and by requesting snack items for themselves from other teachers. If teachers are

unfamiliar with specific signs, then it is appropriate for them to model sign acquisition by asking other teachers to show them the sign or by looking the sign up in a book and sharing the sign with other teachers and children.

- If children are still hungry after finishing their food, then the teacher encourages them to ask for "more" of the food they desire.

Closing

- Teachers encourage children to communicate "all done" and to clear their places when they are finished eating snack.

Opportunities to Embed Goals/Objectives

Cognitive (G:2)	Ask one or two children to assist in setting the table.
Adaptive (B:2)	Ask children to wash hands.
Gross Motor (B:2)	Ask children to sit at snack table.
Social-Communication (D:1.4)	Encourage children to indicate what kind of food they would like.
Social (B:2.1, 2.2)	Encourage children to pass food to each other and to communicate "please" or "thank you" when appropriate.

Examples of goals/objectives for individual children

Child	Goal/objective	Opportunities
Kirsten	Uses 50 words or signs (SC D:1, modified)	Encourage Kirsten to name foods and communicate "more," "please," "thank you," and "done."
	Initiates and maintains interaction with peer (Soc C:1)	Ask Kirsten to find out what snack Amy would like.
		Encourage Kirsten to pass food or serve food to other children.
		Have Kirsten sit next to children who she shows an interest in.
		Encourage Kirsten to ask children to pass food.

Planned Variations

- Ask children to pass serving bowls to each other.
- Discuss tastes, textures, and temperatures with the children.

Vocabulary

- Food items (cracker, apple, cheese, juice, etc.)
- Table-setting items (napkins, cups, etc.)
- More, please, thank you, all done

Peer Interaction Strategies

- Other children are requested to pass snack items to each other and to request items from each other.

Parent/Caregiver Input

- Send information home to children's parents about what kind of signs or words they are using at snack.
- Children's parents can communicate what kinds of food they enjoy at home.

LET'S BLOW BUBBLES

Materials

- Bubble solution
- Bubble wands

Environmental Arrangements

This activity can happen outside or inside, just make sure that there is plenty of space and that the floor surface will not get slippery with bubble solution.

Description of Activity

Introduction

- The interventionist produces a bottle of bubble solution and a handful of wands and begins blowing bubbles where children can see them and/or asks another child to invite some friends to join in blowing bubbles.

Sequence of Events

- Before being given a bubble wand, children are encouraged to ask for one in a way that is appropriate for them.
- Interventionist demonstrates how to blow bubbles.
- Children are each given one turn to immerse their wand in bubble solution and blow bubbles.
- Children are encouraged to request additional turns by asking for them.
- The interventionist helps the children take turns by explaining who is next.
- Children can also be encouraged to try to catch or pop bubbles with their hands or feet or by stomping or jumping.

Closing

- When children are done with the activity or it is time to start another activity, children can return the wands to the interventionist or to another child who has been designated as the interventionist's helper.

Opportunities to Embed Goals/Objectives

Social-Communication (C:2.3, D:2)	Encourage children to request bubble wand. Encourage children to ask for a turn at dipping bubble wand into solution.
	When activity is finished, children are requested to return wands to interventionist or helper.
Cognitive (D:1, 1.1)	Show children how to dip wand into bubble solution and blow bubbles.
	Encourage children to pop bubbles with their hands or feet.
Social (C:1.2, 2.1)	Help children wait for their turn by explaining who is next. Encourage children to communicate to others who will be next and when it is their turn.

Examples of goals/objectives for individual children

Child	Goal/objective	Opportunities
Danielle	Uses 50 single words and signs (Soc D:1, modified)	Wait for Danielle to request bubble wand before handing it to her.
		Encourage Danielle to request turns for dipping bubble wand.
	Imitates motor action that is not commonly used (Cog D:1)	Show Danielle how to dip wand into bubble solution and blow bubbles.
		Encourage Danielle to pop bubbles with her hands or feet.
	Initiates communication with peer (Soc C:2.1)	Encourage Danielle to say or sign who will be next ("your turn") and when it is her turn ("my turn")

Planned Variations

- Put food coloring into bubble solution and encourage children to blow bubbles onto a large sheet of butcher paper for "bubble art."

- Each child can be given his or her own bottle of bubble solution.

- To encourage group interactions, a large amount of bubble solution may be placed into a tub or into the sensory table. Different types of wands or objects with holes may be offered.

Vocabulary

- Bubble(s), wand(s), bottle, solution
- Big, little, high, low
- Blow, watch, pop, jump, stamp, clap
- Hand, mouth, lips, foot
- Peers' names
- Please, thank you
- More, my turn
- Fun

Peer Interaction Strategies

- Provide only a few wands (i.e., fewer than the number of children) and encourage children to share by having one child hold a wand while the other one blows the bubbles. Encourage them to take turns by switching jobs.
- Put bubble solution and wands in the sensory table.
- Have children take turns being in charge of the bottle of bubble solution.

Parent/Caregiver Input

- Send a bottle of bubble solution or a recipe for bubble solution home with each child, and encourage parents to blow bubbles with child at home.

CIRCLE TIME

Materials

- Song cards (8½" x 11") with pictures suggesting short children's songs that incorporate hand or body movements
- Carpet squares

Environmental Arrangements

A large space is needed for the children and interventionists to sit in a circle. A 9' circle works well for a class of 8–10 toddlers and can be demarcated by using carpet cut in the shape of a circle or by placing tape in the shape of a circle on the floor.

Description of Activity

Introduction

Following cleanup of the morning play activities, children are encouraged to bring a carpet square to the circle area, place it on the perimeter of the circle, and sit down on it.

Sequence of Events

- After the children are seated on a carpet square or on an interventionist's lap, song cards are passed out to each child.
- The teacher leading the circle activity asks which child has a specific song card. The child with the song card is encouraged to hold up the card for all of the children to see.
- The teacher sings the song and encourages the children to sing and do the hand or body movements with them.
- This sequence of requesting a card and singing the song is continued several more times, depending on the children's interest level.
- After the last song is sung, an interventionist or a child collects the song cards from the children.
- A basket of books is brought out and passed around (by a child or an adult) from which the children can select a book.
- The teacher assists the children in looking at the books by turning the pages, talking about the pictures, or reading the words. (Some children may look at books individually, whereas others may be willing to share a book with a peer.)

Closing

- After looking at books for 5–10 minutes, the children are requested to return the books to the basket and to go to the sink in order to wash their hands for snack.

Opportunities to Embed Goals/Objectives

Social-Communication (C:2.1, 2.3)	Ask children to bring a carpet square to the circle and sit down on it.
	Ask which child has a particular song card.
	Ask that child to hold up the song card.
	Ask the children to return the song cards and get or choose a book.
Cognitive (C:2, D:1, 2, 2.2)	Encourage children to sing songs and participate in hand or body movements.
Social (A:2.2, 3.2)	Look at books with the children, and talk about the pictures.
	Ask children questions about the pictures.
Adaptive (B:2)	Ask the children to put back books and wash up for snack.

Examples of goals/objectives for individual children

Child	Goal/objective	Opportunity
Matthew	Carries out two-step direction, without contextual cues (SC C:2)	Present Matthew with several two-step directions.
		Ask Matthew to bring a carpet square to the circle and sit down on it, return the song cards and get a new book, and put the book away and go wash his hands at the sink.
	Imitates motor action that is not commonly used (Cog D:1)	Encourage Matthew to imitate actions of songs.
	Uses 50 words or signs (SC D:1, modified)	Encourage Matthew to sing along. Talk about the pictures in the book that Matthew chooses. Show him the signs to words or actions in the book whenever possible.
	Initiates and maintains communicative exchanges with peers (Soc C:2)	Encourage Matthew to look at a book with a friend.

Planned Variations

- Objects suggesting songs can be placed in a bag and children can take turns reaching in to select the object for the next song. (This gives less song selection control to the interventionist.)

- During circle time, a group activity such as Ring Around the Rosy or Duck, Duck, Goose can take the place of songs.

- A planned activity could include providing each child with a photocopied song card and coloring it with markers or crayons. Interventionists and children could hum or sing the song during this activity. The opportunity for increased repetition and to talk about the songs helps children become more familiar with the songs so that they are better prepared for circle time. This may also be an effective way to introduce a new song before circle time.

Vocabulary

- Words from songs
- Carpet square, song card, book
- Sit down, stand up, take, give, sing, read, look at, do
- On top of, sit next to, hold up, take out of, put into
- Everybody, me
- Peers' names

Peer Interaction Strategies

- Select a song that requires a partner, such as "Row, Row, Row Your Boat."
- Children can carry carpet squares together, sit on carpet squares or laps together, and/or look at books together.

Parent/Caregiver Input

- Teachers can send song lyrics home so that parents can practice the songs with their child. Copies of song cards with the words on the back can also be sent home.

- Teachers can make a tape of all of the songs on the song cards to send home with the children.

- Ask parents for favorite songs that they sing with their child at home, or invite a parent to join the circle time and share new songs with children.

- Ask parents to send one favorite book of their child's to school for the week for book time.

- Parents could go on a field trip to the library to help select books for the book basket.

HAPPY BIRTHDAY TO ME

Materials

- Playdough in several colors
- Rolling pins
- Circle cookie cutters (wide mouth canning jar rings)
- Birthday plates or lids for cake pans
- Birthday candles
- Plastic knives
- Birthday candle holders
- Birthday hats
- Streamers
- Tape

Environmental Arrangements

Have playdough available at a table with chairs. Predecorate the classroom with streamers, or have the children assist in decorating. The interventionist has all of the supplies readily available and either sets them out before the activity or asks the children to assist.

Description of Activity

Introduction

- Children can help set up the activity by setting the table with plates, knives, birthday hats, and a predetermined number of candles for each spot.

Sequence of Events

- Children are invited to sit at the "birthday table" and make birthday cakes.
- Interventionist demonstrates how to make playdough into a cake-like shape.
- Interventionist demonstrates how to put candles into cake, counting the number he or she puts in.
- Interventionist then sings the birthday song and blows out the candles.
- Children make cakes, sing songs, and blow out candles.
- Children can also cut up their cakes and serve them to peers or "hungry" teachers or dolls.

Closing

• The interventionist tells the children that the activity will be ending in 3-
  to 5-minutes and that the party is almost over.

• The children assist in putting playdough and party supplies away.

Opportunities to Embed Goals/Objectives

Social (C:1, 2)	Children work together to decorate the activity area.
	Only have one or two rolling pins at the table to encourage negotiation.
	Ask children to show peers how to blow out candles.
	Encourage children to serve each other birthday cake.
Cognitive (F:1.2, G:1.1, 1.2, 2)	Ask children to help set the table by placing an item at each spot.
	Show children how to roll out playdough and cut out cake shape.
	Talk about the colors of the candles and the colors of the playdough.
	Ask children to sort toys when cleaning up the activity.
Fine Motor (A:4, B:2.2)	Encourage children to place candles in candleholders and then in playdough.
Social-Communication (D:1.5)	Ask children whose birthday it is and sing for that person.

Examples of goals/objectives for individual children

Child	Goal/objective	Opportunity
Jack	Uses 50 single words and signs (SC D:1)	Ask Jack to label colors and to name items.
		Encourage Jack to count candles.
	Initiates and maintains interaction with peer (Soc C:1)	Children work together to decorate the activity area.
		Ask Jack to show another child how to blow out candles.
		Only have one or two rolling pins at the table to encourage negotiation.
		Encourage children to serve each other birthday cake.
	Demonstrates functional use of one-to-one correspondence (Cog G:2)	Ask Jack to help set the table by placing an item at each spot.

Planned Variations

- This activity can also happen in the sandbox with real cake pans or similar containers and sticks or colored popsicle sticks.

- Make birthday party invitations with the children before the activity.

- Use salt dough and bake the cakes. Create candle holes in the cakes by pressing beans or other objects the diameter of a candle into the cake before it bakes. When you remove the object, a hole will be available for real candles to be placed in and removed by the child. "Frost" the cake by painting it when it is cool.

Vocabulary

- Peers' names
- Colors
- Numbers 1–5
- Cake, candles, playdough
- Actions: cut, roll, stick in, blow, take out, press, flatten, sing, eat, serve, give

Peer Interaction Strategies

- Ask children to pass utensils to each other.
- Talk with children about toys that they would like for their birthday.
- Encourage children to serve cake to each other.

Parent/Caregiver Input

- Invite parents to join the class for a real party. After the activity, eat real cake and celebrate all of the birthdays that happen that month. Let the kids serve the parents.

Cultural Sensitivity

- Some families do not celebrate birthdays. Make sure that this activity is comfortable for all children and families that would be participating.

PUMPKINS

Materials

- Books about pumpkins
- Pictures of pumpkin patch and vines
- Pumpkins
- Children's pumpkin knives, large spoons, bowls, aprons
- Wagon

Environmental Arrangements

Put books about pumpkins on the bookshelf. Set several pumpkins on the carpet. Cut open one pumpkin and scoop out most of the seeds. Place pumpkin and seeds on a tray. The activity begins on the rug with the interventionist and children reading a book. A wagon is pulled over when the story is finished. Pumpkins will be cut at the table.

Description of Activity

Introduction

- Teacher places the pumpkins on the carpet and invites the children over to hear a story.
- Teacher asks the children to share what they know about pumpkins.
- Teacher reads the story and engages the children in conversation about pumpkins.
- Teacher asks the children if they think a pumpkin is heavy or light.
- Teacher chooses several children to pick up the pumpkins and put them in the wagon to take over to the table.
- Teacher asks the children who would like to help cut open the pumpkins to see what is inside.
- Teacher chooses someone to pull the wagon over to the table.

Sequence of Events

- Children put the pumpkins on the table.
- Children will help put out the tray with the pumpkins and seeds.
- Children put on aprons.
- Children use pumpkin knives to cut out the tops of the pumpkins. The interventionist will provide cues and assistance when necessary.

- Children will use spoons to scoop out the pumpkin seeds.

- Children will spoon the seeds into the bowls.

- Children will separate the seeds for roasting and planting.

Closing

- Interventionist tells the children that the activity will be ending in 3–5 minutes. The timer is set for 5 minutes.

- Children help carry the bowls and pumpkins to the counter.

- Children wash their hands.

- Children wipe off the table.

- Children take off their aprons.

Opportunities to Embed Goals/Objectives for the Group

Cognitive	Have children pick a book.
Social (C:1)	Encourage children to help peers fasten their aprons when assistance is needed.
	Encourage two children to work together on one pumpkin.
	Prompt children to assist peers with the cleanup process.
Adaptive (B:2)	Encourage children to wash and dry hands independently.
Social-Communication (D:1.1, 2.4)	While you cut the top off of the pumpkin and demonstrate how to spoon out the seeds, ask the following questions:
	Which pumpkin do you want to cut? What will be inside the pumpkin? What does it feel like inside the pumpkin? What does it look like inside the pumpkin?

Examples of goals/objectives for individual children

Child	Goal/objective	Opportunity
Julian	Washes hands with soap and rinses with water (Adap B2.1)	Have Julian wash hands after completing his pumpkin.
	Makes comments and asks questions while looking at picture books (Cog G:4.2)	While reading the pumpkin book, engage Julian in the story by pointing to pictures and looking at Julian expectantly and asking questions such as, "What do you think will happen next?" "Can you tell me about this picture?"

Planned Variations

- Make science equipment available (i.e., magnifying glass, color paddles, scale).
- Have other fruit available to cut and compare seeds.
- Cut pieces of pumpkin and other fruit to taste.

Vocabulary

- Peers' names
- Colors (e.g., orange)
- Sizes (e.g., big, little)
- Quality (e.g., heavy, light, wet, dry)
- Location (e.g., in, top, bottom)
- Texture (e.g., smooth, rough, slimy, slippery)
- Temperature (e.g., warm, cold)
- Stem
- Seeds
- Cut

Peer Interaction Strategies

- Limit the number of pumpkins so children will need to take turns and work together cutting and scooping.
- Have children work together to clean up.
- Have children help each other put on and take off aprons.

Parent/Caregiver Input

- Invite parents to participate in a field trip to the pumpkin farm and a hayride.
- Ask parents/caregivers to share their recipes for pumpkin pie, pumpkin cookies, pumpkin seeds, pumpkin bread, and more.

INDEX

Page references followed by *f*, *t*, or *n* indicate figures, tables, or notes, respectively.

Order Form

Set Savings!

____ **Complete AEPS®, Second Edition** | Administration Guide, Test: Birth to Three Years and Three to Six Years, Curriculum for Birth to Three Years, and Curriculum for Three to Six Years—$239.00 • Stock #65614

____ **AEPS® Birth to Three Set** | Administration Guide, Test, Curriculum for Birth to Three Years—$179.00 • Stock #66024

____ **AEPS® Three to Six Set** | Administration Guide, Test, Curriculum for Three to Six Years—$179.00 • Stock #66031

AEPS® Components

____ **AEPS® Administration Guide**
$65.00 • 336 pages • 7 x 10 • spiral-bound • ISBN 978-155766562-1

____ **AEPS® Test: Birth to Three Years and Three to Six Years**
$75.00 • 304 pages • 7 x 10 • spiral-bound • ISBN 978-155766563-8

____ **AEPS® Curriculum for Birth to Three Years**
$65.00 • 512 pages • 7 x 10 • spiral-bound • ISBN 978-155766564-5

____ **AEPS® Curriculum for Three to Six Years**
$65.00 • 352 pages • 7 x 10 • spiral-bound • ISBN 978-155766565-2

____ **AEPS® Child Observation Data Recording Form I** (Birth to Three Years)
$25.00 • package of 10 • 28 pages • 7 x 10 • saddle-stitched • ISBN 978-155766583-6

____ **AEPS® Child Observation Data Recording Form II** (Three to Six Years)
$25.00 • package of 10 • 24 pages • 7 x 10 • saddle-stitched • ISBN 978-155766584-3

____ **AEPS® Child Progress Record I** (Birth to Three Years)
$25.00 • package of 30 • 6 pages • 7 x 10 • gatefold • ISBN 978-155766586-7

____ **AEPS® Child Progress Record II** (Three to Six Years)
$25.00 • package of 30 • 6 pages • 7 x 10 • gatefold • ISBN 978-155766587-4

____ **AEPS® Family Report I** (Birth to Three Years)
$25.00 • package of 10 • 28 pages • 7 x 10 • saddle-stitched • ISBN 978-155766588-1

____ **AEPS® Family Report II** (Three to Six Years)
$28.00 • package of 10 • 24 pages • 7 x 10 • saddle-stitched • ISBN 978-155766589-8

Purchase the CD-ROM
with any **AEPS®** set and save 20% on the CD-ROM!

Forms CD-ROM
PC and Mac compatable
$8^{1}/_{2}$ x 11

English—$249.95
ISBN 978-155766635-2

Spanish—$199.95
ISBN 978-155766812-7

For pricing and other information on AEPSi, visit www.aepsinteractive.com.

Customer number (4 or 6 digits): __ __ __ __ __ __   Title: _____

Field: ○ Birth–Five ○ K–12 ○ Clinical/Medical ○ 4-year College/Grad. ○ Comm. College/Vocational ○ Assn. ○ Comm. Service

Credit Card #: _____ Exp. Date: _____

Signature (required with credit card use): _____

Name: _____ Daytime phone: _____

Street Address: _____ ❑ residential ❑ commercial
Complete street address required.

City/State/ZIP: _____ Country: _____

E-mail Address: _____

❑ Yes! I want to receive special web site discount offers! My e-mail address will not be shared with any other party.

Photocopy this form and mail it to **Brookes Publishing Co.**, P.O. Box 10624, Baltimore, MD 21285-0624, U.S.A.; FAX 410-337-8539; call 1-800-638-3775 (8 A.M.—5 P.M. ET) or 410-337-9580 (outside the U.S. and Canada); or order online at **www.brookespublishing.com**

Shipping & Handling

For subtotal of	Add*	For CAN
$0.01 – $49.99	$5.00	$7.00
$50.00 – $69.99	10%	$7.00
$70.00 – $399.99	10%	10%
$400.00 and over	8%	8%

calculate percentage on product total

Policies and prices subject to change without notice. Prices may be higher outside the U.S. You may return products within 30 days for a full credit of the product price. Refunds will be issued for prepaid orders. Items must be returned in resalable condition.

Subtotal $_____

5% sales tax, Maryland only $_____

6% business tax (GST), CAN only $_____

P.O. customers: 2% of subtotal $_____

Shipping Rate (see chart) $_____

Total (in U.S. dollars) $_____

Shipping rates are for UPS Ground Delivery within continental U.S.A. For other shipping options and rates, call 1-800-638-3775 (in the U.S.A. and CAN) and 410-337-9580 (worldwide). Canadian customers: please place orders by the 9th and 24th of each month.

BA 73 is your source co